A HISTORY OF GKN

By the same author

ACCOUNTANCY AND THE BRITISH ECONOMY 1840–1980: The
Evolution of Ernst & Whinney

INDUSTRIAL ARCHITECTURE IN BRITAIN, 1750–1939

Forthcoming

A HISTORY OF GKN
VOLUME 2

A HISTORY OF GKN

Volume 1
Innovation and Enterprise, 1759–1918

Edgar Jones

Foreword by
Sir Trevor Holdsworth

MACMILLAN
PRESS

First published 1987

Published by
THE MACMILLAN PRESS LTD
Houndmills, Basingstoke, Hampshire RG21 2XS
and London
Companies and representatives
throughout the world

Printed in Great Britain by
Camelot Press Ltd
Southampton

British Library Cataloguing in Publication Data
Jones, Edgar, *1953*–
A history of GKN
Vol. 1 : Innovation and enterprise
1759–1918
1. GKN — History
I. Title
338.7′62′000941   TA57
ISBN 0–333–34594–0

Contents

List of Maps and Figures

List of Tables

List of Illustrations

List of Colour Plates

List of Abbreviations

BCL	Bristol Central Library
BLPES	British Library of Political and Economic Science
BRL	Birmingham Reference Library
BUL	Birmingham University Library
CCL	Cardiff Central Library
DBB	*Dictionary of Business Biography*
DNB	*Dictionary of National Biography*
E	*The Engineer*
EcHR	*The Economic History Review*
GKN	Guest Keen & Nettlefolds
GRO	Glamorgan Record Office, Cardiff
GWR	Great Western Railway
GwRO	Gwent Record Office, Cwmbran
I	*The Ironmonger*
JISI	*Journal of the Iron and Steel Institute*
LNWR	London & North Western Railway
MBA	Midland Bank Archives, London
MPICE	*Minutes of the Proceedings of the Institution of Civil Engineers*
MTL	Merthyr Tydfil Central Library
NER	North Eastern Railway
NLW	National Library of Wales, Aberystwyth
PIME	*Proceedings of the Institution of Mechanical Engineers*
PNB	Patent Nut & Bolt Co.
PRO	Public Record Office, Kew
RR	Rhymney Railway
SRO	Scottish Record Office, Edinburgh
TSWIE	*Transactions of the South Wales Institute of Engineers*
TVR	Taff Vale Railway
USSC	United States Steel Corporation
VCH	*Victoria County History*
S	*of Stafford*
W	*of Warwick*

Foreword

It is perhaps surprising that no thoroughly researched, scholarly history has ever been written about so old, so substantial and so successful an enterprise as GKN.

In the early 1980s as we embarked upon a major and fundamental reconstruction of the company, shedding in the process many of those businesses which had given GKN its long and successful record of almost 230 years, it seemed to me that the past endeavours and achievements by so many should be rigorously researched and recorded, bringing to that task a standard of quality commensurate with their performance.

The history of GKN is at the heart of the industrial history of Britain and of the World's industrial revolution. Starting in 1759 in iron-making and coal-mining, it progressed into steel and its many derivatives, serving the railways, building and construction, auto-motive and other major industries as they emerged and developed through the eighteenth, nineteenth and twentieth centuries.

Its fortunes reflected those of Britain. When Britain led the industrial world in the mid-nineteenth century, so did Guest and Co: when Britain created an Empire, GKN invested there: when Britain was prosperous, so was GKN.

Its history touched the lives of many people, some famous, some high-born, some self-made, some ready-made: a few outstandingly excellent but unknown managers and many thousands of ordinary working people.

No industrial enterprise is more quintessentially British than GKN.

TREVOR HOLDSWORTH

Acknowledgements

I have many people to thank. First, and foremost, Mr John Howard, formerly the group secretary and latterly a director of GKN, has accompanied me on visits to factories, arranged interviews, discussed the execution of the project and commented in detail upon each draft of the text. His extensive and close involvement with the group has proved invaluable. Lord Briggs, whose advice I have sought from the outset, has read the entire study and been a source of encouragement and insight. In addition, I am grateful to the members of the History Committee, set up by GKN to oversee the passage of the book, for their help and specialised knowledge; it included, Sir Trevor Holdsworth (group chairman of GKN), Mr Stephen Lloyd, Mr Michael Chester and Mr Ralph Smallwood. Before his retirement in 1985, Mr Basil Woods was also a member of the committee. The first volume of this history would have contained more errors of fact and judgement but for their corrections and suggestions.

Lord Brookes, life president and former group chairman, discussed at length the modern period of GKN's history, which helped to put the early years into context. I am grateful for his help and hospitality.

The various drafts were read and commented upon by Mr John A. Owen, Works Manager, BSC Dowlais Works. I am deeply indebted to him for his help and advice over the four and a half years of this project. His consistent and enthusiastic commitment to the history of the Dowlais Iron Company and the well-being of Dowlais has a value which is rare today; it has served as an example to me.

I am grateful to Dr Nigel Bowles of Edinburgh University, whose detailed comments on the entire draft have resulted in material improvement. Mr R.E.J. Roberts, Sir Anthony Bowlby and Sir Douglas Bruce-Gardner, who each read the text, made a contribution based upon considerable managerial experience in industry. Those parts of the study dealing with the life of Lady Charlotte Guest were read by Dr Angela John of Thames Polytechnic and those concerning labour and conditions of employment by Dr Howard Gospel of the University of Kent; Mr E.G. Semler, formerly editor of *Chartered*

Mechanical Engineer, commented upon the accuracy of those passages concerned with techniques of mechanical engineering. As specialists in these respective subjects, I am grateful to them all for their corrections and suggestions.

Viscount Wimborne kindly granted me permission to consult the diaries of Lady Charlotte Guest, and the Dowager Viscountess Wimborne most hospitably assisted my researches. I am also thankful to the Earl of Bessborough for providing information about his family and to Sir William Crawshay for his knowledge of the Cyfarthfa Ironworks.

I have received great assistance from the directors and executives of GKN, past and present, whose contributions it is impossible to record in detail. These have included, Sir Barrie Heath (former group chairman), Sir Richard Brooke, Mr J.A. Collier, Mr Emrys Davies, Mr Neville Davies, Mr J.F. Insch, Mr T.H. Keen, Mr E.C. Lysaght, Mr L. Maxwell-Holroyd, Mr G. Moore, Mr L.R.P. Pugh, Mr F.C. Rowbottom, Mr. D. Rowlands, Mr J.C. Sankey, Mr W.E. Simons, Mr R.N.M. Ward, Mr Vincent Wardell and Sir Henry Williams. To those who have helped but not been mentioned, may I offer my apologies.

Amongst the many others who have assisted, I can mention only a few: Mr Colin Baber and Dr Trevor Boyns (both of University College Cardiff); Dr John Booker (Lloyds Bank); Mr W.F. Cartwright; Dr Yousef Cassis (University of Geneva); Mr John Cockcroft; Dr Richard Davenport-Hines (Business History Unit); Mr David Francis (Merthyr Tydfil Central Library); Dr Reiner Fremdling (Freie Universität Berlin); Mr Edwin Green (Midland Bank); Mr Michael Haynes (formerly Director of the Merthyr Tydfil Heritage Trust); Dr John Kanefsky (British Coal); Mr M. McKenzie (National Museum of Wales); Mrs Patricia Moore (Glamorgan Record Office, Cardiff); Miss Elizabeth Rowbottom (European Industrial Services). I am also grateful to the staff of GKN International, whose offices I shared, for providing a companionable atmosphere throughout the execution of this project.

For providing such a wealth of research material my gratitude is owed to the Birmingham Reference Library; Birmingham University Library; British Coal (formerly the National Coal Board); British Steel Corporation; Business Archives Council; Business History Unit; European Industrial Services Ltd; Institution of Civil Engineers; Institution of Mechanical Engineers; Metal Society; National Library of Wales; Rheemco Ltd.; and Sela Fasteners Ltd. (in particular to Mr George Barton, Mr S.A. Brewster and Mr Alan Waterhouse).

The author acknowledges the assistance provided by the publishers, Macmillan, and in particular to Mr T.M. Farmiloe and Ms Pauline Snelson, who guided the book from its inception to the launch. Christine Chambers who typed the manuscript, is owed thanks for her expertise and endurance.

September 1986   EDGAR JONES

Chronology of Events

1759   A partnership was formed to build a single blast furnace beside the Dowlais Brook.

1765   Nathaniel Webb, Thomas Price and William Lewis were the three executive partners in the Dowlais furnace responsible for its operation.

1767   John Guest of Broseley sold his interest in the Plymouth furnace and was appointed manager at Dowlais.

1781   A second blast furnace erected at Dowlais.

1782   John Guest became a partner, buying six shares from Thomas Harris for £2,600.

1785   Sir Josiah John Guest born at Gelligaelog, Dowlais.

1787   John Guest died and was succeeded in management of the works by his son Thomas Guest and son-in-law William Taitt.

1793   A third blast furnace constructed by the Dowlais Iron Co.

1794   The Glamorganshire Canal opened from Merthyr to Cardiff.

1798   A Boulton & Watt steam engine installed at Dowlais to provide blast for the furnaces.

1800   Riots in Merthyr.

1802   The Merthyr Tramroad opened from Penydarren to Abercynon.

1807   With the death of Thomas Guest, Josiah John Guest succeeded to the management of the Dowlais Iron Co.

1815   William Taitt died.

1816   Riots in Merthyr and Dowlais.

1820   Dowlais schools begun in upper floors of the stable building.

1821   Dowlais produced rails for the Stockton and Darlington Railway.

c. 1823 John Sutton Nettlefold opened an ironmonger's shop at No. 8 Red Lion Street, Holborn, London.

1830 The 'Big Mill' laid down at Dowlais to roll rails and bars.

1832 Josiah John Guest elected as Merthyr's first Member of Parliament.

1833 Josiah John Guest and Lady Charlotte Bertie were married.

c. 1834 J.S. Nettlefold set up a woodscrew mill at Baskerville Place, Birmingham.

1835 Arthur Keen was born.

1839 Ifor Works, Dowlais, built – a major extension to the ironworks.

1840 'Little Mill' built at Dowlais.

1845 Dowlais Iron Co. was the greatest ironworks in the world employing 7,300 and operating 18 blast furnaces.

1846 Thomas J. Sloane took out several screwmaking patents in New York.

1848 After protracted negotiations, the Dowlais lease was renewed by trustees on behalf of the third Marquis of Bute.

1851 Sir John Guest, by acquiring two shares from Edward Hutchins, became sole owner of the Dowlais Iron Co.

1851 J.S. Nettlefold observed self-acting machinery at the Great Exhibition.

1852 Sir John Guest died and Lady Charlotte assumed executive control.

1853 Eight week strike by the Dowlais colliers and miners; Nicholas Wood commissioned to produce a report on the Dowlais collieries.

1854 Nettlefold & Chamberlain build their new screw mill at Heath Street, Smethwick; Joseph Chamberlain and J.H. Nettlefold entered the firm.

1855 Lady Charlotte Guest married Charles Schreiber M.P. and gave up the management of the ironworks to the two trustees, G.T. Clark and H.A. Bruce.

1856 Francis Watkins and Arthur Keen set up in partnership.

1856 Dowlais Iron Co. took out the first licence to use Henry Bessemer's process for making malleable iron.

1857 William Menelaus produced his report on the state of the ironworks; work began on constructing the Goat Mill, when completed the most powerful rolling mill in the world.

1858   Watkins & Keen occupied part of the London Works, Smethwick, formerly the premises of Fox, Henderson & Co.

1864   Watkins & Keen floated as the Patent Nut & Bolt Co. incorporating Weston & Grice.

1865   Dowlais converted its first production cast of Bessemer steel; the 'Colly Line' from the works to the collieries near Bedlinog constructed.

1865   Nettlefold & Chamberlain took over James, Son & Avery's King's Norton screw works.

1869   Joseph Chamberlain became a partner in Nettlefold & Chamberlain.

1870   The Patent File Co.'s factory in Heath Street acquired by Nettlefold & Chamberlain and henceforth known as Imperial Mills.

1870   Messrs. Field & Cornforth promoted the St. George's Works of the Birmingham Screw Co.

1871   Dowlais erected its first Siemens-Martin open hearth furnace.

1873   Dowlais Iron Co. one of the founders of the Orconera Iron Ore Co. established to mine and import ore to Britain from northern Spain.

1873   Nettlefold & Chamberlain making 150,000 gross woodscrews a week, or 7,200,000 gross per annum.

1874   Joseph, Walter and Herbert Chamberlain left the partnership of Nettlefold & Chamberlain.

1878   J.H. Nettlefold became senior partner of Nettlefolds.

1880   Flotation of Nettlefolds Ltd. and the take over of the Birmingham Screw Co., Lloyd & Harrison's Stourport works, Manchester Screw Co. and John Cornforth's wire and nail works.

1881   E.P. Martin returned to Dowlais to act as assistant to William Menelaus.

1881   Frederick Nettlefold succeeded J.H. Nettlefold as chairman of Nettlefolds.

1882   William Menelaus died and was succeeded as general manager at Dowlais by E.P. Martin.

1886   Nettlefolds' Castle Works at Wellington sold, and an acid Bessemer plant and rolling mills set up at Rogerstone.

1888   Construction began on the blast furnaces at Dowlais-Cardiff, East Moors, Cardiff.

1890 The sinking of Abercynon colliery began.

1891 J.A. Kenrick succeeded Frederick Nettlefold as chairman of Nettlefolds.

1891 Profits earned from coal sales by Dowlais Iron Co. exceed those from both iron and steel making.

1892 G.T. Clark retired from the management of the Dowlais Iron Co. and was replaced by E.P. Martin.

1892 British Screw Co.'s Leeds factory comes into operation.

1898 Nettlefolds acquired the British Screw Co. from its owners, the American Screw Co.

1899 The Dowlais Iron, Steel & Coal Co. was promoted as a private limited liability company, wholly owned by Lord Wimborne.

1901 The Patent Nut & Bolt Co. merged with the Dowlais Iron, Steel & Coal Co. to form Guest, Keen & Co. under the chairmanship of Arthur Keen.

1901 Imperial Mills, Coverack Road, Newport opened by Nettlefolds.

1902 Guest, Keen & Co. amalgamated with Nettlefolds to form Guest, Keen & Nettlefolds.

1902 GKN took over the Cyfarthfa steelworks and collieries.

1902 E.P. Martin retired as general manager of Dowlais and was succeeded by William Evans, formerly of Cyfarthfa.

1905 Work began on new blast furnace plant at Dowlais.

1910 Cyfarthfa steelworks closed.

1915 Most of GKN's steelworks, collieries and factories became Controlled Establishments.

1915 Arthur Keen died and was succeeded as chairman by his eldest son, Arthur T. Keen.

1917 Cyfarthfa again produced pig iron.

1918 Arthur T. Keen died unexpectedly and the Earl of Bessborough became chairman of GKN.

Introduction

Although formed in 1900–02 from constituents which dated either from the mid-eighteenth or mid-nineteenth centuries, Guest, Keen & Nettlefolds (GKN) remained a company not widely known to the general public. Unlike some multinational groups such as Unilever, Ford or BP, it has never become a household name, a fact which is explicable in terms of the nature and style of the business. With the exception of Nettlefolds, whose woodscrews reached the consumer through a network of wholesalers, the company and its predecessors have never dealt to any significant extent with the man in the street. Supplying bulk iron and steel products to railway companies, shipbuilders and the engineering industry as a whole, and for a period selling coal to merchants, GKN became one of Britain's manufacturing giants without ever engaging the attention of the mass of the population. Whilst its companies have operated at the heart of the Industrial Revolution, the group appears to have grown in an unspectacular manner to occupy a leading place in British business history. The absence of ostentatious display should not be taken to imply a lack of substance. Not only for those thousands employed in its factories, mines and ironworks was GKN important. Whole communities, such as Merthyr and Smethwick, benefited from its presence, while the iron and engineering industries profited from the training schemes and technical advances pioneered by its managers.

Today, however, very little remains of the three companies who in 1900–02 came together to form Guest, Keen & Nettlefolds. The Dowlais Iron Co. (the Guest element) comprised steelworks in Cardiff and Dowlais and an extensive holding in the coal mines of South Wales; the Patent Nut & Bolt Co. (the Keen element) consisted of two nut and bolt factories near Birmingham and an ironworks with a colliery at Cwmbran, near Newport; and Nettlefolds owned a large woodscrew mill at Smethwick with a steelworks at Rogerstone. Because of nationalisation, but, more significantly, the changing demands of the modern economy, many of these operations have ended and none of these industrial sites remain within the GKN

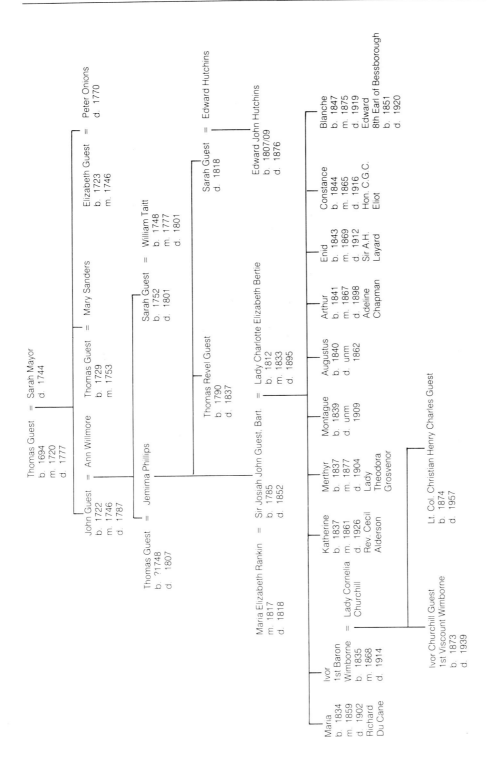

Figure 1 A simplified family tree of the Guests

group, the woodscrew mill at Heath Street, once a key component, being the last divestment.

Of the three elements which formed GKN, the Guests were the oldest. John Guest was appointed manager of the Dowlais Iron Co. in April 1767. The single blast furnace belonging to the company had been constructed in 1759 and was funded by a partnership of eight, many of whom were Bristol merchants with little or no knowledge of iron making. By saving his salary, in 1781 Guest was able to purchase a six-sixteenths share in the firm for £2,600, which in turn was inherited by his eldest son Thomas. He too took an active part in the management of the business, though it was his son, Sir [Josiah] John Guest, who was responsible for raising the Dowlais Iron Co. to the foremost position among British ironworks. Precipitated into pro-prietorial office at the age of twenty-two by the death of his father, he recruited the ablest engineers and ploughed profits into expansion and technical innovation, whilst taking an active part in improving communications from Dowlais to Cardiff. Josiah Guest was one of the outstanding figures in the history of GKN, an entrepreneur of vision who cared deeply for his family firm. His debilitating illness and death in 1852 brought his wife, Lady Charlotte, into the active management of the company and for three years she was, in effect, the executive head of the business. A woman of drive, determination and high intelligence, her role at Dowlais, judged by the standards of the mid-Victorian period, was quite exceptional.

The retirement of Lady Charlotte Guest in April 1855 for all practical purposes ended the family's direct control of the business since Sir Ivor Bertie Guest, later Lord Wimborne, who inherited the firm, took no direct interest in either the operational decisions or strategic policy making, though he did remain the final arbiter on questions involving heavy capital expenditure. Career managers and professionally-qualified engineers, principal among whom were G.T. Clark, William Menelaus and E.P. Martin, now ran the Dowlais Iron Co.

Arthur Keen, the architect of the two mergers which created GKN, originally set up in business with Francis Watkins in 1856. Whilst the Guest family, now members of the aristocracy, steered the Dowlais Iron Co. into the period of its greatest triumph, the men who founded the second component in GKN were of a very different social class. Keen was the son of a yeoman farmer and Watkins a foreman from America. The latter had acquired the British patent rights for an automatic bolt-making machine and, being unable to sell them, decided to become a manufacturer himself in conjunction with Keen, whose friendship with Thomas Astbury, a wealthy ironfounder, provided a source of finance. In 1864 the business was floated as a public limited liability company, the Patent Nut & Bolt Co. (PNB), and in the following year they took over Weston & Grice, nut and bolt makers of West Bromwich, who also owned an ironworks and colliery at Cwmbran. It was the need, later in the century, to obtain steel-

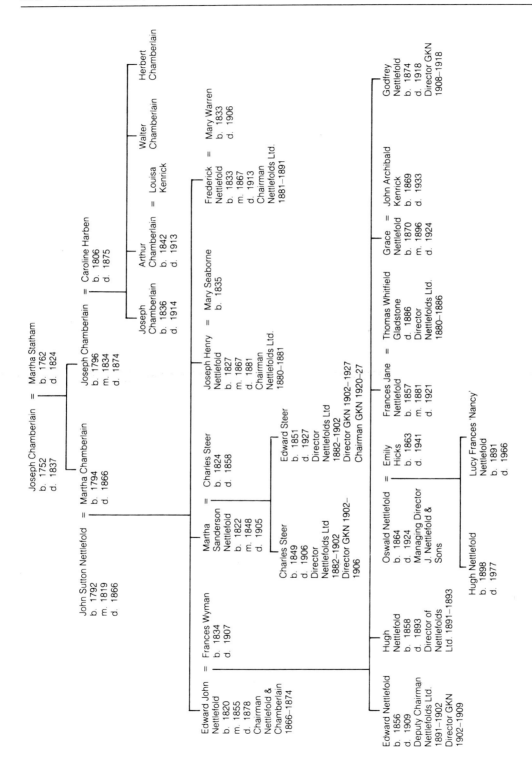

Figure 2 A simplified family tree of the Nettlefolds

making technology which led Arthur Keen to propose an amalgamation with the Dowlais Iron Co. Lord Wimborne, the sole proprietor, wishing to relinquish his responsibility for such a large and increasingly complex business, agreed to the sale and the consequent formation of Guest, Keen & Co. in 1900.

The third component, Nettlefolds Ltd., which joined Guest, Keen & Co. in 1902, was also begun as a partnership, Nettlefold & Chamberlain. The founders, John Sutton Nettlefold and his brother-in-law Joseph Chamberlain Senior (whose son, the Liberal politician, joined the company) established a purpose-built woodscrew factory at Smethwick in 1854. They soon became the leading screw manufacturer in Britain and in 1880, on taking over several competitors, floated the business as a public limited liability company. Growth continued, and in 1887, following a path of vertical integration, Nettlefolds opened their own steelworks at Rogerstone with a wire-drawing mill nearby at Tydu.

The Great War produced no dramatic change in the operations or organisational structure adopted by GKN. By 1918 the group had scarcely altered in shape from its formation in 1900–02. In essence, it remained committed to coal mining, steelmaking and the manufacture of fasteners. Exhibiting a considerable degree of vertical integration, GKN remained a UK-based company, having no overseas manufacturing plant, but maintained a healthy level of exports, principally to the Empire. Major changes occurred at a senior level of management during the Great War. Arthur Keen died in 1915, and when the death of his son and successor, Arthur T. Keen, followed in 1918, the chairmanship fell to the Earl of Bessborough, an aristocrat, who was in effect a non-executive leader. It was a seriously weakened main board which entered the 1920s, as many of the experienced directors of the Edwardian period had either died or retired.

The principal products of the three companies that formed GKN were all initially made of iron and, by the end of the nineteenth century, steel. Once it had adopted the puddling and rolling processes, the Dowlais Iron Co. was able to make bar iron, the demand for which rose dramatically from the 1840s. For this was the period when a network of railway lines was laid down throughout Britain and the Guests became one of the principal suppliers of rails at home and in export markets. In time, steel was specified rather than bar iron, and in order to maintain their position as rail manufacturers, the Dowlais Iron Co. constructed Bessemer converters and open hearth furnaces. The PNB also included railway companies among their leading customers; they sold them wrought iron fishplates, spikes, nuts and bolts and cast iron sleepers and chairs. In addition, they produced a multiplicity of fasteners for the engineering trades of the Midlands. For Nettlefolds the gimlet-pointed woodscrew, forged and cut from iron, later steel, wire was their chief source of profit. Turning woodscrews out in a myriad of lengths and gauges, they became the world's largest maker and supplied not only Britain but also the Empire.

Although the products themselves may not have altered greatly over the period of this study, the means by which they were manufactured were subject to considerable change. The technology by which pig iron was made underwent continuous modification, enabling ironmasters to manufacture ever larger quantities at lower unit costs. They were not so successful in improving the refining processes and puddling remained virtually unaltered from the time of its conception by Henry Cort. The substitution of steel (a form of iron which possessed the tensile strength of wrought iron and compression properties of cast iron) solved the problem and resulted in the mass production of a metal which could be shaped into a variety of uses. Like the blast furnace, the rolling mill was subject to repeated advances. The Dowlais Iron Co. laid down a succession of larger and more powerful mills, culminating in the Goat Mill which in 1857 was the biggest in the world.

Whilst the technology for making both woodscrews and nuts and bolts by mass-production methods initially came from America, both the PNB and Nettlefolds were responsible for modifying these pioneering designs to increase their operating speeds and to turn out higher quality fasteners. Although Nettlefolds refused to sell their machines to competitors either at home or abroad, the PNB had considerable dealings in the acquisition and sale of patents. Not only did they purchase licensing rights from American manufacturers, and then sub-license Continental producers, they also patented their own machines and sold them throughout Europe, and on one occasion bought the rights to a German nut-making machine which they subsequently sub-licensed to the Upson Nut Co. of Connecticut.

This is not exclusively a history of GKN, its products, technology and customers, for an accurate evaluation of its performance requires comparison with the group's competitors. It is difficult, for example, to assess the efficiency of the Dowlais Iron Co. in the late nineteenth century without reference to, say, the steelworks erected in the Middlesbrough region or the advances being achieved by the latest American and German works. There is almost as much to be discovered about business success from those that failed as from those that prospered. The reasons why GKN sold or closed certain subsidiaries help to explain why other parts of the group continued in operation, as the gradual winding down of Cyfarthfa steelworks after its acquisition in 1902 showed. Because companies which have crashed cannot commission histories, and because successful groups sometimes exhibit a reluctance to speak of their failures, this is a subject from which there is still much to learn.

This history seeks to identify those factors which enabled the various components of GKN to be successful for such long periods of time. The eighteenth and nineteenth centuries offered no safety nets to the weak performer. Governments did not support companies fallen upon hard times, nor were there other institutions from which assistance might be expected. For much of this period, these businesses were partnerships relying on internally generated funds and were precluded from appealing to the stock market for investment capital. The Guests, Keens and Nettlefolds survived simply because they consistently earned profits. The crucial question, therefore, is how? Through an examination of the principal areas of business activity outlined above, this study seeks to provide an answer.

At this moment the discipline of business history has largely resolved itself into the study of individual companies, or biographies of their chief executives, rather than industries or specific themes which influenced business, such as governmental controls, accounting developments, the rise of the professional manager or the importance of organisational structures.[1] While there have been histories of major companies involved in textiles (notably Courtaulds),[2] chemicals (ICI),[3] food and soap (Unilever),[4] glass (Pilkingtons),[5] oil (BP and Burmah),[6] coal (sponsored by British Coal),[7] and steel (Colvilles),[8] to date, no study has been published of a large group which has combined iron and steelmaking with coal mining and engineering.

To a certain extent, the intricate nature of some company histories has been mitigated because the business in question has been associated consistently with a single industry, albeit, a complex one. This is particularly true of small and medium-size enterprises without the resources or expertise to diversify far beyond their prime activity. The same cannot be said of GKN. Through acquisition and internally-generated expansion, the group has been involved in coal mining, iron and then steel making, and a variety of engineering trades. Doubtless, this policy was evolved by several generations of managers and owners as a source of strength. Not putting every egg in the same basket has an age-old appeal, whilst the advantages provided by vertical integration over the control of inputs were also clearly perceived.

By beginning as early as 1759 and then pursuing a range of activities, GKN offers the historian an opportunity to take a cross-section through the Industrial Revolution and subsequent periods of economic growth. As in a picaresque novel, the fortunes of the company can be followed from its conception as a single water-powered blast furnace in remote Merthyr Tydfil, to the adoption of steam engines to provide the blast and drive the rolling mills, the sinking of deep pits rather than open cast mines, the acquisition of the Bessemer patent for making steel and its replacement by the open hearth furnace and the switch from acid to basic technology. At Smethwick both Nettlefolds and the Patent Nut & Bolt Co. gained economies of scale by introducing self-acting machinery and were thereby able to undercut their competitors, many of whom they

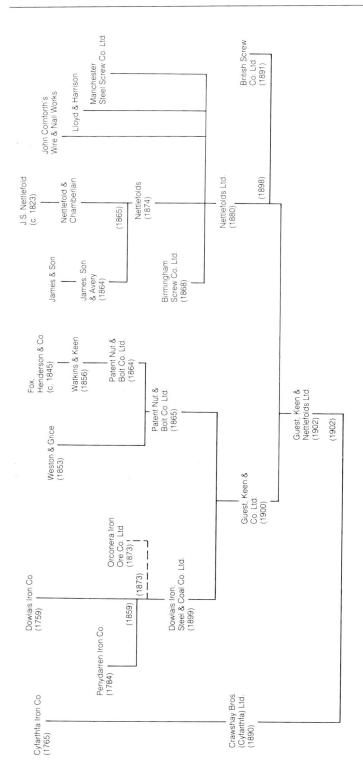

Figure 3 A simplified genealogical table of GKN, 1759–1918

subsequently took over.

There was a considerable measure of geographical contiguity about the three companies which merged to form GKN: both the Dowlais Iron Co. and the PNB owned collieries and ironworks in South Wales, whilst Nettlefolds had its steelworks at Rogerstone and a mill in Newport. The woodscrew and nut and bolt factories of the PNB were close neighbours in the Midlands. As a result, this history also assumes the shape of two regional case studies, South Wales, where coal mining and the first iron and steel works flourished, and the Midlands, the focus for the fastener, forgings and general engineering business. It is impossible, for example, to separate the fortunes and growth of Merthyr Tydfil from its four ironworks. They were responsible for the construction of its canal and early railways, owned most of the housing in the town, built many of the schools, chapels and institutions and assisted with the public health reforms of the 1860s. This study examines the nature of the economic and social conditions in these areas, and seeks to explain their evolution, identifying those considerations which encouraged the creation of businesses there. Among the particular attractions of Smethwick, for example, were web-like rail communications for the distribution of fasteners to wholesalers, the availability of semi-skilled and skilled labour, and proximity to both customers and suppliers.

Moreover, this is the story of a major business enterprise, a history of an institution. The formation and development of GKN from its roots in the Dowlais Iron Co. represents the transformation of a partnership limited in essence to Glamorgan and Bristol into an international group, the scale of whose diverse activities have now demanded the creation of a devolved, multi-divisional structure with central strategic control and operational monitoring, supported by a number of specialist head office departments. Important stage posts along this evolutionary road included the resort to limited liability following the Companies Acts of 1856 and 1863, the formation of a holding-subsidiary company relationship after the mergers of the Edwardian and inter-war periods, and in the mid-1960s the creation of 'Sub-groups' arranged according to product or territory.

Crucial indicators of the performance of a business are of course profit figures which in turn need to be related to turnover and the value of the assets employed. Whilst company legislation (particularly after 1948) has compelled businesses to reveal these statistics and the basis on which they have been calculated, there was no such requirement during the nineteenth century. As a result the production of profit figures generally remained a practical guide for management, which already possessed an intuitive understanding of the company's financial condition, and were not recorded in a systematic and standardised form. Technical problems surrounding the valuation of assets, an allowance for depreciation and the costing of manufacturing processes had yet to be solved and so introduced a further element of uncertainty to the figures. Accordingly, for individual factories and certain periods these statistics are not available. Others, such as output of specific products, numbers employed and salaries, have often not survived purges of limited office space. Hence, despite widespread searches, no precise measure of the workforce employed by Nettlefolds nor the annual production of woodscrews exists for the nineteenth and early twentieth centuries.

GKN, among the longest-lived of Britain's major manufacturing companies, survived and prospered over some two hundred years because it has been able to modify or re-direct its activities in tune with developments in the economy as a whole. Through internally-generated funds and periodic resort to the money markets, GKN, a large company, has been able to keep pace with new technologies and fresh patterns of demand. But this very success, resulting in a diversity of products and several changes in direction, makes the history of GKN one of considerable complexity, and suggests that it may be interpreted as a revealing insight into Britain's industrial experience.

References

1. Geoffrey Jones (Editor), *British Multinationals: Origins, Management and Performance*, Gower (1986) and R.P.T. Davenport-Hines (Editor), *Markets and Bagmen: Studies in the History of Marketing*, Gower (1986).
2. D.C. Coleman, *Courtaulds*, 2 Vols., Oxford (1969), Vol. 3, Oxford (1980).
3. W.J. Reader, *Imperial Chemical Industries, A History*, Vol. 1, Oxford (1970), Vol. 2, Oxford (1975).
4. Charles Wilson, *The History of Unilever*, 2 Vols., London (1954), Vol. 3, London (1968).
5. T.C. Barker, *The Glassmakers*, London (1977).
6. R.W. Ferrier, *The History of British Petroleum*, Vol. 1, Cambridge (1982); T.A.B. Corley, *A History of the Burmah Oil Company*, London (1983).
7. M.W. Flinn, *The History of the Coal Industry 1700–1830*, Vol. 2, Oxford (1984).
8. Peter L. Payne, *Colvilles and the Scottish Steel Industry*, Oxford (1979).

Part I

Iron in South Wales, 1759–1850

1 *The Guests and Foundations at Merthyr, 1759–93*

The Dowlais Iron Works was established at Dowlais, near Merthyr Tydfil, in September 1759 when a partnership was formed between a group of merchants and ironmasters to construct a single blast furnace. After the Hirwaun ironworks, set up in 1757 by John Maybery of Powicke Forge, Worcestershire, it was only the second coke-fired furnace to be erected in South Wales, and for power it relied upon a waterwheel set in front of a dam laid across the Dowlais Brook. Whilst not one of the original nine partners, John Guest was appointed as the works manager in April 1767 and subsequently saved sufficient of his salary to purchase a shareholding in the firm, his family ultimately gaining complete control of the enterprise. From this remote and speculative venture, established at a time when Britain was in the initial throes of an industrial revolution, a mighty ironworks rose and prospered. In these early days, however, it was by no means certain that the infant enterprise would be nurtured through to adulthood.

THE PARTNERSHIP OF 1759 AND THE FIRST FURNACE

On 19 September 1759 Thomas Lewis (1699–1764) and eight others (Thomas Price, Richard Jenkins, Thomas Harris, John Curtis, Nathaniel Webb, John Jones, Isaac Wilkinson and Edward Blakeway)[1] formed a partnership to establish 'the business of an ironmaster and iron manufacturer'. They agreed[2] 'to build a certain ffurnace or ffurnaces for smelting of iron oar, iron mine or stone, into pig iron, in the Parish of Merthir Tidvil, in the County of Glamorgan . . . And for the selling and uttering of iron made, wrought, or manufactured'. The success of this enterprise critically relied on the purchase in 1757–58 of two leases which granted them mineral rights over property belonging to the Dowager Viscountess Windsor. The lease of 1748 permitted its holder, or his servants,[3]

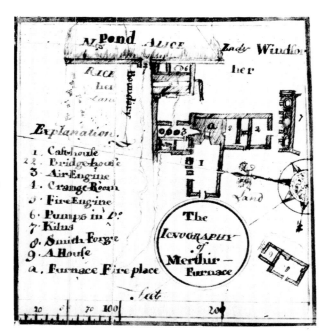

1 A plan of the Dowlais furnace in 1763. The waterwheel on the brook by the dam is not shown. Water was pumped back into the pond by the atmospheric engine ('6'). The three pistons ('3'), which provided the blast to the furnace ('a') through a single tuyère, were driven by an eccentric crank. The iron flowed from the furnace to pig beds within the cast house ('1'). The kilns ('7') were for calcining iron ore and for making coke.
(*Glamorgan Record Office*)

agents, and workmen, to dig for, make, and sink pits, and to make trenches, ditches, gutters, ponds, and levels, and to erect limekilns for burning of lime, engines, banks, stanks, sluices, and all other conveniences for the better scouring for getting, having and obtaining all such iron mine, coal and stone, and the earth and rubbish raised out of the said Works.

The first lease, acquired by Thomas Lewis, as well as providing land in Dowlais and Tor-y-Fan, also gave 'full power and liberty to dig for or[e] raising stones whatsoever that shall be found upon any part of their freehold estates for building of furnace or furnaces'.[4] In the second, obtained on 6 July 1758, Lewis secured a piece of land[5] 'towards building and erecting an air engine or engines or any other works or buildings whatsoever (except dwelling houses) and furnace there . . . All situate lying and being within the said Parish of Merthyr Tidvil and adjoining a brook there called Dowlais'. In addition, the partnership took out a further lease from Lady Windsor in June 1763 that provided an extra twenty two acres on which the Dowlais Co. proposed to erect blast furnaces, forges, mills, engines, store houses, kilns and coalhouses.[6]

The two principal leases included a fixed annual rental of £26, with an extra £5 consequent upon the 1763 agreement, which in retrospect was to prove unrealistically low, based on the value of land in an agrarian economy. Doubtless the speculative and then novel nature of the undertaking had prevented Lady Windsor, the owner of the freehold, from inserting a royalty clause on the coal and ore to be mined or iron manufactured. When the agreement of 1763 was signed, it was confirmed that the whole arrangement should expire in 1848; the 1757 lease, valid for 99 years, commenced on 1 May 1749 when Thomas Morgan of Ruperra came to an agreement with Herbert, Viscount Windsor.[7] It had, in turn, been subject to a sub-lease to Thomas Rees and David John, both yeomen of Merthyr, who on 20 September 1757 assigned the property to Thomas Lewis of Newhouse, Llanishan, Monmouthshire, a leading member of the Dowlais partnership.[8] In 1759, therefore, the company had 89 years in which to operate their blast furnace, secure in the knowledge that their rental would never rise above £31 per annum.

Despite the clauses allowing him to 'work coal, iron ore, limestone, sandstone and fire-clay', Morgan reportedly used the Dowlais property merely as a hunting ground.[9] Charles Price in his 'Recollections' of *circa* 1800 suggested that a furnace, whose blast was provided by a waterwheel on the Dowlais brook, had been erected in 1757 and was producing pig iron for two years before the partnership led by Webb, Lewis and Price.[10] Yet it seems more likely that construction followed the partnership arrangement of 1759 when sufficient funds would have been available for such a capital-intensive and uncertain venture. Why was it then that, for the first ten years of the main lease, nothing tangible had been undertaken? The Merthyr and Aberdare regions had, in fact, been centres of iron production during the Tudor period.[11] A number of Sussex ironmasters suffering from shortages of charcoal had then moved to these thickly wooded valleys. The exhaustion of suitable timber during the reign of Elizabeth I resulted in the closure of these works, so that any pool of skilled iron workers had long since disappeared from the Welsh valleys when the first coke-fired furnaces were established in the late 1750s.

THE TECHNICAL BREAKTHROUGH

Why also should men of means have considered it a fair risk to sink capital in an ironworks situated in an area remote from established centres of population and which had no recent tradition of industrial endeavour or entrepreneurial genius? The question of location may be answered by reference to the 1757 lease, which permitted[12] 'workmen to dig for, make and sink pits and to make trenches and ditches, gutters and levels, and to erect engines . . . and all other conveniences for the better scouring, getting, having, and attaining all such ironstone and coal'. The two essential materials required for the manufacture of pig iron were coal (to be converted into coke) and iron ore; that limestone, needed as a flux in the blast furnace, also occurred

in the area was a bonus. 'Farmers', Charles Wilkins recalled in 1867, 'often brought a sack of lime to Mr. [John] Guest and for ½d. they received a sack of coal in exchange. The load generally borne on a horse consisted of three sacks'.[13] The fact that fast-flowing streams ran down the valley (in a region of high rainfall) permitted the installation of waterwheels to pump bellows for the blast and to drive hammers and rolling mills. In addition, streams could be dammed and then released to scour the hillside for the easier removal of iron ore and coal. Thus, Merthyr with its extensive mineral deposits and advantages of terrain possessed both the basic ingredients and the power sources necessary for a number of emergent ironworks.

The crucial technical innovation which allowed deforested districts, such as the Welsh valleys, to recommence iron making in the mid-eighteenth century had been pioneered by Abraham Darby I (1678–1717) as early as 1709.[14] He demonstrated at Coalbrookdale that it was possible to use coke as the fuel in the blast furnace, though for over fifty years charcoal continued to be favoured by ironmasters. Quaker exclusiveness, fear of competition too, and teething troubles all played a part in keeping the secret within the Quaker circles for some time.[15] Moreover, the slow diffusion of coke technology had other causes. Ironmasters were, of course, already situated in areas of forest rather than coal, and coal of a suitable quality, so that it was not until the mid-eighteenth century, when supplies of timber were running low and orders for iron multiplied because of the Seven Years War, that entrepreneurs set up furnaces in regions where minerals rather than trees proliferated. The rapid diffusion of smelting by coke, rather than charcoal, can be adequately explained in terms of the widening differential in costs between iron produced by the two methods.[16] Charcoal prices increased sharply during the mid-eighteenth century (because of growing scarcity and multiplying demand), so that those using coke could save as much as £1.50 to £2.00 per ton of pig iron in the 1750s.[17] The setting up of the great ironworks at Carron in 1760,[18] for example, and of the large furnace at Seaton, near Workington, both using coke, were instances of the geographical shifts which occurred in the industry as a result of the new technology.

Although charcoal was believed to have been used at Dowlais in the early days,[19] and the 1757 lease mentioned the possibility of 'charcoal' being employed,[20] it seems certain that the blast furnace was fed with coke from the outset.[21] This being so, Dowlais may claim to have been the second coke-fired furnace to have operated in South Wales, being preceded by that erected at Hirwaun in 1757.[22] The attraction of Merthyr was its geology and the provision of water power, while the delay in exploiting these opportunities resulted from lags in technical innovation, combined with the remote situation of the village and its lack of communications.

It was significant that most of the main characters in this story were outsiders; few had Welsh blood, a fact which had both a technical and a financial dimension. Isaac Wilkinson and John Guest had each come from the Coalbrookdale region of Shropshire. Situated in the Severn Valley and populated by Darbys, Guests and Wilkinsons, it served as a practical seminary in the art of smelting and refining; the village, and its neighbours, was the crucible of metallic technology, where ideas were tested, information exchanged and whence a new race of ironmasters dispersed. When John Guest needed more managers he sent to the Calcott Works, near Broseley, owned by Thomas Homfray. The latter's three sons, Jeremiah (1759–1833), Thomas (1760–1825) and Samuel (1763–1822), visited Dowlais and were then interviewed by Anthony Bacon at Cyfarthfa. Bacon then contracted them to build a forge which he would supply with pig iron and coal.[23] In time, the arrangement was dissolved and the three Homfrays established the Penydarren Ironworks, close to Dowlais. In the mid-eighteenth century, therefore, a circle of ironmasters flourished, like today's professional cricketers playing on the county circuit, competing with one another, but either great friends or hostile rivals.

The enigmatic and migratory Isaac Wilkinson seems to have been born in Shropshire, the son of a yeoman farmer.[24] After practical experience in the iron industry in Cumberland, Wilkinson worked in the 1730s as a chief caster or 'potfounder' at the Backbarrow Iron Co., Furness, another partnership in which the Quaker religion of its members and marriage ties led to close connections with several Bristol merchants.[25] His own furnace and forge, acquired in 1748, at Wilson House, near Grange-over-Sands,[26] Furness, was not a great success. So in 1753 he moved from there to Bersham to operate a furnace with his son John and a group of Liverpool gentlemen. Concentrating chiefly on cast iron objects, they made heaters, sugar rolls, water pipes and, under pressure of demand created by the Seven Years War, cannon.[27] Disposing of the plant to his sons, John and William, following financial failure, Isaac moved to Merthyr after only eight years at Bersham. Between 1757 and 1771 he was associated with the activities of no less than three iron partnerships in South Wales. Having discerned that this was a region of economic growth – an eighteenth century equivalent of a present-day silicon valley – he used his technical experience as a bargaining factor. The Dowlais furnace was the first venture in the area with which Wilkinson was associated though he sold his one-sixteenth share to Nathaniel Webb in March 1762.

In the following year he formed a partnership with John Guest, whom he had already met in Shropshire, and obtained a lease from the Earl of Plymouth which gave them permission to erect 'certain ffurnaces, fforges, mills, pothouses or other works for the making and manufacturing of iron'.[28] The agreement was to run from 1 May 1765 for ninety-nine years at an annual rental of £60.

3   A smelting (or cast) house at Broseley (1788), also by Lowry, the village in which John Guest lived and worked as an iron founder. Molten metal is being channelled from a furnace into beds of sand to allow the iron to solidify in conveniently sized blocks.
(*Trustees of the British Museum*)

Once the single blast furnace, powered by a waterwheel,[29] was erected, John Guest returned to his native Broseley and made only the occasional visit to Merthyr to see how his investment was faring.[30] He did, however, leave his brother, Thomas Guest (b. 1729), to keep a closer eye on its management. Because neither Isaac Wilkinson nor John Guest were able to devote much time to the running of the Plymouth venture, and because Mr Terry, the company's agent, who also served as the manager proved to be incompetent, the firm soon ran into difficulties. Charles Wood, the consulting engineer employed by Anthony Bacon to build the nearby Cyfarthfa ironworks, visited Plymouth regularly to purchase castings needed in the construction: one order, costed at £5 15s. per ton delivered to Cyfarthfa, included four hammers, 120 furnace bars, three anvils and twenty two bearing bars.[31] It soon became apparent to Wood that the Plymouth works was in a parlous state:[32]

> Mr. Terry tells me that their coal byes them in 2s. per ton getting & 2s. carriage & 4½d. per ton coaking . . . Their bellows are growing bad, their pypes too streight & tuere too small, the wind [blast] rebounds back . . . Their scrap iron they put into the furnace again, which in my opinion, is another piece of mismanagement, as it would be more profit to sell it for what the metal byes therein . . . So that upon the whole they are certainly by these short blasts working to a loss.

Further, he discovered that 'there is not any want of either mine or coal' and confirmed in conversation with Nathaniel Webb, then manager of the Dowlais works, that the Plymouth furnace was structurally sound but lacked competent 'management'; 'their blast is weak, their coal too far coked, so much to destroy the strength of it'.[33]

Since the business was in essence well founded, Bacon instructed Wood to approach the proprietors, Wilkinson and Guest, with a view to purchasing the furnace. Because of the expense and time that it took to construct an ironworks, Bacon was anxious to begin trading in South Wales so that his Cyfarthfa works, once completed, would have an established clientele on which to build. John Guest journeyed from Broseley reaching Merthyr on 26 June 1766 to discuss a possible sale.[34]

The first act of Wilkinson and Guest on arriving in Merthyr was to visit Thomas Guest 'to demand a sight of the books, which had been refused them some time ago'.[35] As they were found to have been kept in an irregular manner,[36] Wilkinson set about calculating potential profitability of the Plymouth furnace. Assuming a weekly output of 14 tons of pig iron, he estimated that the following expenses would be incurred:[37]

	£	s.	d.
Coals, 70 tons @ 4s. per ton	14	0	0
Ironstone (49 tons)	9	16	0
Limestone (16 tons)	3	4	0
Wages	5	6	0
Rent, stock, wear and tear	7	5	0
Total £	39	11	0

Given that a ton of pig iron commanded £4 5s. 0d. in the market place, the works could expect to make a profit of £19 19s. 0d. a week.

Although Wilkinson and Guest had leased the land for the furnace from the Earl of Plymouth, they did not possess sufficient capital themselves for the plant and machinery. It cost £2,000 to build the works, a sum which was raised by the sale of ten £200 shares: John White & Co. (seven), Edward Blakeway (two) and Francis Evans (one).[38] To raise further capital the partnership was expanded when twenty shares of £205 were issued: John White & Co. (seven), William Perritt (four), Edward Blakeway (two), Francis Evans (one), and Sarah Guest, daughter of John and subsequently second wife of William Taitt (one), Isaac Wilkinson and John Guest taking three and two shares respectively.[39] The two founding partners and owners of the lease retained the management of the Plymouth furnace.

In response to Bacon's offer, Guest replied that he wanted[40]

> £100 for each share, exclusive of the advance, which he says is £150 per share more and he and Mr. Wilkinson will assign over the lease from Lord Plymouth of the premises, with the management and all other advantages they were to have and was reserved to each in their articles of co-partnership.

During the negotiations, Guest lowered his price for the two shares to £160 but refused to accept anything less than £300 for the advance.[41] Wood conducted the discussions through Wilkinson, who observed that 'John Guest is very fickle and uncertain to deal with and hard to fix',[42] a judgement which was soon confirmed by the latter's desire to retain a half share in the company 'with an intent', Wood supposed, 'to have the management'.[43] To this Bacon was not prepared to agree. In the event Guest accepted £884 10s. for his entire interest in the partnership to be paid in two instalments.[44] The exchange of documents took place in Bristol whence Wilkinson and Guest had journeyed in July 1766.[45]

On his return to Merthyr, Wood called upon Thomas Guest to inform him that the transaction was completed.[46] Shortly afterwards, he received a note from Mr Terry to say that £1,792 9s. 11d. was needed to be spent on the Plymouth furnace to keep it in blast.[47] Wood himself calculated that if 700 tons of iron were sold to Cyfarthfa at

1790, for instance, Taitt came to an agreement with Messrs. Harrisons, Gordon & Stanley to act as commission agents for him in London (taking five per cent on orders from new clients and two and a half per cent on those from existing customers). A considerable trade seems to have been conducted through agents in the North: John Fletcher, a Manchester ironfounder, John Rigby of Hawarden Foundry, Flintshire, who acted as a factor for the Liverpool area, and others in Newcastle and Gateshead. Dowlais also sold freely to the Bristol region, either to ironfounders such as Walter Swayne or merchant houses such as Messrs. Harford & Co.[90] Success at Dowlais in the decade before the outbreak of the French Revolutionary Wars appears, therefore, to have been based on a determined and skilfully conducted sales policy which to a certain extent compensated for a failure to innovate in new technology (p. 27).

MERTHYR AND ITS FOUR IRONWORKS

The establishment of four major ironworks (Cyfarthfa, Dowlais, Penydarren and Plymouth) at Merthyr was, in many respects, akin to the rise of the oil industry in Texas during the 1880s and 1890s. Just as the latter served as a powerful generator of wealth for the American economy, so the first coke-fired ironworks provided an important impetus to growth during the Georgian age in Britain.

Neither the settlements which arose on the back of ironworks, nor those created by a proliferation of oil wells in America, were, in their respective pioneering phases, suitable places for women and children. Richard Webb, son of Nathaniel, observed in 1777 that the business at Dowlais had been from the outset[91] 'carried on in a very dangerous manner and became very profitable to the partners . . . and continued in such as flourishing state and condition until and at the time of the death of the said Nathaniel Webb [1771] and for several years afterwards'. As a result, Merthyr, which before industrialisation had been 'a small village, inhabited by shepherds and farmers',[92] grew with the features of an American goldrush settlement. To Henry Skrine, a visitor in 1798, it appeared as a 'curious place . . . an inconsiderable town in the midst of an obscure district' which 'has swelled of late into great commercial importance, from the ironworks established there by two great proprietors, who have employed a large capital in them with spirit and success'.[93] Fast-growing, unplanned, it was a shanty town in which disease was endemic and poverty lay just beneath the surface, threatening to break out at the slightest misfortune. To Malkin's eyes in 1804 it appeared as[94] 'a mountain valley, overspread, as far as the eye can reach, with the comparatively commodious habitations of masters, agents, engineers and workmen . . . peopled in the teeth of every obstacle, and . . . the triumph of fact over probability'. With such rapid growth, involving

the recruitment of much labour, concern for housing and sanitation was minimal. Rows of cramped stone houses were constructed piecemeal for the ironworkers and miners. 'These cottages', Malkin concluded,[95]

> were most of them built in scattered confusion without any order or plan. As the works increased more cottages were wanted, and erected in the spaces between those that had been previously built, till they become so connected with each other as to form a certain description of irregular streets . . . These streets are now many in number, close and confined, having no proper outlets behind the houses. They are consequently very filthy for the most part, and doubtless very unhealthy.

The population of Merthyr, estimated by Malkin in 1802 as being upwards of 10,000, was then far larger than that of Cardiff;[96] in fact, the 1801 census gave Merthyr's population as 7,705 at a time when Cardiff had only 1,870 inhabitants. 'No place in the kingdom', suggested Manby in 1802, 'has had so rapid an increase in trade and population in the same number of years'.[97] This demographic explosion was, in part, explained by the influx of farm labourers from

4 A general view of Merthyr Tydfil in 1811 from the north by John George Wood. The Glamorganshire Canal is on the extreme right, while the plume of smoke in the middle distance was probably from the Plymouth Works. (*British Library*)

5 A pencil sketch of the Cyfarthfa ironworks from the Brecon road by J.M.W. Turner who visited Merthyr Tydfil in 1798. The large waterwheel which provided power for the blast is clearly shown. The River Taff is in the foreground. (*Trustees of the British Museum*)

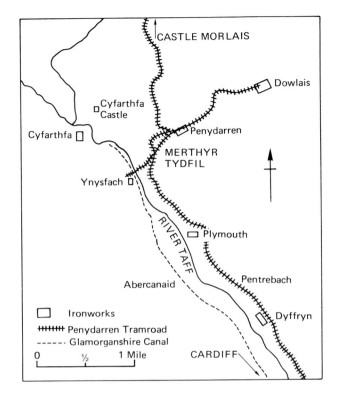

Figure 5 The four principal ironworks in Merthyr (c. 1820). There are also subsidiary works shown.

rural Wales and there was, in addition, a more limited migration of skilled workers from further afield, but possibly the largest group of workers came from the nearby English counties.[98] The ironworks at 'Mirthyr Tidfill', observed Fox in 1796, 'have brought from different parts of the country such numbers of workmen and their families, as to create a consumption of the great quantities of the necessaries of life, and cause a public market once a week.[99] In the eighteenth century it was still from the ranks of the men bred from the soil, rather than those of the town, that labour for the iron industry was recruited, so that furnaces and forges often stopped during the summer months to allow workers to assist with the harvest.[100]

Although jobs in the new industrial towns often brought harsh and unhealthy conditions of employment and housing, for many born into rural communities they represented a real improvement. Wages were generally higher, and if the worker were prepared to acquire technical knowledge or skills, he could advance still further. Industrialisation provided a broader range of opportunities for the farm labourer who, in exceptional circumstances, could make his fortune.

The language spoken at the four ironworks was almost entirely Welsh, despite the fact that 'the number of Englishmen among them is very considerable'.[101] This was doubtless because the original core

6 The Cyfarthfa ironworks in 1811 by John George Wood. Four blast furnaces are shown on the left hand side with casting houses in front of them. (*British Library*)

of workers were local men – John Guest when he became manager of the Dowlais Iron Co. felt it desirable to learn Welsh – and in later periods because the foremen and managers would have been Welsh speaking.

The frightening impact made by the ironworks on the uninitiated

7 A sepia wash drawing by Thomas Hornor (fl. 1800–44) of un-named rolling mills in Merthyr (*c.* 1817). If the buildings in the far distance represent Merthyr, then the outline of the terrain would suggest Cyfarthfa. However, the shape of the roofs and their chimneys bear a considerable similarity to the view of Penydarren by Wood (plate eight). (*Elton Collection, Ironbridge Gorge Museum Trust*)

8 A soft ground etching of the Penydarren Ironworks in 1811 by John George Wood. The stream in the foreground is presumably the Dowlais Brook, while the buildings to the right are rolling mills.
(*British Library*)

visitor was captured by Malkin's description of Cyfarthfa, then the largest in the world:[102]

> His [Richard Crawshay's] house is surrounded with fire, flame, smoke and ashes. The noise of the hammers, rolling mills, forges and bellows incessantly din and crash upon the ear. Bars and pigs of iron are continually thrown up to the hugely accumulating heaps that threaten to choke up every avenue of access . . . The machinery of this establishment is gigantic; and that part of it, worked by water, among the most scientifically curious and mechanically powerful to whom modern improvement has given birth.

His vivid impressions were matched pictorially in the *Views of South Wales* (1817–19) by Thomas Hornor, whose watercolours of the town's rolling mills revealed the searing glare of iron passing through the rolls. On the back of one of these drawings Hornor wrote:[103]

> At night the view of the town is strikingly singular. Numbers of furnaces and truly volcanic accumulations of blazing cinders illuminate the vale, which combining with the incessant roar of the blasts, the clangour of ponderous hammers, the whirl of wheels, and the scarcely human aspect of the tall gaunt workmen seem to realise without too much aid from fancy many of our early fears.

The chronologies of the three ironworks that competed with Dowlais may be outlined briefly.[104] The early story of the Plymouth Ironworks, situated in the southern part of the town on the east bank of the Taff, has already been mentioned (p. 8), but in 1784 it passed from the Cyfarthfa group under Bacon to his brother-in-law, Richard Hill, in whose family's possession the works remained until 1862.[105] The Penydarren Ironworks which lay close to Dowlais but nearer to Merthyr and on the other side of the Brook, had been established in 1784 by Thomas Homfray and his three sons, Jeremiah, Thomas and Samuel,[106] encouraged to move to South Wales from Broseley by John Guest 'when he saw that the iron business was expanding'.[107] Finally, and by 1793 most important of all, there was Cyfarthfa. Its first blast furnace had been erected in 1765 under the direction of Anthony Bacon (d. 1786), who was then in partnership with William Brownrigg.[108] However, in 1786 the ambitious and self-made Richard Crawshay succeeded in buying his way into the Cyfarthfa partnership, also obtained a lease on its forge, and in 1787 completed his coup by purchasing its blast furnace.[109] Cyfarthfa, unlike the other three ironworks, was situated in the western half of Merthyr, on the northern bank of the Taff. Dowlais then had the distinction of being the oldest of the quartet, the pioneer on whose success the others had taken the courage to begin.

WAR AND TECHNICAL INNOVATION

How, then, did these various ironworks fare during the period from 1759 to 1793? First, a distinct correlation existed between war (with the extra demand it created for munitions) and the establishment of these works.[110] Hirwaun, Dowlais and Plymouth had all been founded during the Seven Years War (1756–63), which also encouraged the setting up of Cyfarthfa. The construction of the Penydarren Ironworks occurred during the American War of Independence (1775–83), which not only increased the demand for armaments but hindered the import of Swedish and Russian iron. This conflict also prompted Bacon to extend his manufacture of cannon at Cyfarthfa, to lease the Plymouth Ironworks in 1777 and the Hirwaun Furnace in 1780. By 1788 there were some thirteen blast furnaces in South Wales making 10,000 tons of pig iron per annum.[111] Whilst it seems unlikely that the economy as a whole benefited from these wars as some have claimed,[112] the metal industries derived short-term advantages from increased demand that, in turn, permitted them to invest heavily in plant.[113] For those ironworks engaged in coke smelting, revenues exceeded costs by on average more than £2 per ton of pig iron during the 1760s and by £1–£2 per ton in the 1770s. The Dowlais furnace, an especially favourable example, had profits of nearly £2,500 in 1764 on an initial investment of £4,000.[114]

However, the beneficial effects of these wars have to be set against the drawbacks usually associated with the return to peace when a crash often followed the sudden reduction in demand. The Peace of Paris, for instance, signed in February 1763 to end the Seven Years War, introduced a few months of continued prosperity, but in July came the inevitable slump.[115] A long period of sluggish trade resulted, in which the unhappy relations with the American colonies played an important part in reducing the level of British exports. In the years before the outbreak of the American War of Independence, iron-masters had to accept that some of their markets, for the time at least, ceased to exist and others needed to be found if production were to continue at comparable levels. At Dowlais, though an indenture dated 24 December 1765 mentioned profits being made from 'cannon balls or bulletts . . . for the use of the King's Majesty's Navy or Army',[116] this was then a declining market. In 1767, for example, the Coalbrookdale Co. used its surplus to make iron rails to replace those of wood for its wagon ways.[117] Throughout this depressed period, Dowlais continued to specialise in the production of pig iron and castings; given the costs of entry it would not have been prudent to diversify into the bar iron trade.[118]

Again, the years immediately after the American Wars were unfavourable for the iron industry, as surplus capacity brought a depression in 1783–85. In August 1782 John Guest wrote to William Beeby, a Dublin merchant, to encourage him to sell their goods:[119]

> I have shipped on board the *Success* of Captain Griffith Francis 17 tons of dark grey pig iron which I have consigned to you as per inclosed bill of lading to sell for my account and as I shall have a pretty large quantity yearly to dispose of I shall be very glad to consign it to you if you think you can dispose of it.

Nevertheless the re-opening of trade with the United States offered a considerable measure of compensation and markets recovered. After 1783, for example, Dowlais exported iron in small quantities to America, the shipments being taken down the valley passes to the port at Cardiff by mule train.

Progressive industrialisation and the fillip provided by war in general kept both prices and demand high in the iron industry. Although it has often been asserted that Henry Cort's invention of a puddling and rolling process in 1784 had permitted a rapid expansion in the output of wrought iron which was generally converted into bar iron,[120] Professor Charles Hyde has demonstrated that it was the 'potting and stamping process', patented in 1761 and 1763 by the Wood brothers, which enabled British producers to capture a substantial share of the domestic bar iron market in the period 1760–90.[121] By this method pig iron taken from the refinery was broken into small pieces and placed in clay crucibles or pots with a flux (to absorb the sulphur) and heated in a coal-fired reverberatory furnace. The high temperature oxidised the carbon and broke the pots, the metal being removed from the furnace to be re-heated in a coal-fired chafery and consolidated under a forge hammer.[122]

Charles Wood introduced the potting and stamping process at Cyfarthfa in 1766, though its adoption on any significant scale was delayed until the 1770s.[123] Forges employing the potting process consistently had average costs at least £2–£3 per ton lower than those achieved at charcoal forges. In 1787, for instance, Cyfarthfa could produce bar iron at £12.12 per ton, while the Backbarrow Forge, using charcoal, had costs of £17.50.[124] Dowlais, which until the first decade of the nineteenth century remained primarily a producer of pig iron, did not adopt the potting and stamping process, introducing its successor 'puddling and rolling'.

In the puddling process, patented by Henry Cort in 1784,[125] the fuel did not come into contact with the molten metal and was, therefore, unable to contaminate it with impurities. Heat generated by a coal fire was reflected off the ceiling of the furnace on to the metal, and decarburisation was accelerated by stirring. Unlike potting, no fluxes were needed; decarburisation proceeded faster than in potting because the metal could be stirred and, if the pig iron had a sufficiently low silicon content, preliminary refining could be eliminated, thereby making puddling a one-stage process[126] (see p. 73). Peter Onions of Merthyr patented a method for producing bar iron of remarkable similarity to puddling in 1783,[127] though it

specified consolidation by hammering rather than rolling. Whilst the Dowlais Ironworks experimented with the Onions technique in 1783, practical difficulties prevented its commercial exploitation there.[128] Indeed, the puddling process patented by Cort had teething troubles and its diffusion was, as a result, considerably delayed. Richard Crawshay who in May 1787 took out the second licence (by which he agreed to pay a royalty of £0.50 per ton of bar iron produced) issued by Cort[129] subsequently attempted to encourage other ironmasters to adopt the process in a circular.[130] The response, by September 1788, was noted:[131] 'The ironmasters are all silent. I have not one line of answer. We must expect little to avoid disappointment'.

Only six ironworks had put Cort's patent into practice by 1790, and they included Penydarren, which in 1788 had started puddling. This resistance to the new method was in part because it required much improvement, and before 1790 offered only minor cost advantages over the potting process. Richard Crawshay, therefore, may take much credit for persevering with the method, for his correspondence with James Cockshutt (d. 1819), the manager of Cyfarthfa between 1788 and 1792, reveals that puddling did not become an unquestioned commercial success at Cyfarthfa until nearly four years after its introduction.[132] As late as December 1791 he remarked that Cyfarthfa was 'in complete readiness for stamping and hammering again' and that he was prepared to abandon puddling if necessary.[133] The turning point came when James Cockshutt was dismissed and Crawshay himself took control.

Although most of the technical difficulties had been slowly overcome, the cost incentive to introduce the technique did not occur

11 A watercolour of rolling mills at Cyfarthfa in 1825 by Penry Williams. (1802–85) Sets of grooved rolls stand in the foreground and a re-heating furnace is in operation on the right. (*Cyfarthfa Castle Museum*)

until the French Revolutionary Wars created a great expansion in demand.[134] Between 1790 and 1798, bar iron output at Cyfarthfa increased from about 2,300 tons to around 6,000 tons, while variable costs fell from £12.3 per ton to slightly under £11 per ton.[135] The improvements made to the puddling process by Crawshay made it the cheapest means of producing bar iron in the mid-1790s; at the same time variable costs for the potting process rose from roughly £11–£12 per ton in the late 1780s to £15 and more by the end of the decade.[136] Hence, Samuel Smiles could observe with the benefit of hindsight that Richard Crawshay, 'the first of the great ironmasters who had the sense to adopt the methods of manufacturing iron invented by Henry Cort', had shown that 'as respects mere money-making, shrewdness is more potent than invention, and business faculty than manufacturing skill'.[137]

Accordingly, Cyfarthfa established a lead over its three rivals at Merthyr. Malkin remarked in 1804 that 'Mr. Crawshay's ironworks are now the largest in the kingdom; probably, indeed, the largest in Europe; and in that case, as far as we know, the largest in the world'.[138] There were three blast furnaces at Cyfarthfa in 1796 and six by 1803, when over 2,000 were employed there. The ranking of the others may be determined from the Merthyr parish book, which in 1796 rated Penydarren at £3,000 per annum, Dowlais at £2,000 and Plymouth at £750.[139] Penydarren and Cyfarthfa had extended their activities to include the manufacture of bar iron and both had introduced Cort's process. Dowlais, like Plymouth, remained primarily a producer of pig iron: in April 1792 Crawshay ordered 1,000 tons of pigs from them at £4 per ton, and in the same year Samuel Homfray of Penydarren entered into a contract with Thomas Guest for a supply of pig iron.[140] Although under John Guest output at Dowlais had grown from 500 tons at the end of 1760 to 1,000 tons per annum in 1763, and rose to 2,000 tons under the management of Thomas Guest in 1790,[141] this rate of acceleration did not match that of its major rivals. The Dowlais Iron Co. was gradually falling behind and had already slipped behind Penydarren in the rankings.

The source of resistance to innovation among the Dowlais partners is uncertain. Dissatisfaction with the failure to extend the firm's range of activities mounted, and in November 1792 Taitt, Cowles, and John and Thomas Guest (who between them held ten of the sixteen shares) offered to sell their combined interest to William Lewis for £25,000.[142] Agreement was not reached and in December 1792 the partners asked Richard Crawshay whether he would purchase the whole works for £60,000.[143] Possibly short of capital himself, and yet to perfect the puddling process, he sensibly refused their suggestion. His supremacy at Merthyr was then unquestioned, and it was only after his death and changes in management that the Dowlais Iron Co. was to present a serious challenge to the might of Cyfarthfa. Dowlais needed to invest in puddling furnaces and rolling mills and if it were to expand further required steam power to overcome the limitations imposed by waterwheels.

SUMMARY

The business success of the Dowlais Iron Co. in its early years relied on the combination of technical expertise and mercantile investment. John Guest provided the practical drive and determination to operate the furnace, while his fellow partners contributed capital and arranged markets for its pig iron and castings. The crucial innovation was the ability to smelt iron with coke, rather than charcoal, which freed the industry from its reliance on the forest and resulted in considerably reduced costs. Output rose consistently under the impetus provided by industrial growth and the demands of war. However, by 1793 the Dowlais partnership had fallen behind its rivals in South Wales through a consistent lack of investment, and dissatisfaction had revealed itself among the progressive members of the firm. Having reached the limits imposed by the use of water power, the ironworks had not followed Crawshay's advance first into potting and stamping and then puddling and rolling. An initial lead at Dowlais had been squandered, it appears, because of the early form of committee management and subsequently by the reluctance of one or more partners (presumably William Lewis) to invest further.

By the time the French Revolutionary Wars broke out in 1793, causing an explosion in the demand for iron (weapons, cannonballs and so forth), the four ironworks at Merthyr Tydfil had established themselves, and had some thirty years experience to draw upon. Cyfarthfa under 'King', as he was known, Richard Crawshay led the field. Through the activities of these and various other ironworks in the region, South Wales had 13 blast furnaces in operation by 1788 with an annual output of 10,800 tons, representing 15.7% of Britain's total, figures that by 1796 had risen to 25 furnaces, 34,400 tons and 27.4% respectively.[144] At this latter date when the total number of blast furnaces was estimated at 144, only two or three were still using charcoal in contrast to 1788 when 53 out of a total 77 were coke fired.[145] In addition, the scale of operations had in many cases altered dramatically. Ironworks, sited near supplies of ore and coal, and now beginning to be powered by steam engines rather than waterwheels, functioned as integrated units where the furnace, forge and mill, hitherto, often distinct and dispersed, had been brought together in one site. Thus, ore extracted in the neighbourhood, smelted with coke from locally mined coal, could be refined and rolled into its finished form as bar iron at the same works.

References

1. John Lloyd, *The Early History of the Old South Wales Iron Works, 1760–1850*, London (1906), pp. 23–24; NLW, Ms 6093E. Papers relating to South East Wales Ironworks, 19b, Dowlais Iron Works (*c.* 1825).
2. Lloyd, *Early History*, p. 24.
3. Lloyd, *Early History*, p. 21.
4. *Morgannwg*, Vol. III (1959), J. England, 'The Dowlais Works 1759–93', p. 42.
5. Ibid., p. 42.
6. Ibid., pp. 30–31; John A. Owen, *The History of the Dowlais Iron Works 1759–1970*, Newport (1977), p. 12; England, 'The Dowlais Works', p. 44.
7. Lloyd, *Early History*, pp. 20–22; Charles Wilkins, *The History of Merthyr Tydfil*, Merthyr Tydfil (1867), p. 139; *Morgannwg*, Vol. XII (1968), John Davies, 'The Dowlais Lease 1748–1900', p. 38.
8. Davies, 'The Dowlais Lease', p. 39; Lloyd, *Early History*, pp. 22–23.
9. Charles Wilkins, *The History of the Iron, Steel, Tinplate and other Trades of Wales*, Merthyr Tydfil (1903), p. 35.
10. GRO, D/DG Section C, Box 8, 'Remarks on the Commencement of the Dowlais Furnace by Charles Price' (*c.* 1800).
11. *Archaeologia Cambrensis, The Journal of the Cambrian Archaeological Society,*

No. XXXIV, April 1863, W. Llewellin, 'Sussex Ironmasters in Glamorganshire', p. 83.

12.   Lloyd, *Early History*, p. 22.
13.   Wilkins, *Merthyr*, p. 147.
14.   T.S. Ashton, *Iron and Steel in the Industrial Revolution*, Manchester (1968), p. 31; T.K. Derry and Trevor I. Williams, *A Short History of Technology*, Oxford (1960), p. 147; John Randall, *History of Madeley including Ironbridge, Coalbrookdale and Coalport*, Madeley (1880), p. 60.
15.   Charles Wilson, *England's Apprenticeship 1603–1763*, London (1965), p. 301.
16.   Charles K. Hyde, *Technological Change in the British Iron Industry 1700–1870*, Princeton (1977), pp. 61–62.
17.   Ibid., p. 62.
18.   R.H. Campbell, *Carron Company*, Edinburgh (1961), pp. 29–36; Ashton, *Iron and Steel*, p. 37.
19.   Wilkins, *Merthyr*, pp. 147–9.
20.   D. Morgan Rees, *Mines, Mills and Furnaces, An Introduction to Industrial Archaeology in Wales*, London HMSO (1969), p. 65; Owen, *Dowlais Iron Works*, p. 10.
21.   *Coke Oven Managers Association Bulletin*, Vol. XXX, No. 3, R.A. Mott, 'Coke Making in Wales', p. 6.
22.   W.E. Minchinton (Editor), *Industrial South Wales 1750–1914*, London (1969), Introduction, p. xii.
23.   Wilkins, *Iron, Steel and Tinplate*, p. 56.
24.   L.S. Pressnell (Editor), *Studies in the Industrial Revolution presented to T.S. Ashton*, London (1960), W.H. Chaloner, 'Isaac Wilkinson, potfounder', p. 24.
25.   J.D. Marshall, *Furness and the Industrial Revolution*, London (1958), pp. 20–25.
26.   James Stockdale, *Annales Caermoelenses: or Annals of Cartmel*, Ulverston (1872), pp. 209–210.
27.   Alfred N. Palmer, *John Wilkinson and the Old Bersham Iron Works*, Wrexham (1899), pp. 11–12; A.H. Dodd, *The Industrial Revolution in North Wales*, Cardiff (1951), p. 135.
28.   Lloyd, *Early History*, p. 72.
29.   Wilkins, *Iron, Steel and Tinplate*, p. 42; *Glamorgan Historian*, Vol. 5, Cambridge (1968), Margaret Stewart Taylor, 'The Plymouth Ironworks', p. 186.
30.   GRO, Charles Wood's Diary No. 2.
31.   Ibid., No. 1, 17 June 1766.
32.   Ibid., No. 2, 25 June 1766.
33.   Ibid., 26 June 1766.
34.   Ibid., 27 June 1766.
35.   Ibid.
36.   Ibid., 28 June 1766.
37.   Ibid.
38.   Ibid., 14 September 1766.
39.   Ibid.
40.   Ibid., 27 June 1766.
41.   Ibid., 29 June 1766.
42.   Ibid.
43.   Ibid.

44. Ibid., 9 July 1766.

45. Ibid., 27 June 1766.

46. Ibid., 14 July 1766.

47. Ibid., 28 July 1766.

48. Ibid., 31 July 1766.

49. Ibid., 10 August 1766.

50. Wilkins, *Merthyr*, p. 141.

51. John Randall, *Our Coal and Iron Industries and the Wilkinsons*, Madeley (1879), p. 39; see also, *The Severn Valley: Series of Sketches*, Madeley (1882), p. 319.

52. Owen, *Dowlais Iron Works*, p. 13.

53. GRO, Charles Wood's Diaries, 22 May 1766, p. 41.

54. Ibid., 26 June 1766.

55. Ibid., p. 15; Madeleine Elsas, *Iron in the Making, Dowlais Iron Company Letters 1782–1860*, Cardiff (1960), p. vii.

56. Wilkins, *Merthyr*, p. 143; *The Engineer*, Vol. XXVI, 17 July 1868, 'The Early History of the Iron Trade in South Wales', p. 39.

57. Wilkins, *Merthyr*, p. 144; MTL, Revd. J. Hathren Davies, 'The History of Dowlais' (1891), p. 6.

58. Lloyd, *Early History*, pp. 23–24.

59. Chaloner, 'Isaac Wilkinson', p. 43.

60. BCL, *The Bristol Directory* (1785), pp. 18, 25, 30; *Sketchley's Bristol Directory* (1775), pp. 22, 41, 54.

61. John Latimer, *The Annals of Bristol in the Eighteenth Century*, Bristol (1893), pp. 442–443.

62. A.H. John, *The Industrial Development of South Wales 1750–1850*, Cardiff (1950), pp. 31–32.

63. Samuel Smiles, *Industrial Biography, Iron Workers and Tool Makers*, London (1863), p. 129.

64. J.P. Addis, *The Crawshay Dynasty, A Study in Industrial Organisation and Development 1765–1867*, Cardiff (1957), pp. 1–2; John, *South Wales*, pp. 24–25.

65. François Crouzet (Editor), *Capital Formation in the Industrial Revolution*, London (1973), Crouzet, 'Capital Formation in Great Britain', p. 173.

66. John, *South Wales*, p. 14.

67. J.T. Barber, *A Tour Throughout South Wales and Monmouthshire*, London (1803), p. 180.

68. Crouzet, *Capital Formation*, Sidney Pollard, 'Fixed Capital in the Industrial Revolution in Britain', pp. 146–147.

69. P.L. Cottrell, *Industrial Finance 1830–1914*, London (1980), pp. 30–31.

70. Alan Birch, *The Economic History of the British Iron and Steel Industry 1784–1879*, London (1967), pp. 198, note 6.

71. John, *South Wales*, p. 35.

72. Pollard, 'Fixed Capital', p. 150.

73. Ibid., p. 157.

74. Addis, *Crawshay Dynasty*, p. 156 ss.

75. John, *South Wales*, p. 43.

76. Owen, *Dowlais Iron Works*, p. 15.

77. NLW, Mayberry Collection, No. 3968, Indenture between Robert Price and John Guest, 19 August 1782; GRO, D/DG, John Guest to J. Hawkins, 22 July 1782 (Copy Letters 1782–94); Madeleine Elsas, *Iron in the Making*, p. 81.

78. Elsas, *Iron in the Making*, p. viii, 238; England, 'The Dowlais Works', p. 51.

79. Ashton, *Iron and Steel*, p. 22.

80. M.W. Flinn, *Men of Iron, The Crowleys in the Early Iron Industry*, Edinburgh (1962), p. 3.

81. GRO, D/DG Plans No. 1, 'The Iconography of the Merthir Furnace' (*c.* 1767); R.A. Mott's Re-drawn Plan and Letters, 29 July 1963; Plan No. 2; D/DG Section C, Box 6, Charles Price's 'Remarks'.

82. Lloyd, *Early History*, p. 29.

83. Owen, *Dowlais Iron Works*, p. 12.

84. MTL, Henry Murton, 'Recollections of Dowlais, its Works and Workpeople 1808–1812' (1873), p. 2.

85. MTL, Revd. Hathren Davies, 'History of Dowlais', p. 6.

86. Owen, *Dowlais Iron Works*, p. 16.

87. England, 'The Dowlais Works', p. 51; Elizabeth Havill, *Transactions of the Honourable Society of Cymmrodorion* (1983), 'William Taitt and the Dowlais Iron Co.', p. 102.

88. Wilkins, *Merthyr*, p. 175.

89. England, 'The Dowlais Works'., p. 54.

90. Ibid., p. 55.

91. GRO, D/DG E 112/2096/135.

92. T.E. Clarke, *A Guide to Merthyr-Tydfil, the Traveller's Companion*, Merthyr Tydfil (1848), p. 15; see also, W. Sotheby, *A Tour through parts of Wales*, London (1794), pp. 15–16; and *Tours in Wales (1804–1813)* by Richard Fenton, Edited by John Fisher, London (1917), for a description of Merthyr in 1695, p. 346.

93. Henry Skrine, *Two Successive tours throughout the Whole of Wales*, London (1798), p. 48.

94. Benjamin H. Malkin, *The Scenery, Antiquities and Biography of South Wales*, London (1804), p. 170.

95. Ibid., p. 177.

96. Ibid., p. 176.

97. G.W. Manby, *An Historic and Picturesque Guide from Clifton through the Counties of Monmouth, Glamorgan and Brecknock*, Bristol (1802), p. 187.

98. Minchinton, *Industrial South Wales*, p. xiv.

99. John Fox, *General View of the Agriculture of the County of Glamorgan*, London (1796), p. 7.

100. Ashton, *Iron and Steel*, p. 197.

101. Malkin, *Scenery, Antiquities*, p. 179.

102. Ibid., p. 178.

103. Quoted from F.D. Klingender, *Art and the Industrial Revolution*, London (1972), p. 116, plate 17; the watercolour is held at the Ironbridge Gorge Museum Trust in the Arthur Elton Collection.

104. Merthyr Tydfil Teachers' Centre Group, *Merthyr Tydfil A Valley Community*, Cowbridge (1981), pp. 282–289.

105. Rees, *Mines, Mills*, p. 70.

106. *Glamorgan Historian*, Vol. 3, Cambridge (1966), Margaret Stewart Taylor, 'The Penydarren Ironworks 1784–1859', p. 75.

107. Wilkins, *Merthyr*, p. 156.

108. Addis, *Crawshay Dynasty*, pp. 1–2.

109. Ibid., pp. 8–10.

110. John, *Industrial Development of South Wales*, pp. 32–32.

111. Minchinton, *Industrial South Wales*, p. xii.

112. *EcHR*, Vol. VII (1955), A.H. John, 'War and the English Economy 1700–1763', pp. 329–344.

113. Crouzet, *Capital Formation*, pp. 214–215.
114. Hyde, *Technological Change*, p. 63.
115. Ashton, *Iron and Steel*, p. 132.
116. England, 'The Dowlais Works'., p. 48.
117. Ashton, *Iron and Steel*, p. 134.
118. England, 'The Dowlais Works'., p. 52.
119. GRO, D/DG, Letters Out Going 1792–1794, August 1782, p. 13.
120. Phyllis Deane, *The First Industrial Revolution*, Cambridge (1965), p. 107.
121. Hyde, *Technological Change*, p. 77; see also Charles Hyde, *EcHR*, Vol. XXVII, 'Technological Change in the British Wrought Iron Industry 1750–1815', pp. 197–200.
122. Hyde, *Technological Change*, pp. 83–84.
123. Ibid., p. 86.
124. Ibid., p. 87.
125. Patent No. 1420, 14 February 1784.
126. Hyde, *Technological Change*, p. 89.
127. Patent No. 1370, 7 May 1783; see C.W. Roberts, *A Legacy from Victorian Enterprise, The Briton Ferry Ironworks and the Daughter Companies*, Gloucester (1983), pp. 21–22.
128. Owen, *Dowlais Iron Works*, p. 15; Hyde, p. 90.
129. Hyde, *Technological Change*, p. 91.
130. GwRO, Letter Book of R. Crawshay, 1 January 1788 – 3 November 1797, Circular dated July 1788.
131. Ibid., R. Crawshay to Samuel Jellicoe, 12 September 1788.
132. Ibid.; Hyde, *Technological Change*, p. 96; see also GRO, Cyfarthfa Mss Account Books 1791–98, and 1802–06; C. Reginald Andrews, The Story of the Wortley Ironworks, Nottingham (1975), pp. 46, 51.
133. GwRO, Letter Book, R. Crawshay to Henry Cort, 24 December 1791.
134. Ashton, *Iron and Steel*, pp. 142–53.
135. Hyde, *Technological Change*, p. 101.
136. Ibid.
137. Smiles, *Industrial Biography*, p. 128.
138. Malkin, *Scenery, Antiquities*, p. 266.
139. Wilkins, *Merthyr*, p. 162.
140. England, 'The Dowlais Works', p. 54.
141. *Merthyr Historian*, Vol. I (1976), J. Owen, 'Chronological Date Sequence of Events for the Dowlais Ironworks', pp. 7–8.
142. GRO, D/DG Dowlais Iron Co. Letter Book 1792–93, 29 November 1792.
143. Ibid., 11 December 1792, p. 72.
144. Ashton, *Iron and Steel*, p. 98; J.C. Carr and W. Taplin, *History of the British Steel Industry*, Oxford (1962), p. 6.
145. W.K.V. Gale, *Historic Industrial Scenes, Iron and Steel*, Hartington (1977), p. 10.

2 *War and Expansion at Dowlais, 1793–1815*

War in the eighteenth century had in general been a driving force for the creation and expansion of ironworks, and the period 1793–1815 was no exception. Initially, however, war with Revolutionary France had the opposite effect, contributing as it did to the commercial crisis of 1793 which brought an end to the wave of investment that had begun in the early 1780s.[1] For the next three years the price of iron remained fairly steady, increased supply (the product of a decade's growth) being able to cope with rising demand. Then, in 1796, the price of imported iron rose by about 30 per cent[2] – the result of higher customs duties and the interruptions to trade with the Baltic nations caused by the war at sea[3] – which in a climate of swelling orders ensured huge profits for British ironmasters. Successive increases, during 1797 and 1798, in the duty on foreign bar iron were deliberately designed to encourage the home industry. The tariff on imported bar iron had been £2.81 per ton in the period 1782–95 but rapidly mounted to £6.49 by 1813 and had the effect of pricing the Swedish and Russian product out of the UK market.[4] Hence one ironmaster declared in 1798 that no fewer than twenty one blast furnaces had been constructed since 1796 and that a further nineteen were nearing completion.[5] In Glamorgan alone nine blast furnaces were built between 1796 and 1800, five new ironworks being established in South Wales in 1799–1802.[6]

On the demand side, repeated orders for ordnance, small arms and munitions from the government were of major significance, apart from the need for all the varied metallic objects required in the assembly of vessels, gun carriages and encampments. In May 1798, for instance, William Taitt wrote 'we have an offer of making a large quantity of guns and 4 and 6 pounders if we can immediately set about them'.[7] Whilst on the supply side, the possibility of a break in trade with the Northern nations (Sweden and Russia), which provided a substantial proportion of the iron required by the smaller metal trades of Sheffield and the Black Country, was a factor in stimulating increased output and the discovery of new methods of production.[8] The actual severance of trade with those countries in 1800–01 added greatly to the orders placed with British ironworks.

It might have been expected that the temporary conclusion of peace in October 1801 would have resulted in loss to ironmasters and unemployment for workers. In 1801 and 1802, during this breathing-space, the secondary iron trades certainly suffered, but the impetus derived from coke technology and the much expanded markets now available to British makers were sufficient to carry them across the gulf to the Napoleonic Wars. In 1801–02 twenty two new blast furnaces came into production and a further twenty five were under construction.[9] The resumption of hostilities in May 1803 gave the promise of fresh prosperity to the industry. The years 1797–1803 coincided with a period of major investment in iron which peaked during 1799–1802.[10] Against this background of expansion, Richard Crawshay erected two furnaces at Ynysfach in 1801 to the design of Thomas Jones, thereby supplementing the output of his huge Cyfarthfa works,[11] which by 1803 made[12]

> upon average, between sixty and seventy tons of bar iron every week, and has lately erected two new additional furnaces, which will soon begin to work, when he will be able to make, one week with another, 100 tons of bar iron. Mr. Homfray makes weekly, on a moderate average, fifty tons of bar iron and upwards, and is now extending Penydarren and its buildings, which will soon be completed; he will then make at least eighty tons per week. The Dowlais Iron Works . . . are on as large a scale of those of Penydarren, and about to be augmented in an equal proportion. Those of Mr. Hill [Plymouth] make thirty tones of iron weekly and upwards; additional buildings are now erecting, which, when finished, will make at least forty tons per week.

The establishment of a forge and foundry at Cwmbran in 1800 alongside the Monmouthshire and Brecon Canal by F.J. Blewitt of Llantarnam Abbey,[13] and the construction of a blast furnace at Brymbo, Denbighshire in c. 1796[14] were other features of this war-induced expansion in the iron industry. Although John Wilkinson had purchased the Brymbo Hall estate in 1792,[15] its actual development was delayed until the mid-1790s. Aiming at an annual target of 4,000 tons of pig iron, Wilkinson set plans in motion to build two blast furnaces, the first, 'Old Number One', being completed in c. 1796[16] and the second not so long afterwards.[17]

While the French Revolutionary Wars had corresponded with a dramatic expansion in the British iron industry, the Napoleonic Wars, 1803–15, did not generate comparable levels of investment, even in good years such as 1806 and 1809.[18] Although imports of Swedish and Russian iron continued to decline (from 17,194 tons in 1806 to 8,816 in 1809)[19] and the armed forces still demanded high qualities of ordnance, the general disruption of trade created by Napoleon's Continental System prevented any sharp increase in demand. The latter was designed to exclude British exports from France and her Continental allies in an attempt to ruin her trade and promote a financial crisis. The American embargo from December 1807 to March 1809 and the subsequent period of restrictions had in fact produced a fall in exports to the United States of no less than 50 per cent, ironmasters being only partially compensated by the speculative boom in trade with South America; the collapse of this bubble late in 1810 led to the temporary trade depression of 1811.[20] In 1812 the downturn cleared and a substantial increase in output occurred in South Wales and Staffordshire where the iron industry was most closely associated with those trades dependent upon exports.[21] Moreover, by this time Sweden had been forced by Napoleon into war against Britain and the sudden fall in imports of bar iron from the Baltic provided a gap for English forges to fill until mid-1812. From then till 1815, when peace returned, British ironmasters prospered in spite of the restoration of relations with Sweden and Russia in 1813, because tariff defences had been strengthened by a pound increase on the duty to £6 9s 10d per ton.

In general, these twenty years of uneven war-induced expansion had promoted widespread investment in iron, and in the puddling process in particular. While only five British forges had used puddling before 1795, fifteen adopted the technique in 1795–1805 and thirty-seven more followed suit before the end of the Napoleonic Wars.[22] High levels of profit encouraged both investment and a rapid growth in output. The consistent ploughing back of these swollen profits ensured a rapid accumulation of capital within ironworks. At Cyfarthfa, for instance, the capital value of the plant rose from £14,000 in 1790 to £160,000 by 1813[23] – an annual growth rate of 11.17 per cent – while at Kirkstall Forge, near Leeds, it mounted from £1,800 in 1799 to £29,578 by 1808, at an average annual increase of 10.18 per cent.[24] Rates of the order of ten per cent were not uncommon, though some such as Newton, Chambers & Co. (1793–1821) and J. Marsh & Co. (1813–38), both of Sheffield, achieved 12.6 per cent and 17.6 per cent respectively.[25]

VERTICAL INTEGRATION AND INNOVATION

The immediate history of relative decline at the Dowlais Iron Co. had been a product of lack of investment in the latest technology. The greater level of demand created by the war encouraged the partners to expand and, in doing so, narrowed the gap that had opened between them and Cyfarthfa and Penydarren. Nevertheless, pig iron remained the sole product, and in 1796 they agreed to sell 2,000 tons per annum (almost their total output) to the Crawshays for five years. In that year

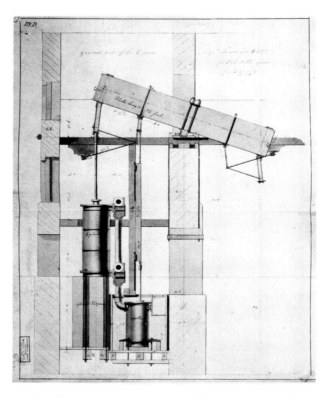

12 A diagram of the Boulton and Watt beam-engine ordered by William Taitt for the Dowlais furnaces in 1798. (*Birmingham Reference Library*)

the company's capital had still only reached £20,000, at a time when Cyfarthfa was worth eight times that sum.

Although the adoption of steam power was indeed critical for the long term development of the Dowlais Iron Co., this was not because, as some historians have argued, coke smelting only became a manifestly superior technique after steam engines had been introduced to provide the blast for furnaces.[26] Hyde has shown that coke furnaces produced iron more cheaply than those using charcoal at a time before anybody had purchased a Boulton & Watt engine.[27] According to his estimates, the total cost of making a ton of pig iron at Dowlais in 1764 was £2.52, a figure that had risen to £3.73 in 1770–75.[28] These costs were significantly lower than at charcoal-fired furnaces and were achieved long before steam was introduced at Dowlais. Similarly, Crawshay, whose works were served by the River Taff, could happily rely on water power, and constructed a mammoth 50ft waterwheel to provide the blast for his three furnaces. When completed in about 1785, it was believed to be the largest in Britain and was designed by Watkin George, who had trained as a carpenter, but eventually became a partner at Cyfarthfa in 1792.[29]

While by no means crucial for the initial diffusion of coke-smelting technology, the steam engine permitted the subsequent development of large, integrated ironworks in which the weight of machinery could no longer be driven by waterwheels. 'The period 1788 to 1790', suggested Scrivenor in 1854, 'may be considered a new era in the history of the manufacture of iron, arising from the more general use by ironmasters, of the double power engine of Mr. Watt'.[30] An interim stage (when Newcomen 'fire-engines' were installed to pump water into reservoirs to feed a waterwheel)[31] was overtaken at Dowlais in 1798 at a cost of £1,382 when William Taitt ordered a double-acting steam engine with a 40ins cylinder from Boulton & Watt.[32] This superseded the cylinder blower (whose piston was driven by water power) that had been patented by Isaac Wilkinson, as Taitt wrote to Boulton & Watt in November 1798 that[33] 'I have now to say that our old engine will be stopped on Monday next 26th inst. and I hope in 7 or 8 days the new one will be at work, as everything is completely ready for it'. The continued expansion of the ironworks prompted them to buy a second engine in 1803 (36ins cylinder)[34] and a third with a 50ins cylinder in 1810.[35] Steam technology was not introduced with such rapidity at Cyfarthfa because of adequate alternatives. As late as 1849 an eyewitness could report that,[36]

> These extensive works are chiefly carried on by water power, the supply being procured from the River Taff at a considerable distance up the valley, but steam is used when in summer the water fails. The machinery is very large and ponderous. Those of the waterwheels are 36 feet in diameter, and the flywheels, which are 60 feet in circumference and of prodigious weight, make ordinarily 70 revolutions in a minute.

Thus, the fortunate provision of running water, which gave Crawshay an early advantage over Dowlais in the pre-steam era, restrained him from investing in the latest power technology, though in 1788 he had apparently purchased a Boulton & Watt engine.[37] The Guests had no option, if they wished to expand, but to buy steam engines and it was their mechanical improvement that held the key to providing drive for rolling mills and blast for furnaces.

The wish to duplicate plant was not the sole reason for purchasing a Boulton & Watt engine, for the nature of coke smelting and coal mining made its fuel relatively cheap. Only the larger pieces of coal could be coked and used in the furnace (p. 41), the 'small coals' and 'slack', or coal dust, had limited uses but had to be removed from the mine, otherwise they would hinder the cutting of the remaining deposits. It was this coal that could be used to fuel the boilers of steam engines.[38]

In addition, the steam engine was much more reliable than the waterwheel – in periods of short rainfall or extreme cold when streams froze, the latter could be rendered useless. Charcoal furnaces needed to be shut down for at least four months of the year;[39] and though coke furnaces, on occasion, had to be blown out for repairs, they could be operated (particularly when steam engines provided a stronger and more regular blast than had been possible with waterwheels) continuously for periods of several years; Truran reported in 1855 that furnaces at Dowlais possessed an average life of eleven years before requiring to be re-lined, the longest period he had experienced being eighteen years.[40]

The other decision which allowed the Dowlais Iron Co. to ascend the ranking of South Wales ironworks was taken in 1801 when they chose to adopt Cort's puddling and rolling process and whole-heartedly entered the market for bar iron. No longer did they remain suppliers of pig iron to their larger rivals. Henceforth the company could compete for orders on an equal basis with integrated works like Cyfarthfa. Taitt had been the protagonist in favour of this strategy and had in part financed the expenditure from his own pocket: he wrote in September 1802 to his son-in-law to explain that the demands of the works prevented him from visiting his dying daughter.[41]

The introduction of rolling mills multiplied the number of iron products that the Dowlais Iron Co. could manufacture. A list of products made at Dowlais in 1816 mentions thirty three distinct shapes and sizes, including eight gauges of 'rounds' and six of 'flats'.[42] The range of specialised shapes permitted by the introduction of grooved rolls was vastly greater than had been possible using hammers and stamping.[43] Following this capital investment, the Dowlais Iron Co. began its recovery. In 1811 John Wood recorded that the company lay third if ranked according to the annual output of bar iron: Cyfarthfa (11,000 tons), Penydarren (7,000), Dowlais (5,000), and Plymouth (4,000). Considerable economies of scale existed for rolling mills (in contrast to puddling where greater output was achieved by duplicating plant rather than increasing the size or complexity of operations). The average output of rolling mills in South Wales rose from 5,300 tons in 1812 to 8,400 tons in 1817 at a time when the smallest mill in the region produced over 4,000 tons annually and the largest, which was Cyfarthfa, attained an output of about 13,500 tons per annum.[44]

Even after Dowlais had improved its pig-making facilities and set up its own puddling furnaces and rolling mills, demand for bar iron still often outstripped its capacity. In 1806, for example, the company recorded purchases from other producers which amounted to almost a third of total sales:[45]

500	tons of pig iron from Cyfarthfa
240	tons of pig iron from Beaufort
1,000	tons of bar iron from Penydarren
152	tons of unspecified iron from Beaufort
1,892	tons, total known purchases

Yet as capacity at Dowlais expanded (and after the 1815 post-war boom crashed into a slump), the practice of buying iron from rivals declined in absolute and percentage terms.

By 1800 the three blast furnaces at Dowlais had attained an annual output of 3,000 tons of pig iron.[46] The construction of puddling furnaces and rolling mills enabled them to manufacture 5,432 tons of bar iron and tramplates in 1806.[47] Profits which had stood at £1,900 for the year ending 31 March 1793, rose accordingly, reaching £4,000 in 1804.[48] A fourth blast furnace was erected in 1808 (with an average weekly make of 50 tons) by which time four refinery fires, twenty puddling and ten balling furnaces had been constructed.[49] A profit of £9,846 in 1810 was improved upon during the remainder of the war and achieved a peak of £16,528 in 1814.[50] When a fifth furnace came into operation in 1815, the Dowlais Co. was able to produce 15,600 tons of pig iron per annum,[51] while the quantity of coal consumed had fallen to four tons per ton of pig iron.[52] Local stone was used in the construction of these structures and, being raised nearby on the Common, the cost of materials did not serve as a brake on the building of bigger furnaces.[53]

Larger, more efficient blast furnaces were permitted by coke-smelting and the introduction of the steam engine. Coke could support a much heavier 'charge' than charcoal so that in the nineteenth century the dimensions of the furnace were chiefly determined by the strength of the blast needed to support combustion.[54] The problem was solved by the application of ever more powerful and reliable steam engines. Later in the century as an inexpensive means of assisting the smelting process engineers sometimes added coal to the coke in the furnace (large coals to prevent crushing, which in turn would inhibit the flow of the blast). However pig iron produced by this means contained a higher level of impurities (these being partially removed by the coking process) and required further refining before being puddled.

A further incentive to construct larger blast furnaces was provided by the knowledge that unit costs fell with increases in size. A blast furnace with dimensions 25ft by 10ft by 10ft required 1,000 square feet of masonry and encompassed a volume of 2,500 cubic feet; if its dimensions were increased to, say, 40ft by 15ft by 15ft, the volume would increase by a factor of 3.6 to 9,000 cubic feet, while the square footage of masonry would rise by a smaller factor of 2.4 to 2,400 square feet.[55]

Gains could also be made on overheads. The construction of a second furnace of greater size presumably would not, for example, have increased managerial costs. A cashier would have been required whether there were one or two furnaces and might need an assistant only if a further five or six furnaces were erected. The same would have been true of certain buildings (offices, stables, workrooms for fitters, blacksmiths and so forth). Potential economies of scale awaited should an ironmaster decide to expand certain sections of plant. To operate a single furnace it was necessary to invest considerable capital in mines, tramways, housing and roads, and these would not require duplication if a second or third furnace were added.

There was a marked increase in the size of blast furnaces being constructed in the late 1790s. The coke blast furnaces of the 1750s and 1760s had stood about 25ft high, roughly the same size as charcoal furnaces.[56] Ironmasters using coke began to experiment with larger structures in the late 1770s but the first major increase in their dimensions came during the 1790s in South Wales. Gilbert Gilpin, who toured the region in 1796, noticed that most of the coke furnaces he visited were 50–60ft high and produced an average of 1,500 tons per annum.[57] By 1805 furnace output at Dowlais had reached approximately 2,100 tons per annum, a figure well above the national average.[58]

The investment in additional blast furnaces and the expansion of the works' puddling and rolling capacity resulted, according to Clarke's calculations, in Dowlais overtaking Penydarren (whose three blast furnaces had an annual output of 7,800 tons) by 1815, but it still remained some way behind Cyfarthfa.[59] The Plymouth Works had grown considerably and now equalled Penydarren in output.[60]

MINING OPERATIONS: COAL AND IRON ORE

The occurrence of bituminous coal, iron ore and limestone in proximity to one another and their easy extraction lay at the basis of Merthyr's prosperous iron industry. Robert Clutterbuck's description of operations at Penydarren in 1799 revealed the importance of the combination of mineral deposits in the Merthyr region:[61]

> After the ore has been exposed to calcination in these kilns by the continuance of a uniform red heat, it is removed to the furnaces and thrown together with limestone unburned, in the proportion of one ton of ore to one and half cwt. of lime. This compound generally requires twelve hours for complete fusion, during which time the furnace is supplied with fresh quantities of ore and limestone as the charge is already put in contracts in size . . . the average consumption is computed at about a hundred tons of ore in twenty four hours, and produces about one third of its weight in metal, which still contains many impurities.

In the early days coal was not mined there by sinking pits and extracting the mineral through underground passages. Because it occurred in outcrops near the surface the technique of 'scouring' proved to be an effective means of preparation. Mountain streams were dammed to considerable heights at such places as Twyncarno and the debris swiftly cleared away, the ensuing rush of water scouring iron ore and coal from the sides of the valley. These minerals by their greater weight would sink to the bottom of the stream.[62] The accumulated tips of spoil, dumped into Dowlais Brook, were also removed during spells of heavy rainfall by opening the sluices of the larger ponds to produce a torrent of sufficient force to wash away a level or large tip.[63] The method caused much damage and generated a considerable number of lawsuits.[64] Given the limitations of water power, and the fact that the Dowlais Ironworks was sited on the same brook as the Penydarren Co., but further upstream, the latter often complained that the former had taken a disproportionate share of the water. In May 1784, for example, a lease was drafted between John Guest and the Homfray brothers giving the former rights of passage for his wagons and horses, while the latter were allowed to divert water from a certain spring, provided that they left a supply for a nearby house and sufficient 'in dry seasons for injection of water for the fire engine at Dowlais furnace'.[65] There was insufficient coal on the Penydarren land so several veins had to be leased from Dowlais. In 1786 Guest granted the Homfrays a seven-year lease permitting them 'liberty to exploit the coal and make use of water issuing forth from veins of coal for the purpose of watering cokes and cokeyards at Penydarren furnace; at an annual rent of £140.8.0d. with an additional rent of 6d. per ton for coal taken in excess of 5,616 tons'.[66] Quarrels and lawsuits followed over the interpretation of these mining agreements. Wilkins, who on occasion exaggerated, suggested that coal at Dowlais, being nearer the outcrop than at Penydarren, could be obtained at one shilling per ton, while their rivals had to pay three times as much.[67]

Mining was not generally performed by company employees but by contractors who had specific agreements to supply the works. In 1793 Harry Thomas, a miner at Dowlais, agreed,[68]

> to raise 1,500 tons of Little Vein Mine [iron ore] in a work he is to open near his house – of which mine not more than 300 tons is to be raised in open works and engages to raise 50 tons per month . . . in consideration of which the said Dowlais Company engage to pay the said Harry Thomas five shillings per ton for every ton of ironstone delivered at the pit mouth and three shillings per ton for every ton of good coals delivered into a wagon at the rail road or on the furnace bank.

Even in the early days when coal was primarily mined to feed the ironworks, some was sold to consumers outside Merthyr.[69] Around 1810 Richard Crawshay sent coal to Cardiff by the Glamorganshire Canal (p. 47) where it sold for about 10 shillings per ton.[70] As John

Guest had more coal than required for his furnaces but was short of lime, 'he surmounted the difficulty', according to Davies,[71] 'by bartering one commodity for another. As limestone was abundant in the vicinity, the Cwm Taf Fawr and Cwm Taf Fechan farmers burnt lime for their personal use in their own small kilns on the mountain side'. The juxtaposition of ironstones and coal measures within neighbouring bands of strata was of crucial importance. Certain types contained sufficient carbonaceous matter to enable them to be calcined (that is, roasted as a preliminary to smelting) without the addition of fuel; these were called 'blackband'.[72] The Revd. Evans visiting Merthyr in 1803 observed that the local ores if properly mixed were suitable for most iron products:[73]

> The ores of the district are of a greyish or brownish black colour . . . and of so brittle a nature, as not to be worked with advantage alone to give it tenacity therefore for wire and other purposes, they make use of a red ochreous ore from Furnace [sic] in Lancashire . . . and by a proportionate mixture of the two, they produce iron of every quality from the Spanish blade to the Swedish bar, adapted for the different purposes of making wire or sheathing wheels.

The 'mine', as ores were then termed, was extracted in the same fashion as coal; scoured by damming streams and subsequently hewn by labour from patches, drifts or levels. So long as deposits occurred near the surface the techniques required to extract them remained simple, characterised by repetitious and strenuous toil.

MANAGEMENT AND ITS POLICIES

The turn-around evident in the fortunes of the Dowlais Iron Co. cannot be seen simply in terms of economic fluctuation and the progressive introduction of coke technology as changes in the organisation and management of the company were also of conse-quence. During December 1791 and January 1792 the output of the blast furnaces declined to 126 and 97 tons respectively because of the poor state of repair into which they had been allowed to fall.[74] To modernise the works, early in 1792 Robert Thompson was appointed 'Manager, Superintendent and Agent' for twenty one years at an annual salary of £250 together with all profits above that sum which accrued from a one-sixteenth share. Thompson succeeded in improv-ing the productivity of the furnaces and made the mines safer but his precipitate departure in 1799 brought Josiah Guest into prominence and by 1807, when he took complete charge, the plant had been brought to a good state of repair, though it seems that this had been achieved not without considerable financial strain. *The Gentleman's Magazine* recorded that in 1806 the Dowlais Co.[75]

> produced yearly about 5,000 tons of iron, and were on the death of the proprietors, in considerable pecuniary embarrassment. Mr. Thomas Guest died in 1807. The entire management then devolved upon Sir J.J. Guest who, by his extraordinary capacity for business, his mechanical ingenuity (to which many of the most important improvements in the working of iron are to be attributed), and by a judgement in mercantile transactions rarely equalled not only cleared the firm of debt, but raised the produce of the mines in a few years to no less than 68,000 tons.

Too much blame should not be placed on the shoulders of Thomas Guest as his earlier attempts to make the works more efficient had been blocked by the conservative partners (likely to have included those resident in Bristol whose appreciation of its problems was comparatively remote) who were anxious to maximise profits in the short term, refusing in April 1783 to allow him to 'raise the stack of the furnace'.[76] His failure to modernise the plant was possibly conditioned by earlier frustrations.

When Thomas Guest died on 28 February 1807, having developed an obstruction of the neck and bladder, control of the Dowlais Ironworks passed into the hands of his eldest son, Josiah John Guest (1785–1852), then only twenty-two, but set to become one of its most successful managers. Alexander Kirkwood, a nephew of William Taitt (who owned eight of the sixteen shares), was instructed to assist the youthful Guest.[77] This was probably because Taitt, who had despaired of Thomas Guest, also had few hopes of Josiah whom he described as inattentive and possessing deplorable handwriting.[78] The death of Kirkwood from tuberculosis on 6 January 1814 and the demise of the dictatorial and energetic Taitt on 20 November 1815 made Josiah Guest's authority undisputed.[79] He inherited the eight shares to add to the one he already held, whilst Thomas Revel Guest (1790–1837), his younger brother, owned another. William Lewis had increased his holding from two to six shares by the time of his death in 1802 and these were inherited by a nephew, Wyndham Lewis MP (1779–1838).[80] Although the latter had trained as a solicitor and later became a barrister, he sold his legal practice in High Street, Cardiff, and devoted much of his business energy to the Dowlais Iron Co. Described as a 'grave melancholy man'[81] Wyndham Lewis founded the banking firm of Lewis & Guest, with branches in Merthyr and Cardiff. His wife, Mary Ann, née Evans, who subsequently married Disraeli, persuaded him to enter politics and in 1821 he won the seat for Glamorgan Borough, though the Marquis of Bute ensured that his uncle Lord Patrick Crichton-Stuart defeated him at the next election. Wyndham Lewis became MP for Aldeburgh in 1826 and in 1835 for

13 Thomas Revel Guest (1790–1837), a partner and the company's agent based principally in Ireland. (*Glamorgan Record Office*)

Maidstone. His share of the Dowlais Iron Co. was inherited by his younger brother, the Revd. William Price Lewis (p. 240).

In attempting to characterise the behaviour and activities of John, Thomas and Josiah Guest, William Taitt, Richard Crawshay, the Homfrays and other South-Wales ironmasters, the term 'entrepreneur' is most fitting. Of humble origins (not normally farmers, like Guest, but more commonly from the secondary metal trades), they were often as demanding of themselves as of others; business was their consuming interest and they continued to lead the simple lives to which they had become accustomed and to which there was little alternative. They practised a stringent personal economy and rigid austerity to maximise their savings. Withdrawing each year from their firms only a small part of the profits for their personal needs, they paid themselves small salaries. The case of the Walker Brothers was perhaps extreme: starting with a wage of ten shillings per week, it was fifteen years before they allowed themselves a dividend of £140, about 2.5% of their foundry's value.[82] Entrepreneurs consistently ploughed back most of their profits in order to finance expansion. At Cyfarthfa in the 1790s Richard Crawshay systematically re-invested any surplus each year. In 1821 William Crawshay I (1764–1834) wrote in characteristic vein to his son that profits were to be 'left on the spot . . . to support that which created it'.[83] During wartime this often produced a considerable re-investment – in excess of a 15–20 per cent return on capital employed, and at Cyfarthfa in 1796–97 reached a startling 52 per cent.[84] Losses were correspondingly rare, except in the lean years after 1815 and even during periods of reduced trade profits remained respectable.[85]

The fact that so many of these entrepreneurs were also members of Non-conformist sects reinforced their tendency towards abstinence; hard work and thrift discouraged them from a sybaritic lifestyle or a conscious attempt to ape the upper classes, even when they had made a fortune.[86] Prevented by the 1673 Test Act and the 1661 Corporation Act from entering the universities, professions, or from holding civil, corporate or military office, dissenters were encouraged to enter commerce or industry in the newer settlements where the trade guilds had yet to establish their authority. In South Wales the spiritual energies of the ironmasters found general expression in the Methodist movement. Whilst the wealthiest of them all, Richard Crawshay, adhered to the established church, most of his contemporaries were followers of Wesley.[87] The Guests (from John onwards) lent their weighty influence to his teachings. Thomas always exhibited 'the gravity and strong religious convictions which characterised the brethren in the early epoch of Wesleyanism'.[88] 'Gruff in speech, brusque, not interested in frivolity', he showed a greater concern for Wesleyan preaching than iron making and gave much money to the chapels of Merthyr.[89] Josiah Guest 'showed less of sectarian influences than his brother, Thomas [Revel] Guest, who, though rather wild in his youth, became, like his father, a local preacher'.[90] Isaac Wilkinson and his son, William, were both members of the Presbyterian chapel in Wrexham but gravitated towards Unitarianism, while John Wilkinson, founder of Brymbo, has variously been described as a Unitarian, Churchman, Methodist and unbeliever.[91]

LABOUR PROBLEMS

The operation of an integrated ironworks brought with it new problems of labour. The men employed in the forges and furnaces had, by virtue of their number, the power, if properly organised, to challenge the master's authority. Accordingly, in 1810 when the price of wheat rose following bad harvests and a depression occurred in the iron industry (the price per ton falling from 12s. 0d. to 10s. 6d.), Josiah Guest reduced his men's wages and prompted the first organised strike at Dowlais.[92] For two weeks the works were at a complete standstill. Then those men who, through hardship, decided to accept the revised, lower rate began to drift back to work; Josiah Guest 'rewarded these by allowing them to select their own [puddling] furnaces – a course that was the cause of much ill-feeling among the men . . . Within about five weeks all had returned'.[93] This strike set the pattern for much of the nineteenth century, sharp movements in wages or food prices often provoking industrial action, a response invariably resisted by the management at Dowlais (see p. 276). At this stage, however, trade unionism had not been established in Merthyr and the first strike of 1810 was a genuinely spontaneous mass-movement triggered by hardship. Guest, in common with many other ironmasters, attempted to maintain a healthy surplus for re-investment and as a safeguard against the vicissitudes of the trade cycle. He believed that if the cost of provisions rose too fast this put powerful pressures on wages which would, in turn, erode profits and bring an end to prosperity in the manufacturing sector. He was, therefore, an advocate of restraint in times of shortage and careful budgeting in periods of plenty.

TRANSPORT PROBLEMS: THE GLAMORGANSHIRE CANAL

The most pressing problem facing the four Merthyr ironworks in 1793 was the absence of an efficient transport system to the port of Cardiff. Merthyr, situated at the head of the sparsely populated Taff valley, had never developed any form of communication suitable for frequent consignments of bulky, low-value goods. Iron was conveyed to Cardiff by trains of pack mules, a slow, inconvenient and, in times of adverse weather, impossible journey. The first attempt to improve matters had been made in 1767 by Anthony Bacon who organised a local subscription to repair the road from Merthyr, through Caerphilly, to Cardiff.[94] However, without the regular income available to a turnpike trust for maintenance and suffering under the heavy traffic generated by the ironworks, the route soon fell into disrepair. The first turnpike proper was authorised by an Act of 1771 which permitted the extension of the Cardiff-Taffs Well road to Merthyr. Significantly, both William Lewis and John Guest became trustees,[95] while the General Turnpike Act of 1785 included Jeremiah and Samuel Homfray – ironmasters concerned to have a say in the operation of this lifeline. Yet roads, as the canal promoters argued, were not suited to their traffic. As the output of the ironworks rose, so bottlenecks and jams resulted. The limitations of road haulage were obvious: 'coals were conveyed to Cardiff on horses and mules, each carrying a load of 130 lb, a woman or lad having charge of three or four. Iron was taken to the port in wagons each laden with two tons and drawn by four horses'.[96]

The answer to the transport problems of Merthyr was not found until 1794 when the Glamorganshire Canal was opened. Samuel Smiles summarised the reasons for its construction:[97]

> The distance of Merthyr from Cardiff, the nearest port, being considerable, and the cost of carriage being very great by reason of the badness of the roads, Mr. Crawshay set himself to over come this great impediment to the prosperity of the Merthyr Tydvil district; and in conjunction with Mr. Homfray of Penydarran [sic] Works, he planned and constructed the canal to Cardiff, the opening of which gave an immense impetus to the iron trade in the neighbourhood.

Led by Crawshay, the ironmasters of Merthyr, together with some prominent Brecon people, joined forces in 1790 to obtain an Act[98] to construct a navigation from their town to a shipping place on the River Taff below the Old Quay.[99] The first major canal in Wales, it had an authorised capital of £60,000, the principal shareholders being: Richard Crawshay (£9,000)[100] and his family (£3,500), the Harfords of Mellingriffith (£6,000), the Homfrays (£1,500), Richard Foreman of Penydarren (£1,000), the Hills of Plymouth (£1,500), together with William Taitt (£1,000) and Thomas Guest (£500).[101] Although proprietors, neither Guest nor Taitt were appointed to the first committee of management; possibly Richard Hill of the Plymouth Ironworks, who had been selected, represented their interests.[102]

Construction began in August 1790 from the Merthyr end; there being no company engineer, a group of the leading proprietors checked the work at regular intervals. The canal was initially opened as far south as Pontypridd, and finally completed to Cardiff on 10 February 1794 when a 'fleet of canal boats arrived from Merthyr laden with the product of the ironworks there'.[103] This represented a

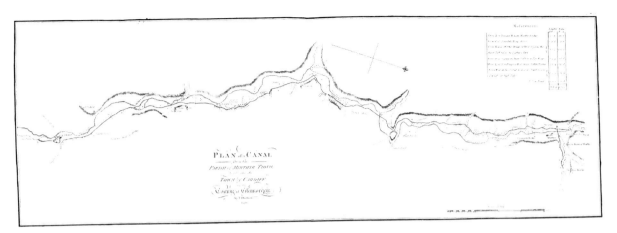

PLAN of a CANAL

14   A plan of the Glamorganshire Canal showing its route from Cardiff to Merthyr. (*The Trustees of the Science Museum*)

considerable constructional achievement as the waterway descended some 543ft in its twenty-five miles, requiring 51 locks, many of them in pairs, and one near Nantgarw was a triple.[104] With the digging of the branch to Aberdare in 1798, the total cost rose to £103,600,[105] the original estimate being £48,288 exclusive of land. Its effect was to facilitate greatly 'the means of conveying so ponderous an article of commerce to market'.[106]

Originally, a branch to Dowlais had been planned, but when the scheme was abandoned by Crawshay, using his controlling interest, Taitt and Guest, who had now joined the committee, withdrew temporarily. They then built a tramroad from their ironworks to the cut at Merthyr at a cost of around £3,000 to which the canal company offered £1,000 in toll credits as compensation.[107] This was completed by June 1793.[108] In April 1792 a tramroad from the limestone quarries at Gurnos to the Dowlais line was authorised by the shareholders and though Crawshay had been asked to build it, the construction was actually undertaken by Hill. In January 1799 William Taitt, Samuel Homfray for the Penydarren Co., and Richard Hill Junior for the Plymouth Co. signed an agreement for the laying of a tramroad 'from the limestone rocks at Castle Morlais to Crag Evan Leyson'.[109]

The completion of the Glamorganshire Canal, argued Phillips in 1802,[110]

has opened a ready conveyance to the vast manufactory of iron established in the mountains of that country, and many thousand tons are now annually shipped from thence . . . a commodious dock has also been formed at the end of the canal, where vessels of large burthen may lie afloat . . . on the banks of the dock, spacious warehouses are erected by the proprietors of the ironworks. At Merthyr Tidwell these various operations diffuse a spirit of exertion through the country, and will bring into action talents that hitherto lain dormant.

An indication of the character of traffic using the canal was given by the first toll charges:[111] 'Iron-stone, iron-ore, coal, limestone, lime and all kinds of manure – 2d. per ton per mile. Stone, iron, timber, goods, wares, merchandise and other things – 5d. per ton per mile'.

Although Richard Crawshay operated the navigation almost as a subsidiary of the Cyfarthfa Ironworks, it was extensively used by his three competitors. In June 1793 both the Dowlais and Penydarren companies were granted leases for land beside the canal at Merthyr to erect wharves.[112] A request from the Dowlais Co. in October 1809 'to have the water out of the pond near the Navigation House for the purpose of making a bason to *ship coal'* was granted.[113] Speaking of Cardiff in 1818 a *Directory* observed that,[114]

> from this town there are not less than 100,000 tons wrought iron of best manufacture shipped annually for London and other places; the bulk of which is made at Merthyr Tydfil, and brought down from there by a curious navigable canal . . . the canal . . . is brought through a mountainous country with a wonderful ingenuity. Coals are good and cheap, being delivered at half-a-guinea per ton.

The improved transport link between the ironworks in Merthyr and the port of Cardiff was crucial in allowing them to produce ever larger quantities of manufactures. Writing in 1831, Priestley believed that 'the chief object of this navigation and the railways with which it is connected is to facilitate the export of the vast quantity of coal, iron-stone, and other ores and minerals which are worked in great abundance on its line, and in particular at Merthyr Tidvile and its immediate vicinity'.[115]

To improve their transport facilities further, in 1794 William Taitt bought two sloops, *The St. Pierre* and *The Castle*, to carry shipments to Bristol; while during the Napoleonic Wars two brigs, *The Industry* and *The Mary Ann*, operated a regular schedule to London from Cardiff, returning with general merchandise.[116]

THE MERTHYR TRAMROAD

Such was the volume of iron being made at the four Merthyr ironworks that congestion occurred on the Glamorganshire Canal prompting a search for an additional form of transport – the Merthyr Tramroad.[117] For though it represented a great improvement on the existing roads, a canal was in many ways not an ideal solution to the region's transport needs, as evidenced by its comparatively fast decline once the railways had been built (see p. 102). The mountainous nature of the terrain between Cardiff and Merthyr made it an arduous and time consuming journey.[118] Delays could easily result if water shortages combined with heavy traffic flows. Indeed, its narrowboats, which carried 20 tons (increased to 24 when the channel was deepened) were not capacious by British standards[119] – 40 tons being a good average load.

In an *Address* printed for circulation in January 1799, William Taitt complained that Richard Crawshay had consistently operated the Glamorganshire Canal for his own advantage. Tolls, set at 5d. per ton in September 1794,[120] he complained, were too high and the £1,000 credit offered to the Dowlais Iron Co. as part payment for their tramroad, took nearly three years to accumulate so that the 'interest of our money expended on the road amounted to nearly one half of this same one thousand pounds worth of tonnage'.[121] In addition, Taitt claimed, the produce of Cyfarthfa, Penydarren and Plymouth 'was made into bar iron, which very much reduced the quantity', while Dowlais making pig iron was disadvantaged by high tolls levied by weight.[122] In June 1797 the canal company lowered their definition of a hundredweight from 120 to 112 lbs which further had the effect of increasing tolls for the Dowlais Iron Co.

Accordingly Crawshay's rivals, Guest, Homfray, Hill and William Lewis of the Pentyrch Ironworks, near Cardiff, presented a Bill to Parliament in 1799 for the laying of a tramroad from Cardiff to Merthyr.[123] The prospect of losing its monopoly stirred the canal company into vociferous opposition. The Bill was withdrawn when on 18 January 1799 Taitt of Dowlais, Hill of Plymouth and Homfray of Penydarren privately agreed to build a tramroad from Merthyr to Abercynon. Because, by the terms of the Glamorganshire Canal Act, those proprietors whose works lay within four miles of the navigation could build tramroads to it without extra Parliamentary approval, construction, under the engineer George Overton, proceeded forthwith. Since the 1790 Act did not specify to which point such tramways should be laid, they chose a ten-mile route south to Abercynon, on the opposite, eastern side of the valley to the canal. As a counterbalance to Crawshay's control of the waterway, the ownership of the tramroad was divided almost equally among the three ironworks: Dowlais five shares, Penydarren five and Plymouth four; the Pentyrch ironworks also held one share.

Work began in 1800 with Richard Hill of Plymouth responsible for the overall direction of the project. The nine-and-a-half miles were completed in 1802, its iron rails set on stone blocks with a gauge of 4ft 4ins.[124] All three main companies used the tramroad (one horse pulling five loaded trams, hauling a total payload of ten tons of iron). Moreover, the Merthyr, or Penydarren, Tramroad achieved fame because on 21 February 1804 it was used by Richard Trevithick to operate his first steam locomotive (his design, dated 1803, for a locomotive to be run at Coalbrookdale appears never to have been implemented),[125] which pulled, as he wrote,[126] 'ten tons of iron, five wagons and 70 men riding on them the whole journey. Its above 9

miles which we perform'd in 4 hours and 5 mints . . . The engine
while working, went nearly 5 miles per hour'. An accident to the
locomotive prevented its return to Merthyr until the evening.
Although it continued in use for several weeks, rails tended to break
under the weight,[127] and the locomotove was converted into a
stationary engine for pumping water, winding coal and driving a
forging hammer at the Penydarren ironworks. This was the first
occasion on which a steam locomotive had hauled a load on rails, pre-
dating the Stockton & Darlington adventure by 21 years.[128]

The Merthyr Tramroad continued to be an important means of
carrying iron to Cardiff until the construction of the Taff Vale Railway
(p. 99) rendered its horse-drawn wagons obsolete. Being firmly
committed to the steam-hauled freight train, Lady Charlotte Guest
sold the 5/9ths share that Dowlais held in the tramroad company.[129]

SUMMARY

Occurring in the setting of industrialisation, the French Revolutionary
and Napoleonic Wars produced, on balance, a favourable economic
climate for the British iron makers. High profits and rising demand
encouraged the ironworks of South Wales to invest heavily in
puddling and rolling plant to the extent that the process was for a
time known as the 'Welsh method'. With tariff walls to keep out
overseas competitors, British producers were able to gain complete
control of their home market. South Wales, which produced only
11,300 tons of pig iron in 1788 (16.2 per cent of national output), grew
fastest and became the country's leading iron-making district with an
output of 140,000 tons in 1855, 35.4 per cent of the nation's total.[130]
The proportion generated by Staffordshire rose from 9.8 per cent in
1788 to 31.6 per cent in 1815 while Shropshire, the traditional charcoal
region, declined from 35.6 per cent to 12.6 per cent over the same
period. This territorial shift was accompanied by a concentration in
ownership. Of the 249 coke blast furnaces operating in Britain during
1810, 102 (or 40 per cent of the total), belonged to the fifteen largest
firms, and by 1815 these fifteen accounted for 53 per cent of coke pig
iron output.[131] The process of concentration was even more pronounced in the refining sector. Hyde has estimated that South Wales
and Staffordshire were responsible for roughly three-quarters of total
output by the end of the Napoleonic Wars. As there were then only
seven rolling mills in South Wales (Cyfarthfa and Dowlais being
among the largest) and around eight in Staffordshire, the bar iron
trade was dominated by about fifteen firms.[132]

By introducing puddling furnaces and rolling mills, and leaving it
sufficiently late that they missed potting and stamping, the Dowlais
Iron Co. finally embraced the new coke technology in all its forms.
Although behind Cyfarthfa in the technical race to implement

puddling, and still smaller in size, by 1815 Dowlais had adopted the complete range of processes possible in the manufacture of bar iron. For the iron industry, through a series of innovations, some minor, had been transformed from reliance on charcoal and water power to one in which coke and steam power were crucial ingredients. Coke-fired blast furnaces, coal-fired refineries and puddling furnaces, and steam engines to provide the blast and to drive the new rolling mills and hammers typified the modern ironworks.

During the period 1775–1815 conditions were, in general, highly propitious for the British iron industry. Demand for iron grew so rapidly that periods of stability alternated with price rises, in spite of the tremendous growth in output achieved by the new and expanding works. It was partly for this reason that works without the latest technology could perform reasonably well. Even before investing in the wrought iron trade, Dowlais could earn substantial surpluses by supplying pig iron to their neighbours, such was the demand for iron products. In this economic climate they were able by the judicious re-investment of profits to expand and diversify. This was a bold decision, for the construction of new blast furnaces, or puddling furnaces and rolling mills, were capital intensive projects and could not be diverted to other uses if markets collapsed. After 1815, when output rose faster than demand and prices were set on a long-term decline, circumstances altered dramatically, and ironmasters, if they wished to survive, had to remain at the head, or near the front, of the technical race.

References

1. Crouzet, *Capital Formation*, pp. 207–208.
2. Ashton, *Iron and Steel*, p. 143.
3. Crouzet, *Capital Formation*, p. 209.
4. H. Scrivenor, *History of the Iron Trade*, London (1854), p. 128.
5. Ashton, *Iron and Steel*, p. 144.
6. Crouzet, *Capital Formation*, p. 209.
7. GRO, D/DG, William Taitt to Robert Thompson, 22 May 1798, 1798–1799, f. 134; Elsas, *Iron in the Making*, p. 118.
8. Ashton, *Iron and Steel*, p. 145.
9. Ibid., p. 146.
10. Crouzet, *Capital Formation*, p. 209.
11. Wilkins, *Merthyr*, p. 202; John B. Hilling, *Cardiff and the Valleys*, London (1973), p. 44.
12. Scrivenor, *Iron Trade*, p. 123.
13. 'History of the Cwmbran Works' (typescript); Aubrey Byles, *The History of the Monmouthshire Railway and Canal Company*, Cwmbran (1982), p. 13.
14. Luther Griffiths, 'The Story of Brymbo' (GKN typescript, 1974), p. 4; *The Brymbo Works Magazine*, Vol. I, June 1920, p. 44.

15. Griffiths, 'Story of Brymbo', p. 3; D. Morgan Rees, *The Industrial Archaeology of Wales*, Newton Abbot (1975), p. 61.

16. Although it has been widely stated that the first blast furnace at Brymbo came into operation in 1798, an excise return, dated 1796, recorded that 884 tons of pig iron had been made at Brymbo in that year suggesting that 'Old Number One' had been erected around 1795–96.

17. Griffiths, 'Story of Brymbo', p. 4; *The Brymbo Works Magazine*, Vol. I, December 1920; J. Kent Smith, 'Number One', p. 112.

18. Crouzet, *Capital Formation*, p. 210.

19. Ashton, *Iron and Steel*, p. 147.

20. Ibid., p. 150.

21. Ibid., p. 152.

22. Hyde, *Technological Change*, p. 106.

23. Addis, *Crawshay Dynasty*, pp. 88, 173; John, *South Wales*, p. 41.

24. Rodney Butler, *The History of the Kirkstall Forge through Seven Centuries 1200–1954*, York (1954), pp. 27, 29, 110.

25. Quoted from Crouzet, *Capital Formation*, p. 199; *Thorncliffe, A Description of Newton, Chambers & Co. Ltd.*, Sheffield (n.d.).

26. Phyllis Deane, *The First Industrial Revolution*, Cambridge (1965), p. 101; see also Ashton, op. cit., p. 69.

27. Hyde, *Technological Change*, p. 69.

28. Ibid., p. 60.

29. John B. Hilling, *Cardiff and The Valleys*, London (1973), p. 39.

30. Scrivenor, *Iron Trade*, p. 88.

31. England, 'The Dowlais Works', p. 52.

32. BRL, Boulton & Watt Collection, Portfolio 704, Plan and View of the Engine, 17 July 1798.

33. BRL, B & W Collection, Box 3 'T', letter, 22 November 1798.

34. GRO, D/DG, Boulton & Watt to Dowlais Co., 17 July 1803, 1802–03, ff. 401, 402; Elsas, *Iron in the Making*, p. 179; Clarke, *A Guide to Merthyr-Tydfil*, p. 27; Owen, *Dowlais Iron Works*, p. 21.

35. BRL, B & W Collection, Portfolio 678, Plan of the Blowing Engine, 22 June, 1810.

36. Jules Ginswick (Editor), *Labour and the Poor in England and Wales 1849–1851, The Letters to the Morning Chronicle, Vol. III, The Mining and Manufacturing Districts of South Wales*, London (1983), p. 41.

37. D.J. Davies, *The Economic History of South Wales prior to 1800*, Cardiff (1933), p. 139.

38. Hyde, *Technological Change*, p. 70.

39. Ibid., p. 71.

40. William Truran, *The Iron Manufacturers of Great Britain*, London (1855), p. 78.

41. BM, Add Ms. 58835 F.159, William Taitt to Frank Mallalieu, 6 September 1802; Havill, 'Taitt', p. 111.

42. John George Wood, *The Principal Rivers of Wales Illustrated*, London (1813), p. 56.

43. GRO, D/DG Letter Book, 1816, 'Prices of Iron at Dowlais Works, Glamorganshire, 3 October 1816'.

44. Hyde, *Technological Change*, p. 125; GRO, D/DG, Letter Book, 1817, Gilbert Gilpin to William Wood, 23 September 1817.

45. M.J. Daunton, *The Welsh History Review*, Vol. 6, Cardiff, June 1972, 'The Dowlais Iron Company in the Iron Industry 1800–1850', p. 19; Clarke, *A*

Guide to Merthyr-Tydfil, p. 27.

46. Owen, *Dowlais Iron Works*, p. 20.
47. Hathren Davies, 'History of Dowlais', p. 9.
48. Owen, *Dowlais Iron Works*, p. 21.
49. Murton, 'Recollections', p. 5.
50. GRO, D/DG, Section E, Box 2, Profit and Loss Account Summary 1810–1855.
51. Hathren Davies, 'History of Dowlais', p. 9.
52. Owen, *Dowlais Iron Works*, p. 22; Rees, *Industrial Archaeology*, op. cit., p. 50.
53. CCL, Bute MSS, Box XVI, No. 9, Letter Robert Beaumont to Lord Bute, 26 October 1839.
54. Hyde, *Technological Change*, p. 73.
55. Ibid., p. 74.
56. Ibid., p. 110.
57. BRL, Boulton & Watt MSS, Assay Office, Birmingham, Iron Trade Box, Ms 23, 'Mr Gilpin's Memorandum Book', October 1796.
58. GRO, D/DG, Letter Book, 1817, Gilbert Gilpin to William Wood, 23 September 1817.
59. Clarke, *A Guide to Merthyr-Tydfil*, p. 27.
60. Ibid., p. 28.
61. *Glamorgan Historian*, Vol. 3, Cambridge (1966), T.J. Hopkins, 'Robert Clutterbuck's Tour through Glamorgan', p. 203.
62. Wilkins, *Iron, Steel, Tinplate*, p. 45.
63. Murton, 'Recollections', p. 10.
64. NLW, Ms 6093E, Papers relating to South-East Wales Ironworks, Case against Guest & Evans, for scouring over the period 1777–82, p. 14.
65. NLW, W.T. Morgan (Compiler), A Schedule of the Mayberry Collection, Vol. I, Draft Lease, Guest to Homfrays, 26 October, 1782, p. 27.
66. NLW, Ibid., No. 134, October 1785, pp. 29–30; *Glamorgan Historian*, Taylor, 'Penydarren Iron Works', p. 76.
67. Charles Wilkins, *The South Wales Coal Trade and its Allied Industries*, Cardiff (1888), p. 69.
68. NLW, Ms 6093E, op. cit., No. 18, Agreement between Harry Thomas and the Dowlais Iron Co., 9 February 1793.
69. M.W. Flinn, *The History of the British Coal Industry, Vol. 2, 1700–1830, The Industrial Revolution*, Oxford (1984), p. 11.
70. Wilkins, *South Wales Coal*, p. 67.
71. Hathren Davies, 'History of Dowlais', p. 15.
72. F.J. North, *Coal and the Coalfields in Wales*, Cardiff (1931), p. 198.
73. Revd. J. Evans, *Letters written during a Tour through South Wales in the Year 1803*, London (1804), p. 92.
74. England, 'The Dowlais Works', p. 56.
75. *The Gentleman's Magazine*, Vol. XXIX, January–June 1853, Obituary J.J. Guest, p. 91.
76. England, 'The Dowlais Works', p. 56.
77. Hathren Davies, 'History of Dowlais', p. 9.
78. Havill, 'Taitt', p. 111.
79. Ibid., the valuation of Taitt's estate by the Perogative Court of Canterbury in December 1815 amounted to £60,000 (PRO, L IR26/659/540).
80. GRO, D/DG Section E, Box 1, 'Statement of Shares 1816–1838'; Roger L. Brown, 'The Lewis' of Greenmeadow' (typescript, 1984), pp. 11–19.

81. Ashton, *Iron and Steel*, pp. 209–210.
82. A.H. John (Editor), *The Walker Family, Iron Founders and Lead Manufacturers 1741–1893*, London (1951), pp. v, 2–9.
83. Addis, *Crawshay Dynasty*, pp. 155–156.
84. John, *South Wales*, p. 41, n. 2.
85. Crouzet, *Capital Formation*, p. 196.
86. Ibid., p. 189; Arthur Raistrick, *Quakers in Science and Industry*, Newton Abbot (1968), p. 43.
87. Raistrick, *Quakers*, pp. 36–37; Ashton, *Iron and Steel*, p. 221.
88. Wilkins, *Merthyr*, p. 177.
89. Hathren Davies, 'History of Dowlais', p. 8.
90. Wilkins, *Merthyr*, p. 177.
91. Ashton, *Iron and Steel*, p. 222.
92. Ness Edwards, *The Industrial Revolution in South Wales*, London (1924), p. 62.
93. Wilkins, *Iron, Steel*, p. 126.
94. Wilkins, *Merthyr*, p. 151.
95. Charles Hadfield, *The Canals of South Wales and the Border*, Cardiff (1960), p. 90.
96. Wilkins, *Iron, Steel*, p. 67.
97. Smiles, *Industrial Biography*, p. 131.
98. 30 Geo. III *c.* 1782, R.A., 9 June 1790; Joseph Priestley, *Historical Account of the Navigable Rivers, Canals and Railways of Great Britain*, London (1831), p. 282.
99. Hadfield, *Canals of South Wales*, p. 90.
100. Addis, *Crawshay Dynasty*, p. 16.
101. NLW, Ref 92B, Glamorganshire Canal Co., Minutes of the Proprietors 1790–1836, pp. 1–3.
102. Ibid., 30 June 1790, p. 7.
103. *Archaeologia Cambrensis*, No. XLI, January 1865, p. 94.
104. *Merthyr Historian*, Vol. I, 1976, J. Gross, 'The Glamorganshire Canal', pp. 42–43.
105. D.D. and J.M. Gladwin, *The Canals of the Welsh Valleys*, Oakwood (1974), p. 16.
106. Revd. J. Evans, *Letters*, p. 72.
107. NLW, Proprietors' Minutes, 1 June 1791, pp. 22–23.
108. Owen, *Dowlais Iron Works*, p. 17.
109. NLW, Mayberry Collection, Vol. I, No. 109, 18 January 1799, p. 124.
110. J. Phillips, *A General History of Inland Navigation*, London (1805), pp. 595–596.
111. Priestley, *Historical Account*, p. 283.
112. NLW, Proprietors' Minutes, 5 June 1793, p. 51.
113. Ibid., 10 October 1809, p. 331.
114. GRO, *A Complete Directory and Guide to the Towns and Castles of Cardiff and Caerphilly*, Cardiff (1818), pp. 4–5.
115. Priestley, *Historical Account*, p. 284.
116. Owen, *Dowlais Iron Works*, p. 20.
117. Rees, *Mines, Mills*, p. 69; Stanley Mercer, *Transactions of the Newcomen Society*, Vol. XXVI (1947–9), 'Trevithick and the Merthyr Tramroad', pp. 89–91.
118. Hadfield, *Canals of South Wales*, p. 93.
119. Henry R. de Salis, *Bradshaw's Canals and Navigable Rivers of England and Wales*, London (1904), p. 22.

120. GRO, D/DG Section G, Water, *An Address to the Landowners and others in the vicinity of the Glamorganshire Canal*, by W. Taitt, 28 January 1799, pp. 1–2.
121. NLW, Proprietors' Minute Book, 30 September 1794, p. 80.
122. GRO, D/DG, *Address*, op. cit., p. 3.
123. Stuart Owen-Jones, *The Penydarren Locomotive*, Cardiff (1981), pp. 6–7; Hadfield, *Canals of South Wales*, p. 97.
124. Bertram Baxter, *Stone Blocks and Iron Rails*, Newton Abbot (1966), p. 219.
125. Owen-Jones, *The Penydarren Locomotive*, p. 21.
126. Quoted from ibid., p. 9.
127. D.S.M. Barrie, *A Regional History of the Railways of Great Britain, Vol. XII, South Wales*, Newton Abbot (1980), p. 32.
128. D.S.M. Barrie, *The Taff Vale Railway*, Godstone (1950), p. 6.
129. *Merthyr Historian*, Vol. I, 1976, J. Gross, 'The Merthyr Tramroad', p. 55.
130. Hyde, *Technological Change*, p. 114.
131. Ibid., p. 124.
132. Ibid.

3 *Supremacy in Iron, 1815–40*

The ending of war in 1815, as in earlier periods, brought a slump: in the case of iron Britain suddenly found itself with excess capacity. Despite attempts by regional groupings of ironmasters to secure agreements to maintain values, prices fell as firms competed for dwindling orders.[1] In the Midlands, for example, pig iron for the forge had sold at £6 a ton in 1814, but fell to £3.75 in 1816 and remained at £5 or below for seven of the nine years after 1814.[2] Some ironworks closed while others were sold at a fraction of their original worth. In the trough of the depression, 1816, William Hood, the Dowlais Iron Co.'s London agent, wrote to Josiah Guest that[3]

> the demand you have had is from speculations to America, which being now completely glutted with iron and British goods, the demand will cease. From Liverpool alone there is 15 million of property exported, which will not be got back for some years and you will find no small distress will be prevailing in the spring when merchants are expecting remittance. There is no channel for a large consumption of iron in the spring but to America, the East India demand being now nearly over for this season, and France and others on the Continent [exhausted by war] have not the means to purchase large quantities. Of foreign iron there has been a large quantity of Sweeds exported to India, in consequence of the bad quality of the British that [has] been exported for some years and I think that the British iron will run a great risk of losing that market.

DEPRESSION AND GROWTH AT DOWLAIS

Profits at Dowlais, which had risen in real terms from 1810 to 1815 (Table 3.1), slumped in the next two years and only recovered in 1818. At Merthyr, a policy of wage cuts agreed between the ironmasters in 1816 produced a series of strikes culminating in a riot during October, the Royal Glamorgan Militia being called out.[4] Greatly outnumbered, the Volunteers were put to flight and Josiah Guest was besieged at Dowlais House. The matter was settled peacefully a few days later, when reinforcements arrived and the ironmasters promised that there would be no further reductions in wages.

Table 3.1 Profits from the Dowlais Iron Co., 1810–40

	£	Adjusted £		£	Adjusted £
1810	9846	6419	1825	20000	
1811	10983	7554	1826		
1812	11470	7007	1827	22619	22778
1813	11973	7089	1828	16538	17156
1814	16538	10753	1829	4711	4916
1815	15021	11564	1830	12570	13302
1816	10953	9235	1831	17221	18070
1817	11873	9002	1832	16613	18156
1818	21187	15275	1833	21652	24438
1819	25801	20141	1834	50097	50183
1820	23177	20084	1835	51836	61344
1821	10404	10435	1836	67711	71125
1822	16393	18650	1837	129160	136967
1823	34870	35727	1838	77413	79154
1824	16730	16418	1839	85024	74848
			1840	78066	76162

Source: GRO, D/DG, Section E, Box 2, Profit and Loss Account Summary 1810–50. Figures adjusted by Gayer, Rostow and Schwartz's index of commodity prices, 1821–25 = 100.

Elsewhere a similar pattern of hardship and recession emerged. The ironworks at Brymbo, which had been almost entirely involved in the manufacture of weapons during the war, suffered greatly in the 1816 slump and this, together with litigation over John Wilkinson's will, forced the trustees to let the works to John and James Thompson in 1818 at an annual rental of £1,500.[5] In general, the small, non-specialist or badly-managed businesses failed, and, though experiencing a period of reduced make and financial stringency, Dowlais and its three Merthyr rivals advanced into the 1820s when an upswing in the trade cycle brought a brighter economic climate.

On a wave of recovery, Josiah Guest built the Dowlais Co.'s fifth blast furnace in January 1817 for £2,000.[6] Numbers 6 and 7 followed in August (at a total cost, including wages, of £4,577), together with No. 3 blast engine (£4,000).[7] The eighth blast furnace was erected in April 1821, and cost £1,200, a ninth in 1822, and in the following year yet another came into operation.[8] The annual make of iron rose to 22,287 tons,[9] when the weekly yield of each of the ten furnaces

Cyfarthfa and a further four nearby at Ynysfach.[20]

In tune with the iron industry's frenetic growth, Josiah Guest constructed a second plant, the Ifor Works, adjacent to the original enterprise. Built during 1839, it was named after his eldest son, Ivor Bertie Guest (1835–1914), and concentrated all the trades and facilities needed by a large, integrated ironworks. Engineers, fitters, smiths and moulders were housed there, though, in time, rising orders and the limitations of space imposed by the hilly nature of the site dictated that it, too, enter iron making by the construction of blast furnaces.[21]

The outcome of these developments was that Dowlais surpassed Cyfarthfa as the principal ironworks in Merthyr, and South Wales. This change in league positions was well illustrated by the quantities of iron sent annually down the Glamorganshire Canal (Table 3.2) in the twenty years before the construction of the Taff Vale Railway. Since most of the iron was shipped through Cardiff and the navigation (supported as far as Abercynon by the Merthyr Tramroad) formed the only efficient link, these tonnages provided a reliable indication of levels of output at the respective ironworks. In 1817, for example, Dowlais, Penydarren and Plymouth operated roughly on a par, Cyfarthfa being considerably larger. Yet, during the 1820s, Dowlais drew away from the two smaller competitors and grew at a faster rate than Cyfarthfa. It first exceeded the output of the last in 1830 when Dowlais shipped 27,647 tons of iron by canal[22] at a time when the combined traffic from Cyfarthfa and Hirwaun totalled 19,892

15 A watercolour by Penry Williams of Cyfarthfa in 1825. The 'Castle' rolling mills were situated on the left, the blast furnaces in the middle distance and puddling furnaces to the right.
(*Cyfarthfa Castle Museum*)

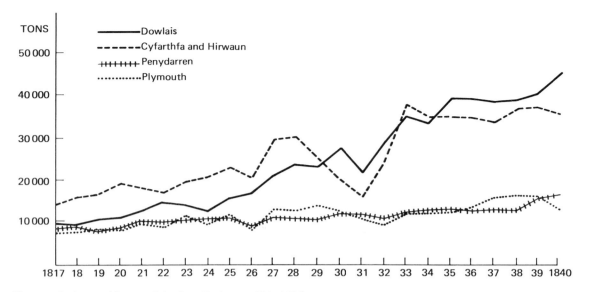

[Source: Scrivenor, History of the Iron Trade, pp. 124, 257.]

Figure 7 Iron carried on the Glamorganshire Canal 1817–40

tons.[23] Nevertheless, Dowlais did not establish its supremacy beyond doubt until the mid-1830s; they despatched 39,145 tons of iron by the Glamorganshire Canal in 1835 and 45,218 tons in 1840, in comparison with the 35,090 and 35,507 tons respectively sent by Crawshay.

In December 1834, when it had become clear to the inhabitants of Merthyr that Dowlais had surpassed Cyfarthfa, some voters, who had a preference for the Crawshays, protested when Josiah Guest stood for re-election as the town's MP (see p. 87). Lady Charlotte recorded in her journal that Richard Hill had remarked,[24] 'if Dowlais Works had not made more iron, than Mr. Crawshay's, we should never have heard of this opposition in the borough'. Although slight growth could be detected at Plymouth and Penydarren from the traffic figures, their operations remained at a lower level, shipments in 1840 reaching 12,922 and 16,130 tons respectively.

PRODUCTIVITY AND PRODUCTS

Rising profits at Dowlais had not been achieved simply by doubling up plant in a repetitive manner so that earnings increased in a direct relationship with output. Technical innovation was a crucial factor in this tale of sustained business success. In 1810 it was estimated that each furnace at Dowlais produced on average 50 tons of iron per week and that the highest make for that period was 75 tons. The corresponding figures for 1820 were 62 and 109 tons, for 1830 78 and 126 tons, and for 1840 reached 88 and 136 tons (Table 3.3).[25] Josiah Guest had not simply been able to build bigger and better blast

Table 3.2 Iron sent down the Glamorganshire Canal, 1817–40 (tons)

Year	Cyfarthfa*	Dowlais	Penydarren	Plymouth	Total
1817	14191	9936	8275	7095	39497
1818	15707	9695	8834	7377	41613
1819	16646	10796	7549	7633	42624
1820	19007	11112	8687	7947	46753
1821	18057	12568	10009	9949	50583
1822	17133	14554	9926	8825	50438
1823	19452	14025	10240	10920	54637
1824	20399	12594	10358	9499	52850
1825	23063	15851	10611	11269	60794
1826	20206	16601	8691	7836	53334
1827	29312	20726	10369	12907	73314
1828	30011	23575	10223	12976	76785
1829	24768	23352	10085	13534	71739
1830	19892	27647	11744	12177	71460
1831	15465	22075	11819	10498	59857
1832	24668	29395	10582	9200	73854
1833	37380	35072	12150	12093	96695
1834	34952	33477	12752	12073	93254
1835	35090	39145	12834	12631	99700
1836	34654	39286	12537	13573	100050
1837	33580	38914	12834	15353	100681
1838	36986	39361	12707	16143	105197
1839	37009	40495	15540	15762	108806
1840	35507	45218	16130	12922	109777
Totals	613125	585470	265486	270192	1734283

*The Cyfarthfa totals also include iron manufactured at Hirwaun.

Source: 1817–20, Small notebook 'J.J. Guest' in possession of Lady Wimborne; 1821–40, Scrivenor, *Iron Trade*, op. cit., pp. 124, 257.

furnaces, for 'in the South Wales district', observed Truran, who was employed at Dowlais as an engineer,[26] 'the ironmasters have taken advantage of the generally mountainous character of the locality to erect the furnaces on hill sides, having back ground on a level with the furnace top, over which the materials are wheeled direct into the furnace'. Four of the more recent furnaces by virtue of their size did, however, require a waterbalance lift which had a capacity of up to 500 tons.[27]

Greater outputs per furnace were achieved, moreover, with reduced consumption of coal. In 1823 four tons of coal were needed to make one ton of pig iron, a figure that fell to between two and three tons by 1839.[28] Such efficiencies must, in part, have been won by the adoption of J. Beaumont Neilson's invention in 1828 of the hot blast process. By

Table 3.3 Productivity at Dowlais 1790–1855

Year	Number of blast furnaces	Per blast furnace	
		Average weekly make (tons)	Highest weekly make (tons)
1790	2	20	29
1795	3	27	44
1800	3	36	50
1805	3	42	63
1810	4	50	75
1815	4	58	92
1820	7	62	109
1825	11	66	98
1830	11	78	126
1835	13	85	130
1840	17	88	136
1845	18	101	190
1850	18	102	170
1855	18	116	180

Source: William Truran, *The Iron Manufacture of Great Britain*, London (1855), p. 66.

passing the blast through a chequer-work of hot bricks before it entered the furnace, the amount of coke needed as fuel was reduced and the smelting process accelerated and, just as important, in an age of cheap coal, this permitted greater quantities of iron ore to be converted in each operation.

William Truran, an engineer at Dowlais, argued that the impact of Neilson's invention had been overstated by some enthusiasts particularly in areas such as South Wales where high quality coal was available:[29]

> Without intending any disparagement of the hot blast, which unquestionably is a most meritorious invention, we must protest against this wholesale system of attributing to it powers which it does not possess. That the hot blast under certain circumstances has effected a saving in the consumption of fuel, and also augmented the weekly make, we freely admit. But the saving of fuel and increase of make due to its employment is not generally one-fourth of the quantity which writers have asserted.

He suggested that considerable gains in productivity had already been achieved with the cold blast method. The quantity of coal required to coke and ore, it would have been difficult to have improved this yield to any significant extent.

An area of major expansion at Dowlais, in the three decades after the Napoleonic Wars, occurred in the market for rolled products, which in turn required that the number of puddling furnaces had to be increased; for puddling was the crucial stage in the lengthy process by which raw material was converted into iron rod, bar or rail. It was labour intensive, but also highly skilled, and later in the nineteenth century when the number of puddlers fell short of demand, encouraged valiant but unfulfilled efforts at mechanisation (p. 269). Something of the complexity and physical dexterity required of the process was revealed by a description of 1849–50:[53]

> a puddling furnace is an oven or a coffer of brickwork, about eight feet long and about four feet wide, having a tall chimney. Into one of these several pieces of the broken refined iron are thrown, and the heat is supplied by coal or coke, and powerful streams of blast. To work each furnace there are two persons, 'the puddler' and his 'underhand'. They work in three courses, so that each set has eight hours' continuous labour. After subjection to the fire for three-quarters of an hour the iron melts, and gives off copious quantities of gas, boiling up with a frothy appearance. The puddler now . . . stirs about the mass until it has arrived a proper consistency . . . After a while the iron loses the sandy crumbling nature, and begins to clot and cohere . . . and the entire mass is divided into five parts, rolled up.

The hot iron ball was then carried in a pair of huge pincers by the 'shingler' to the 'squeezers' where the metal was compressed on an anvil. Formerly this was performed with a heavy hammer, but the advent of steam power allowed this work to be undertaken by a plate hinged to the anvil and driven by an eccentric wheel. In this manner a rough bar of wrought iron was fashioned for rolling into any manner of cross-sections or weights.

The 'gentleman puddler' was the highest paid workman; he needed considerable skill and physical strength. High temperatures made it an uncomfortable occupation, while the fumes and noxious gases that were evolved represented a health hazard. Dowlais and the other integrated ironworks could continue to expand only so long as men came forward to learn these exacting tasks. The shortage of puddlers and the failure to devise a mechanical substitute was to encourage the adoption of the Bessemer converter in the late 1850s as steel possessed all the tensile properties of wrought iron but could be refined from pig iron without the time-consuming toil of puddling (p. 272).

In the first half of the nineteenth century it was the growing demand for rails, more than any other product, which promoted the duplication of puddling and ironmaking plant at Dowlais. Even by

1821 the Dowlais Iron Co. had achieved a reputation for the manufacture of rails, a specialism for which they were to develop a world-wide reputation. In May of that year Thomas Meynell, chairman of the Stockton & Darlington Railway committee, wrote to Josiah Guest to obtain his opinion:[54] 'The committee . . . will esteem it a great favour if you will do me the honour to communicate to me your opinion of the comparative value and advantages of *Tram*-roads and *Rail*-roads, as constructed on the most improved principles'. In November they were sent a specification for wrought iron rails and asked to tender.[55] Unfortunately the identity of those companies supplying tender prices was concealed from the full committee of the railway. The price of £12 0s. 0d. per ton for malleable iron rails at Cardiff may well have been offered by the Dowlais Co.[56] However, they did not win one of the contracts, these being granted to M. Longridge of the Bedlington Iron Works, near Newcastle, to supply wrought iron rails, and the Neath Abbey Iron Co., to supply cast iron rails.[57] The choice between wrought and cast iron for the rails caused the directors much difficulty and, in the event, more than four-fifths of the track consisted of the former. Although these were purchased from the North-east, and had been rolled in the Bedlington Works, it appears that the pig iron, at least, from which they had been refined was purchased from South Wales.[58] The original contract to supply the Liverpool & Manchester Railway was shared by Thompson, Forman & Co. of Penydarren and James Bradley & Co. based in the Midlands.[59] Subsequent contracts were directed to Bradley & Co. and also to the Bedlington Iron Co. Thus from the entry of the railway companies into the rail market the ironmasters of South Wales played an important part, even if in certain cases they were no more than suppliers of basic material to rollers. Their expertise as producers of tramplates and rails for tramroads ensured that they would always be considered for orders.

In 1830 the Big Mill at Dowlais, a very specialised piece of machinery, was laid down to take on the work of rolling rails for an apparently limitless market. So great was the demand for railway track that in 1840 it was supplemented by the Little Mill which had two mill trains and was supplied by eleven puddling furnaces.[60] The introduction of larger, more powerful mills capable of rolling complicated sections of greater weights than before represented a major innovation in iron technology.

It was claimed that the first wrought iron rails had been rolled at the Penydarren Works.[61] For Dowlais America was from the first an important market. Thomas Evans wrote to Josiah Guest in 1832 to inform him that:[62] 'we are at work on the American rails, and they turn out very well, a gentleman from the United States is here inspecting the work, and highly approves of them. Mr. Ogden has given the remaining 250 tons to Bagnall to make at £8 5s. 0d. per ton'. By 1836–37 Dowlais was producing 20,000 tons of rails a year. Among

3   A view looking north-east up the valley to the Dowlais furnaces by George
Childs (fl. 1826–73) in 1840. Standing in front of them in a line of buildings
are the mills and forges, while No. 6 blowing engine house stands above the
furnace tops in the middle distance. The parish road (foreground) was a right
of way through the works.
(*National Museum of Wales*)

its early customers in the UK were: the London & Southampton Railway (1835), Manchester, Bolton & Bury Canal Railway (1836), Liverpool & Manchester Railway (1836) and the London & Birmingham Railway (1836). Overseas contracts included the Baltimore & Susquihanna Railway (1835), Harlaam Railroad, New York (1835), Berlin & Leipzig Railway (1836), St. Petersburg-Pauloffsky Railway (1836), New Orleans & Nashville Railway (1836) and the Wilkins Ferry Railroad (1836).[63] The company also supplied the Navy Board and the East India Co.

In November 1836 Lady Charlotte Guest recalled how 'after dinner I went with Merthyr [her name for Josiah] to the Upper Mill to see them try the rolls for a new sort of rail which Mr. Brunel talks of laying down on the Great Western Road'.[64] In the following year, when the company made record profits and the market for rails boomed, Lady Charlotte recorded that[65]

> Thomas Evans returned from London and called upon me – He has taken 2,000 tons of Southampton rails at a melancholy price of £8 7s. 6d. *Mine* iron and *delivered* [good quality iron and including transport costs] – we have now though at low prices about 8,000 tons of rail to make and I cannot help hoping that the trade has reached the utmost point of depression.

A month later, in a happier mood, she noted that orders were 'pouring in very fast and the price [of pig iron] has advanced from £6 to £7'.[66] The growing volume of output encouraged a degree of mechanisation:[67]

> We proceeded to the bottom of the forges where, under the rail shed, they have got a small steam engine for sawing off the hot ends of the rails, which is now done tediously by hand . . . Today the saw acted beautifully and the effect is certainly surprising. It cuts through a heavy rail from 3 to 9 seconds, and all the time the saw, which goes at about 1,000 revolutions a minute, throws off sparks.

Josiah Guest and his fellow managers must take the credit for perceiving that the market for rails would expand and endure and backing their judgement with a series of capital-intensive projects. The death of William Crawshay in August 1834 and the passing of control at Cyfarthfa to one less committed to the long-term development of the business (in contrast to Josiah Guest's careful and sustained investment in Dowlais) formed a major part of the explanation for a reversal in the relative fortunes of the two ironworks.

MORE COAL AND DWINDLING IRON ORE

From the 1820s the Dowlais Iron Co. began to experience what was to prove a problem throughout the nineteenth century, shortages of coal. The surface deposits, or those that outcropped near the surface, and which could be extracted by simple levels or drifts had largely been exhausted by the third decade of the century. The quantity of coal needed to make a ton of finished iron, though reduced by efficiencies in blast furnace management, had increased because of greater mechanisation in the works which, in turn, required the widespread use of steam power. Coal for coking and coal to fuel boilers and locomotives became a vital commodity. To satisfy these pressing needs in 1823–27 the Brewhouse Coal Level was driven into the mountain side and the Rhas-Las Drift opened, two very large workings.[68] The Brewhouse Level had its entrance adjacent to No. 10 blast furnace in the heart of the works. Ultimately it was used as a general entrance to the mountain for horse-drawn wagons and an outlet for drainage water. Originally it had been dug as a coal and clay level 2,992 yards long and from it two side drifts were driven to extract the lower four-feet coal.

The nature of the lease system of ownership, however, did not encourage methods designed to extract the maximum amount of coal and there appears to have been much wastage. Because it was apparent that the deposits were extensive and the company's lease was due to expire in 1848 with only a slim chance of renewal, Josiah Guest chose to remove the best coal as quickly and cheaply as possible, even if this involved the loss of substantial quantities. Both coal and iron ore were mined by patch workings, a system which Robert Beaumont, Lord Bute's agent, reported in 1826 'wholly destroys the surface . . . and the works take no pains to restore the greensward but wherever they have worked, the whole surface is rendered totally valueless for ever'.[69] When extracted in levels, often too great an area of coal was removed with insufficient support for the roof. In an effort to remove coal as quickly as possible, the distance between each stall, commonly four yards, was increased to seven, which in turn put too great a pressure on the supporting pillars.[70] A collapse, or 'crush' resulted in the loss of more distant masses of coal obstructed by rock falls. 'Another source of error and loss', observed Beaumont, was the 'continual changing of the person who has charge of the coal mines. Within the last six or seven years they have had some three or four persons managing and directing the works'.[71] Beaumont, who might well have had reason to exaggerate, estimated that between 1834 and 1838, a period in which the Dowlais Iron Co. had extracted 1,041,666 tons of coal by this method, some 1,519,305 tons had been wasted and were now irretrievably lost.[72] The system of mining in levels did, of course, keep Josiah Guest's fuel costs down produce is coal' observed Clarke in 1849; 'great quantities are shipped from Swansea, Neath and Cardiff; from Cardiff alone, in 1846, there were shipped 490,000 tons'.[93] Although overseas sales of Welsh coal were to prove immensely profitable by the end of the nineteenth century (p. 341), they were as yet negligible, less than 65,000 tons a year being exported in 1840 and 1841.[94]

AGREEMENTS AMONG THE IRONMASTERS

Although earlier associations designed to regulate prices and output had never proved effective over long periods of time, the emphasis placed on these meetings declined in the 1820s and 1830s. The interdependence that had once existed between the four Merthyr ironworks weakened. After 1820, purchase or sales of large quantities of pig iron between them became less significant as exchanges were increasingly characterised by smaller, irregular dealings in finished iron.[95] This, too, reflected the growth in the scale of the ironworks which could not stockpile in periods of sluggish activity and low prices and thus be able to obtain a higher profit when markets recovered. In 1825, for example, William Crawshay I commented that all acted for themselves 'and without regulation'.[96]

Agreements between ironmasters seem to have had their greatest impact during periods of severest recession. In 1810 William Crawshay I (1764–1834), who succeeded his father, Richard, adopted a shrewd and statesman-like policy in face of both shortages and over supply.[97] Not residing at Cyfarthfa but ruling its affairs from their London warehouse at George Yard, Thames Street, he sought to maintain prices and during the protracted recession of 1813–20 wrote to William Taitt at Dowlais that he was not prepared to enter the ruinous price-cutting war started by Richard Taitt:[98]

> that the Staffordshire Works having inundated the market seek to close the Welsh Works; that William Crawshay Junior will co-operate in local measures to reduce production costs but that sales and prices will be entirely a matter for the writer who confident of his ability to last as long as others, and believing that the crisis is due to the poverty and distress of producers and not overproduction will charge whatever circumstances seem to dictate.

One of the most sacred principles in William Crawshay's policy was the maintenance of a large capital reserve to enable him to hold substantial stocks of iron during depressions, being ready thereby to benefit from an improvement in demand and upward drift in prices. For this reason, in 1820 he objected to his son, William Crawshay II (1788–1867), spending £6,000 on land for the site of Cyfarthfa Castle.[99]

This and its actual construction (which cost £30,000 in 1824–25) consumed valuable capital reserves. Guest at Dowlais, who had yet to achieve Cyfarthfa's size, could not afford such a luxury. In 1821, when price-cutting followed a reduction in orders, Crawshay I was dismayed to discover that Josiah Guest had 'prevailed on the meeting of ironmasters to reduce the price of iron at Cardiff, which policy need not be followed by Cyfarthfa'.[100] In part, Crawshay believed that this was a deliberate assault on Cyfarthfa's position of dominance agreed between its three smaller rivals in Merthyr.[101] His response was to stockpile all that could not be sold at the old price and to use his reserves to sit out the financial siege. By March 1821 he reckoned that £10,000 had been lost by refusing to concur with the price-cutting tactics of Guest, Hill, Frere and others.[102]

During times of plenty William Crawshay I adopted an equally independent course. In the boom years of 1824–25, he might have been expected to take advantage of soaring values, more especially because his ironworks had the greatest output and the largest stocks in South Wales.[103] He consistently refused to join any agreements designed to extort high prices. Believing that it was in the long-term interests of the iron industry, William Crawshay I brought a measure of stability by standing apart, picking and choosing orders, turning away speculative buyers and refusing to panic when prices slumped and left him with large stocks.[104]

Agreements over output and prices seem to have been less common during the 1830s, partly because this was a decade of expansion, but also because the works were better able to look after themselves in periods of recession. Falling prices in 1836 prompted William Crawshay II, seconded by Thomas Guest, to propose that 'it is expedient to reduce the make of iron in Wales'.[105] Lady Charlotte doubted the efficacy of their twenty per cent reduction 'as Shropshire and Staffordshire have extinguished one third [of their furnaces]'.[106] The market, under the stimulus of railway investment, soon recovered. Another restriction on output was agreed in 1840–41 when prices tumbled in the approach of the general depression. Yet an attempt to limit the make of iron during the next slump, 1847, failed, the meeting being poorly attended and unable to reach an acceptable figure. Price and output fixing were features of the pioneering days when new works and their markets were still fragile. From the 1830s, an era of virtually continuous expansion, businesses on the scale of Dowlais did not generally need these protective arrangements; indeed, the collapse of one of the weaker ironworks in time of adversity (Penydarren in 1859) was to be welcomed for the prospect it offered of diminished competition in time of economic recovery.

LADY CHARLOTTE AND SIR JOSIAH JOHN GUEST

Josiah John Guest and Lady Charlotte Elizabeth Bertie, only daughter of the ninth Earl of Lindsey, married on 29 July 1833.[107] Their courtship had been one of extreme brevity and for Lady Charlotte characterised by high emotion. Meeting for the first time in May 1833 at the London home of Wyndham Lewis, a partner in the Dowlais Iron Co., their marriage followed a mere three months later. She was twenty-one and Josiah forty-eight.[108] In 1817 he had married Maria Rankin, who had travelled to Wales from Ireland during the rebellion of 1798. Just nine months after their union, she died, aged twenty-three.[109] Grief-stricken, Josiah concentrated his energies on building up the business and for nearly twenty years abandoned any thoughts of family life.

Lady Charlotte Bertie, who was to prove a remarkable business-woman of courage, application and insight, had experienced a harsh and lonely childhood at Uffington, near Stamford. Her father, sixty-eight when she was born, died six years later and her mother's second

19 Lady Charlotte Guest (1812–95) from a mezzotint by William Walker of the painting by Richard Buckner. (*Glamorgan Record Office*)

20 Sir John Guest from a mezzotint by William Walker of the painting by Richard Buckner. (*Glamorgan Record Office*)

husband, the Revd. Peter W. Pegus, was a man of violent temper with no affection for the young Lady Charlotte.[110] She described this traumatic period in her journal:[111]

> I have been brought up alone and never have associated with children or young persons of my own age, nor had I ever anyone with whom to share my early joys and griefs, and *when anything annoys or delights me I am accustomed to brood over it in the inmost recesses of my own bosom*. Though I know many whom I love and esteem *I have never found a kindred soul to whom the whole of my heart may be opened, being but a reflection of its own*.

The 'kindred soul' was to be Josiah Guest. Given the difference in their ages and the bleak early years of Lady Charlotte's life, he probably served as a father figure as well as a husband. Because Josiah too had suffered much sorrow during his childhood, it provided a common bond and for him an insight into her personality. His mother had died when he was a small boy and the young Guest had been brought up by an old woman, Mari Aberteifi, who was engaged as a nannie.[112] Subsequently, he attended Bridgnorth Grammar School in Shropshire and on his return to Dowlais was instructed by John Evans, the general manager.[113] At the age of twenty-two, the death of his father, Thomas, precipitated Josiah into the management of the business. As in the case of Lady Charlotte, a great determination to succeed appears to have been created by adversity.

Despite the differences of class, education and age, the marriage proved to be an enduring and mutually rewarding union. Recalling the ceremony, at St. George's, Hanover Square, London, Lady Charlotte wrote:[114] 'I could not detach my thoughts from him [during] the whole service, and hardly my eyes . . . a thousand contrasts it drew between his circumstances and my own – and what had I done to merit the happier fate?' She had experienced a brief romance in May 1833 with the young Disraeli (seeking a rich wife to finance an embryonic political career),[115] who described her as 'very clever, [worth] £25,000 and domestic'.[116] She thought him 'wild, enthusiastic and very poetical' but could not understand why he was trying to get into Parliament.[117] Although they became 'very good friends',[118] Disraeli did not pursue the relationship but subsequently married Mary Anne *née* Evans (1792–1872) the widow of Wyndham Lewis. Fifty years later, in 1880, he, as Prime Minister, recommended Lady Charlotte's eldest son, Sir Ivor Bertie Guest, for a peerage and the latter became the first Lord Wimborne.

Fortunately for Dowlais, Lady Charlotte did not marry Disraeli. Her honeymoon with Josiah Guest was spent on the South coast and at Bristol. Her arrival at Merthyr Tydfil, where she was to live for the next twenty years, was cushioned by nightfall. This relieved Josiah, who was concerned that the nature of the scene, 'far from

picturesque', might cause alarm. 'By the time we reached the house',
she wrote,[119] 'it was quite dark, and the prevailing gloom gave full
effect to the light of the blazing furnaces which was quite unlike all I
had ever before seen or even imagined'.

Once established at Dowlais House, Lady Charlotte Guest took care
to study the practical operation of the business and her knowledge of
the iron industry became sufficiently full for her to write a monograph
on its history.[120] She learned Welsh in order to converse with the local
people and achieved such an understanding that she was able to
translate several medieval texts, including the *Mabinogion* (1846).
Taking on the role of secretary and accountant, Lady Charlotte
devoted a considerable portion of her time to the company. In August
1836 a typical entry in her journal recorded,[121]

> . . . remained at home busy with my books – I had the
> satisfaction of bringing the balance right of the last four months'
> accounts – It has been rather a long job as more than £100,000
> have gone through my hands in that space of time and while in
> London I was too ill to attend at all to the posting of the books.

The story is told that Lady Charlotte, attending a sybaritic society
reception in London, had left instructions that a messenger with news
from Wales should be admitted without hindrance. He arrived
carrying a long tin case containing statements of the year's accounts.
Lady Charlotte, surrounded by aristocratic beauties, then proceeded
to check the figures and calculate the profits exclaiming 'three
hundred thousand pounds'.[122] Whether the incident is apocryphal or
exaggerated, it demonstrates that her commitment to the business was
widely acknowledged. In March 1840 she reported that Josiah was

'now much annoyed that I do not write up all the books as formerly. So I suppose I must return to the old work' and by April she was again drawing up the monthly accounts.[123]

'I have given myself a man's education from the age of twelve when I first began to follow my own devices', Lady Charlotte Guest wrote in October 1836, 'and since I married I have taken up such pursuits as in this country of business and iron making [as] would render me conversant with what occupied the male part of the population'.[124] Her firm grasp of the principles of ironmaking and management were revealed by a further entry from her Journal which described the visit of Charles Babbage, the scientific inventor:[125]

> I told [Mr. Babbage], that I was quite overwhelmed with the magnitude of the subject and felt I could never fully understand it in all its branches as I had once hoped to do, that I might teach Ivor and also that I might be of some use to Merthyr . . . Mr. Babbage [assured] me that it was a discouragement he had often felt himself on those very subjects in which he had been most successful . . . He placed also strongly before me the necessity of looking at great leading points and not allowing myself to be discouraged and perplexed by comparatively insignificant details – There is much truth in this – It has been always trifles that overset men – The other day I almost cried finding that I did not yet know all the parts of the punching machine. Yet so long as I know the principles on which the machine acted – its efficacy etc I believe it was very immaterial whether or not I could construct one like it.

During the boom year of 1836 Lady Charlotte Guest made one of her visits to Bristol, through whose mercantile community the Dowlais Iron Co. conducted much of its business. Enjoying the success of the company (in that year the works had earned a profit of £67,711), she recorded in her journal that,[126]

> I should have been much more pleased at seeing the effect of commercial industry had there not been a studious avoidance of every allusion to trade and a great dislike expressed to Bristol where all this wealth was accumulated – This I consider very bad taste – I hope I shall never be ashamed of the Iron Trade.

It was remarkable that influential sections of English society took such a disdainful view of industry in the very period when Britain led the world in manufacturing and was experiencing quite unprecedented economic prosperity and growth. To have set herself against such ingrained snobbery and moved to Dowlais revealed that Lady Charlotte was a woman of originality and resilience.

The keeping of a journal, from which these references are taken, also demanded considerable commitment. It had begun with a small pocket diary when Lady Charlotte was ten,[127] and continued with much fuller entries until she was seventy-nine. Although serving as a 'memoranda of the principal things' that struck her, she also believed that a 'journal must be equally interesting in after times to its author whether that person be of decided genius or of none whatever'.[128] It was not, however, kept with a view to future publication and was written as a personal and apparently truthful record of events. The reliability of the journals may be attested by Lady Charlotte's appreciation of the dangers:[129] 'there is always the chance of the *future* disclosing more than necessary and of erroneous notions being conveyed by the careless and often ambiguous manner in which, one who keeps a journal of thoughts and sentiments must often be liable to express himself'.

POLITICS AND CHARTISM AT DOWLAIS

Not only did Sir John Guest provide houses, churches, schools, library and educational facilities for his workers, serve as chairman of the local railway company and the first Merthyr Board of Health, he also sat as the borough's first Member of Parliament, for, in a sense, Dowlais, the township, was his family's creation. To have called it 'Guest-town' would not have been inappropriate. When the 1832 Parliamentary Reform Act redistributed the nation's seats to recognise the new industrial centres and the decline or disappearance of some rural settlements, Merthyr became a parliamentary constituency and there was little doubt that Josiah Guest would hold the seat. In 1826 he had been elected as MP for Honiton as a Liberal,[130] and though losing his seat there in 1831, Josiah Guest supported a reformist doctrine to the extent that he could be termed a Radical.[131] His radicalism was not unqualified, however: returned unopposed by the voters of Merthyr Tydfil in 1832 (there were about 500 who satisfied the property requirements and most were well-to-do shopkeepers),[132] he won their support because he advocated the principles of cheap and efficient government, free trade, *laissez-faire*, the abolition of the Corn Laws (to keep food prices and, therefore, wages low) and further reform of Parliament.[133] He espoused the views that an enlightened man of business might be expected to hold at that time; his opposition to universal suffrage, trade unions and Chartism was complete.

Josiah Guest defended his seat in 1837 when he defeated John Bruce Bruce (who subsequently changed his name to Bruce Pryce) of Dyffryn by 309 votes to 135;[134] and was returned unopposed in 1835, 1841, 1847 and 1852, the last as a token of respect of a man virtually on his death bed.[135] Not given to oratory, nor particularly regular in his attendance at the Commons, he nevertheless, 'served frequently upon important committees, and generally voted upon the great questions of the day'.[136]

In 1837 Josiah Guest had agreed to contest the seat for Glamorganshire, having been promised a baronetcy if he should stand. In the event he lost and Lord Adare (later the third Earl of Dunraven) was returned. To enter the contest he had been required to resign as MP for Merthyr and after his defeat Guest was swiftly re-elected to his former constituency.[137] On 14 August 1838 Lord Melbourne recommended the award of a baronetcy and henceforth he was known as Sir John Guest.[138] It is striking and almost out of character that he should have sought such an honour. Josiah Guest was not, for example, particularly attracted to the life of the landed gentry and preferred to live an unostentatious life in Dowlais, though in April 1838 he had purchased a house at Sully for £3,500.[139] He entered Parliament not to become a powerful figure in the land but merely to safeguard the interests of his firm and Merthyr. The limited nature of his elevation upset Lady Charlotte who believed that he deserved a peerage.[140] The oddly disdainful view of men of industry restricted him to the baronetcy. His son, who became Lord Wimborne, had scarcely done as much to deserve this honour, but possessed the attributes of the landed aristocracy.

The major political disturbances facing Josiah Guest as both MP and ironmaster occurred in 1831 and later when the Chartists won considerable popular following in Merthyr Tydfil. Common to all these was economic hardship. Recession in the summer of 1831 produced considerable distress and workers from the four ironworks took to the streets in protest. In an attempt to restore order the Argyll and Sutherland Highlanders were called upon and a terrible battle ensued outside the Castle Inn. At least twenty were killed and many more injured, while one of the ringleaders, Dic Penderyn, was hanged at Cardiff. Order was thus restored but the riots helped to stimulate the Trade Union movement (at Dowlais and Plymouth the employers retaliated by locking out members) and was instrumental in gaining Merthyr its parliamentary seat in 1832.

This did not solve the question of militancy, for in December 1838 Lady Charlotte reported that,[141]

> the opinions of a discontented set of idlers who wish to stir up dissension have for some time been gaining ground in the North, where the workmen have been encouraged to hold meetings and sign petitions for the cessation of certain privileges which they dignify by the name of the people's charter.

A meeting was held in Merthyr on Christmas Day and, though there were supposed to be 700 Chartists in the town, few attended.[142] In May 1839 enthusiasm for the People's Charter mounted and the Guests, anxious to influence events in Merthyr, left London for

Dowlais.[143] On their arrival they found that these reports had been exaggerated and all was peaceful. The demonstration held on 20 May proved to be orderly and the procession numbered a mere 200, but 'a good many of our people were on the look out to see them return, but they did not join them, though I believe the hearts of many went with them.'[144]

The peaceful protest of the spring months, however, gave way to riots in October when mobs of Chartists stormed the buildings in Ebbw Vale and Newport.[145] The Guests too believed that they were targets and expecting an attack on Dowlais House sent their children away for safety.[146] 'Last night', Lady Charlotte wrote,[147]

> there were several times from fifty to a hundred special constables all in the house, and the succession of suppers and tea-drinkings that went on amongst all that entered was really a curious thing . . . Our own men are good and true and stick to their work gallantly. It is of the Hill people [Plymouth Ironworks] that apprehensions are alone entertained.

Despite further fears of a Chartist rising in Merthyr, the temperature cooled without further incident. The years 1838–39 were profitable ones for the iron trade so that there was likely to have been full employment in the town and acceptable levels of wages being paid. Thus, in a period when labour unrest correlated with dramatic fluctuations in prices and wages, grievances against the ironmasters would not have been widespread or particularly passionately felt.

Chartism had not entirely disappeared in the meantime: 500 attended a meeting in the market place at Merthyr in August 1840, but the speeches remained 'entirely political (of the usual tenor) without any local or personal allusions'.[148] The depression years 1841–42 encouraged the Chartist cause in South Wales and there were meetings at Caedraw, Dowlais and Heolgerrig.[149] In the summer of 1842 at the height of the agitation the Home Secretary, Sir James Graham, observed, 'you have in Merthyr some dangerous men deeply involved in the Chartist conspiracy, which has given life and impulse to this insurrectionary movement'. The authorities reacted swiftly. Troops were brought into the area; a proclamation was issued against future meetings and the ironmasters of Cyfarthfa and Dowlais dismissed known Chartist leaders. In fact, most of the protagonists were not connected with the iron trade but were tradesmen, members of the middle and upper working classes.

In general the 1840s were prosperous years for the ironmasters and low wage levels did not provide the spark of discontent that the Chartist leaders required for mass support. Yet 1848 did see a fresh outbreak of campaigning, culminating in the presentation of a petition in London,[150] though activity in Merthyr failed to reach the frenetic pitch of 1839. Among the reasons for this lack of enthusiasm may have been concern over the very future of the Dowlais Iron Co. as its lease expired. To have caused a riot at the time when the Guests were struggling to re-negotiate satisfactory terms would have been impolitic and the consequences for Merthyr of the closure of its largest ironworks would have been catastrophic.

SUMMARY

In the twenty years following the peace of 1815, Dowlais succeeded in eclipsing Cyfarthfa as the leading ironworks in South Wales. In certain respects this development was surprising. Cyfarthfa entered the race with a huge initial lead and possessed the advantage of being able to operate the Glamorganshire Canal Co. as a virtual subsidiary. It could manipulate the tolls to suit its own demands for dividends or need for cheap transport. At first the patrician response of William Crawshay I to falling prices denuded Cyfarthfa of some capital reserves, while Dowlais and the other Merthyr ironworks accepted many of the orders he rejected on grounds of excessive price reductions.[151] William Crawshay II, his son, invested considerable sums in farms and in 1825 expended a further £30,000 on the construction of Cyfarthfa Castle.[152] It appears that insufficient investment had been made in the ironworks in the mistaken belief that economy and retrenchment were of paramount importance.[153] This was a policy from which William Crawshay III dissented; he wrote to his father in 1832 that 'new and more up to date engineers' should be employed at Cyfarthfa because their 'iron is inferior to Dowlais and certainly not the best made'.[154] A

22 Cyfarthfa Castle, designed by Robert Lugar in a watercolour by Penry Williams (1825). The ironworks was down the hill to the left and plainly in view from the Castle windows.
(*Cyfarthfa Castle Museum*)

new mill was erected at Cyfarthfa in 1833[155] but on the whole capital investment had been neglected so that in 1839 there were still only seven blast furnaces (together with four at Ynysfach), while Guest had seventeen with one under construction.[156]

The time and effort required to perfect the puddling process and set up rolling mills had also cost Cyfarthfa dear. The Crawshays bore the expense of applying the new technology, while Guest, who imported these improvements wholesale to Dowlais, did not have to incur these sums. Unfairly, in a sense, the true innovator was penalised and Josiah Guest was able to take full advantage of the trials and tribulations at Cyfarthfa.

Josiah Guest, who had consistently undercut the Crawshays during the latter years of the Napoleonic Wars and throughout the 1820s, had invested heavily in new plant and was continually searching for greater efficiencies. He determinedly recruited talented engineers and managers, and placed consistent emphasis on technical innovation. It was also suggested that 'Guest and Bailey are pushing their works because they have short leases, but that pushing manufacture of pig iron at Cyfarthfa would only increase an unwieldy stock and encourage the men to demand higher wages'.[157] The expiry of the Dowlais lease in 1848 certainly influenced their mining methods and may well have tempted them to opt for short-term profits though Sir John Guest still nurtured the hope that renewal was possible and strove to bring about a settlement with the Marquis of Bute. Overall, his business strategy was tailored to produce growth through expansion and greater efficiencies and was achieved in the main by capital investment and the recruitment of able managers. This altered only towards the end of 1847.

References

1. Ashton, *Iron and Steel*, p. 153.
2. Hyde, *Technological Change*, p. 135.
3. GRO, D/DG, Letter Books 1816 (3), W. Hood to J.J. Guest, 4 January 1816, f. 98.
4. Bryn Owen, *Glamorgan – Its Gentlemen and Yeomanry 1797 to 1980*, Risca (1983), pp. 20–21.
5. Griffiths, 'Story of Brymbo', p. 5.
6. GRO, D/DG, Section C, 'Notes giving dates of commencement of furnaces, 1817–1818'.
7. Ibid.
8. Revd. H. Davies, 'History of Dowlais', p. 10.
9. Wilkins, *Iron, Steel*, p. 101.
10. Owen, *Dowlais Iron Works*, p. 25.
11. Scrivenor, *Iron Trade*, op. cit., pp. 24, 127.
12. Wilkins, *Iron, Steel*, op. cit., p. 87.
13. Owen, *Dowlais Iron Works*, p. 26.

14. NLW, Schedule No. 593(a), Walter Williams to R. & W. Crawshay & Co., 3 December 1831, p. 898.
15. David Ricardo, *On the Principles of Political Economy and Taxation*, London (1821), Introduction by R.M. Hartwell, Harmondsworth (1971), p. 17.
16. Ibid.
17. Guest, 'Journal', Vol. V. January 1835 – November 1837, 6 September 1837, Lady Charlotte recorded that a further advance of 10 shillings had brought iron to £9 per ton, p. 578; Bessborough, Earl of, *Lady Charlotte Guest, Extracts from her Journal 1833–1852*, London (1950), p. 58.
18. Guest, 'Journal', Vol. V, January 1835 – November 1837, 9 October 1835, p. 135; Bessborough, p. 39.
19. Peter Mathias, *The First Industrial Nation*, London (1968), p. 280.
20. David Mushet, *Papers on Iron and Steel*, London (1840), p. 415.
21. Owen, *Dowlais Iron Works*, p. 32.
22. Scrivenor, *Iron Trade*, p. 124; Gladwin, *Canals of the Welsh Valleys*, p. 82.
23. Slightly different figures are quoted by Hadfield (*Canals of South Wales*, p. 105) for 1830 – Dowlais 29,621 tons, Cyfarthfa 21,312, Plymouth 13,046 and Penydarren 12,582 tons, though the disparities are too small to affect the conclusions.
24. Guest, 'Journal', Vol. IV, May 1833 – February 1835, 22 December 1834, p. 431.
25. William Truran, *The Iron Manufacture of Great Britain*, London (1855), p. 66.
26. Ibid., p. 24.
27. Ibid., p. 25.
28. Owen, *Dowlais Iron Works*, p. 31.
29. Truran, *Iron Manufacture*, p. 85.
30. Ibid., p. 86.
31. William Fairbairn, *Iron its History, Properties, and Processes of Manufacture*, Edinburgh (1861), p. 55.
32. GRO, D/DG, Letter Book 1836 (1), Blunt & Duncan to Guest Lewis & Co., 12 March 1836, f. 297; Elsas, *Iron in the Making*, p. 94.
33. GRO, D/DG, Letter Book 1836 (2), William Fairbairn to Guest Lewis & Co., 21 May 1836, f. 69; Elsas, *Iron in the Making*, p. 201.
34. Owen, *Dowlais Iron Works*, p. 31.
35. Hyde, *Technological Change*, p. 154.
36. Ibid.
37. *Explorations in Economic History*, Vol. 10, No. 3 (1973), Charles K. Hyde, 'The Adoption of the Hot Blast by the British Iron Industry: A Reinterpretation', pp. 282–283.
38. John, *South Wales*, p. 156.
39. Hyde, 'Reinterpretation', p. 288; Andrew Ure, *Dictionary of Arts*, p. 1110.
40. Hyde, 'Reinterpretation', p. 292.
41. Ibid., p. 290.
42. John, *South Wales*, p. 156.
43. Owen, *Dowlais Iron Works*, p. 26.
44. Ginswick, *Labour and the Poor, Vol. III, South Wales*, p. 25.
45. Ibid., pp. 22–23.
46. Elsas, *Iron in the Making*, pp. 64–68 contains correspondence concerning the enticement of workers and entreaties for the return of men to those works where they were still contracted.
47. Hyde, *Technological Change*, p. 142; Cardiff Central Library, Bute Mss, XIV, p. 12.

48. Hyde, *Technological Change*, p. 142.
49. Alan Birch, *The Economic History of the British Iron and Steel Industry 1784–1879*, London (1967), p. 190; Hyde, *Technological Change*, p. 143.
50. Hyde, *Technological Change*, p. 170.
51. Cardiff Central Library, Bute Mss MIV, p. 21; GRO, D/DG, Section C, Box 4; Section E, Box 2; Hyde, p. 170.
52. Truran, *Iron Manufacture*, p. 139.
53. Ginswick, *Labour and the Poor*, p. 26.
54. GRO, D/DG Letter Book 1821 (3), T. Meynall to J.J. Guest, 13 May 1821, f. 279; Elsas, *Iron in the Making*, p. 171.
55. GRO, D/DG Letter Book 1821 (1), J. Cairns to J.J. Guest, 1 November 1821, f. 340; op. cit., p. 173.
56. PRO, SAD 1/6, 29 December 1821, pp. 7–9; G.R. Hawke, *Railways and Economic Growth in England and Wales*, 1840–70, Oxford (1970), p. 215.
57. Hawke, *Railways*, p. 216.
58. Ibid.; John, *South Wales*, pp. 103–104.
59. Ibid., p. 217; John, *South Wales*, p. 103.
60. Owen, *Dowlais Iron Works*, p. 32.
61. *PIME*, Vol. 68 (1905), p. 355.
62. GRO, D/DG Letter Book 1832 (1), Thomas Evans to J.J. Guest, 13 January 1832, f. 306; Elsas, *Iron in the Making*, p. 92.
63. Elsas, *Iron in the Making*, pp. xviii–xix.
64. Guest, 'Journal', 5 November 1836, p. 399.
65. Ibid., 15 July 1837, p. 526.
66. Ibid., 18 August 1837, p. 568.
67. Ibid., 10 January 1837, p. 424; 11 January 1837, pp. 427–428; Bessborough, *Lady Charlotte Guest*, p. 43.
68. Owen, *Dowlais Iron Works*, p. 30.
69. Daunton, 'Dowlais Iron Company', p. 49.
70. CCL, Bute Mss, Box VI.1 'Report on the Mines of Dowlais, 1839', pp. 26, 29.
71. Ibid., p. 3.
72. Ibid., pp. 47–8.
73. Ibid., p. 60.
74. GRO, D/DG Section D, Box 2, 'Delivery and Cost of Coal from under the Brewhouse Level, 1827'.
75. Ibid., 'Cost of Coal raised month ending 19 April 1828'.
76. Ibid.
77. Guest, 'Journal', Vol. IV, 22 October 1834, pp. 365–366.
78. M.W. Flinn, *History of the British Coal Industry*, p. 100.
79. NLW, Schedule of the Mayberry Collection, Vol. I, No. 151 (1825), pp. 320–321.
80. Ibid., pp. 322–323.
81. Roger L. Brown, 'The Lewis' of Greenmeadow' (typescript, 1984), p. 11.
82. Owen, *Dowlais Iron Works*, p. 31.
83. David Mushet, *Papers on Iron and Steel*, London (1840), p. 307.
84. Ibid., pp. 846–847.
85. CCL, Bute Mss, Box VI.1, 'Report, 1839', pp. 10, 11, 14.
86. Truran, *Iron Manufacture*, p. 12.
87. Ibid., p. 6.
88. GRO, D/DG Letter Book 1833 (1), William Chessell to Richard Wood, 22 February 1833, f. 189; Elsas, *Iron in the Making*, p. 93.

89. Wilkins, *South Wales Coal*, p. 181.
90. J.H. Morris and L.J. Williams, *The South Wales Coal Industry 1841–1875*, Cardiff (1958), p. 2.
91. Wilkins, *South Wales Coal*, p. 76.
92. Ibid., p. 77.
93. Clarke, *A Guide to Merthyr-Tydfil*, p. 6.
94. Morris and Williams, *South Wales Coal Industry*, p. 3.
95. Daunton, 'Dowlais Iron Company', p. 20.
96. Ibid., p. 26.
97. *National Library of Wales Journal*, Vol. VII (1951–52), J.D. Evans, 'The Uncrowned Iron King (The First William Crawshay)', p. 12.
98. Schedule of Cyfarthfa Papers, Vol. I, compiled by J.D. Evans, No. 25, W. Crawshay I to W. Taitt, 18 March 1813, p. 41.
99. Evans, 'Iron King', p. 19; Schedule, Vol. II, W. Crawshay I to W. Crawshay II, 5 August 1820, p. 676.
100. Schedule, No. 56, W. Crawshay I to W. Crawshay II, 22 November 1821, p. 685.
101. Ibid., W. Crawshay I to W. Crawshay II, 23 November 1821, p. 686.
102. Schedule, Vol. II, No. 71, W. Crawshay I to W. Crawshay II, 8 March 1821, p. 691.
103. Evans, 'Iron King', p. 26.
104. Schedule, Vol. II, No. 61a, William Crawshay I to William Crawshay II, 16 December 1820, p. 687.
105. Daunton, 'Dowlais Iron Company', p. 31.
106. Guest, 'Journal', Vol. V, 11 December 1836, p. 418.
107. *DNB*, Vol. XXXII, London (1890), p. 321; *History Today*, Vol. XXIII, No. 1, January 1973, David Jones, 'Lady Charlotte Guest', pp. 38–46; Dorothy P.H. Wrenn, *Welsh History Makers*, London (1976), 'Lady Charlotte Guest', p. 58.
108. Bessborough, *Lady Charlotte Guest*, p. 5.
109. Wilkins, *Iron, Steel*, p. 101.
110. Bessborough, *Lady Charlotte Guest*, p. 1.
111. Guest, 'Journal', Vol. I, March 1822 – April 1828, 29 August, p. 96.
112. Revd. H. Davies, 'History of Dowlais', p. 9.
113. *MPICE*, Vol. XII (1852–53), Memoir of Sir J.J. Guest, p. 163.
114. Guest, 'Journal', Vol. IV, May 1833 – February 1835, 11 August 1833, p. 14.
115. Robert Blake, *Disraeli*, London (1966), pp. 94–95.
116. William Moneypenny, *The Life of Benjamin Disraeli, Earl of Beaconsfield*, Vol. I 1804–1837, London (1910), p. 232.
117. 'Journal', Vol. IV, 18 May 1833, p. 1.
118. Ibid., p. 2.
119. Ibid., 15 August 1833, pp. 21–22.
120. Ibid., 2 June 1837, she visited the British Museum to research this history, p. 494.
121. Ibid., 19 August 1836, p. 330.
122. John Randall, *The Severn Valley*, Madeley (1882), pp. 319–320; quoted from Roebuck, *History of the Whigs*.
123. 'Journal', Vol. VI, November 1837 – March 1941, 24 March 1840, p. 390; 4 April 1840, p. 396; Bessborough, *Lady Charlotte Guest*, pp. 110–111.
124. 'Journal', Vol. V, 21 October 1836, p. 390.
125. Ibid., 5 September 1836, pp. 347–348.
126. 'Journal', Vol. V, 25 August 1836, p. 338.

meeting in October 1833, Hill chaired discussions in Merthyr designed to approve a speculative plan for a line from London via Gloucester, Usk, Pontypool and Crumlin to join the Merthyr Tramroad; in the event the scheme was aborted, but the notion of constructing a railway to Merthyr took hold. On 12 October 1834 Lady Charlotte Guest recorded in her journal that[17]

> Mr. Brunel of the Thames Tunnel, accompanied by Mr. Frere, came here in the evening. They are to make a survey of a railroad from Merthyr to Cardiff, and Merthyr got up soon after six this morning, in order that he might have a *very* early meeting with them on the subject.

As a preliminary to setting up a rival organisation, R.J. Hill, Thomas Revel Guest, Thomas Charles and Walter Coffin (a leading colliery owner) resigned from the canal committee in June 1835, their places being taken by two Crawshays and Rees William. On 12 October 1835 at the Castle Inn, Merthyr, the Taff Vale Railway Co. was formally inaugurated with Josiah and Thomas R. Guest both on the provisional committee,[18] the latter being elected its treasurer *pro tempore*.[19] Having obtained an estimate of £190,649 from Brunel as the cost of construction, they secured an Act of Incorporation on 21 June 1836, despite concerted opposition from the canal company.[20] The purpose of the enterprise was succinctly stated in the preamble to the Act:[21]

> the making of a Railway from Merthyr Tydfil to Cardiff, with a Branch therefrom, to communicate with the tramroad leading to the several iron works of Pen-y-darren, Dowlais, and Plymouth, and an nother branch [sic] to the collieries called Lancaiach . . . would be of great public convenience by opening an additional, certain and expeditious means of conveyance to the sea for the extensive Mineral and other Produce of the Places and Works mentioned, also for the Carriage to the said Works from the Port of Cardiff of Iron Ore and other Mineral Produce used in the Fabrication of Iron, and for the Conveyance of Passengers and Goods to and from the said Towns.

The first section of the railway, between Cardiff and Navigation House, Abercynon, was opened in October 1840, and had been engineered by Brunel.[22] Reaching Merthyr on 12 April 1841,[23] it became in Clarke's words 'the great connecting link between the ironworks and the English markets'.[24] Josiah Guest was elected the chairman of the Taff Vale Railway in July 1836 with Walter Coffin as his deputy; T.R. Guest also served on the board, while Edward John Hutchins, a nephew of Josiah, had been appointed treasurer.[25] Although the railway was originally single track and standard gauge (to reduce costs in the mountainous and restricted terrain), the rising

volume of traffic soon determined that the line be doubled;[26] work on this began in 1845 and was largely complete by 1861.[27] The reciprocal nature of freight carried by TVR goods trains was reinforced by a resolution passed on 13 October 1841:[28]

> That for every ton of ore carried up the line to Merthyr at the present rates the [railway] Company are ready to convey down to Cardiff a like quantity of iron at the rate of 1d. per ton per mile (locomotive included) on condition that the wagons, to be provided by the freighters shall at the least carry up $4\frac{1}{2}$ tons of iron ore and return with as much iron as they shall have taken up of iron ore.

Although Josiah Guest was chairman and T.R. Guest sat on the board (who together with E.J. Hutchins owned 60 of the 160 shares originally allocated), the fact that there were ten other directors, two of whom were members of the Great Western board, resulted in the company being run, to all appearances, impartially to users. Whilst the Crawshays had been able to dictate to the other proprietors of the canal, Guest was never in a position to run the TVR for the sole benefit of the Dowlais Ironworks. In December 1851 the directors turned down a request from Sir John for a reduction in the rates on iron and iron ore because 'neither the past dividends nor the future prospects of the railway' warranted such a policy.[29] Further, a dispute over charges and the construction of a branch to the Dowlais Works had, in fact, arisen at the outset. 'The ultimate point of difference', wrote Lady Charlotte in January 1842,[30] was that the TVR expected the Dowlais Co. to pay for the locomotive power required to haul empty freight trains back to Merthyr once they had transported their iron to Cardiff. There was a mounting back carriage in iron ore, and to a lesser extent general goods, though it had yet to attain the flow of iron products from Dowlais. The TVR offered to grant them an allowance of 20,000 tons on top of the actual north-bound traffic but this, in certain circumstances, would still leave room for an imbalance and saddle the Dowlais Iron Co. with a substantial bill. Taking the worst possible case, Lady Charlotte calculated,[31]

> supposing 50,000 tons of iron went down, (by the railway) but only 5,000 tons of goods etc. went up (add to that the 20,000 tons admitted by the Railway) there would be a shilling per ton loss on half the whole quantity sent down, amounting to 25,000 shillings or £1,250 per annum [which would have represented an increase of one shilling per ton on the existing canal rates]. But this is an extreme example to have taken as in general I expect our back carriage, with the 20,000 tons allowed by the Railway, will be fully equal to the quantity of iron taken down.

As most of the high quality local ore had been mined and increasing quantities had to be brought from Westmorland, the company's back carriage would equal and then possibly exceed that of finished iron to Cardiff.

In the event, agreement was reached in February 1842 and it was resolved that the TVR would convey the company's iron products at the standard tonnage rate and undertake[32]

> to provide wagons for bringing down any excess of iron over the iron ore and goods going up to the extent of 20,000 tons per annum at the charge of one-eighth of a penny per ton per mile, and should the excess of iron over the iron ore and goods be more than 20,000 tons per annum and it be found necessary to be taken up the Railway empty . . . the Railway Company to be allowed to load them with any materials or goods going up the Railway paying the Dowlais Co. at the rate of $\frac{1}{8}$ of a penny per ton mile on the weight of the goods so carried for the use of the wagons.

The second contentious matter was the branch railway; authorised in June 1837, it was conceived in part as an inclined plane which would run from the main line south of the Merthyr terminus to the Dowlais Works, and then continue to the limestone quarries at Morlais.[33] In January 1842 it was arranged with Walter Coffin and Christopher

James, delegates from the TVR, that the railway company were to deposit shares to pay for the land on which the branch would be laid, but that the Dowlais Iron Co. must pay for its construction. The latter were permitted to recover this expenditure after 1844 from charges that would accrue to the TVR. In addition, the railway agreed to 'carry the *whole* of the iron [from the Dowlais Co.] down at 2/– per ton (which would bring the carriage of it per railway to the same amount as per canal), allowing for it 1/– per ton' that being the sum they would be obliged to pay the Merthyr Tramroad Co. on existing contracts.[34] Thus, the canal was charging 3s. to transport a ton of iron from Merthyr to Cardiff, the TVR 2s. and the tramroad 1s. for the part journey to Abercynon. Nevertheless, the scheme to construct the incline and branch to Dowlais floundered, and it was not until the passing of the Dowlais Railway Act in 1849[35] that construction began. The line was laid to the ironworks itself and was complete in August 1851.[36] Although intended for freight by the Dowlais Iron Co., it also served a small number of passenger trains until early in 1854 when several derailments cast doubt upon the safety of an inclined section for this service.[37]

Despite the protracted and sometimes bitter dispute over the Dowlais Branch (Sir John actually resigned from the TVR board in January 1840 on this issue but was re-elected in August after a fresh agreement had been concluded),[38] the completion of the railway to Cardiff was of crucial importance in the business success of the Guests during the 1840s. As well as easing congestion on the waterway, it broke the near monopoly of the canal and forced them to cut their tolls. In September 1841 the Glamorganshire Canal Co. lowered tonnage rates by 50 per cent, being able to sustain such a loss in revenue because of the great increase in the volume of traffic which had occurred over the last forty years; in September 1844 a further reduction of $2\frac{1}{2}$ per cent on gross rates was implemented,[39] so that those who continued to ship goods by narrowboat benefited as well as railway customers. By the mid-1840s the Dowlais Iron Co., which was the TVR's largest freight account, consigned around 70,000 tons of goods annually by the railway. Of the iron carried on the TVR, 80 per cent belonged to the Guests, and in one year their bill for its conveyance amounted to £25,641.[40]

Traffic on the TVR rose dramatically as the value of this novel form of transport became widely appreciated. Coal shipments increased astronomically from 41,669 tons in 1841 to 152,100 tons by 1843 and reached 560,000 tons by 1850.[41]

However, the conflict of interest that emerged (low transport costs versus high profits for shareholders), prompted Sir John Guest to resign from the chairmanship of the Taff Vale Co. in May 1847.[42] Regretting the decision, and in the context of the imminent expiry of their lease, Lady Charlotte observed of the railway:[43]

It was his creation and through almost overpowering difficulties he carried it through, and made it prosper. I feel as if thus another link were broken that binds us to dear Wales. How bitterly I have cried over it all, during the afternoon. Yet I know his judgement is correct in this matter.

Sir John was succeeded by his deputy chairman, Walter Coffin,[44] until the completion of the G.W.R.'s link along the Bargoed Taff Valley and the Dowlais Iron Co. remained one of the principal customers of the TVR.

RAIL PRODUCTION AT DOWLAIS

Not only did the railways specifically provide the Dowlais Iron Co. with a means of transporting bulk goods at low cost to Cardiff, in general terms they also generated a vast and seemingly insatiable demand for iron goods, and in particular rails. 'The impulse given to the iron trade by the construction of the railroads' noted a handbook for *Travellers in South Wales* (1860) 'was nowhere more felt than in this [Merthyr] district'.[45]

Between 1830 and 1870 the promotion and growth of railway companies resulted in some 30,000 miles of track being laid throughout Britain to form routes totalling 15,000 miles.[46] Most important of the 'backward-linkage' effects generated by this activity were those for wrought iron manufacture, and principally for rails and their components such as fishplates and chairs; the associated demand for bridges, station fixtures, locomotives and rolling stock, whilst important, was for the iron industry less significant.[47] In Britain the production of pig iron for new lines and replacements reached a peak in the mid and late 1840s (significantly the period when profits at Dowlais climbed to a peak). During the years 1844–51 17.9 per cent of all pig iron produced in Britain went into permanent-way materials for British companies. As just over one-third of the output from British ironworks was exported, 17.9 per cent represented 28.6 per cent of the pig iron consumed at home; in 1848, the peak year, the respective percentages were as high as 30 per cent and 40 per cent.[48]

Whilst this railway-induced demand for iron cannot be considered to be the sole or over-riding cause for the up-turn in the British iron industry after 1844,[49] its influence in South Wales, where ironworks concentrated on permanent-way products, was of greater significance. Although Professor Hawke has asserted that the railways 'were not essential to the existence of the iron industry . . . nor were they responsible for technical advances and external economies in the finishing processes and rolling mills',[50] there were exceptions especially in those regions, such as Merthyr, where ironworks focused on the mass production of rails, and to a lesser extent, chairs, fishplates and cast iron fixtures. It seems likely, for instance, that refinements to Neilson's hot-blast technique were prompted at Dowlais because of the rising scale of operations, while improved rolling methods were encouraged by the high volume of orders that they won. The introduction of a steam-powered saw (p. 75), the laying down of the Big Mill in 1830, Little Mill in 1840, and the opening of the Ifor Works in 1839 were all crucially influenced by booming rail orders.

Because Sir John Guest was chairman of the Taff Vale Railway, the Dowlais Iron Co. seems to have been excluded, on grounds of propriety, from being the main supplier of rails. He competed for orders during the initial period of tender (in July 1839 an order for 1,500 tons of rails at £9.14 per ton was accepted from the Pentwyn & Golynos Iron Co.),[51] but did chair the sub-committee set up to determine 'the shape and size of rail' to be employed.[52] An entry in the TVR minute book for December 1839 recorded that the Dowlais Iron Co. were granted six per cent interest 'from the delivery of the permanent rails . . . to the date of payment',[53] though the quantity appears to have been small. When there was a need for replacements, and Sir John had resigned from the board, the Dowlais Iron Co. could compete successfully for orders and in August 1848 secured a contract to supply 500 tons of rails at £5 10s. per ton.[54] The company was particularly well placed to supply customers throughout South Wales and it is doubtful whether English or Scottish ironworks ever sold many rails in this region.

The Dowlais Iron Co. was a specially favoured supplier in the South of England, explained, possibly, by its proximity to Cardiff and Bristol. During the 1840s customers included the South Eastern Railway,[55] Great Western Railway (by whom they were particularly favoured, presumably because of the connection with Brunel), Dover & Eastern Counties Railway and the Brighton, Croydon & Dover Joint Railway.[56] In addition, the Merthyr ironmasters extended their activities into the Midlands and North throughout this period. The Sheffield & Rotherham Railway ordered rails from Dowlais in 1842,[57] and according to Whishaw they also supplied rails to the North Midland Railway.[58] In the mid-1840s, for example, the Midland Railway was buying rails from Cyfarthfa. The Newcastle & Carlisle Railway patronised the Ebbw Vale Iron Co. and Dowlais, while the Preston & Wyr, the York & North Midland and the Eastern Counties Railways were all supplied by the Crawshays.[59] The only region of England not successfully held by ironmasters from South Wales was the North-east where the rise of a thriving local industry displaced them.

The very character of this booming demand for iron was of importance in shaping production at Dowlais. In this period of experiment, when the railway system was created by a host of independent companies, occasionally competing over similar routes, no standardised form of rail emerged. They varied considerably in their cross-section (double-headed, flat-bottomed, even inverted 'U' shapes) and, weights – the lines belonging to the Midland Counties Railway employed rails of 78lbs per yard, while those of the Newcastle & Carlisle Railway varied from 42lbs to 82lbs per yard.[60] The trend was towards longer rails and heavier sections so that renewals necessitated a greater demand for pig iron. In 1837, for example, the Dundee & Arbroath Railway chose 48lb rails and in 1840, having experienced the intensive use of their line, the Edinburgh & Glasgow opted for ones of 75lbs.[61] Chairs and fishplates increased in weight proportionally and so added to the orders for pig iron. Further, rails did not last as long as engineers had initially predicted, the ever increasing number of trains accelerated renewals as they cracked or wore under the strain. In the 1880s wrought iron rails of heavy section had on average to be replaced every nine to twelve years,[62] so that those lighter variants which characterised the 1830s and early 1840s would have possessed a shorter life expectancy with some compensation for less intensive use. Indeed, the widespread introduction of the tougher and more expensive steel rail in the early 1870s (p. 273) did not necessarily result in a drastic reduction in replacements as trains, running at higher speeds with heavier loads and often operating at greater frequency, increased the level of wear and need for renewal. Suffice it to say that the huge profits earned at Dowlais in the 1830s and 1840s were built on a substantial and sustained demand for rails of many types. Indeed, so great was the variety and level of orders for rails that Guest had to sub-contract rolling work to Penydarren during the early 1840s.

EXPORTS FROM DOWLAIS

By 1850 British ironmasters had established a world dominance in the market for cheap, mass-produced iron. For the industry as a whole, exports rose from about 13,000 tons (sixteen per cent of total production) in 1815 to 59,000 tons in 1830 (45 per cent);[63] thereafter they increased to represent 60 per cent of total pig iron output by 1870.[64] Whereas pig iron exports grew at the remarkable rate of 11 per cent per annum between 1821 and 1870, wrought iron (including rails) reached the still impressive but lower level of nearly 7.5 per cent.[65] Both figures exceeded the average yearly growth rate recorded for British pig iron production (5.6 per cent) and revealed an increasing reliance on overseas sales. The three principal markets for British ironworks were America, France and the German states. During the 1820s the success of the Dowlais Iron Co. in selling to Germany was determined by price and quality. George Uhthoff, the company's agent in Hamburg, claimed that Welsh bar iron could compete there only by charging significantly lower prices than the high quality

Swedish charcoal iron.[66] When, in 1836, iron prices in Britain jumped (bar iron by more than 30 per cent, and pig iron by about 50 per cent), this brought about a reduced level of British exports. The Goldschmidt brothers, merchants in Frankfurt, wrote to Dowlais 'we regret, that the present high price of iron in your country prevents our handling new specifications of iron, as this article is now cheaper here'.[67]

In the mid-1840s, the construction of a railway network in Germany and the inability of domestic suppliers to respond fully to this extra demand, opened the door to British manufacturers of rails. The Dowlais Iron Co. was among the first to enter. Their customers included: the Berlin-Saxon Railway (1841), Leipzig & Dresden Railway (1842), Saxony & Bavaria Railway (1842) and the Lower Silesia Railway (1844).[68] From 1840 to 1844 Germany, then in the throes of a railway-construction boom, bought nearly 50 per cent of all British pig iron exports and nearly 25 per cent of all bar-iron exports, most of which were rails.[69]

After 1843–44 when the German iron industry had acquired the latest British technology and, under the stimulus of railway demand, expanded its output, Dowlais and the other British exporters found it harder to sell there. German ironmasters substituted their own product for imports.[70] At this point Dowlais sought other markets and discovered to their delight that Russia would serve their purposes equally well.

Having already supplied the St. Petersburg-Pauloffsky Railway in 1836, the Dowlais Iron Co. was able to attract a growing volume of orders because of a fortunate combination of circumstances in Russia: after the mid-1840s economic activity there noticeably brightened,[71] though their own iron industry remained backward and, until the 1860s, stagnant.[72] Lady Charlotte recorded in September 1843 that[73]

> Merthyr had a long consultation with Evans and Davies . . . about an order for engines for the Russian Government which Kitson [George Kitson, company's agent on the Continent] has written about. They want us to undertake the supply of them, though they know we do not make any ourselves, but, as we make their rails, they fancy they can rely upon our doing well for their interest, at a slight profit for our trouble, by making contracts with first rate engine makers in England for them. The affair could be a lucrative one but attended with some risk.

A few months later Thomas Evans, the company's managing agent, returned from Russia to announce that on their way through Poland he and Kitson had secured an order for 12,000 tons of rails at £6 per ton. They had, however, lost the Russian bridge contract but did not regret this as it 'was taken at a very low price'.[74] In August 1844 Kitson completed a considerable coup by obtaining an order for 50,000 tons of rails in Russia 'on advantageous terms'. This represented,

Lady Charlotte believed, 'the largest contract of the kind ever made'.[75] In January 1852, after the lease renewal had been settled, but when Dowlais suffered from a shortage of orders, Lady Charlotte was relieved to sign a contract with the Russians for 'some 60,000 to 70,000 tons of iron to make at a price which, though very low, may not be entirely unremunerative, and we shall be able to keep the works on, and our people employed and fed'.[76]

From the scale of the business connected with Russia, and the combined volume of work for Germany and America in the 1830s and early 1840s, it would appear that exports from the Dowlais Iron Co. exceeded the national average of around 35 per cent of total output. The company was not involved in the French market but did on occasion sell rails to other Continental customers such as the Genoa & Turin Railway (6,000 tons in 1847), and the Dutch Railway Co. (1,000 tons in 1841), the Sardinian government (3,000 tons in 1847), the Hanoverian government (2,500 tons in 1846), and other sundry orders and the Canada Railway Co. and the Atlantic & St. Lawrence Co. (1,600 tons in 1847).[77]

PROFITS AND OUTPUT

By the early 1840s Dowlais was widely credited as being the largest ironworks in the world. It employed around 5,000 people in 1840, while Cyfarthfa had 3,000 and Plymouth and Penydarren each had about 2,000 workers.[78] In 1845 it was calculated that the eighteen blast furnaces belonging to the Guests produced 74,880 tons a year, including time for repairs, holidays, closures and so forth,[79] and the eleven at Cyfarthfa made 45,760 tons.[80] By this time the workforce at Dowlais had risen to 7,300. Clarke observed of the ironworks in 1848 that it constituted 'by far the largest establishment of the kind either in this district or in any country on the face of the globe'.[81] Something of the scale of the enterprise is captured by *The Morning Chronicle* in 1849–50:[82]

> The general view of these works is very imposing. Fourteen blast furnaces [excluding the Ifor Works], fifty feet high, stand at the head of an area disposed in a curve something like the form of a horseshoe. Below these stand the refineries, and further down again, the mills and forges, with their hundred chimneys spouting forth fire. Large engine-houses and regulators (huge globes of iron for equalising the current of blast) stand on the north side of the works. Crossing at several points are pipes of cast iron, varying in diameter from six to thirty-six inches, which convey blast to the furnaces, water for cooling the machinery, the workmen's tools and for other uses, and steam to supply the requisite power for the wheel work, squeezers, shears and saws,

used in the several processes through which metal passes. Besides the workmen engaged in the mills, hundreds are employed in loading and unloading trams, breaking and pulling iron, excavating and building, pulling down and repairing and in diverse other occupations, carried on in the open air.

Because the plant was deliberately run down in the belief that the lease would not be renewed in 1848, H.A. Bruce (a trustee appointed after the death of Sir John Guest) argued that 'the production of iron at Merthyr probably reached its height in 1847, but I question whether the yield of 1851 exceeded that of 1846'.[83] He calculated that the four Merthyr works made a total of 204,339 tons in 1846, of which 184,608 tons were sent to Cardiff.[84] Dowlais produced 87,251 tons of iron, Cyfarthfa 56,278 tons, Plymouth 35,198 tons and Penydarren made 25,612 tons.

Table 4.1   Profits at Dowlais, 1840–50

	£	Adjusted £		£	Adjusted £
1840	78066	76162	1846	159070	184965
1841	47293	48406	1847	172747	178848
1842	55206	62169	1848	104827	128150
1843	15335	19240	1849	15768	21337
1844	31157	38418	1850	3778	5140
1845	59039	71330			

Source: GRO, D/DG Profit and Loss Account Summary 1810–35. Figures adjusted by the Gayer, Rostow & Schwartz index of British commodity prices, 1821–25 = 100.

Consistently high profits were earned throughout the 1840s by the Dowlais Iron Co. (Table 4.1), until fear of closure prompted the run down of the works. While the decade has gained the epithet, the 'hungry forties', and did indeed produce considerable hardship for many, the continuing expansion evident at Dowlais was a positive feature of the period. Nevertheless, the slump of 1841–43,[85] with a particularly severe depression for the iron industry in 1843,[86] resulted in lower levels of profit for the Guests. These were difficult years epitomised by reduced outputs, wage cuts and retrenchment.[87] In contrast the harvest crisis of 1847, exacerbated by a banking panic,[88] seemed not to affect the performance of Dowlais. The negligible profits of 1849–50 were solely explained by the partial dismantling of the works (see p. 114). Large sums had to be expended to bring the works back to life and to up-date machinery that had been allowed to fall into disrepair or obsolescence. 'The expenses have been enormous', conceded Lady Charlotte in November 1850,[89]

25 John, the second Marquis of Bute (1793–1848) by Sir Henry Raeburn (1756–1823). (*In a private Scottish Collection*)

Dowlais Iron Co. was that Lord Bute became determined to extract as much as possible from the Guests, first as a compensation for the unrealistically low royalties charged over the previous 99 years and secondly to contribute to finance the modernisation of Cardiff's docks. The obsessional distrust and suspicion of this myopic and solitary aristocrat overwhelmed any sound business principles in dealings with the Guests and produced a series of half truths, broken promises and fruitless deals.

Formal negotiations over the renewal of the lease began in about 1841, but there was little agreement for two years. In April 1843 Lady Charlotte recorded with despair that the company had received a letter from Lord James Stuart to say that,[94]

> Lord Bute did not intend to ratify the agreement he had made through Stephenson in July . . . The idea of leaving Dowlais in

five years, when all seemed so nearly settled, and the many questions of property are quite enough to disturb the placidity of anyone.

The cat and mouse game continued and in July 1845 fresh proposals were received from the Marquis. But 'they were as we expected quite preposterous', wrote Lady Charlotte:[95]

> 4/6d. per ton royalty on pigs and 7/– on bars, dead rent of £9,000 per annum. A very insufficient quantity of mining ground assigned for so large a concern, and a fine of £80,000 for renewing the lease, which was to be for 21 or 42 years certain!!!

The rejection of these terms was followed by a revival of the suggestion that Dowlais be turned into a joint stock company.[96] The works were then valued at £950,000 but the plan, which had first been raised in May 1841,[97] was considered impractical, possibly because of the large sums involved. A flotation would presumably have raised sufficient capital to enable them to renegotiate the lease and bring the works back into a state of proper repair.

Despairing of the unreasonable and unpredictable behaviour of Lord Bute, from the summer of 1843 the Guests became resigned to leaving Dowlais.[98] In April 1845 they considered purchasing Canford Manor, a picturesque Gothic house and estate near Wimborne, Dorset, for their retirement.[99] The mansion, built by Edward Blore (1787–1879) in 1826, was being offered for sale by Lord de Mauley.[100] A complicated settlement and a requirement to obtain an Act of Parliament resulted in the transaction being delayed until October 1846 when Sir John Guest successfully purchased the manor for £335,000 and additional lands at Canford for £19,000.[101] It is unlikely that he would have spent such a considerable sum on a country estate so far from South Wales, had he not believed that the Dowlais lease would lapse. Sir John had the example of the declining fortunes of the Crawshays after the construction of Cyfarthfa Castle to see the effect of diversification into farming and gracious living. Canford was intended as a distraction and retirement home for Sir John who was already suffering from poor health (p. 115).

Lady Charlotte, who was as distressed as anyone at the thought of leaving Dowlais, prepared for the break by involving herself in the Wimborne estate. After an abortive collaboration with the architect Thomas Hopper (1776–1856), whom Lady Charlotte rejected because 'he has not the slightest taste in Gothic decoration',[102] Sir Charles Barry (1795–1860) was commissioned to carry out extensions and modifications to the house. As one of the leading architects of the day, responsible no less for the design of the Houses of Parliament, his fee was not small and the alterations, undertaken by Cubitts, the builders, amounted to £30,000, a sum that Sir John considered extravagant. By July 1849, work was sufficiently advanced for the Guests to occupy Canford and the improvements were finally completed in 1850.

By March 1847, Sir John had given up any thoughts of remaining at Dowlais and expressed a 'willingness to dispose of his plant at a fair value either to Lord Bute or any person to whom he might grant a lease of the minerals'.[103] He was particularly upset by the thought that the Crawshays might take over the new lease.[104] Nevertheless, Sir John persevered with discussions only to be met by 'vague, unsatisfactory and discouraging' replies from Lord Bute, whom Lady Charlotte accurately described as being 'narrow-minded and arrogant'.[105] In November 1847, the Guests finally concluded that it would be wise to abandon the works:[106]

> if the lease could be had on really advantageous terms it would be well to take it; but that, looking at the profits (which have been large), for the last few years on the one hand, and on the other, the heavy responsibilities and enormous payments to Lord Bute, which a new lease would involve, that it would be very imprudent to Merthyr to accede to anything like exhorbitant or even *high* terms; say that the profits have been £50,000. Of this the royalties demanded by Lord Bute would absorb £25,000 leaving on the other £25,000 for the lessees. But the capital &c., in the works if withdrawn would yield £15,000, so that the £25,000 to be expected on renewal would only give a gain of £10,000. So the question is, whether such a sum considering our position, and more than, independence, Merthyr's own age, and his children's youth, with the great difficulty of finding people to

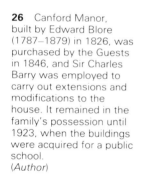

26 Canford Manor, built by Edward Blore (1787–1879) in 1826, was purchased by the Guests in 1846, and Sir Charles Barry was employed to carry out extensions and modifications to the house. It remained in the family's possession until 1923, when the buildings were acquired for a public school. (*Author*)

manage a concern of such magnitude, is adequate to the risk and anxiety. All were inclined to consider it not so, but that under all the circumstances of the case it would be better and happier for us if our connection with Dowlais closed with the present lease.

Her grief at the prospect of abandoning the ironworks was heartfelt and on the solstice of 21 December 1847, Lady Charlotte spent, as she described it, *'the longest* day' of her life touring the site with her husband. 'I wanted once more', she declared,[107]

while they were in full operation, to go through the dear old works, leaning as old on my dear husband's arm. I knew it to be my last day at Dowlais in its glory. I knew that if I came there again ever before the lease expired, some parts of the works would be stopping (as the work of dismantling it is to begin forthwith).

In February 1848 Edward Hutchins, who managed the ironworks in Sir John's absence, wrote to him at Canford to say that three blast furnaces had been blown out and that they were about to dismantle the blowing engines.[108] A large quantity of rails and mechanical equipment were brought up from the mines for sale and coal trams were piled high round the pit tops.[109]

Then, quite unexpectedly (and as a result of such accidents the course of history appears to be altered dramatically), forty-four days before the lease expired on 18 March 1848, the Marquis of Bute died.[110] Lady Charlotte was visiting friends at Bournemouth when Lady Shrewsbury remarked that,[111]

'there is a report in the paper that Lord Bute is dead, that he died suddenly at Cardiff Castle'. I shrieked rather than exclaimed 'Lord Bute!' My agitation was so great that I could hardly breath[e]. Tears stood in my eyes and for many minutes I trembled violently.

RENEWAL OF THE LEASE AND THE DEATH OF SIR JOHN GUEST

John Patrick, Third Marquis of Bute (1847–1900), was but a year old when his father died, the only child from a second marriage to Sophia (d. 1859), daughter of the Marquis of Hastings. Accordingly, all negotiations passed into the hands of the Bute trustees. They instructed John Clayton, a solicitor, to secure an agreement, and in broad terms a settlement was reached on 21 April 1848, ten days before the expiry of the lease. By such fortuitous and fortunate timing, the future of the Dowlais Iron Co. was saved. The news spread swiftly to South Wales and when Sir John and Lady Charlotte Guest returned to Merthyr on 11 July, the town gathered to celebrate the impending renewal:[112]

> The latter part of our progress was certainly the most brilliant and the most enthusiastic. Here were several arches, and flags put across the road for us to pass under. At the Lodge was a triumphal arch, made of flowers and evergreens and flags and constructed really with a great deal of taste . . . When the carriage stopped Mr. Jenkins read aloud the congratulatory address of the people to my husband . . . They [the crowd] then gave a number of cheers, some for him, some for me, some for the children, for the works, the trade, the prosperity of Dowlais.

In fact, the formal agreement did not take place until the beginning of 1853, because discussions over the exact boundaries of the mineral rights proved protracted.[113] Whilst this problem was clarified by a local Act[114] and the lease, which was to run for 52 years, drawn by November 1852, its ratification was delayed by Sir John Guest's death later in that month.[115] It had to be redrawn for Lady Charlotte's authorisation and was signed by her on 18 January 1853. Reasonable in its provisions, the renewal fine was only £2,000 (in contrast to the £10,000 Lord Bute had demanded in 1847 and the £80,000 of 1845), and the rent for the Common was set at £5,000 a year. A higher scale of royalties were introduced (9d. per ton for coal consumed at the works, and 1s. for coal sold) with a sliding scale for iron bars.[116]

Sir John Guest had endured ailing health throughout the 1840s and the strain imposed by the question of the lease weakened him further. Having gone to Canford to rest, he realised that death was near and in September 1852 decided to return to Dowlais where he had been born. There, on 26 November 1852, he died.[117]

His had been a remarkable career; educated at Bridgnorth Grammar School, he had started work at Dowlais and been precipitated by events into its management in his early twenties. Responsible for its dramatic growth and prosperity, Sir John well understood the elements of a successful business strategy – the need to be competitive, which in turn dictated a requirement for cheap transport and low raw material costs. Like a number of ironmasters, he believed that wages needed to be restrained if growth were to continue, in order to maximise profits, which, in turn, allowed the construction of additional plant and machinery. Others such as Thomas Attwood, a Birmingham banker and industrialist, argued that high wages were beneficial, as they would raise consumption and thereby stimulate manufacturing. His views may have been conditioned by the fact that Birmingham's industry was characterised by small-scale units of skilled workers, and therefore often well paid, in which the distinction between masters and men was less pronounced.[118] Those like Guest, who employed vast numbers, many of whom performed simple labouring tasks, and whose plant was capital intensive were pre-disposed towards a low wage economy. Their products, which were not in general purchased by members of the public, were sold to other manufacturers, large companies and customers overseas and could compete successfully only if they were priced as low as possible.

In the obituary for *The Gentleman's Magazine* it was stated that Josiah John Guest had been 'a man of great mental capacities, a good mathematician, and a thorough man of business'.[119] He had the gift of being able to select managers of ability; as a result Dowlais became one of the great training schools of the iron industry and a place where many inventions were devised and tested. During the 1830s, Guest appointed a head engineer called Brunton who erected a blast engine which produced high pressure steam and condensed exhaust gases. Brunton was also the first to ventilate a pit by the exhaustion of air.[120] Two other key managers appointed by Guest were the brothers, John and Thomas Evans. Their father, John Senior, a gifted engineer, had worked for a time at Dowlais but eventually ran a forge and mill for Messrs. Bailey at Nant-y-glo.[121] Thomas Evans, a confidant and childhood friend of Guest until the former's death in 1846, was the senior manager, concerned with policy making and travelled the world as a salesman. John Evans (d. 1862), a tough engineer capable of handling the rough spirits in the works, was a direct understudy to his brother at Dowlais and commanded the day to day manufacturing activities.

In addition, Sir John Guest served as Merthyr's first MP (p. 87) and retained the seat until his death. He was elected a Fellow of the Royal Society in June 1830, became a Fellow of the Geological Society and from 1834 was an Associate of the Institution of Civil Engineers. Nevertheless, the baronetcy that he received in August 1838 might be regarded as inadequate public recognition of a career as one of Britain's outstanding industrialists. Like Arthur Keen, the creator of Guest, Keen & Nettlefolds, Sir John was one of the principal figures in the history of the company.[122] The inscription on the plaque (designed by Sir Charles Barry and composed by Lady Charlotte), which marked his grave in St. John's Church, Dowlais, read:[123]

27   John Evans (d. 1862), manager of the Dowlais ironworks and right-hand man to Sir John Guest. (*Mr. P.G. Simons*)

> Beneath rests the mortal part of Sir Josiah John Guest . . . who through honest paths placed himself at the head of the Iron Manufacture of Great Britain, raised into importance this populous and flourishing district, and was himself an example of what, in this free country, may be attained by the exercise of skill, energy and perseverence.

SOCIAL AND SANITARY QUESTIONS AT MERTHYR

Described in 1849 as 'a rude and shapeless cluster of dwelling houses, inhabited principally by workmen employed in the iron trade',[124] Merthyr Tydfil had undergone rapid and unregulated growth during the first half of the nineteenth century. The population had risen from 7,705 in 1801 to 22,083 in 1831, 34,977 in 1841 and reached 46,378 in 1851.[125] The arrival of workers and their families from other parts of Wales, the border counties of England and from Ireland was the principal cause of this demographic explosion. In the period 1841–47, the balance of births over deaths was a mere 3,657 which suggested that 64 per cent of the increase in population in those seven years (about 10,000) resulted from immigration.[126] Births exceeded deaths by 1,729 between 1848 and 1853, when the population grew by 7,000; the difference, 5,271, or 75 per cent of the total increment, was represented by immigration. Because the four ironworks at Merthyr had expanded at such a rate and required vast numbers of labourers (to mine the coal and iron ore, feed the furnaces, assist the puddlers, fetch and carry, and operate the rolling mills) the town grew in an unbalanced fashion. Obviously enough, the dominance and size of the various works explained 'the large numerical preponderance of the *working classes*', recorded Dr. William Kay, the first (temporary) Officer of Health, appointed in 1853,[127] and the 'very limited number of persons occupying the middle and upper stations, in its local society'.[128] Of the 46,000 inhabitants, he calculated that a mere 6,000 could be described as middle or upper class. Death rates were high. The average life expectancy for trades-people was thirty-two, but for miners and ironworkers it was a mere seventeen years.[129] The cause was twofold: the nature of employment, and the sanitary condition of the town.

Dr. White, the medical officer at the Dowlais Ironworks, argued that 'the most frequent diseases amongst the workmen are – muscular rheumatism, indigestion, "fever-cold" and affections of the lungs especially asthma, all due to the nature of their avocations, and the cold and changeable character of the climate'.[130] Edward Davies, one of the surgeons at the Dowlais Works, spoke of the dangerous nature of employment there:[131]

> Not only are his [founders, refiners, puddlers, ballers, or rollers] duties laborious and exhausting to an extent which affects the duration of life, but he is continually subject to accidents of a highly dangerous kind. What between the casualties above and underground, the very streets are thronged with the maimed and mutilated. In a distance of a hundred yards I once saw three men moving in different directions, two of whom had lost a leg and the other both legs . . . During the years 1841 to 1847, inclusive, the deaths by accidents and violence in *Merthyr alone* averaged fifty a year.

The high infant mortality rate (between 1848 and 1853 47.4 per cent of deaths in Upper Merthyr and 46.6 per cent in Lower Merthyr were of children under five years)[132] was ascribed by Dr. White to 'the impure atmosphere of a small, overcrowded and ill ventilated home, surrounded by collections of filth'.[133] There were no privies in Merthyr, inhabitants having no choice but to 'throw night-soil and slops into the streets or river'.[134] 'It would appear', recorded Sir Henry de la Beche in his *Report on the Sanitary Conditions of Merthyr Tydfil* (1845), that[135]

> the Dowlais Iron Co. undertake to carry away the ashes (containing other refuse) from the doors of the inhabitants of Dowlais at the rate of one penny per week for each house. The money seems stopped out of the wages paid, the greater part of the population of Dowlais being under control, and in the pay of the company. It remained, however, an ineffective and woefully inappropriate response to the public health question.

In general the mawkish condition of Merthyr was attributed to 'the vicious construction of houses, the inadequate supply of water, the absence of drainage, defective ventilation, and the necessary consequences, the accumulation of filth, atmospheric impurity, and also the extensive and fatal prevalence of disease'.[136]

Repeated and terrifying outbreaks of cholera appear to have been the cause of sanitary improvements in Merthyr. It had first struck the town in 1832 where conditions for its breeding proved to be widespread. Of the 600 infected, around 160 died, but still the disease was not taken seriously.[137] Cholera struck with greater ferocity in May 1849 and continued to ravage the population until the end of the year. In its survey of the town, *The Morning Chronicle* calculated that from July to October the pestilence attacked 3,624 people of whom 1,524 died, which represented 'one death in every twenty-eight of the entire population'.[138] In July 1849, Lady Charlotte had written in her journal,[139]

> I am sorry to say that the accounts of the cholera at Dowlais are fearfully bad. They are beyond anything I could have imagined, sometimes upwards of twenty people dying in one day, and eight men constantly making coffins.

A report by T.W. Rammell, researched in May 1849 at the height of the cholera infection, prompted the formation of the Merthyr Board of Health in 1850 with Sir John Guest as its first Chairman.[140] In September 1851 it was proposed to form a joint stock company to provide a safe water supply and by November applications for shares to the value of £20,000 had been received, mainly from the ironmasters. The Local Board of Health could not agree to the scheme and the company's Bill which had already been submitted to

Parliament was taken over by the Board. Yet the Merthyr Waterworks Act, passed in June 1852, proved to be a false dawn and nothing resulted.[141]

The value of reforms had, in fact, been demonstrated by Mr. Hill of the Plymouth Works whose 300 spacious cottages had[142]

> pumps which supply water, ovens for baking, and covered privies. At the approach of the cholera ventilators were put in the ceilings, and proper arrangements made for the daily removal of house refuse. Not less than 1,100 of the workmen were living in these houses, of whom only 25 died of cholera; whilst of 1,700 workmen, who resided in the ill-ventilated and waterless town of Merthyr, 150 died of the disease.

A visitor to the district in 1852, E.F. Roberts, observed the most appalling conditions in the vicinity of Dowlais:[143]

> In the face of the wall on the road-side (on the top of which a kind of parapet was built in front of the houses) were several openings. In these mounds of human odure, and the disgusting aspect of the whole made me marvel that in the neighbourhood of the largest works in the country, perhaps in the world – in the broad open day, offensive to the sight and the smell the apathy of proprietorship could be so great as to neglect the drainage facilities here opened – such as is rarely seen in any town, village or city in the kingdom.

Inevitably the cholera struck again. On 11 September 1854 Dr. Dyke reported a case in Merthyr. Memories of the 1849 visitation were fresh, and a panic spread. John Evans, the Dowlais Works manager, recorded on 20 September that[144]

> we have had twenty-one deaths since Saturday and the disease is spreading. The people are so frightened that they are leaving the place in droves especially the Irish, amongst whom so far it has been most fatal . . . It is with the greatest difficulty that we carry on the mills and other departments.

In the event, 424 died. A few lessons were learned as the Merthyr Board of Health set about demolishing the worst tenements, ensuring that new dwellings were properly constructed. Inspectors of Nuisances were empowered to 'enforce the removal of refuse by scavengers', while roads were 'macadamized, stone gutters formed, pavements laid, and an unlimited quantity of pure water supplied to nearly a thousand houses'.[145]

It would be wrong to conclude that the Guests and the other ironmasters had been oblivious to the need for reform, though their lack of enthusiasm in the first four decades of the nineteenth century reflected an unyielding attitude towards profit making, the need to be competitive and a refusal to accept responsibility for the health of their employees. It was an uncompromising place where the fittest alone could survive. The belief that their lease would not be renewed would also have discouraged the Guests from investing valuable capital in sanitary schemes during the 1840s. Only after the shock of the 1849 cholera did the ironmasters exhibit a real concern for action. In October 1853, for example, Lady Charlotte, who was then managing the Dowlais ironworks, recorded,[146]

> it was reported that a case of cholera had broken out in Merthyr which if true is a most awful thing. In the last visitation (1849) the loss of life here was most fearful. Sanitary and cleansing measures and precautions against overcrowding are being slowly adopted – But there is so much to do, it will be long before anything effectual can be accomplished.

Lady Charlotte Guest then calculated that £1,900 was needed to provide a supply of pure water to Dowlais and wrote to the Merthyr Board of Health offering 'to do it at our own expense'.[147] Further negotiations followed and, in view of the costs having risen to £3,000, Lady Charlotte asked that the Board refund the Dowlais Iron Co. the entire sum after the work had been completed.[148] In the event, a dispute arose over the expense and the ultimate control of the system, which prevented agreement.[149] She then decided to proceed with her own scheme funded by the Dowlais Co.[150] This was postponed, however, and it was probably only after news of the cholera outbreaks at Cardiff in March 1854 that preventative measures were taken.[151]

The crucial improvements to Merthyr's sanitation were undertaken by the Board of Health after the election of G.T. Clark (p. 262) as a member in April 1857.[152] Already the resident trustee of the Dowlais Iron Co., he had worked as an engineer on the Great Western Railway, served as an Inspector of the General Board of Health and was conversant with the latest drainage and water-supply systems. A Bill for the construction of the Merthyr Tydfil Waterworks was promoted by the Local Board of Health in January 1858 and became law in May. Construction of filter beds at Penybryn, together with the provision of standpipes throughout the town, proceeded and was complete by January 1861; the reservoir opened in October 1862.

The death rate at Merthyr fell from 36 per 1,000 in 1851–52 to 25 per 1,000 in 1866. The mortality of children under 5 years was reduced from 527 per 1,000 to 434, and the average age at death rose from $17\frac{1}{2}$ to $24\frac{1}{2}$ years.[153] Despite the improvements to the town's water supply little had been done to improve its sewage facilities. Cholera duly returned to Merthyr in August 1866. In just 58 days the disease killed 115 people.[154] Ironically, G.T. Clark had already persuaded the Local

Board of Health to initiate a major programme of sewer construction in July 1865.[155] As a result some 34 miles were constructed by 1867 and 55 miles by September 1868, allowing householders to install lavatories for the safe disposal of waste. This done, cholera was finally banished from Merthyr.

If the prevalence of disease in Merthyr during the 1830s and 1840s gave it the worst record of health standards in England and Wales, excepting Liverpool,[156] why were so many men and their families prepared to risk illness and death to live there? The Irish, for instance, came in droves to escape the rural poverty of their island[157] and later in the century, when the Dowlais Iron Co. began purchasing iron ore from Vizcaya, a Spanish community arose in the town. Because some of the skilled jobs offered by the ironmasters were more highly paid than other forms of manufacturing, and because the average wage in the iron industry represented a considerable improvement on farm labouring (the least well rewarded occupation), there were financial incentives in moving. Migration increased in times of economic prosperity; the Brecon Road leading to Merthyr from the North was known as the wages barometer of the town.[158] This circumstance produced considerable social problems. Large numbers of single men, working far from their homes, earning an industrial wage boosted by the hazardous nature of their employment, created conditions where drunkenness, violence and prostitution flourished. The very worst housing conditions in Merthyr were the tenements of 'China' at Pont Storehouse, the district between the High Street and the River Taff, where 1,500 beings were crammed in 1845; a large proportion were criminals, vagrants and prostitutes.[159] Indeed, continual shortages of labour at the ironworks in the period up to the 1820s had obliged managers to employ those on the run from the law. Furnaces had, on occasion, to be blown out when there were insufficient men to work them and 'once lost would be with difficulty regained'.[160]

Although Sir John Guest sponsored the building of schools, churches and chapels (and when disease reached fearful and endemic proportions was also prepared to organise and fund schemes for improved sanitation) he deemed this insufficient. Like other employers, he felt compelled to try to raise the morals and manners of his employees, instilling in them values of 'respectability'; a wish expressed at Dowlais by the grant of loans to privileged workers so that they could buy their homes from the company.[161] In addition, to encourage thrift, Guest opened a savings bank in September 1852 for his workers though initially it proved difficult to persuade many to subscribe.

Sir John stressed sobriety and preferred to employ teetotallers.[162] In 1831, when the number of beer houses in Merthyr and Dowlais was multiplying, he ordered that 'no person employed in our service must have anything to do with keeping a public house or beer shop and if any person does so he must be warned to leave one of the two'.[163]

Such stern injunctions to encourage sobriety and industry were also laid down at Hill's Plymouth Works and the Pontypool Ironworks in 1865.[164] John Evans, and his brother Thomas, the works manager and managing agent respectively at Dowlais, rewarded those workmen who became teetotallers in 1840 with a new hat valued at 24 shillings.[165] In 1848 John Morgan, a puddler of Mountain Hare, was dismissed by the company for keeping a beer house; Guest maintained that Morgan would tempt his fellows to drink at his house after work.[166] In 1852 Guest succeeded in his efforts to close the 'Walnut' public house, which was 'considered the greatest nuisance', situated as it was near the gates to the Ifor Works.[167] During the 1850s the Dowlais manager argued that the provision of good housing would encourage the development of a sober and law-abiding citizenry:[168]

> If a workman has a comfortable house over his head, he will by degrees regard air, water and drainage as necessaries of life. He will save money. He will insist upon having some time at his disposal for reading, gardening, and the society of his wife.

In the past, the 'truck system' and similar methods of payment were introduced as a means of controlling drunkenness, tying workers to the company, and as an encouragement to thrift. The Dowlais Co. had opened their 'company shop' in 1797 and employees were paid in one-pound notes issued by the company that could be exchanged there for goods. This, in part, compensated for the lack of coin and the shop itself was needed in the absence of established retail outlets. Although some entrepreneurs managed their shops at a profit and, in effect, defrauded their workers (which resulted in their prohibition under the Truck Act of 1832), the Dowlais shop was occasionally operated in deficit. This resulted from speculative purchases of food in a time of shortage, based on the view that prices would rise higher still – when they actually fell a loss resulted.[169] On one occasion the Dowlais workmen complained that the truck system was unfair and the company agreed after an investigation that they could in future exchange their 'money-note' for food at their shop or use it at an outside grocer. But when a vote was taken, the men decided against this option and returned to the exclusivity of the old system.[170] Debts caused Josiah Guest to abandon the enterprise in 1823, though it reopened in 1828 until legislation compelled its closure.

The lengthy gap between payments (at Dowlais the men were paid once a month) originated with the truck system, the object being to compel them through shortages of ready cash to depend on the company shop for the supply of necessities.[171] Josiah Guest also subscribed to the view that the more infrequently men were paid, the less drunkenness there would be. Lady Charlotte graphically described the heavy drinking and violence that occurred on pay day. In

28 The Dowlais stables built in 1820, but allowed to fall into disrepair before being partially restored by the Merthyr Tydfil Heritage Trust (with financial assistance from GKN and BSC), and shown here before work began. (*Author*)

December 1852 she discussed the possibility of drawing up wages every six weeks 'the object being to get steadier work – much time being always lost in the first week in the month' from heavy drinking.[172] In fact they reduced the number of pay days to eight in 1853,[173] and in June 1859 the interval between payments was increased to 10–12 weeks.[174]

Judged by the mortality statistics, not only was Merthyr one of the least healthy towns in Britain, it grew in the early decades of the nineteenth century with lamentably few educational and social facilities. In this respect, however, the ironmasters did more to improve the lot of the inhabitants than local or central government. Josiah Guest had opened a school for the children of his employees in the upper floor of the Dowlais Stables in 1820 and the following year it was attended by around 200 boys and 100 girls.[175] Rising numbers and the need for workers who could read, write and understand technical problems led to the construction of a purpose-built school. This, which incorporated a reading room and library was completed in 1844 at a cost of £7,000;[176] and in 1846 an infants' school was added.[177] In October 1848 the first night school for boys and workmen was established, though it remained exclusively for employees of the Dowlais Co. The average attendance each evening numbered 110 during the first winter, but increased to 150; its subjects included reading, writing, cipher, history, geography and grammar.[178] In 1849–50 *The Morning Chronicle*'s reporter observed of Merthyr that,[179]

the workmen were almost entirely helpless with regard to the instruction of their children. The private schools were utterly incompetent and insufficient . . . Great praise is due of late years to Sir John and Lady Guest, who, fortified by the assistance of the Legislature in giving a power to the employer to create an

29 The Guest Memorial Hall, designed in 1854 by Sir Charles Barry, but not completed until 1863 as a library and reading rooms for the workers of the Dowlais Iron Co. (*Author*)

educational fund out of the wages of the workmen, have rendered infinite service to the cause of social advancement in Dowlais.

In 1853 Lady Charlotte Guest decided as part of a lasting memorial to her husband to build a new school at Dowlais to incorporate all the educational requirements of the works and instructed Sir Charles Barry, whom she had previously employed at Canford, to prepare the plans.[180] The Dowlais Central Schools were completed in 1855 at a cost of £20,000 and offered places for 650 boys and girls, and 680 infants.[181] A form of central heating was provided by hot air pumped from an engine house in the ironworks through underground ducts to the school itself.[182] That Lady Charlotte should have employed Barry for this building, and in 1854–55 to design the Guest Memorial Hall (a library and reading room for employees, not actually completed until 1863),[183] revealed a conviction that industrial districts were no less fitting environments for fine architecture than, say, the capital city. In this respect, Lady Charlotte was in the vanguard of contemporary thought.[184] The enthusiasm manifested by the Guests for school building led Dowlais to be called the 'Prussia of South Wales',[185] for that continental state placed special emphasis on the value of tuition. Although Sir John had initially organised the workers' education and subsequently offered wholehearted support, Lady Charlotte was the driving force behind many of the educational projects funded by the Dowlais Iron Co. in later years. In 1827 he had himself commissioned the construction of St. John's Church, Dowlais, at a cost of £3,000 and gave to many local chapels. In addition, he founded a Mechanics

Institute in 1829 at Dowlais in which weekly lectures were delivered principally on mineralogy and metallurgy.[186]

The school system established at Dowlais by Lady Charlotte was developed by G.T. Clark who regarded education as a means of disciplining the minds of his workers and instilling a capacity for 'painstaking industry combined with good moral conduct'. Clark appointed only those certificated teachers whose philosophical approach met with his approval, and preferred those who had been educated in the company's schools. In 1881 he could claim that 'almost all the workforce had been through his schools, and certainly all the clerks'.[187] Such an employment policy, coupled with compulsory deductions from wages to support the school, led to high enrolment figures, though these concealed heavy absenteeism and early withdrawal.

SUMMARY

By 1850 Merthyr had established itself as one of the key iron-making districts in Britain and was the pre-eminent producer of rails. Of the four ironworks there, Dowlais was the principal. Despite the problems caused by the renewal of the lease, it remained the largest, possessed the ablest managers and retained a considerable capital reserve, and so possessed the necessary elements to effect a full recovery. In 1823 it was estimated that Wales and Monmouthshire accounted for 42.93 per cent of Britain's total pig iron production, rising to 44.59 per cent in 1830. Although output continued to rise, its percentage decline (falling to 38.8 per cent in 1839 and 36.16 per cent in 1847,[188] representing 720,000 tons)[189] was not due to any inherent weakness but simply reflected the growth of the iron industry in Scotland, Northumberland and the North-west. In 1850, reported Astle,[190]

> the four establishments of Dowlais, Penydarren, Cyfarthfa and Plymouth had 47 blast furnaces with forges and mills in proportion. Their combined annual produce approximated to 225,000 tons . . . no pig iron was sent away, but all worked up at home into rails and bars. The number of hands employed numbered nearly 18,000 and the wages paid exceeded £20,000 per week.

The Dowlais Ironworks, its very size and awesome power, seemed to manifest the very qualities of the Industrial Revolution, of man against nature. 'This narrow valley', observed Cliffe in 1848,[191]

> is blocked up to a great extent by the enormous black banks of cinders &c., compared with which the largest railway embank-

ments are mere pigmies. Additions are of course constantly being made to these banks . . . As the 'tips in progress are formed of hot cinders, they are on fire from nearly top to bottom – glow like lava. Rivulets of *hot* water wash the bases of these gloomy banks. The scene is strange and impressive in broad day-light, but when viewed at night is wild beyond conception. Darkness is palpable. The mind aids reality – gives vastness and sublimity to a picture lighted up by a thousand fires. The vivid glow and roaring of the blast furnaces near at hand – the lurid light of distant works – the clanking of hammers and rolling mills, the confused din of massive machinery – the burning headlands – the coke hearths, now if the night be stormy, bursting into sheets of flame, now wrapt in vast and impenetrable clouds of smoke – the wild figures of the workmen, the actors in this apparently infernal scene – all combined to impress the mind of the spectator wonderfully.

The thirty-five years from 1815 had, however, seen a fundamental change in the iron industry. Until that time rapidly growing demand had kept prices high and provided readily available surpluses for technical experiment and expansion. After 1815 the pattern changed. The rapid growth in demand continued but output increased even more quickly producing a sustained fall in prices. Railway booms had produced short periods of high prices, but they had also been accompanied by depressions lasting sometimes for five or six years. Ironmasters had to innovate if they wished to survive in an economy of ever tougher competition.

The most rapid diffusion of new techniques often occurred during periods of slump, when cost cutting became an imperative for commercial survival. The initial wave of adoption for Neilson's hot blast process took place in 1835–45 at a time when iron prices fell sharply.[192] Ironmasters were able to introduce these new techniques because the nature of the innovations had changed significantly since the late eighteenth century. With the exception of the hot blast method and rolling-mill design, none of the advances after 1815 (taller furnaces, the Cowper stove, waste heat and gas recovery systems, 'pig-boiling', the Nasmyth steam hammer, or the Rastrick boiler) represented a fundamental departure from previous practice.[193] The risks associated with these innovations were relatively small and they did not require heavy inputs of capital. The ironmaster could adopt the new technique initially on a limited basis with relatively low expenditure. The only major exception to this pattern was the installation of heavy mills capable of rolling rails and structural ironwork. Powerful engines and their boilers and the complex arrangement of rolls required considerable planning and expenditure, such that many ironworks declined to undertake such a step, apart from installing mills capable of rolling crude billets. The really heavy investment at Dowlais, and the other major ironworks, had been made when the puddling furnaces were laid down and duplicated and when the largest blast furnaces were constructed.

References

1. Lady Charlotte Guest, 'Journal', Vol. V, January 1835 – November 1837, 24 September 1837, pp. 592–593; Bessborough, *Lady Charlotte Guest*, p. 60.
2. Ibid.
3. E.E. Edwards, *Echoes of Rhymney*, Risca (1974), p. 24.
4. Wilkins, *Iron, Steel*, p. 187.
5. Guest, 'Journal', Vol. V, 23 September 1837, p. 592.
6. Clarence S. Howells, *Transport Facilities in the Mining and Industrial Districts of Wales and Monmouthshire*, London (1911), p. 11.
7. Hadfield, *Canals of South Wales*, p. 107.
8. Ibid., p. 110.
9. Evan J. Jones, *Some Contributions to the Economic History of Wales*, London (1928), p. 55.
10. NLW, Ref. 92A Glamorganshire Canal Minute Book, No. 1, 11 September 1818, p. 489.
11. Ibid., 21 September 1820, p. 535.
12. Ibid., 2 October 1823, p. 596.
13. Ibid., 2 June 1824, p. 604.
14. NLW, Ref. 92B Glamorganshire Canal Minute Book, No. 2, 1836–1944, 9 March 1838, p. 8.
15. Ibid., 3 June 1840, p. 24.
16. D.S.M. Barrie, *The Taff Vale Railway*, Godstone (1950), p. 6.
17. Guest, 'Journal', Vol. IV, 24 October 1834, p. 356; Bessborough, *Lady Charlotte Guest*, p. 36.
18. PRO, Taff Rail 684/1, TVR Directors Minute Book, Vol. I, October 1835 – May 1844, 12 October 1835, item 1.
19. Ibid., 23 October, 1835, item 4.
20. 6 Wm. IV c. LXXXII; Barrie, *TVR*, p. 6; see also *Merthyr Historian*, Vol. 1 (1976), V.L. Wilding, 'The Railways to Merthyr Tydfil', pp. 72–73.
21. Barrie, *South Wales*, pp. 6–7.
22. Guest, 'Journal', Vol. VI, 8 October 1840, pp. 464–465; Bessborough, *Lady Charlotte Guest*, p. 116.
23. PRO, Taff Rail 684/1 Minute Book, 26 March 1841, item 647.
24. Clarke, *A Guide to Merthyr-Tydfil*, p. 16.
25. PRO, Taff Rail 684/1 Minute Book, 16 July 1836, item 24, item 26.
26. Charles F. Cliffe, *The Book of South Wales*, London (1848), p. 14.
27. Barrie, *South Wales*, p. 116.
28. PRO, Taff Rail 684/1, TVR Minute Book, 26 March 1841, item 647.
29. PRO, Taff Rail 684/3, TVR Minute Book, Vol. III, September 1849 – May 1856, 5 December 1851, item 781.
30. Guest, 'Journal', Vol. VIA, March 1841 – August 1843, 26 January 1842, pp. 119–120.
31. Ibid.
32. PRO, Taff Rail 684/1, 21 February 1842, item 907.
33. Ibid., 22 August 1837, item 181.

34. Guest, 'Journal', Vol. VIA, 14 January 1842, p. 110.
35. 12 & 13 Victoriae, cap. 61, Royal Assent 28 July 1849.
36. PRO, Taff Rail 684/3 TVR Minute Book, Vol. III, 8 August 1851, item 665; 15 October 1851, agreement finalised for the Dowlais Branch, item 733.
37. *The Railway Magazine*, Vol. LXXXI, No. 484, October 1937, 'The Dowlais Railway', pp. 291–292.
38. PRO, Taff Rail 684/1 TVR Minute Book, 17 January 1840, item 456; 4 August 1840, item 497.
39. NLW, Ref. 92B Glamorganshire Canal Co. Minute Book, op. cit., 17 September 1841, p. 31; 11 September 1844, p. 47.
40. Wilkins, *History of Merthyr Tydfil*, p. 185.
41. Evan Jones, *Contributions*, p. 69.
42. PRO, Taff Rail 684/2, TVR Minute Book, Vol. II, May 1844 – August 1849, 4 May 1847, item 2869.
43. Guest, 'Journal', Vol. VII, June 1844 – March 1848, 2 May 1847, p. 608.
44. PRO, Taff Rail 684/2, 31 August 1848, item 2989.
45. *A Handbook for Travellers in South Wales*, London (1860), p. 70.
46. T.R. Gourvish, *Railways and the British Economy 1830–1914*, London (1980), p. 20.
47. J.B. Snell, *Mechanical Engineering: Railways*, London (1971), p. 79.
48. M.C. Reed (Editor), *Railways and the Victorian Economy*, Newton Abbot (1969), B.R. Mitchell, 'The Coming of the Railway and United Kingdom Economic Growth', pp. 22–23.
49. Mitchell, 'Coming of the Railway', p. 23.
50. G.R. Hawke, *Railways and Economic Growth in England and Wales 1840–1870*, Oxford (1970), p. 245.
51. PRO, Taff Rail 684/1, TVR Minute Book, 17 July 1839, item 402.
52. Ibid., 10 April 1839, item 376.
53. Ibid., 20 December 1839, item 451.
54. PRO, Taff Rail 684/2, TVR Minute Book, Vol. II, 2 August 1848, item 3279.
55. Hawke, *Railways*, p. 223.
56. Elsas, *Iron in the Making*, p. xviii.
57. Ibid.
58. F. Whishaw, *The Railways of Great Britain and Ireland*, London (1840), p. 372.
59. Hawke, *Railways*, p. 226.
60. Bryan Morgan, *Civil Engineering: Railways*, London (1971), pp. 74–75.
61. Reed, *Railways and the Victorian Economy*, Wray Vamplew, 'The Railways and the Iron Industry: A Study of their Relationship in Scotland', p. 36.
62. I.L. Bell, *The Iron Trade of the United Kingdom*, London (1886), p. 34.
63. Hyde, *Technological Change*, p. 144.
64. Ibid., p. 172.
65. Rainer Fremdling, 'British Exports and the Modernisation of the German Iron Industry from the 1820s to the 1860s' (typescript), p. 5.
66. Ibid., p. 8; Elsas, *Iron in the Making*, pp. 122–123; GRO D/DG Letter Books, 1822 (2), f. 538–545; 1823 (5) ff. 269–275.
67. GRO D/DG Letter Book 1836 (2) f. 246; Elsas, *Iron in the Making*, p. 128.
68. Elsas, *Iron in the Making*, p. xviii.
69. Fremdling, 'British Exports', p. 11.
70. Fremdling, 'British Exports', pp. 8–10.
71. M.E. Falkus, *The Industrialisation of Russia 1700–1914*, London (1972), pp. 31–32.

72. Ibid., pp. 40–41.
73. Guest, 'Journal', Vol. VIB, August 1843 – October 1845, 4 September 1843, p. 513; Bessborough, *Lady Charlotte Guest*, p. 155.
74. Ibid., 16 December 1843, pp. 572–573; Bessborough, *Lady Charlotte Guest*, pp. 157–158.
75. Ibid., 22 August 1844, p. 22.
76. 'Journal', Vol. IX, February 1851 – September 1853, 30 January 1852, p. 271; Bessborough, *Lady Charlotte Guest*, p. 288.
77. Elsas, *Iron in the Making*, pp. xviii–xix.
78. *Robson's Commercial Directory of London and the Western Counties . . . and South Wales*, Vol. II, London (1840), p. 48.
79. *The Engineer*, Vol. XXVI, 17 July 1868, 'The Early History of the Iron Trade in South Wales', p. 243.
80. *Slater's Directory for South Wales* (1850), p. 63.
81. Clarke, *Guide to Merthyr-Tydvil*, p. 27.
82. Ginswick (Editor), *Labour and the Poor in England and Wales*, Vol. III, pp. 20–21.
83. H.A. Bruce, "Merthyr Tydfil in 1852", *A Lecture delivered to the Young Men's Improvement Society at Merthyr Tydfil*, Merthyr Tydfil (1852), p. 5.
84. Ibid.
85. Ashton, *Iron and Steel*, p. 153.
86. Truran, *Iron Manufacture*, p. 169.
87. Guest, 'Journal', Vol. VIA, 14 December 1841, p. 95.
88. Mathias, *First Industrial Nation*, p. 230.
89. Guest, 'Journal', Vol. VIII, 20 November 1850, pp. 759–760; Bessborough, *Lady Charlotte Guest*, p. 251.
90. Owen, *Dowlais Iron Works*, p. 35.
91. Ibid., p. 39.
92. GRO D/DG Section C, Box 4, 'Cost of Materials and Iron made at Dowlais 1845–52'.
93. *Victorian South Wales Architecture, Industry and Society*, The Victorian Society, Seventh Conference Report (1969), J. Mordaunt Crook, 'Patron Extraordinary: John, 3rd Marquis of Bute' (1847–1900), pp. 3–4.
94. Guest, 'Journal', Vol. VIA, 29 April 1843, pp. 447–448; Bessborough, *Lady Charlotte Guest*, p. 143.
95. Ibid., 23 July 1845, p. 188; Bessborough, *Lady Charlotte Guest*, p. 163.
96. Ibid., 15 October 1845, pp. 255–256; Bessborough, *Lady Charlotte Guest*, p. 168.
97. Ibid., Vol. VIA, 3 May 1841, p. 16.
98. Ibid., 3 July 1845, p. 175.
99. Ibid., 30 April 1845, p. 145.
100. J. Pouncy, *Dorsetshire Photographically Illustrated*, London (1857), p. 89.
101. Guest, 'Journal', 6 October 1846, p. 506; Bessborough, *Lady Charlotte Guest*, p. 183; Bournemouth Reference Library, Nora Parsons, *The Manor of Canford Magna*, Swanage (1974), p. 9.
102. Guest, 'Journal', Vol. VII, June 1844 – March 1848, 1 October 1847, p. 702.
103. Ibid., 1 March 1847, p. 593.
104. Ibid., 28 March 1847, p. 598.
105. Ibid., 31 October 1847, p. 710.
106. Ibid., 27 November 1847, pp. 722–723; Bessborough, *Lady Charlotte Guest*, p. 199.

107. Ibid., 22 December 1847, p. 735.
108. Ibid., 23 February 1848, pp. 775–776.
109. Revd. Hathren Davies, 'History of Dowlais', p. 17.
110. *Burke's Peerage and Baronetage*, London (1975), p. 426.
111. Guest, 'Journal', Vol. VIII, 20 March 1848, p. 8; Bessborough, *Lady Charlotte Guest*, p. 205.
112. Ibid., 11 July 1848, p. 89.
113. Revd. Hathren Davies, 'History of Dowlais', p. 60.
114. 11 & 12 Victoriae cap. 20, Royal Assent 31 August 1848.
115. Bessborough, *Lady Charlotte Guest*, p. 310.
116. Revd. Hathren Davies, 'History of Dowlais', p. 60.
117. Ibid., 26 November 1852, p. 496; Bessborough, *Lady Charlotte Guest*, p. 301. *DNB*, Vol. XXIII, London (1890), pp. 319–321.
118. Asa Briggs, *Victorian Cities*, Harmondsworth (1968), pp. 184–189.
119. *The Gentleman's Magazine*, Part 1 (1853), pp. 91–92; Wilkins, *Iron, Steel*, pp. 116–117.
120. Wilkins, *Iron, Steel*, p. 123.
121. Ibid., p. 257.
122. Obituaries of Sir John Guest were published in: *The Times*, 9 December 1852, p. 8; *The Gentleman's Magazine*, Vol. XXXIX, Part 1 (1853), pp. 91–92; *MPICE*, Vol. XII (1852–53), pp. 163–165.
123. *Illustrated London News*, Vol. XXVII, No. 766, 20 October 1855, p. 476.
124. *Hunt & Co.'s Directory and Topography of Glamorganshire*, London (1849), p. 53.
125. Census; Cliffe, *Book of South Wales*, p. 127.
126. T.W. Rammell, *Report of the General Board of Health on a Preliminary Inquiry into the Sewerage . . . and Sanitary Condition of the Town of Merthyr Tydfil*, London (1850), p. 14.
127. William Kay, *Report on the Sanitary Condition of Merthyr Tydfil*, Merthyr Tydfil (1855), p. 4.
128. Ibid., p. 10.
129. Owen, *Dowlais Iron Works*, p. 41; *Merthyr Historian*, Vol. II (1978), Joseph Gross, 'Water supply and Sewerage in Merthyr Tydfil 1850–1914', p. 68.
130. Kay, *Sanitary Conditions of Merthyr Tydfil*, p. 52.
131. Ginswick, *Labour and the Poor*, p. 39.
132. Kay, *Sanitary Conditions of Merthyr Tydfil*, p. 15.
133. Ibid., p. 53.
134. Rammell, *Report of the General Board of Health*, p. 48.
135. MTL, *Report of the Health of the Towns Commission into the Sanitary Conditions of the Labouring Population of Great Britain by Sir Henry de la Beche*, P.P. 1845, XVIII, p. 319.
136. Kay, *Sanitary Conditions of Merthyr Tydfil*, pp. 58.59; Rammell, *Report of the General Board of Health*, p. 48.
137. Owen, *Dowlais Iron Works*, p. 41.
138. Ginswick, *Labour and the Poor*, p. 11.
139. Guest, 'Journal', Vol. VIII, March 1848 – February 1851, 31 July 1849; Bessborough, *Lady Charlotte Guest*, p. 230.
140. Gross, 'Water Supply', p. 69.
141. Ibid.
142. Ginswick, *Labour and the Poor*, p. 62.
143. E.F. Roberts, *A Visit to the Environs of Merthyr Tydfil and the Iron Works in 1852*, London (1853), p. 31.

144. GRO, D/DG Letter Book, 1854, J. Evans to Lady Charlotte Guest, 20 September 1854, f. 473; Elsas, *Iron in the Making*, p. 73.

145. NLW, *Second Annual Report on the Sanitary Conditions of Merthyr Tydfil*, Merthyr Tydfil (1867), p. 89.

146. GRO, Microfilm Reel 129, Diary of Lady Charlotte Guest 1852–54, 8 October 1853, p. 159.

147. Ibid., 17 October 1853, p. 161.

148. Ibid., 18 November 1853, p. 180.

149. Ibid., 22 November 1853, p. 181.

150. Ibid., 21 December 1853, p. 192.

151. Ibid., 26 March 1854, p. 225; 28 March, p. 227.

152. Gross, 'Water Supply', pp. 69–71.

153. NLW, *Second Annual Report*, (1867), p. 90.

154. Owen, *Dowlais Iron Works*, p. 44.

155. Gross, 'Water Supply', p. 73.

156. *The Morning Chronicle*, 4 March 1850.

157. Ginswick, *Labour and the Poor*, pp. 64–65.

158. W.R. Lambert, *Drink and Sobriety in Victorian Wales c. 1820–c. 1895*, Cardiff (1983), p. 28; C.H. James, *A Lecture on Wages delivered before the Total Abstainers of Merthyr Tydfil*, Merthyr Tydfil (1851), p. 12.

159. Sir Henry de la Beche's Report, p. 322; Lambert, p. 31.

160. NLW, Cyfarthfa Mss, William Crawshay to Crawshay Junior, 19 January 1814; see also GRO, D/DG Letter Book, T. Bridge to W. Taitt, 2 June 1815; Addis, *Crawshay Dynasty*, pp. 60, 73, 125; Lambert, *Drink and Sobriety*, p. 36.

161. Lambert, *Drink and Sobriety*, p. 35; Weetch, Kenneth Thomas, 'The Dowlais Ironworks and its Industrial Community 1760–1850' (M.Sc.(Econ) thesis, University of London, 1963), pp. 53–54, 144.

162. GRO, D/DG Letter Book (1872) (2), Robert Napier to William Gardner, 27 April 1827, f. 573; Elsas, *Iron in the Making*, p. 25.

163. GRO, D/DG Letter Book 1831 (1), J.J. Guest to E.J. Hutchins, 28 February 1831, f. 568; Elsas, *Iron in the Making*, p. 79.

164. Lambert, *Drink and Sobriety*, p. 39.

165. Ibid; *The British Temperance Advocate*, 15 February 1840.

166. Lambert, *Drink and Sobriety*, p. 39; GRO, D/DG Letter Book, J.J. Guest to John Evans, 15 August 1848, f. 987.

167. Ibid.; ibid., J.J. Guest to John Evans, 28 April 1852, f. 158.

168. G.P. Smith, 'Social Control and Industrial Relations at the Dowlais Iron Company c. 1850–1890' (University of Wales (Aberystwyth) M.Sc. thesis, 1982), p. 116; R.A. Church, *The History of the British Coal Industry, Volume 3, 1830–1913*, Oxford (1986), p. 279.

169. Revd. J.H. Davies, 'History of Dowlais', p. 7.

170. Ibid.

171. Lambert, *Drink and Sobriety*, p. 41.

172. GRO, Reel 129, Diary, 27 December 1852, p. 9.

173. Ibid., 28 December 1852, p. 12.

174. Lambert, *Drink and Sobriety*, p. 41; *Cambrian*, 10 June 1959.

175. Owen, *Dowlais Iron Works*, p. 24.

176. Wilkins, *Iron, Steel, Tinplate*, p. 108.

177. *National Library of Wales Journal*, Vol. IX, (1955–56), Leslie Wynne Evans, 'Sir John and Lady Charlotte Guest's Educational Scheme at Dowlais in the Mid-Nineteenth Century', pp. 266–267.

178. Owen, *Dowlais Iron Works*, p. 41.
179. Ginswick, *Labour and the Poor*, pp. 79, 80.
180. *The Builder*, Vol. XVIII, No. 902, 19 May 1860, pp. 305–07; No. 903, 26 May 1860, pp. 322–4.
181. Owen, *Dowlais Iron Works*, p. 49.
182. Wynne Evans, 'Educational Scheme', p. 273.
183. Owen, *Dowlais Iron Works*, p. 50.
184. Edgar Jones, *Industrial Architecture in Britain 1750–1939*, London (1985), pp. 80–105.
185. Owen, *Dowlais Iron Works*, p. 25.
186. Ibid.
187. G.P. Smith, 'Social Control and Industrial Relations at the Dowlais Iron Company *c.* 1850–1980', pp. 71–81; Church, *Coal Industry*, p. 294.
188. Bell, *Iron Trade*, p. 9.
189. Carr and Taplin, *British Steel Industry*, p. 7.
190. John G.E. Astle, *The Progress of Merthyr*, Merthyr Tydfil (1879), pp. 9–10.
191. Cliffe, *The Book of South Wales*, pp. 128–129.
192. Hyde, *Technological Change*, p. 200.
193. Ibid., p. 210.

Part II

Engineering in the Midlands, 1850–1900

5 *The Origins of Nettlefold &*
Chamberlain 1823–80

On 1 May 1851, Lady Charlotte Guest, with her daughter Maria, attended the opening ceremony of the Great Exhibition in the Crystal Palace situated in Kensington Gardens.[1] The Dowlais Iron Co. had loaned series of specimens illustrating the manufacture of iron[2] and these would have been displayed in the south-west galleries, along with other items illustrating coal mining and the metallic industries.[3] The exhibition had been conceived not simply as a way of demonstrating British superiority in manufacturing but was, in the words of Prince Albert, President of the Commissioners, appointed to organise the event, 'to give us a true test and living picture of the point of development at which the whole of mankind has arrived'.[4] The engineering trades were equally well represented and there were a variety of machines on display to show their precision and self-acting properties. Machinery for drilling, boring, shearing, punching, planing and slotting, together with their products, were arranged in the north-west corner of the mighty hall of iron and glass.[5] It was here that an inspired John Sutton Nettlefold first considered applying the latest mechanical techniques to the manufacture of woodscrews. Britain's industrial and trading competitors also exhibited, so that Germany, France, Belgium, Russia and America all had sections.

The Crystal Palace itself, a huge glasshouse, designed by Joseph Paxton, had been fabricated in Birmingham. The 9,000,000 square feet of glass were supplied by Chance Brothers of Smethwick,[6] and the cast iron columns and beams which formed its skeleton had been manufactured by Fox, Henderson & Co., whose London Works were also, if misleadingly, situated in Smethwick. In the case of the ironworks, the detailed specifications had been drawn by [Sir] Charles Fox (1810–74), while George Henderson (1783–1855) organised the production of the components in their foundry. Not long afterwards the London Works were acquired by Arthur Keen and served as the headquarters for his Patent Nut & Bolt Co., and subsequently of Guest, Keen & Nettlefolds.

BEGINNINGS OF THE BUSINESS

John Sutton Nettlefold (1792–1866) began his manufacturing career far from the Midlands at Sunbury-on-Thames, where he used the power generated by a waterwheel to make woodscrews. By 1823 he had opened a small ironmonger's shop at No. 8 Red Lion Street, Holborn, and it was three years later that he decided to purchase the water-powered mill, for in the meantime Nettlefold had acquired a British patent (taken out in 1817 by John Gerard Colbert, a watchmaker of Winsley Street, Marylebone)[7] to make screws with a buttress thread, which made it easier to drive them in and harder to take out,[8] an important innovation as they remained blunt-ended. In April 1826 he issued a price list for his 'patent screws'; there were 184 different varieties in gauges from one to twenty-four and in length from $\frac{1}{4}$ to 4 inches, and were offered in iron, brass or copper. They were by no means inexpensive, the smallest screws selling at 8d. (presumably for a dozen) and the largest at 16s. 0d.[9] When a new list of brass and copper screws was published in July 1852, the total number of variations had fallen to 127, though it is unlikely that such a reduction applied to iron screws which generated the greatest demand. Handwritten additions to the 1852 advertisement indicated that Nettlefold increased the range of brass and copper screws to 199 not long afterwards – presumably following the construction of his new screw mill in 1854.

However, to be closer to suppliers of raw materials (wrought iron and brass wire) and better able to compete, Nettlefold decided to transfer his manufacturing operations to Birmingham, the centre of the screw trade, and by 1834 established a steam-powered factory at Baskerville Place. He set up his offices in an adjacent building, No. 14 (later altered to 16) Broad Street. At the same time his eldest son, Edward John Nettlefold (1820–78), was admitted to the partnership.[10] A ledger listing their Birmingham factory's customers during the 1840s reveals that the majority were based in that city (including Thomas Belliss, Westley Richards, Abel Stokes, Chance Bros., Henry Cox, William Undell & Co., Lingham Bros., James Cartland, Henry Shaw, Rabone Bros. & Co., Chas. Mardiwitz and Pickford & Co.), while others were in Southampton (H. & J. Lankester), Manchester (Michael Atkinson), Glasgow (P. & W. McLellan and Wm. McGeoch), Sheffield (B. Huntsman) and Bristol (James & R. Godwin).[11]

By 1834 John Sutton Nettlefold had also moved his London wholesale firm to more fashionable premises at 54 High Holborn, London, where J.S. Nettlefold & Sons remained until 1928 when expansion occasioned a transfer to a new building in Euston Road, opposite the former LNWR terminus. During the 1830s the family business continued to prosper with a shop in London and a factory in Birmingham but growth was limited by the repetitive hand-work

30 John Sutton Nettlefold (1792–1866), the founder of Nettlefold & Chamberlain.

required in the manufacture of woodscrews.

A private journal, kept from 1834 to 1854, which included sums set aside for 'deteriorations' (depreciation), indicated that the Nettlefold business was for the most part a thriving concern (Table 5.1). Nevertheless, their profits reached a peak in 1846 which suggested that if dramatic growth were to be sustained a major initiative needed to be implemented.

Table 5.1   John Sutton Nettlefold's Profit and Loss Account 1834–52

		£			£
June	1834	138	June	1844	213
	1835	254		1845	1,387
	1836	657		1846	2,303
	1837	206		1847	754
	1838	427		1848	(1,439)
	1839	(100)		1849	(586)
	1840	658		1850	(998)
	1841	38		1851	1,578
	1842	(45)		1852	2,043
	1843	(69)			

Figures in brackets indicate a loss.
Source: J.S. Nettlefold, Private Journal 1834–54, pp. 30–5; loose working papers within.

The crucial innovation was the purchase in 1854 of the Sloane patent for the manufacture by automatic machinery of woodscrews with gimlet points (until then screws had a blunt end which made them more difficult to drive in). It has been widely stated that J.S. Nettlefold observed American screw-cutting lathes in operation at the Great Exhibition of 1851 and that a shortage of capital caused the three-year delay between the scheme's conception and its implementation in Birmingham.[12] Whilst a number of self-acting machines were indeed on display at the Crystal Palace, those for making woodscrews were not of advanced design:[13]

> the head is raised in a die by pressure; the worming is effected by a screw, which traverses the back of the spindle, and forces the clams containing the blank or uncut iron forward against small cutters, which rip or cut out the thread. Slitting is done by small circular saws.

Further, the stands filled by the United States did not contain any machinery for making woodscrews, though a model of one for making nails and spikes was on display.[14] Circumstantial evidence suggests that the idea of using automatic machinery may have been crystallised in J.S. Nettlefold's mind whilst he was visiting the exhibition and that

31 An automatic pointing and threading machine (left) and an automatic screw turning and slotting machine (right) mounted on a common base. (*Museum of Science and Industry, Birmingham*)

he might have met Thomas J. Sloane there or, at least, someone who knew him or of his invention.

America had stolen a technical lead in the design of machine tools by the mid-nineteenth century. As early as August 1839, Lady Charlotte Guest recalled a trip to Birmingham where[15]

> Merthyr [Sir John Guest] came home and fetched me to see a new process of making screws by machinery. The invention is by Dr. Hull, an American, and the American Minister, Stephenson and Mr. Vanworst were looking at the same time that we were there. The whole thing was done by machinery even to the feeding of the machines of which there were four different ones. The first formed the rough shape of the screw. The second perforated the head and made it true. The third sawed the nick across the head. The fourth cut the thread by means of a circular file.

In 1842 an American mechanic called Cullen Whipple patented a thread-cutting machine in which all the operations were automatic and in the following year patented a further two self-acting machines, one for turning the heads of blanks, and one for removing burrs after slotting and eventually assigned his rights to the New England Co. of which he was a leading promoter.[16] However, the screws produced under Whipple's several patents remained blunt-ended, and William

G. Angell (1811–70) of their competitor, the Eagle Screw Co., realised that if automatic machinery could be arranged to produce gimlet-pointed screws there was an excellent chance of capturing a major share of the market. When he heard that the New England Co. had refused to purchase the patents taken out in 1846 by Thomas J. Sloane of New York to manufacture pointed screws (No. 4704, 20 August, and No. 4864, 24 November), Angell took them up, having first decided that they differed significantly from those devised by Whipple, thereby minimizing the chances of any legal action.[17] The decision proved to be commercially sound. Not only did the Eagle Screw Co. establish a powerful position in the United States, it also began exporting to Britain. The threat imposed by the American-made pointed screw may well have spurred J.S. Nettlefold into action, or at least caused him to accelerate his plans to acquire the British rights to the Sloane patents.[18] In the event the Eagle Screw Co. merged with the New England Screw Co. in 1860 changing its name to the American Screw Co. and Angell was elected as president. Shortly afterwards it acquired the Bay Screw Co. and became the largest manufacturer in the United States. Thirty years later it decided to challenge Nettlefolds' monopoly in Britain (p. 212).

If business survival was the spur, then cost was the problem for J.S. Nettlefold as the initial price for exclusive rights in Britain, together with sufficient machines to begin to exploit its potential, was set at £30,000. In addition, he needed to build a new type of factory to ensure that a sufficient number of screw-cutting lathes could produce such economies of scale to support the increase in overheads. After debating and planning for three years, and possibly when the force of American competition started to hit hard, J.S. Nettlefold decided to risk a substantial capital investment. He needed, however, to obtain £10,000 from his wife's brother, Joseph Chamberlain Senior, who had a shoe manufacturing, or cordwaining, business at No. 36 Milk Street, London, and which entitled him to an equal share in the screw-making firm.[19] Nettlefold & Chamberlain was therefore a family partnership using accumulated savings and profits to fund a modern industrial enterprise. Chamberlain Senior, who was noted for his capacity for hard work, had a precise and cold manner but possessed a strength of character which made him quite implacable when he had determined upon a particular course of action.[20] His son, Joseph Chamberlain Junior (1836–1914), inherited many of those traits, as his record in management was to demonstrate, for his father, having resolved to remain in London to run his own business, sent the young Joseph to look after his interests in Birmingham. Subsequently Chamberlain Senior moved to the Midlands, settling at Moor Green Hall and became a partner in Smith & Chamberlain, brassfounders.

Similarly, J.S. Nettlefold, who continued to manage his wholesale ironmongers in Holborn could not spare sufficient time to oversee developments at the new Midlands factory, so he arranged for his

son, Joseph Henry Nettlefold (1827–81), a mechanical engineer, to serve as its works manager under the supervisory gaze of Edward J. Nettlefold (1820–78).

Having made the crucial decision to introduce automatic screw-cutting lathes, it was imperative that Nettlefold & Chamberlain build a factory in which they could be effectively operated. They found a site in Heath Street, on the border of Birmingham and Smethwick, which was served both by the Cape Arm of the Birmingham Canal Co. and was close to the London & North Western Railway's station at Soho.[21] It was sufficiently near to the centre of Birmingham and their office, mill and warehouse at Baskerville Place not to be inconvenient, and by virtue of its situation in a still rural area,[22] offered scope for expansion. The first mill, constructed in 1854, consisted of two one-storey sheds (219ft long and 50ft wide) joined together by a common centre wall. The provision of brick cellars, which increased the building costs considerably, was an important innovation, for it allowed them to house the shafting beneath the machinery which was driven by belting from below. This was a much safer system than the almost universal practice of installing the shafting just below the

32 (left) Joseph Chamberlain (1836–1914) photographed in early life when a partner in Nettlefold & Chamberlain.

33 (right) Joseph Henry Nettlefold (1827–81).

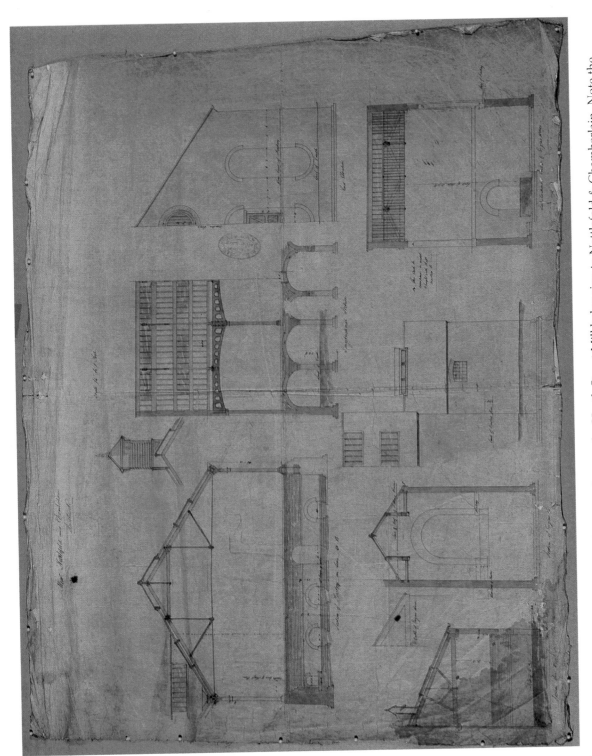

7 Unsigned plans produced in 1863 for extensions to the Heath Street Mill belonging to Nettlefold & Chamberlain. Note the decorative louvred ventilator and recessed panels to the end elevation.
(European Industrial Services)

and packing cases; the ground floor served as a packing room, general office and store for galvanised screws; the first floor held wrapping and sorting rooms and stocks ready for wrapping, while the top storey was fitted as an order department for screws destined for France.

The canal arm was the principal means of obtaining coals for the boilers to drive the machinery and to take packaged screws to the railway depot for distribution throughout Britain and overseas. Horse-drawn wagons were used for local deliveries.

The premises at 16 Broad Street and Baskerville Place (which in reality were one) had not altered much since their acquisition in 1834. An office of three storeys fronted Broad Street and by 1872 accommodated twenty to thirty clerks, Joseph Chamberlain Junior, who had become a partner in 1869, being the manager and Herbert Chamberlain, a younger brother, the chief clerk.[32] Adjacent to the offices and entered from Baskerville Place was a two-storey mill which manufactured special screws and performed the pattern work. Unlike the top-lit and well ventilated mills at Heath Street, this factory conformed to the traditional pattern of screw works in the Midlands and was widely regarded as being unhealthy.[33] Across the Birmingham Canal, over a wooden bridge, was a four-storey warehouse. The top floor contained brass screw stock and bolts and nuts; the third floor held the manager's office, iron-screw stock and labels for both Nettlefold & Chamberlain and James & Avery (see p. 148); seconds and japanned screws were stored on the second floor, where town orders were also executed; the ground floor was for receiving goods from the works, packing and despatching.[34]

As well as the Birmingham offices and mill and the main works at Smethwick, Nettlefold & Chamberlain had acquired a further three factories by the 1870s. They purchased a screw mill from James, Son & Avery at King's Norton (p. 147) and has also integrated vertically into wire drawing and rolling. In 1869 they bought Gibson's Ashtree Works at the Cape, Smethwick, and under its new name, the Imperial Wire Co., it became Nettlefold & Chamberlain's first wire mill. Until then they had obtained their supplies from Messrs. Thomas & Leonard Jenkins's Milton Works, but their consumption of five loads of 30 cwts daily made it increasingly necessary for them to have their own wire-drawing facilities close at hand.[35] The Imperial Mills, too, had a wharf on the canal arm to receive coil, which was drawn into various gauges of wire for the screw machines at Heath Street and King's Norton.

Originally Nettlefold & Chamberlain purchased their bar iron from various manufacturers in Staffordshire, but at some point in the 1860s they bought land at Hadley Castle, near Wellington, Shropshire, from their solicitor, R.D. Newill, for an ironworks. There they erected a blast furnace and puddling furnaces together with rolling mills to convert bar iron to coil. The wire needed to make woodscrews had to

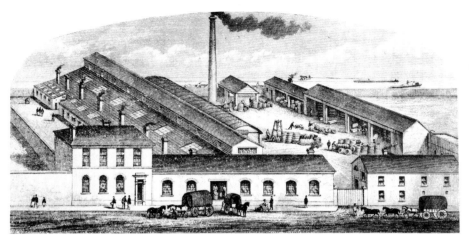

36 The Imperial Wire Co. belonging to Nettlefold & Chamberlain. Coil was delivered to the works by narrowboat and then drawn into the various gauges of wire required in the manufacture of woodscrews. The plant was eventually transferred to Heath Street when they acquired the premises formerly belonging to the Patent File Co. of Sheffield.

be of high quality and uniform gauge which explained why they were determined to obtain as much control as possible over the input of materials to the main works. The existence of a mock turret near the ironworks gave rise to its title, the 'Castle ironworks', and also provided Nettlefold & Chamberlain with their distinctive trademark.

The introduction of automatic machinery transformed the wood-screw trade hitherto characterised by laborious and repetitive hand operations. W.C. Aitken suggested in 1878 that,[36]

> inventive skill has been largely exercised in this country and America in perfecting the machines, and those now in use here are American and self acting. The attendance of women in the former dirty occupation of 'screw grinding', as it was called, is entirely got rid of, and they are now employed in tending the machines, a number of which can be managed by one female.

By revolutionising the manufacturing process, the automatic lathe permitted a dramatic increase in output. In 1865 Birmingham produced 130,000 gross woodscrews a week, of which Nettlefold & Chamberlain manufactured 90,000 gross, which was more than the total national output for 1850.[37] By 1873 they were making 150,000 gross weekly or 'seven million two hundred thousand gross of screws per annum'.[38] Nettlefold & Chamberlain had achieved such a standing in the industry that a party from the Institution of Mechanical Engineers visited the Smethwick screw works in July 1876. The machinery was of special interest:[39]

> The length of wire to form the screws is cut off by machines, which also upset one end by a blow to form the head. These 'blanks' then pass to a machine in which the head of each is turned, the blank being held in a revolving chuck, and the tool

brought up to it, and the nick is then cut across the head by a small circular saw; the supply of the blanks to the machine is by a self-acting feed, and the chuck holds and releases the blank by self-acting means. After being sorted and examined, the blanks next pass to the screwing or 'worming' machine, in which each is

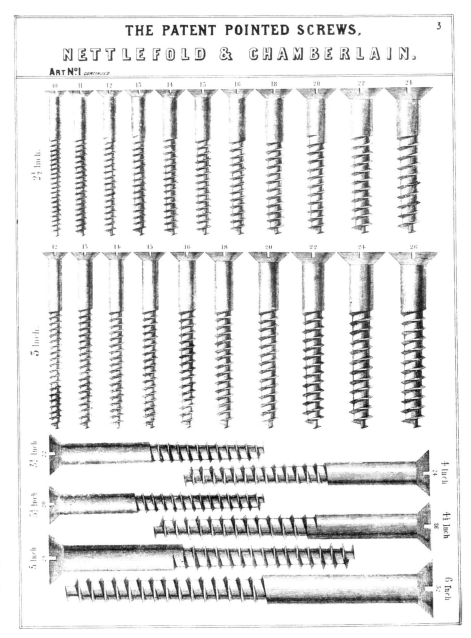

37 A page taken from Nettlefold & Chamberlain's second catalogue (1871) showing some of the sizes of gimlet-pointed, iron woodscrews which they manufactured.

gripped by the head end in a revolving jaw; and after the other end has been turned off to a point by one tool, the thread is cut by a traversing tool, taking a succession of cuts of increasing depth.

The screw mill had by 1876 been extended to cover $1\frac{3}{8}$ acres and contained over 2,000 machines, turning out about $\frac{1}{2}$ million screws an hour. Because they were self-acting, one woman could attend several of them, having only to charge the hoppers with blanks and replace the cutters as they became worn.

Although the original Sloane machines had been assembled in America, replacements and additional screw-cutting lathes (called 'A' and 'B' machines) were all made at Heath Street.[40] Regular maintenance required that they be capable of building their own machines for the small circular saws employed for cutting the nicks in the screw heads which could, on average, cut about 1,000 screws before needing to be replaced. Some 4–5,000 of these saws were consumed each day.[41] Although they could be re-used several times, the works needed facilities for stamping blanks, cutting the teeth and hardening and tempering the steel. Being actively involved in the assembly and maintenance of these machines encouraged technical innovation and new designs were generated within the works rather than by the acquisition of patents from overseas. One employee, Mr. Wakefield, for example, patented a forging machine and every quarter would come around the mill 'carrying a bag of money which was a royalty or allowance off them'.[42]

The adoption of mass-production methods and Nettlefold & Chamberlain's dominance of the British market (p. 152) encouraged them to increase the type and number of fasteners. Their catalogue for 1871 revealed 730 varieties of iron screw (891 by 1917),[43] not to mention those in copper or brass, plated, lacquered or galvanised. By this time the company also manufactured a range of nuts, bolts, rivets, hooks, eyes, split linch and cotter pins, washers and hinges. Wire in a range of gauges and coatings was also produced,[44] as was a number of specialist products, including plug and taper taps, Weston's patent differential ratchet braces, and Storer's patent lubricator (in brass for stationary engines and locomotives).[45] Nevertheless, the iron woodscrew, with its countersunk head, remained the staple product on which the success of the business was based.

GROWTH AND COMPETITION

By the mid-1860s, before the transition of power from John Sutton Nettlefold and Joseph Chamberlain Senior to their sons, they took a series of decisions which enabled Nettlefold & Chamberlain to

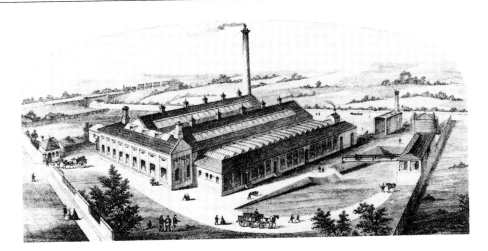

38 The screw mill at King's Norton, formerly owned by James, Son & Avery. It appears to have possessed its own gas plant (top right), and was situated beside the Worcester and Birmingham Canal.

dominate the British and to a lesser extent the world-wide screw market. The purchase of the UK rights to the Sloane patent and the construction of a modern factory were not in themselves sufficient to provide them with the market dominance that they sought. A rival firm, James & Son of Bradford Street, Birmingham, had independently made technological advances, not to the level of the Sloane patent, but far enough to give them a substantial share of the industry's expanded production.[46]

In 1861–62 James & Son had constructed a purpose-built mill (incorporating cellars for the drive shafts as at Heath Street) in King's Norton, Stirchley,[47] then a rural district.[48] This enterprise represented a considerable threat to such ambitions that Nettlefold & Chamberlain held of dominating the Birmingham market in woodscrews. When William Avery, a screw maker, joined the James partnership in 1864 (its style then became James, Son & Avery), he brought with him the patent to a machine which had been successfully manufactured and sold to a Belgian enterprise.[49] When the new firm was in the throes of promoting itself as the British Screw Co. Ltd. in July 1865,[50] it was taken over by Nettlefold & Chamberlain for a reported £100,000.[51] It seems that the acquisition had been preceded by a price-cutting war as the purchase of this business, together with that of John Hawkins (late Messrs. Fox & Hawkins) of Princip Street, Birmingham, who supplied much of the Scottish market was advertised as obviating 'the necessity of further sacrifices in a trade which has already suffered severely from excessive competition'.[52] Although the modern works at King's Norton became an integral part of the firm's manufacturing capacity, the old screw works at Bradford Street, from which James & Son grew, appears to have been closed shortly after the acquisition.

Such, however, was the loyalty to certain brand names that Nettlefold & Chamberlain found that they were unable to sell screws made at King's Norton under their own name and so continued to

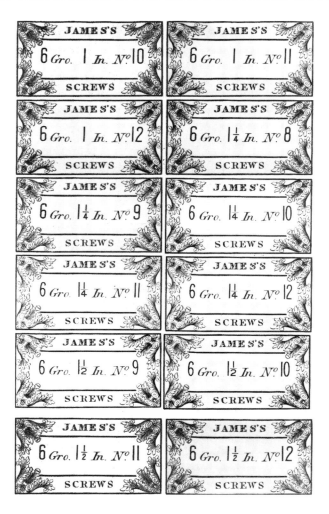

39 A sample of the labels printed by Nettlefolds for woodscrews made at King's Norton retaining the old James & Co. style.

package its products under James & Avery labels.[53] This also had the advantage of preserving an illusion of competition within the Birmingham district – a policy that was re-adopted after the purchase in 1898 of the British Screw Co. in Leeds (p. 220). (The King's Norton works (promoted under the style of the British Screw Co.) had no connection with the British Screw Co. in Leeds, whose name either by coincidence, or perhaps to annoy Nettlefolds, had been selected by its owners the American Screw Co.) Although screws from King's Norton continued to carry a James's label, they were printed on the same bright green paper which characterised Nettlefold's products, though they did not carry the 'castle' emblem.[54]

As Nettlefold & Chamberlain secured an ever larger proportion of the European woodscrew market, so it became necessary to extend the King's Norton works. To increase the capacity of the mill, additional working space was constructed (the bricks having been fired on the site from clay dug from the south-east side of the factory) together with a new foundry and dressing, annealing and carpenters' shops. The site had its own gas plant which was used for lighting,[55] while two beam engines (high and low pressure types) were employed to drive the main shafting and to create the blast for the cupola in the foundry and smith's shop.[56] Water for the boilers was taken from the Worcester and Birmingham Canal which, being adjacent to the works, was also used to deliver screws to Smethwick.[57] Around the mid-1870s the works began to manufacture screw eyes

40 Hand-bending wire goods at King's Norton during the nineteen-twenties.

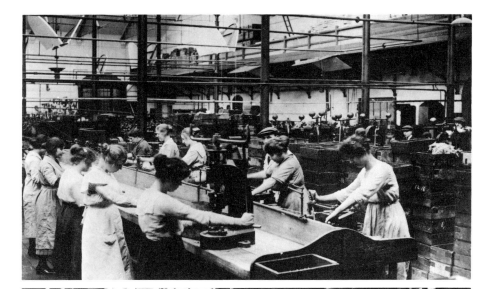

41 The wrapping room at King's Norton shown here in the nineteen-twenties, though the nature of the employment could scarcely have altered since the mid-nineteenth century.

42 Box-making machines in operation at King's Norton. They supplied Heath Street with its packing requirements. Note the canvas blinds to reduce the glare of bright sunlight.

and hooks, cotters, button hooks, scissors, skewers and other products made from wire, for which a further block was erected, facing the Pershore Road. Another extension was made by building a gallery to the south-east wing and this housed screw machines that produced the smallest sizes of screws and printing presses for turning out the many labels needed at all the factories. Box-making machines were also installed when parcel packing was abandoned. Nettlefold & Chamberlain designed and assembled the box-making machines themselves, selling a number to Messrs. Bird & Sons of Birmingham and Cadburys of Bournville.[58] The King's Norton factory developed, therefore, as a specialist plant manufacturing the smallest fasteners wire products, and fashioned all the boxes and labels consumed by the entire business.

Having broadened their screw-making operations, Nettlefold & Chamberlain decided to expand further by vertical integration. The increased volume of production could now justify the purchase of a larger wire-drawing mill in May 1870. The factory lying idle, originally constructed in 1864 by the Patent File Co. Ltd. of Sheffield, situated on the opposite side of Heath Street with a dock on the canal arm, was an obvious acquisition. The consulting civil engineer, Robert C. May (1829–82), who was better known for his work on gasworks, bridges, corn mills and river drainage schemes,[59] had designed the buildings.[60] As laid out in 1865–66 for the Patent File Co., they comprised seven sets of rolls driven by a steam engine with a Siemens regenerative gas furnace and a hardening furnace.[61] The offices and

43 Edward Nettlefold (1856–1909), deputy chairman of Nettlefolds from 1891 to 1902 and a director of GKN until his death.

long as two years.[92] During this period, Chamberlain advocated reducing the discount to 50 per cent which, he calculated, would increase their profits by £20,000–£30,000.[93] This surplus could then be employed to fund the firm when prices were cut to drive their new competitor into insolvency. The only disadvantage he could envisage was that the company would incur the displeasure of the factors during the period of reduced discounts, but felt this would have a minimal impact on their trade as the French, who were supplying Field & Cornforth could spare no 'more than 10,000 gross a week at the present time'.[94] When the Birmingham Screw Co. came into production, Chamberlain estimated that the discount would have to be raised to 75 per cent to defeat them and believed that even at that level the firm could continue to earn profits of 'at least £10,000'. 'I', he added, 'should be content with my share of this for five years while the "meal was cooking". We should have a glorious feast whenever the Company gives up and no more opposition for another five years or so.'[95]

Chamberlain initially outlined the strategy in a series of letters written to J.H. Nettlefold in the month of May 1870.[96] He was receptive to the plan, but both Frederick and Edward Nettlefold remained unconvinced of its efficacy. To persuade them, Chamberlain argued that it was necessary to attack their competitor as soon as they began manufacturing, to prevent them from establishing any reputation: 'on the whole I feel certain that to let the Company get fairly in the market would be to abdicate for ever our position as Screw Kings'.[97] This, he suggested, was the secret of Angell's success in America, 'although in the last recession he stopped up too long and allowed the small companies to take hold so that he has had difficulty in arranging with them'.[98] His reasoning proved effective, as on 20 May Chamberlain replied to J.H. Nettlefold saying 'I am very glad to find by your letter that Fred and Edward have come round to our view . . . it would not be pleasant to have to fight without the full assent of all our partners'.[99]

In an attempt to discourage potential investors in the Birmingham Screw Co., Chamberlain succeeded in getting the following paragraph published in the *Birmingham Daily Post*:[100]

> The Screw Trade
>
> We learn that the works of the late Patent File Company, which have been so long idle, will shortly be set in operation. They have been purchased by Messrs. Nettlefold & Chamberlain, who anticipate an increased foreign demand for their manufactures whenever the competition in the home trade necessitates a reduction in the price. We are informed that this firm have also made arrangements for the erection of large iron mills and furnaces, and have just completed a new wing to their principal factories in Heath Street.[101]

The message was clear; Field & Cornforth could expect a battle and any member of the public considering buying shares in their company could not now be unaware of this fact. After private discussions, Chamberlain reported, 'Mr Keen was very anxious to get a hint as to our intentions but I confined myself to saying that I don't advise my friends to go in at present'.[102] Chamberlain also arranged, after meeting with his managers, that any workman who left the firm to take a job with the Birmingham Screw Co. would never be re-employed by Nettlefold & Chamberlain.[103] In his skilful use of the local press and absolute determination not to be beaten, Chamberlain resembles the fictional character of Arnold Bennett's novel, Denry Machin.[104]

Before committing the firm to a protracted battle with the Birmingham Screw Co., Chamberlain discussed various strategies with his friends in the city and 'the result', as he wrote to J.H. Nettlefold, 'in a few words is to convince me that it is to our interest to *fight* and that we must fight in any case'.[105] He then produced a series of calculations to justify this course of action[106]

Suppose on the one hand we go up to 50% [discount] for two years and then down to 75%, and on the other that we keep at 60% as long as we can. In the latter case we shall lose trade every day till our opponents make say 40,000 gross [a week] and then it will be simply impossible to kill them. And I think that the profits will stand thus

	1st Plan	2nd Plan
1871	100,000	70,000
1872	30,000	60,000
1873	10,000	50,000
1874	10,000	40,000
1875	10,000	30,000
1876	10,000	30,000
	£ 170,000	£ 280,000

He was convinced that a fight on the lines of plan one would defeat the Birmingham Screw Co. and, while profits would be greater in the short term under plan two, they would also 'have half the factory unemployed and a decreasing trade with strong opponents'. 'There is no use flattering ourselves', concluded Chamberlain, 'we have got to smash the new Company'.[107]

The Birmingham Screw Co. began trading but was unfortunate in its timing. Within weeks of its formation, the Franco-Prussian War broke out, greatly increasing Chamberlain's foreign sales and cutting off the Birmingham Screw Co. from its interim supplier. In 1871–72, while the St. George's Works were still under construction, Nettlefold

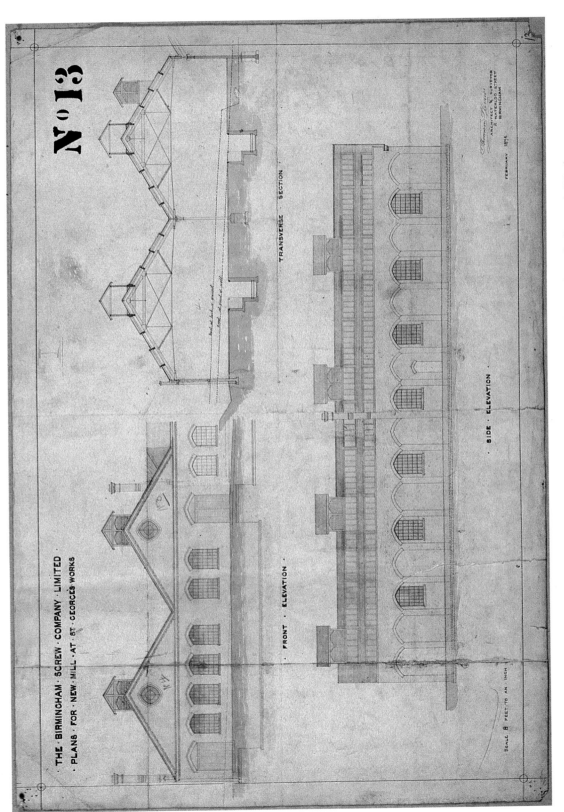

10 Plans (February 1874) produced by Thomson Plevins (1825–97) for the Birmingham Screw Co.'s St George's Works. Designed as a competitor to Nettlefold & Chamberlain, the mills reveal considerable similarities in their structure and execution. (*European Industrial Services*)

& Chamberlain pushed up their prices by as much as 50 per cent by reducing the level of discounts offered to wholesalers. Profits were higher than even Chamberlain had predicted for apart from the beneficial effects of the Continental war, there was an economic boom at home. Yet it was at this stage that Chamberlain decided to leave the business and devote himself wholly to a political career. In 1873 as Mayor of Birmingham and a prospective Parliamentary candidate for Sheffield, he handed the records of his commercial transactions and a précis of his accounting methods to J.H. Nettlefold. With the death of his father, the failure to win the Sheffield seat and his decision to devote more time to his role as Mayor of Birmingham, Chamberlain and his two brothers, Walter and Herbert, sold their half of the partnership to the Nettlefolds in 1874 for a reputed £600,000.[108] After family settlements, Joseph was probably left with £120,000 (which gave him the wealth he required for a full-time political career), a sum not inordinately vast by Victorian standards, but enough to make him very wealthy indeed. Chamberlain was re-elected mayor in 1874 and 1875, his tenure of office being ended only in June 1876 when he became a Birmingham MP. At his death on 2 July 1914 he left £125,495, not much more than he had obtained from the sale of his share of the business.[109] A third brother, Arthur Chamberlain (1842–1913), had joined Nettlefold & Chamberlain shortly after the firm's foundation but departed to join Smith & Chamberlain, brass founders and lamp makers, and established the partnership of Chamberlain & Hookham, manufacturers of electrical fittings.[110]

To commemorate their departure from the business, the Chamberlains organised an enormous works outing. Almost 1,000 employees and their wives were taken by special trains to London to visit the Crystal Palace which had been re-erected on a larger scale at Sydenham.[111] Tea and a three-course dinner were provided, an act of generosity long remembered.[112] Walter Chamberlain was the chief engineer at Heath Street, but also devoted much of his time to overseeing the King's Norton Works where he often harangued the employees, a habit that won him 'an epitaph which would not look well on paper' but which was not recorded.[113]

The Birmingham Screw Co. Ltd. competed with Nettlefold & Chamberlain for nearly ten years and their catalogue revealed that they made a similar, if slightly less varied, range of products – mainly pointed screws in wrought iron, brass and copper in many sizes with different shaped heads.[114] They also produced rivets, nuts, bolts, washers, split linch and cotter pins, hooks and eyes, together with specialist fasteners.

Although the Birmingham Screw Co. was not finally acquired by Nettlefolds until 1880 (when the latter also became a limited liability company, p. 200), the damage had been done by Chamberlain's unyielding strategy, and they never represented a serious threat during the late 1870s. The adoption of mass-production techniques and the introduction of a system of discounts to wholesalers (the crucial elements in the business success of Nettlefold & Chamberlain) drove numbers of small screw makers to the wall. The failure of these was subsequently used by Chamberlain's political opponents in the 1880s as ammunition when he was appointed President of the Board of Trade by Gladstone. Nevertheless, accusations of unfair competition and sharp practice seem by some accounts to have been unfounded. One clergyman at first accused Chamberlain of obtaining his fortune by 'a monopoly secured by the most questionable dodges' but almost immediately afterwards withdrew these charges adding that the worst that could be said of his firm's dealing was that other businesses had suffered from its success.[115] He was possibly the Revd. R.M. Grier, vicar of Rugeley, who wrote to the *Daily News* on 15 November 1884 and observed,[116]

> Up to a recent period I believed the story so industriously circulated about the way Mr. Chamberlain realised his wealth, and when a friend of his challenged the truth of it I had no doubt that it could easily be verified. I was quickly, and I need hardly say agreeably, undeceived. Having made careful inquiries both of his friends and opponents in Birmingham, I could find no foundation whatever for the attacks which had been made upon him as a man of business. I had been given to understand that copies of a threatening circular to the small screw manufacturers, whom he is supposed to have deliberately ruined, were extant and could be produced. I could not discover one.

It is tempting to ask why a vicar from Rugely should concern himself with these questions, and what sources of information would have been available to him to check the veracity of the statements? Yet, ten days later, A. Stokes & Co., screw and rivet manufacturers of Green Street, Birmingham, wrote to the *Daily News* to support Joseph Chamberlain, and quoted from their own experience of being approached by his firm with a view to an amalgamation:[117]

> our firm having been established in the trade for nearly half a century has had every opportunity of knowing the details of all those transactions and their results, and we unhesitatingly affirm that Mr. Chamberlain's actions were highly beneficial to those connected with the trade, and beneficent to those whose businesses were purchased on such liberal terms; also to those who, like ourselves, remained in trade as well as his own firm.

The evidence of these two published letters must be treated with caution as they may have been written by those who for other reasons were sympathetic to Chamberlain. For balance, it would be interesting to have heard the testimony of the small firms which failed to match the low prices offered by Nettlefold & Chamberlain and had collapsed or been taken over as a result.

After the Chamberlains withdrew from the firm in 1874, managerial responsibilities had to be re-arranged. Edward Nettlefold had become chairman both of Nettlefold & Chamberlain and J.S. Nettlefold & Sons when his father had died in 1866. The vacuum created by Joseph Chamberlain's departure allowed J.H. Nettlefold to take additional responsibilities at Heath Street.[118] He had originally been employed in the Holborn office, but moved to Smethwick to help plan the extensions there and serve, in effect, as works manager. A mathematician of considerable ability, J.H. Nettlefold was elected a member of the Institution of Mechanical Engineers in 1860.[119] When Edward Nettlefold died in 1878, J.H. Nettlefold became the new chairman of Nettlefolds and was the prime mover in the promotion of the firm as a limited liability company (p. 199).

SUMMARY

Thus it was in a period of twenty-six years that a small screw-manufacturing business in Broad Street, Birmingham, could be transformed into a major, integrated concern with world-wide customers and a virtual monopoly of the British market. While other screw makers continued to prosper at home, they were not of a scale to challenge Nettlefolds, and would eventually retire from the trade or be taken over. Having seen the introduction of mass-production methods, the construction and development of a substantial manufacturing site at Smethwick (with a smaller, specialist factory at King's Norton, and rolling mills at Hadley Castle), Joseph Chamberlain and his brothers resigned from the partnership. It continued under the management of Joseph Nettlefold, whose relatives joined the firm. By 1880 when the take-over of their biggest and closest rival, the Birmingham Screw Co. Ltd., was imminent, it became clear that further expansion could only be financed by the promotion of a limited liability company. That decision initiated a further round of acquisitions and enabled them to grow almost unhindered into the twentieth century.

References

1. Lady Charlotte Guest, 'Journal', Vol. IX, February 1851 – September 1853, 1 May 1851, pp. 47–48.
2. GRO, D/DG, Section C, Box 8, Miscellaneous, Letter to Lady Charlotte Guest from the Crystal Palace Co., 26 August 1854.
3. Robert Hunt, *Hunt's Hand-Book to the Official Catalogues . . . of the Great Exhibition*, Vol. I, London (1851), pp. 28, 47 and plan.

4. Quoted from C.H. Gibbs-Smith, *The Great Exhibition of 1851*, London HMSO (1981), p. 9.

5. *Hunt's Hand-Book*, pp. 527–28.

6. Raymond McGrath and A.C. Frost, *Glass in Architecture and Decoration*, London (1961), p. 45.

7. Patent No. 4117, 13 May 1817, for 'Certain Improvements in the Method or Methods of making screws of Iron, Brass, Steel or other Metals for the use in all kinds of Wood Work'; *The Ironmonger*, 10 February 1923, p. 96.

8. C. Anthony Crofton, *The Nettlefolds, A Genealogical Account of the Family of Nettlefold* (1962), pp. 27–28.

9. *New List of Prices of Patent Screws sold only by J.S. Nettlefold, No. 8 Red Lion Street, Holborn*, with handwritten note: 'This list printed April 1826. I am now selling for ready money at the Counter by this List.'

10. *The Hardware Trade Journal*, 25 May 1934, p. 304.

11. Typewritten list of early Customers.

12. Elsa Steer, *Threads from the Family Tapestry* (privately printed, 1957), p. 33.

13. *Hunt's Hand-Book*, Vol. 1, pp. 94–95.

14. Ibid., Vol. II, p. 772.

15. Guest, 'Journal', Vol. VI, November 1837 – March 1841, 30 August 1839, p. 270; Bessborough, *Lady Charlotte Guest*, pp. 94–95.

16. H.W. Dickinson, *Transactions of the Newcomen Society*, Vol. XXII (1941–42), 'Origin and Manufacture of Woodscrews', p. 85; 'A Short History of the Woodscrew' (typescript); *The Woodworkers Journal*, No. 2, February 1953, 'A Short History of the Woodscrew', p. 73.

17. Dickinson, *Transactions of the Newcomen Society*, p. 86.

18. United States Patent Office, Thomas J. Sloane of New York, Improvement in Machinery for cutting the threads of Pointed Screws, Patent No. 4864, 24 November 1846, Reissue No. 110, 8 March 1848; Ibid., Improvement in Wood-Screws, Patent No. 4704, 20 August 1846, Reissue No. 107, 22 February 1848; Ibid., Machine for Arranging and Feeding Screw-Blanks, Patent No. 7958, 25 February 1851, Reissue No. 234, 29 March 1853.

19. *DBB*, Vol. 1, London (1984), Peter T. Marsh, 'Joseph Chamberlain', pp. 643–44; Denis Judd, *Radical Joe, A Life of Joseph Chamberlain*, London (1977), pp. 14, 17.

20. 'How Mr. Chamberlain made his Fortune, The Romance of the Pointed Screw' (typescript n.d.), p. 1.

21. Ordnance Survey 6 ins to 1 mile, Staffordshire Sheet, LXXII (1890).

22. 'Recollections of the Screw Department' (typescript, compiled 1927), Mr. E. Castle, p. 1.

23. Jones, *Industrial Architecture*, p. 101.

24. Messrs. Nettlefold & Chamberlain, E.6., Transverse Section of a Mill, Transverse Section through Arch and Band Holes, signed Thomas Chatfeild Clarke, Architect, 137 Leadenhall Street.

25. *The Builder*, Vol. LXIX, No. 2735, 6 July 1895, Obituary T.C. Clarke, p. 15.

26. Nettlefold & Chamberlain, Transverse Section No. 5 Bay (1863).

27. *The Architect's, Engineer's and Building-Trade's Directory*, London (1868), p. 105.

28. Birmingham University Library (BUL), JC 1/17/1, Press Cuttings.

29. Nettlefolds Ltd., Directors Minute Book, No. 1 (1880–86), 20 April 1880, p. 7; 2 May 1882, p. 154.

30. *Price List and Drawings of the Articles manufactured by Nettlefold & Chamberlain*, Birmingham (1870), inside cover.

31. 'Recollections', Mr. A. Weare, p. 9; *VCHS*, Vol. XVII, Oxford (1976), p. 113.
32. Ibid., Mr. John Dinnis, p. 21.
33. Ibid., Mr. Joseph Tetley, p. 12.
34. Ibid., Mr. John Dinnis, p. 21.
35. Ibid., Mr. Hughes, p. 19; *VCHS*, Vol. XVII, op. cit., p. 113.
36. G. Phillips Bevan (Editor), *British Manufacturing Industries, Guns, Nails, Locks, Woodscrews, Railway Bolts and Spikes*, London (1878), W.C. Aitken, 'Wood Screws', p. 60.
37. *Birmingham Daily Post*, 4 July 1914.
38. Aitken, 'Wood Screws', p. 63.
39. *PIME*, Vol. 27, July 1876, pp. 327–28.
40. 'Recollections', Mr. Thomas Burns, p. 5.
41. *PIME*, Vol. 27, p. 328.
42. 'Recollections', Mr. E. Castle, p. 3; Mr. A. Weare, p. 10.
43. *GKN, Nettlefolds Price List and Drawings*, 17th Edition (1917).
44. *English Mechanic and Mirror of Science*, 1 January 1869, Advertisement, p. vii.
45. *Price List and Drawings* (1870) and (1871).
46. *DBB*, Vol. 1, p. 644.
47. *An Outline History of Guest, Keen & Nettlefolds* (c. 1925), p. 29.
48. 'Recollections', Mr. E. Phillips, p. 25.
49. Ibid., Mr. R. Earp, p. 28.
50. Printed letter from Nettlefold & Chamberlain announcing the acquisition, 1 July 1865.
51. Ibid.
52. *The Engineer*, Vol. XX, 14 July 1865, p. 16.
53. 'Recollections', Mr. E. Castle, p. 3; Mr. J. Dinnis, p. 21.
54. 'Book of sample labels', pp. 35–38.
55. 'Recollections', Mr. Phillips, p. 26.
56. Ibid., Mr. Earp, p. 30.
57. Plan of the freehold Property situate in the Parish of King's Norton . . . belonging to Nettlefolds Ltd., (1883).
58. 'Recollections', Mr. Earp, p. 29.
59. *The Engineer*, Vol. LIV, 4 August 1882, Obituary, p. 89; *MPICE*, Vol. LXXIII (1883), Memoir, pp. 367–68.
60. Various plans and elevations signed by Robert C. May, 3 Great Queen Street, Westminster, February–March 1864.
61. Various plans for the rolling shop and furnaces, signed by S.H.F. Cox, agent and contractor of Sheffield, 1865–66.
62. Patent File Co., Contract No. 3, Drawing No. 15, details of the Front Elevation, 15 March 1864.
63. General Plan of the heating furnaces, rolling shops, signed S.H.F. Cox, 26 March 1866.
64. BUL, Neville Chamberlain Papers 1/6/12; Letter J. Chamberlain to J.H. Nettlefold, 21 March 1870.
65. Ibid., 1/6/3/11, 20 May 1870.
66. *Outline History*, p. 27.
67. *Nettlefolds Ltd. Iron and Wire Department Price List*, (1884).
68. Birmingham University Library, Chamberlain Papers, JC 1/18/2, Joseph Chamberlain's Business Notebook 1866–74, 31 May 1870.
69. Ibid., 30 June 1870, p. 27.
70. *DBB*, Vol. 1, pp. 644–45.

71. 'Recollections', Mr. A. Weare, p. 9; Mr. J. Dinnis, p. 22.
72. *DBB*, Vol. 1, p. 645.
73. 'Recollections', Mr. Weare, p. 9.
74. 'How Mr. Chamberlain made his Fortune', p. 7.
75. *The City Press*, 15 March 1913.
76. BUL, JC 1/18, 2 Notebook, *passim*.
77. *Prix-Courant et Album des Manufactures de Nettlefold & Chamberlain*, (1878).
78. 'Recollections', Mr. Weare, p. 10.
79. *Lista de Precos e Desenhos de Artigos fabricados por Nettlefolds*, (1871).
80. BRL, Obituary Notices Birmingham and London, 1864–1904, collected by G.H. Osborne, *Birmingham Gazette*, 24 November 1881, J.H. Nettlefold, p. 192.
81. BUL, JC 1/18, Notebook, 9 September 1869.
82. *DBB*, Vol. 1, p. 645.
83. 'Recollections', Mr. Weare, p. 10.
84. Ibid., Mr. Joseph Tetley, p. 16.
85. Ibid., Mr. E.H. Jackson, p. 7.
86. BUL, J.C.L. Add. 3042, Add. 143, Note on Taxes, 18 August 1870.
87. Ibid.
88. *DBB*, Vol. IV, London (1985), David J. Jeremy, 'Sir Josiah Mason', pp. 179–82.
89. Ibid., Vol. 1, p. 646.
90. *The Builder*, Vol. LXXIII, No. 2,858, 13 November 1897, p. 403; *The Architect's, Engineer's and Building-Trade's Directory*, London (1868), p. 131.
91. Birmingham Screw Co. Ltd., Drawing No. 31, Cross section and Transverse sections through Mill; Ibid., Transverse Section and Ground Plan, October 1870, Thomson Plevins.
92. BUL, Papers of Neville Chamberlain, 1/6/3/11 Letter Joseph Chamberlain to J.H. Nettlefold, 20 May 1890.
93. Ibid., 1/6/3/1, 7 May 1870.
94. Ibid.
95. Ibid.
96. Ibid., 1/6/3/1–11.
97. Ibid., 1/6/3/3, 10 May 1870.
98. Ibid.
99. Ibid., 1/6/3/11, 20 May 1870.
100. Ibid., 1/6/3/13, 23 May 1870.
101. Ibid., 1/6/3/14, 24 May 1870.
102. Ibid., 1/6/3/10, 19 May 1870.
103. Ibid., 1/6/3/13, 23 May 1870.
104. Arnold Bennett, *The Card*, London (1911), Harmondsworth (1975).
105. BUL, 1/6/3/18, (n.d.).
106. Ibid.
107. Ibid.
108. Judd, *Radical Joe*, p. 52.
109. *DBB*, Vol. 1, p. 648.
110. Ibid., Barbara D.M. Smith, 'Arthur Chamberlain', pp. 633–4.
111. 'Recollections', Mr. Weare, p. 11; Mr. E. Phillips, p. 26.
112. Ibid., Mr. Earp, p. 30.
113. Ibid.
114. Birmingham Screw Co. Ltd., *Illustrated Catalogue and Price List* (1876).

115. 'How Mr. Chamberlain made his Fortune' (typescript), p. 5.
116. Louis Creswicke, *The Life of Joseph Chamberlain*, Vol. 1, London (1904), p. 29.
117. N. Murrell Marris, *Joseph Chamberlain: the Man and the Statesman*, London (1900), p. 43.
118. *DBB*, Vol. IV, London (1985), Edgar Jones, 'Joseph Henry Nettlefold', pp. 428–31.
119. *PIME*, Vol. 33 (1882), Memoir, pp. 9–10.

6 *Arthur Keen and the Patent Nut & Bolt Co. 1856–1900*

Arthur Keen (1835–1915) was, in a sense, the creator of Guest, Keen & Nettlefolds. The architect of the mergers which brought together its three principal parts in 1900–02, he was the first chairman of GKN and served in that office until his death on 8 February 1915.[1] Neither an inventive engineer (he had no professional qualifications) nor an expert on steel-making (he had not studied metallurgy or any other science at a technical institute or university), Keen was in essence an authoritarian businessman, an indefatigable worker with an obsessional passion for growth, whether internally generated or by acquisition. He possessed a shrewd eye for a take-over and through an extensive network of contacts in industry, finance and various trade and professional associations was able to build a mighty empire from modest beginnings. Occupying an intermediate stage between the entrepreneur who owned his own business and the professionally-trained manager who pursued his career by promotion through various companies, he was the founder of the Patent Nut & Bolt Co. and its chief executive without possessing ultimate financial control. In the mould of Joseph Chamberlain or J.H. Nettlefold, Arthur Keen exhibited qualities of drive and vision but was not without a trace of ruthlessness.

THE FOUNDATIONS: WATKINS & KEEN AND WESTON & GRICE

The foundation of the Patent Nut & Bolt Co. and, in effect, the 'Keen' element of Guest, Keen & Nettlefolds may be traced back to 1856. It was most likely to have been in that year that Arthur Keen formed a partnership with Francis Watkins to set up as makers of fasteners.[2] The introductions had been effected by Thomas Astbury, a wealthy iron-founder and cannon manufacturer,[3] whose daughter Hannah, Keen was to marry in Smethwick Chapel (Church of England) on 2 September 1858.[4] His marriage, as a report in the *Birmingham Gazette & Express* subsequently related,[5]

44 Arthur Keen (back row left) and his son and successor Arthur T. Keen, standing, presumably, on the steps of the former's Birmingham house 'Sandyford'. Front row (left to right): Arthur, Mrs. A.T. Keen (nee Willan), M.H. Keen, Mrs. A. Keen (nee Astbury) and Dora. (*Mrs. M.H. Dent*)

improved his worldly prospects very notably. It is said of him that a scene in a play where a shrewd Scotsman made successful love to his master's daughter gave him the line upon which he was soon to act with such excellent results.

Until embarking on a career in business, Keen had led an inauspicious life. Born on 23 January 1835, the son of Thomas Keen (d. 1867), a yeoman farmer and innkeeper in Cheshire, he had apparently received only a limited education before joining the London & North Western Railway at Crewe, probably as a clerk. Promotion at the age of twenty-two brought him the post of goods agent at Smethwick where he became acquainted with the leading manufacturers in the district.[6] Having decided to resign from the security of employment with a railway company for the precarious world of business, Keen joined forces with Francis Watkins. In about 1856 the latter had crossed to Britain to try to sell the British rights of a patent nut-making machine, but being unable to find a purchaser and having insufficient capital himself, concluded an arrangement whereby Thomas Astbury would fund his future son-in-law in a partnership. Apparently it was Astbury with his knowledge of industry, rather than Keen, who appreciated the value of the invention and perceived its commercial potential. Watkins & Keen, as the new firm was styled, took premises at Victoria Works, Rolfe Street, Smethwick, and thereby became neighbours of Thomas Astbury & Sons. Such was the efficiency of the American machinery they installed and the ability to undercut competitors that within two years a policy of expansion had resulted in the workforce rising to 500[7] and by 1880 was over 1,000.[8] As in the case of Nettlefold & Chamberlain, it was a patent purchased from the United States which had provided them with the initial technological lead over their competitors.

Owing to the financial failure in October 1856 of Fox, Henderson & Co., structural and railway engineers, the London Works, Cranford Street, Smethwick, became vacant.[9] Thomas Astbury & Sons occupied part of the London Works in 1858, and Watkins & Keen followed them there around 1860, and six years later took over the entire premises when they moved into that section formerly used by Astburys. From this base, Arthur Keen built his manufacturing group and, in time, the small two-storey offices there became the headquarters of GKN.[10]

In April 1864 Watkins & Keen was floated as a limited liability company with a capital of £200,000 divided into 10,000 shares of £20 each. The conversion was arranged by David Chadwick (1821–95), a Lancashire accountant who specialised in company promotions, this

45 A general view of London Works, originally owned by Fox, Henderson & Co. and subsequently the principal factory of the Patent Nut & Bolt Co. The two-storey building in the left middle-distance appears to have been the stables. The pig iron stacked in the foreground was for castings or puddling.

being his first venture outside the Manchester and Sheffield regions.[11] The Patent Nut and Bolt Co. was duly registered under the Companies Act of 1862 on 3 June 1864 and Arthur Keen and Francis Watkins were appointed as joint managing directors.[12] Samuel Thornton, formerly Mayor of Birmingham (1848–49) became the chairman, and Alderman Henry Davis Pochin (1824–95), a merchant of Broughton Old Hall, Manchester and subsequently Mayor of Salford, was his deputy.[13] The first auditors were David Chadwick himself[14] in conjunction with Edward Carter, a Birmingham accountant.[15]

Shortly after the flotation of the company, Arthur Keen entered into negotiations for the acquisition of Weston & Grice, owners of the Stour Valley Works, Grice Street, West Bromwich[16] – a bolt and nut factory with its own rolling mills for railway fasteners, fish and fang bolts and spikes – and of the Cwm-Bran Iron Co., near Newport. The partnership of Weston & Grice had been founded in 1853 when [Sir] Joseph Dodge Weston (1822–95)[17] and James Grice (d. 1889) set up the Midlands bolt works and subsequently acquired the adjacent rod mill from Messrs. Gregory & Pearson.[18] Weston, the son of a Bristol merchant, had joined his father's firm, which presumably also owned the Cwmbran ironworks, foundry and coal mines, and subsequently married one of Keen's daughters. Having a blast furnace, puddling furnaces and rolling mills, it could make bar iron as well as castings. To provide a captive outlet for these products, Weston, together with Grice, may have decided to open the Stour Valley works in West Bromwich, situated near the centre of the fastener trade.

In September 1864, Arthur Keen reported that terms were being discussed for the acquisition of Weston & Grice.[19] In November, the Stour Valley Works and the Cwmbran Foundry were valued at £50,169 (of which machinery and fixtures accounted for £17,026, and materials and work in progress £23,882).[20] At an extraordinary general meeting of the PNB in January 1865, it was agreed to raise £200,000 by issuing a further 10,000 shares (this also being arranged by David Chadwick), 2,500 of these to be allotted to Weston & Grice and the remainder offered for sale.[21] An analysis of the shareholders in May 1865, after the Patent Nut & Bolt Co. (PNB) had merged with Weston & Grice (Table 7.1, p. 201) reveled that the greatest number came from the West Midlands (66.92 per cent) and then from the North West (22.46 per cent), of which 20.94 per cent came from Manchester, the hub of Chadwick's financial network.[22] Analysed by occupation, manufacturers made the largest investment (44.43 per cent of the total shareholding), merchants contributed 13.01 per cent, commercial organisations 9.65 per cent and unoccupied males (gentlemen) 24.45 per cent.[23]

Under the terms of the acquisition, new buildings were to be erected at Cwmbran and installed with the latest nut and bolt-making machines from London Works. They estimated that[24]

46 An aerial view of both London Works in the foreground and the Heath Street Works (c. 1950s).

within four months the buildings and machinery will be in complete operation and capable of turning out from 25 to 30 tons of nuts, bolts and spikes per day; at a profit over the London and Stour Valley Works of at least £1 per ton. This advantage arises from the difference in the price of iron, coal and carriage.

It was soon confirmed that they planned to spend £4,000 on buildings and £6,000 on machinery at Cwmbran and that a target of £12–£15,000 in profits had been calculated for the works once in operation.[25] As a result of the union, J.D. Weston was appointed a director of the PNB (and in 1876 was elected the non-executive chairman)[26] and Edwin J. Grice, who managed the Stour Valley Works, became a joint managing director along with Keen and Watkins.[27]

'The fruitful principle of the division of labour is now driving the making of bolts and nuts out of the engineering workshop', reported *The Engineer* in 1865 after visiting the PNB's premises in Smethwick,[28]

and an inspection of these works affords a strong contrast to the time when the forging of a few bolts and nuts was a good day's work for a skilled smith . . . belonging to the same company and situated on the same line of railway, the London Works at Smethwick and the Stour Valley Works at West Bromwich are practically one. At each of these establishments upwards of 1,000 hands are employed.

The crucial innovation was the application of automatic machinery to take the place of laborious and often skilled techniques by hand. 'Remarkably ingenious and complete self-acting machinery', observed *The Engineer*,[29]

> is employed for these purposes also ['for stamping or rolling nuts, forging bolts and rivets, for tapping and screwing']. They are principally attended to by boys and girls, as but slight manual exertion is required. A number of skilled machinists are, however, employed to look after the tools, and to at once effect slight repairs.

Most of the machines employed at the Cwmbran Ironworks to produce nuts, bolts and spikes had been made at the company's London Works. Like Nettlefolds, therefore, once an initial patent had been obtained from the United States, further technical development, together with routine maintenance, took place within the business. Expertise was not generally bought in, and, in fact, the PNB actually sold machines on a royalty basis to other manufacturers on the Continent (p. 184).

The extent of the transition from skilled methods by hand to self-acting machinery was revealed in Émile Zola's description of a Parisian bolt and rivet factory. The great strength and expertise required to fashion a single rivet from a short length of bar iron was contrasted with the simple ease of producing a machine-made version:[30]

> when the bar was white hot he [Goujet] seized it with his tongs and with his hammer knocked it into regular lengths on the anvil tapping gently as though it were glass. Then he put the sections back into the fire, whence he took them out one by one to work them up. He was making hexagonal rivets. He put the pieces into a heading frame, flattened the top to make a head, tapped the six sides, then threw down the finished rivets, still red-hot, and they gradually darkened and faded on the floor. He did the operation with unbroken hammering, swinging a five-pound hammer in his right hand, finishing a detail with each tap, turning and working the iron so skilfully that he could go on talking and looking at people.

The immense human effort needed to forge a rivet by hand was highlighted when Goujet conducted his visitor into an adjoining building where his master had installed the latest steam-powered machinery:[31]

he raised his voice to shout explanations, then went on to the machines: mechanical shears which devoured bars of iron, taking off a length with each bite and passing them out behind one by one; bolt and rivet machines, lofty and complicated, making a bolt-head in one turn of their powerful screws; trimming machines with cast-iron flywheels and an iron ball that struck the air furiously with each piece the machine trimmed; the thread-cutters, worked by women, threading bolts and their nuts . . . Meanwhile Goujet had come to a halt in front of one of the rivet machines, and he stood dreaming with bowed head and attentive eyes. The machine was turning out forty-four milli-meter rivets with the unruffled ease of a giant . . . The stoker took a piece of iron out of the furnace, the striker placed it in the frame which was continually watered so as to keep the steel tempered, and when the job was done and the bolt fell out with its head as round as if it had come out of a mould. In twelve hours this blasted plant would turn out hundreds of kilograms of them.

In this way the traditional method in which every nut and bolt was a 'sort of speciality in itself' (to such an extent that each bolt with its corresponding nut had to be marked as belonging to one another)[32] was replaced by uniformity and precision.

The merger of the two nut and bolt-making factories, in such close proximity, appears to have been followed by a degree of rationalisa-tion, as in 1873 Samuel Griffiths could report that the London Works concentrated upon 'all kinds of engineer's black and bright bolts and nuts, coach screws, rivets and washers, also every description of bolts and nuts used by ship builders, agricultural implement makers, telegraph engineers, railway carriage and wagon builders',[33] while the Stour Valley Works 'are devoted exclusively to the manufacture of railway fastenings such as fish bolts, fang bolts, and spikes in their endless variety . . . the whole of these articles are made from iron rolled and puddled on the premises. The works also contain a foundry for casting railway chairs'.[34] A fall in gross receipts by about £20,000 for 1866 was attributed to the need to modernise the plant, as[35]

much of the machinery purchased by the company from Messrs. Watkins & Keen and Messrs. Weston and Grice was not in efficient working order, many of the parts required renewal and altering to modern improvements. We therefore in accordance with our Report and recommendations of 9 January 1866 took advantage of the slack time to improve and perfect the whole of the machinery at each works and the improvements made although they have increased your capital account have effected a savings of at least 10% in comparison with our former working.

GROWTH AND ACQUISITION TO 1900

Profits for the Patent Nut & Bolt Co., after some disposals, for the year ending 31 December 1866 were £19,505[36] and the auditors recommended that £5,000 be set aside for depreciation.[37] In 1869 they rose to £26,632,[38] but curiously in a year of buoyant trade they fell to £22,551 in 1870.[39] Unfortunately the minute books of the company do not record overall profit figures after 1870 and it has proved impossible to construct a series from other sources.

Table 6.1 PNB Co. individual factory profits 1868–71 (£)

Years	London Works	Stour Valley	Cwmbran	Midland Works	Total
1868	10046	18888	13157	—	42081
1869	9065	13167	14050	178	36465
1870	8379	17231	11249	1421	38280
1871	14223	10454	1932	644	27253

These are gross figures and do not include deductions for depreciation or taxation.

Source: PNB Minute Book, No. 2, 29 February 1872, item 1647.

In the same way that Nettlefold & Chamberlain gained a virtual monopoly of the woodscrew market, Arthur Keen sought to dominate the nut, bolt and rivet trade in the Birmingham area through a policy of price-cutting and selected take-overs; his aim, according to the *Birmingham Gazette & Express*, 'has consistently been to absorb or exclude, and it was so managed that in exclusion his competitors were absolutely disarmed'.[40] During 1869 the PNB purchased the business and moveable plant of T.F. Griffiths, Son & Co.'s Midland Nut & Bolt Works, Soho.[41] They decided to continue operating the factory under the name of Griffiths but only as a temporary measure.[42] It was the smallest of the PNB's four main plants as Table 6.1 reveals. Poor profitability at the Midland Works led to its closure in June 1877 during a period of depression[43] and the transfer of its machinery to the London Works. The next acquisition undertaken by the PNB appears to have been the Birmingham Bolt & Nut Co. which had fallen into financial difficulties and was purchased from the liquidators in May 1880 for £2,000.[44]

In January 1882, Arthur Keen argued that it was necessary to spend £10,000 on buildings and plant at the London Works 'with a view to further reducing the cost of production and for the more economic working generally of the increased business at these works'.[45] Keen also bought from Charles Carr the machinery and tools of the Trent

Works, Smethwick, for £800 and arranged to take the factory for two years at a rental of £50 per annum.[46] Whilst the need for space to expand the business presumably had governed this action, the purchase of the Workington Rivet & Bolt Co. in February 1887 for £4,769 had a different rationale. Keen stated that this takeover was designed to facilitate 'the general conduct of the company's business [that is, gain economies of scale and reduce competition] rather than in expectation of profit from operations of the Workington Company itself'.[47] Despite these acquisitions and the growth that occurred at the London and Stour Valley factories, the PNB did not dominate the nut and bolt trade in the way that Nettlefold & Chamberlain exercised almost complete control over the domestic woodscrew industry. Major competitors flourished elsewhere in the Midlands – such as F.W. Cotterill Ltd. (founded *c.* 1810) and John Garrington & Sons Ltd. (1830) both in Darlaston, and Bayliss, Jones & Bayliss (established in 1825) of Wolverhampton.

The competitive situation that existed was doubtless a reflection of the nature of the nut and bolt market. By comparison, the manufacturers of woodscrews sold simply to wholesalers who, in turn, supplied builders, the furniture trade and the public, while consumers of nuts, bolts, rivets and spikes were businesses of a wide variety from shipbuilders, railway companies to engineering concerns of every kind.[48] Like the Dowlais Iron Co., the PNB seems to have specialised in selling to railway companies whose appetite for bolts, nuts, spikes and couplings was seemingly limitless. As Aitken observed in 1878,[49]

> large as are the requirements of the English railways, those of foreign and colonial railways are still larger, and have, for the most part, been supplied by English houses . . . One firm alone, *viz.* the Patent Nut and Bolt Company, which has branches at the Stour Valley Works, near Birmingham and Cwmbran Works, South Wales, can produce 100 tons per day and at the rate of 30,000 tons per annum.

In the warehouse of the London Works, *The Engineer* recorded in 1865 that there had been stored '300 tons of finished hexagon and square nuts, varying in size from $\frac{1}{4}$ in to 3 in in diameter', while 'at the Stour Valley Works not less than 1,250 tons of finished work, principally consisting of railway fastenings, have been turned out in one month'.[50] The reporter was particularly impressed by a fang nut 'used with the bridge rail and more recently in the double-headed rail and chair on the London, Chatham & Dover Railway – principally made at the Stour Valley Works where there are eleven puddling furnaces converting pig iron into wrought iron'[51] and two mills, and at the London Works twelve puddling furnaces and two mills. The Stour Valley Works manufactured galvanised screws for use with wire fencing, which were sold amongst others to the East Indian Railway,[52] while in 1887 that company also placed a major order for cast iron sleepers – these being made at Cwmbran (p. 176).[53]

THE CWMBRAN WORKS AND COLLIERIES

One of the principal elements in the union between Weston & Grice and Watkins & Keen was the ironworks at Cwmbran. In 1871, shortly after the acquisition, it comprised twenty puddling furnaces, ten balling furnaces, a foundry and bolt and nut mills, employing in total 800 men.[54] However, the merger of 1864 did not include the entire Cwmbran site, for J.D. Weston retained his ownership of the Cwm-Bran Iron Co., which comprised two blast furnaces and employed 250, and the Cwm-Bran Colliery which had 700 miners.[55] As these three elements had once formed a single integrated enterprise, it made little sense to divorce the iron-making activities from the refining and manufacturing processes. It may have been reasons of cost which delayed the incorporation of such capital-intensive activities by the PNB. In December 1865, the collieries and blast furnaces were valued with a view to their purchase,[56] but it was not until September 1872 that the first instalment, £10,000, was paid together with £14,500 in bills on account of the balance,[57] which further suggested that considerations of expense had slowed up the take-over.

47 A general view of the nut and bolt works at Cwmbran from the south. Clomendy Road is in the foreground. The three buildings closest to the camera were warehouses, and those behind shops for the production of fasteners. (*National Museum of Wales*)

48 A modern portrayal of puddling. (*National Museum of Wales*)

Figure 8 The Ironworks and Nut and Bolt Plant at Cwmbran, c. 1910

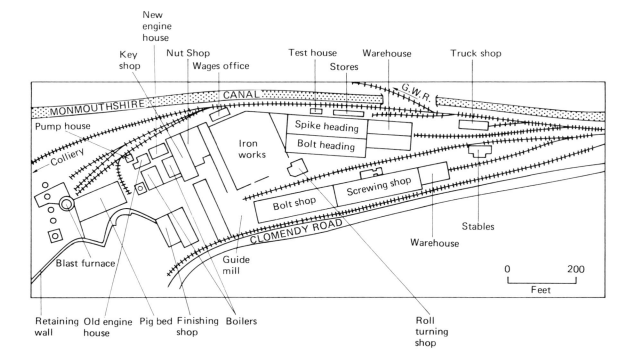

The Cwmbran Works became a principal supplier of bar iron for the nut and bolt works in Smethwick. The acquisition of Cwmbran in 1864 had been accompanied by a decision to lay down a nut and bolt mill there (p. 168) to reduce the cost of transporting basic materials. In addition, it appears that rolling mills were constructed between the original site and the colliery further to the east during the period 1885–95.[58] The whole works, including collieries, employed around 2,000 men in the 1890s.

Initially they seem to have been prepared to tackle a variety of orders. In September 1867, for example, Francis Watkins reported that 'he had been in treaty with Mr. Wassenburger of Vienna for the supply of a large quantity of gun breech forgings amounting to from £12,000 to £20,000 for a government contract'.[59] Yet the installation of self-acting machinery to make nuts and bolts and the company's sustained growth as a supplier of railway fasteners and permanent way fixtures encouraged a degree of specialisation to increase efficiencies and output. Table 6.2 shows how their product range had become focussed by the end of the nineteenth century.

Table 6.2   Principal products from the Cwmbran works 1896–98 (tons)

(1) *Foundry Department*	1896	1897	1898
Cast iron sleepers	23320	20072	18710
Cast iron chairs	7614	16483	8249
Cast iron jaws	660	19	263
Cast iron clips	361	389	279
(2) *Iron Works Department*			
Wrought iron tie bars	3828	2586	4234
Wrought iron cotters	256	124	198
Wrought iron fishplates	481	289	229
Wrought iron bearing plates	1147	947	1379
Wrought iron keys	238	220	294
Steel fishplates	1531	808	212
Steel keys	521	925	793
(3) *Bolt Works Department*			
Wrought iron fang bolts and nuts	3255	2614	2256
Wrought iron fish bolts and nuts	397	409	444
Wrought iron dog head spikes	4165	2975	2148
Steel fish nuts and bolts	434	401	441

Source: GwRO, D.503, Output figures Cwmbran Works 1896–98.

The principal weakness of the Cwmbran works was its iron-making capacity (and this ultimately encouraged the merger with the Dowlais Iron Co., p. 189). The two blast furnaces inherited from the Cwm-Bran Iron Co. were not modern. In 1887 in order that they could meet a contract to supply the East Indian Railway with cast iron sleepers, the

49 A general view from the north at Cwmbran: (left to right) new blast engine house, old blast engine house, pig bed, blast furnace, and hydraulic lift. The Monmouthshire Canal passes close beside the ironworks. (*National Museum of Wales*)

PNB had to purchase 5,000 tons of pig iron (36s. 9d. per ton) from Bolckow, Vaughan Co. Ltd.[60] – of whom Arthur Keen later became a director. In 1890 it was acknowledged that the antiquated bee hive coke ovens and the Shepherd washery could not produce coke of sufficient quality or quantity for the bar iron demands of the fastener mills. Accordingly forty Coppée coke ovens with an improved washery and four boilers (using waste gases for heat) were erected.[61] In the same year, a new blast furnace was also constructed. Nonetheless, by the end of the nineteenth century when a number of integrated, large-scale steelworks had been laid down, single furnaces were at a serious disadvantage. In March 1894 the Cwmbran furnace was blown out because pig iron could be purchased more cheaply from Bolckow, Vaughan & Co. in Middlesbrough than by their own means.[62] In October 1894 Mr. Frederick Rafarel, the general manager at Cwmbran, restated the argument that it would be pointless to blow the furnace in 'as there were no suitable orders in the iron works and the foundry to use up the pigs which would be produced'.[63] Finally, against the advice of Rafarel, in April 1895 Arthur Keen decided to blow in the furnace, possibly because he did not wish to be totally reliant upon outside suppliers for such a basic material.[64] The furnace remained in operation until the merger with the Dowlais Iron Co.

The Cwmbran Works were situated to the north of the town beside the Monmouthshire Canal (from which they obtained water)[65] which was used for transporting iron and coal to and from Newport. In addition, a spur was laid from the nearby GWR Monmouth Valleys line to a network of tracks and sidings linking the colliery with the various parts of the works.[66] Although somewhat isolated from the

50 The stock yard showing a larger number of 'pot sleepers'. (*National Museum of Wales*)

major industrial sites of South Wales (which increasingly congregated along the coast), the Cwmbran Works was well served by both railway and canal.

The Cwmbran collieries were acquired by 1872 by the PNB, not simply as a source of fuel for the ironworks and foundry there, as they were already selling coal to the domestic market. In September 1872, total output was 7,918 tons and the gross profit on sales amounted to £1,400.[67] The profit figure held steadily at just over £1,000 a month for the remainder of the year and during 1873.[68] These, however, were boom years for the Victorian economy, and from then until the late 1890s the trend for wholesale prices was downwards, the fall being particularly marked in the case of coal.[69] Prices tumbled from 32s. per ton (at London) in 1873 to 18s. in 1878, and except for two very unusual boom years, 1900 and 1901, it fluctuated between 16s. and 19s. until just before the Great War.[70] The Cwmbran collieries were pushed into deficit by these price fluctuations. In January 1878 a loss of £1,917 was incurred despite a reduction in wages, an increase in the number of working days and economies effected at the pits.[71] These measures seem to have been sufficient in the long term to pull the collieries back into profitability and in March 1886 the company concluded that it was desirable to increase sales of coal.[72] In June, after a tour of the principal cities of Italy, Grice reported that he had obtained a number of sample orders.[73] In August 1887 to facilitate the company's export business in coal, H.J. Tremellen was appointed as an agent with a salary of £250 per annum and a commission of 1d. per ton on sales above 200,000 tons and ½d. per ton over 225,000 tons.[74]

51 The salaried staff at the PNB's Cwmbran works and colliery. (*National Museum of Wales*)

Yet the policy of pushing coal production to win export orders resulted in diminishing marginal return: in July 1888, the PNB directors were disappointed to discover that 'whilst the quantity of coal got was 13,411 tons in excess of that for the corresponding period of 1887, the cost of working had been increased by 1d. per ton and the profit realised proportionately reduced'.[75] For the six months, January to June 1887, sales from the collieries amounted to £32,234 and yielded a profit of £3,800, the same period in 1888 producing sales of £33,429, but profits of £2,689.[76]

Again, in 1893, the Cwmbran collieries slipped into a loss, this despite an increase in output (p. 180). From January to April a deficit of £2,538 arose on sales of £21,598, which stood in contrast to a profit of £1,681 in the corresponding months of 1892 when sales amounted to £27,138.[77] This, it was argued,[78]

was principally brought about by working out the pillar coal which produced a large proportion of small, and that . . . the introduction of the Long Wall system into the Ebbw Vale Abercarn and Newport Abercarn properties, which would give a much greater proportion of large coal than could be obtained by the system in operation. He hoped also that it would be found possible to work the Hanbury property by Long Wall but at present the roof was too bad to admit of that being done.

The pillar and stall method involved considerable waste; much coal had to be abandoned in the pillars left to support the roof over the roadways and levels, whilst the coal that was worked from the pillars, owing to the pressure of the roof on them, contained, as at Cwmbran, a high percentage of small coal.[79] Matthew Truran, manager of the Dowlais collieries, giving evidence to the *Royal Commission on Coal* in 1871, argued from his experience that 'in many places in taking out pillars they lose more than 60 per cent of the pillars being crushed into small coal'.[80] As workings became deeper so the need to provide larger pillars resulted in greater losses. The longwall system was a response to these inefficiencies.[81] Under this method, a given length of face was hewn in a single line, all the coal being removed in one operation without any pillars being left. As the face advanced, the roadway was moved forward, the excavated area being tightly packed with small coal and waste, the pressure from the roof closing any gap.[82] It made ventilation simpler and more effective; the tortuous direction of an air current through the numerous stalls by a complex, and thus dangerous, arrangement of doorways could be replaced by a more direct method using the working face itself as an airway. Moreover, in the excavated area no cavities were left where gas could accumulate.

The longwall system also permitted economies in working. As the roof behind the collier was supported with tightly packed rubbish there was a saving in timber for propping, which the friable nature of roofs made a particularly high cost in South Wales. A greater proportion of large coal was obtained and even the pressure on the roof over the longwall helped to loosen the coal for the hewer. In 1868 Matthew Truran estimated that the loss of coal (either as small coal or that abandoned in the pillars) had been reduced from 15 to 40 per cent at Dowlais by the change to the longwall system.[83]

The success of the new method was acknowledged in July 1893 at Cwmbran. The cost of producing coal over the six months to 30 June fell from 7s. 0.8d. per ton in 1892 to 6s. 3.2d. in 1893 while output had been increased from 89,921 to 93,342 tons.[84] Rafarel, the general manager, observed that the proportion of small coal had been reduced from 41 per cent at the beginning of the year to 35 per cent and that 'under the longwall system of working which was now being introduced into this colliery he hoped that the proportion of small coal would still be further reduced'.[85] The percentage of small coal declined from 36.09 per cent in August 1893 to 34.83 per cent in December,[86] and by December 1894 had fallen to 30.33 per cent.[87] The loss of 1893 had been turned into a profit by 1894 though this in part resulted from a recovery in coal prices.[88] It may also have been materially affected by a contract to supply the Bristol Gas Co. with 15,000 tons of large coal and 20,000 tons of brush coal obtained in August 1894:[89] the enthusiasm with which news of this order was recorded emphasised the importance of coal sales for Cwmbran's profitability. The extent of the business was revealed by the following statement drawn up for the period 1 January to 11 March 1899:[90]

Cwmbran Collieries (Tons)

By shipment inland and sales to works	42,691
Coal used at colliery boilers	2,746
Loss at washery (shale)	773
Add to stock	4,645
Coal supplied for sale	3,119

EXPORTS AND COMPETITION FROM OVERSEAS

With typical sanguine determination, Arthur Keen sought every means to raise the level of exports from the various works in the PNB group and, where this proved impossible, to license overseas producers who could be persuaded to buy the company's patented machines. It was a two-fold strategy governed by the level of industrialisation achieved in foreign markets and the attitudes of their governments.

Selling the products of the PNB seems to have been most successful in Britain's imperial territories where, in general, domestic manufacturing had scarcely begun. The first sales expedition by the company was conducted to the colonies in 1878–79 when a network of local agents were engaged on a commission basis.[91] But in the case of Australia and New Zealand this soon proved unsuccessful, as the PNB was only able to win 'a small portion of the enormous trade of the Colonies for general bolts and nuts, nearly all of which had been given to Darlaston makers'.[92] Accordingly, they decided to take charge of operations themselves and sent their own representatives to win orders. In 1884 direct sales in Australia and New Zealand amounted to £19,984, a further £4,422 being obtained through agents.[93] Direct sales totalled £54,119 for the period January 1879 to May 1885, while the corresponding figure for orders obtained through merchants working on commission was £20,754. B.J. Cureton, who had undertaken the second sales tour of Australia in 1884–85 reckoned that further business to the value of £12,795 had been obtained. He was asked to consider whether the PNB should establish a manufacturing plant in the colonies; he concluded, for unspecified reasons that this was 'not advisable'.[94]

The question of establishing a nut and bolt works in Victoria, Australia, had in fact been discussed in 1879–80 and when the matter was raised again in July 1886, Cureton argued that the case against such a course was unaltered:[95]

> The tariff remains the same viz 25% ad val [this duty was considered too low to protect an embryonic industry]. No coal has yet been found in the Colony. It all has to be brought from the neighbouring colony of New South Wales, a distance of over 600 miles and the present price in Melbourne is I think about 27/–

per ton. Unskilled men earn about 8/– and skilled men from 12/– to 20/– per day of 8 hours [a higher rate than in the UK]. Working men are difficult to deal with and strikes are a frequent occurrence. There are no workmen skilled in the use of the company's machinery. All would have to be taught or sent from here. The ironmongers may object to the works as being likely to injure their important trade and may refuse to purchase their supplies from them.

For railway fastenings the Colonial Government is the only customer, and works established in the Colony for the manu- facture of those articles would have to depend entirely upon their chance of obtaining the Government contracts, which are submitted to public competition . . .

A small works with an unusually energetic and careful manage- ment might possibly be made to pay if able to make almost everything known to the trade including smith's work and forgings of all descriptions.

In the event, the PNB decided against investing in plant whether on the Continent or in the Empire.

Canada had also been visited by Cureton in 1879–80, though by July 1885 the volume of orders had diminished. Although the PNB reduced its prices in an effort to obtain custom, it was discovered that it could not compete with Canadian and American suppliers, or at least only in 'a few items, and these not leading ones'.[96] The main difficulty was that Canada had, at the request of the United States, introduced a protectionist policy in 1878 (a high tariff of 30 per cent *ad valorem*) to encourage the growth of home production. Factories in Montreal and Toronto, together with others in America, could meet Canada's needs and this led Cureton to conclude that 'unless there is a change in the tariff (which at present seems unlikely) . . . trade in future in bolts and nuts may be considered as hopelessly lost'.[97]

The United States of America was always viewed as a fertile market but, in view of its protectionism, difficult to penetrate. In April 1868 Francis Watkins, calculated that 'we can send nuts and bolts to America at the present tariff, rate of exchange etc. and realise fully 15% to 20% profit'.[98] Yet these expectations were not fulfilled. A comparison of prices in 1885 made it[99]

unmistakably clear that owing principally to the heavy duty of $2\frac{1}{2}$ cents per lb that is payable upon bolts and nuts (which is equal to about £12 per ton) the British manufacturer is completely shut out . . . Trade was found to be in a very depressed condition. The markets were overstocked with goods of all descriptions which were being offered at very low rates.

Like the Dowlais Iron Co. the PNB saw the possibilities of selling to Russia. Such a large country, slow to industrialise, presented a huge market for manufactured goods, but was limited by her lack of foreign exchange. In 1867 an order for 1,500–2,000 tons of fasteners was won[100] and shortly afterwards the PNB considered building a factory there.[101] With a capacity to produce 100 tons of railway fasteners a week (that is 50 tons of fish plates, 10 tons of sole plates, 15 tons of bolts and nuts and 30 tons of spikes), it would have cost £2,500 for the buildings and a further £7,175 in fittings and machinery. The scheme, however, was for the moment abandoned. Then in October 1871, after a visit by Williams and Grice to St Petersburg the matter was re-considered. 'We are convinced', they reported,[102]

> that with the high reputation the company enjoys in St. Petersburg and with the superior knowledge, skill and machinery we should bring to the manufacture, we should soon command a practical monopoly of the Russian trade for fastenings . . . We found that with two exceptions both nuts and spikes were made by hand. We saw many machines of various kinds for making bolts, nuts and rivets, most of them very unsuitable and now lying idle, the few actually in operation were working very badly.

Costings were produced to estimate the effectiveness of a factory in Russia:[103]

> reckoning the price of coal at 21/– per ton, iron at £8 per ton in Staffordshire, fish and sole plate bars at £7 and £8 10s. 0d. respectively in Newport, we estimate the profits to be made as follows, vis.
>
> | | |
> |---|---|
> | On bolts and nuts | £8 per ton |
> | On spikes | £4 per ton |
> | On fishplates | £3 per ton |
> | On sole plates | £3 10s. per ton |
>
> If iron for bolts, nuts and spikes were made and shipped from South Wales [Cwmbran] this would add at least £1 per ton to the profits named.

The reason for the abandonment of the scheme was not recorded.

Continental Europe was a fiercely competitive market for the nut and bolt makers. In 1867 the PNB had been awarded the only silver medal for nuts and bolts displayed at the Paris Exhibition; no golds were given, although bronze medals went to France and Belgium.[104] Given the existence of established competitors in the industrial nations of Europe, it was simpler for the PNB to sell them machines under license than attempt to undercut foreign producers. In 1867, while at the Paris Exhibition, Watkins approached a number of Continental manufacturers including Frederick Krupp, the Prussian steelmakers, with a view to selling them the company's machines under licence.[105] This was in contrast to Nettlefolds whose policy was to refuse to enter into any arrangements over the sale of technology with overseas makers of woodscrews (p. 213).

Francis Watkins was sent to the Continent in 1865 to assess the opposition and returned, having concluded that nut and bolt-making machinery there[106]

> is of a much inferior description to that used by this company or in this country; and although the labour is much cheaper the cost of workmanship is greater. The consequence is that the goods produced are not equal either as regards quality or quantity to those of this country. I found manufacturers ready to entertain the offer of new machinery.

In Belgium, where the PNB had four patents, Watkins visited the Cockerill Co. at Seraing, builders of locomotives, marine and land steam engines, who employed 3,000 workers. As they turned out around one ton of nuts and bolts a day and had not introduced any new machinery since 1857, when they bought a 'Belgium original nut machine' and a "Watkins" original bolt machine', it seemed that they would purchase the rights to the PNB's latest machines. The potential for such sales, argued Watkins, was high for[107]

> large orders for nuts and bolts were being executed there for Russia and Italy; but for the want of proper machinery and management I do not believe the manufacturers are working at a profit, their prices being about the same as those of this country.

Moreover, Watkins suggested that the PNB should sell machines to the German states where they had no patents, for if they refused to deal with them, the Germans would simply copy 'as they can get all the requisite information from our specifications'.[108] He also aroused interest, though he had yet to agree terms, with a bolt manufactory at Charleroi and another at Fouchambaut, the latter using machinery and patents sold to them by Watkins & Keen in 1858–59 and 1863.

The PNB acted, in effect, as an intermediary in the spread of new technology – particularly between America and the Continent. Having toured Europe, Francis Watkins then crossed the Atlantic to assess the competition in the United States. There he examined the latest bolt forging machines and recommended that the PNB immediately set about building these in return for a royalty of £50 per annum for every machine used.[109] The PNB could then start selling them throughout 'the United Kingdom, France, Belgium and other countries', dividing the net profits and royalties with their American inventors. It is not known, however, whether the company purchased the European rights to these American machines.

In May 1884 the PNB bought the UK rights to a German nut-making machine from C.W. Hasenclever & Son of Dusseldorf.[110] According to the specifications, it was able to produce within 24 consecutive working days of ten hours:

> 130,000 hexagon nuts for $\frac{3}{4}$ in. bolts
> 130,000 hexagon nuts for $\frac{7}{8}$ in. bolts
> 100,000 hexagon nuts for 1 in. bolts
> With no more loss of material than 25 lbs in every 125 lbs of iron, so that 125 lbs of bar iron must yield 100 lbs of frazed hexagon nuts.

By September 1884 the machines had arrived from Germany and had been put to work.[111] In December 1886 Cureton announced that he had been able to sell patents for the Hasenclever nut-making machine in the United States to the Upson Nut Co. of Unionville, Connecticut – an unusual example of fastener technology being transmitted from east to west across the Atlantic.[112] In addition, he had licensed Messrs. Inglist Hunter of Toronto to manufacture and sell these machines under a Canadian patent at a royalty to be paid to the PNB of £100 per machine. In November 1890, after a further exploratory visit to the United States, Arthur Keen persuaded the board to purchase a number of American machines for £2,500 which appeared to be more advanced than their British counterparts.[113] In this way, fresh ideas and innovations were diffused among the leading manufacturers in the nut and bolt industry; it was a freer, if not free, exchange of technology than existed in the woodscrew trade, and this was probably a result of a wider and more diverse market supplied by a greater number of producers.

Not simply by acquiring patents from overseas competitors did the PNB maintain its position at the leading edge of technology as the company's engineers sought to refine and improve its own machines. In this way they could reduce their operating costs, and, once protected by patents, they could sell them abroad. Watkins, for example, applied for two American patents in April 1858. One was for a nut-making machine and the other for a bolt and rivet-making machine so that the company then had a total of five patents in the United States.[114] After visiting a number of competitors there, Watkins concluded that[115]

> for making nuts they have machines which work as cheaply as ours but there is a monopoly. These machines are only worked by a few firms namely five. In the manufacture of nuts and bolts there are no machines equal to ours in regard to cheapness of production. The screwing and tapping machines turn out quite

good work but nothing like as fast . . . By building one machine after our own patents and putting them to work successfully we could sell the five [companies] patents at a fair price.

The PNB also sold machines to France and Belgium.[116] In October 1870, after Francis Watkins reported on his experiments to improve the efficiency of a nut-making machine ('I can reduce the cost of small nuts say $\frac{1}{4}$, $\frac{5}{16}$, $\frac{3}{8}$, $\frac{7}{16}$, and $\frac{1}{2}''$ about one half as to labour and fuel'), he patented the invention and suggested that others be obtained to cover America, France and Belgium.[117]

MANAGEMENT AND MANAGERS

Although Samuel Thornton had been appointed chairman of the PNB on its formation in 1864 and Alderman Pochin served as his deputy, real executive authority resided with Arthur Keen and Francis Watkins, the joint managing directors, who were joined in February 1865 by Edwin J. Grice to form a triumvirate. Watkins retired from the board in May 1867 but continued to serve as an overseas salesman.[118] When H.E. Leo, a Manchester merchant and founder director, died in 1869, Frederick G. Grice became the third managing director[119] and took responsibility for the Cwmbran Works. His brother, Edwin, controlled the Stour Valley Works. Although these three, dominated in practice by Arthur Keen, effectively ran the PNB, it was not until March 1875 that their hegemony was formally recognised when a resolution was passed by which the offices of chairman and deputy chairman should be 'merely honorary and that they be rotatory according to seniority'.[120] Under this arrangement Henry Pochin replaced Thornton and Alderman Phillips at Edgbaston became his deputy.[121] In the following year [Sir] Joseph Dodge Weston succeeded to the chairmanship (with Samuel de la Grange Williams of Edgbaston as the deputy)[122] but, despite the resolution, with the exception of the years 1877–79,[123] retained this post until his death in 1895,[124] when Keen replaced him as chairman, making his dominance of the company complete.[125]

Arthur Keen was a man of considerable energy, intelligence and drive. He made business success his life's principal and over-riding goal and pursued it with passion, ruthlessness and considerable acumen, dying in office as chairman of GKN with a sizeable fortune (he left over a million pounds). An obituary described him as 'cautious to a degree, and yet always enterprising, gifted also with an intuitive knowledge of men, and a born organiser, he was throughout his career a strongly-marked personality'.[126] Although Keen may have been slow to make up his mind, once decided he would do everything in his power to achieve that end. He became a figure of immense influence in Birmingham and the Midlands. 'Mr. Keen generally got his way', remarked a contemporary newspaper account, 'both in business and public affairs'.[127] Testimony to his commitment to the onward march of the PNB and his obsession with work was provided by several holidays forced upon him by his doctors. In August 1890, for instance, he announced to the board that,[128]

> his medical adviser considered it essentially necessary for the establishment of his health that he should take a rest from business for a time . . . he had decided . . . to avail himself of the opportunity of joining the members of the Iron and Steel Institute in their forthcoming visit to the United States.

This, in addition, would enable him 'to gain access to the most important works in America connected with the different branches of the iron and steel trades and more particularly those engaged in the manufacture of articles similar to those produced by the company'.[129]

Keen was an entrepreneur *par excellence* – a chief executive, a dealer, a man of determination, whose will to succeed, combined very likely by a fear of failure, drove him to take major risks. A description of his friend, Dudley Docker (1862–1944) another industrialist, could equally well have been applied to Keen:[130]

> a business man unfettered by sentiment, aesthetics or idealism who owned his success to his perfectly honed sense of reality. In fact his power, and his historic interest, came from his sense of possibility. Throughout his life he saw positive possibilities in situations which contemporaries regarded with despair.

The importance of the PNB within the light engineering trades of the Midlands and Keen's dominance of the company led him in 1891 to be elected to the Council of the Institution of Mechanical Engineers, having become a member in 1869, and to his serving as a Vice-president in 1897–1911, despite not being an innovative mechanical engineer himself. Similarly, his membership of the Iron and Steel Institute from 1885, his service on their Council from 1891 and election as a Vice-president in 1895 reflected his standing as a businessman rather than a metallurgist or pioneering steel maker.[131]

The abilities, experience and connections of Arthur Keen were widely appreciated. In April 1880, for example, he was appointed a director of the Birmingham and Midland Bank (later the Midland Bank),[132] and after, in an expansionist policy, it had merged with the City Bank, he became the chairman in 1898.[133] He played an important role in helping the Midland merge with the Sheffield Union Bank and the Yorkshire Banking Co. Retaining this post until 1908, Keen provided able support for [Sir] Edward Holden (1848–1919),[134] the chief general manager, and helped the bank to present an image which appealed to manufacturers. 'His object', was 'to maintain the reputation of the bank for strength and soundness'.[135] When Keen retired, Holden wrote to express his regret and added that[136]

> one of the greatest obligations which I have to you is the great advantages which I have derived in consequence of closely following your methods of doing business. If I have been at all successful in my career as a Banker, it is due to a large extent to my adopting your system, or in other words, by never allowing a transaction to pass without going to the foundation of it.

Thus, qualities including attention to detail and resolution (also said to have been possessed by Joseph Chamberlain) lay at the root of Arthur Keen's appointment to the Midland Bank. Holden then considered the appointment of his son, Arthur T. Keen, to the board:[137]

> I hold no brief whatever for the Keens but only for the Bank. The Keen connection is very far reaching. It goes to a great many accounts in and about Birmingham, and even to Sheffield, and into Yorkshire. Lloyds Bank has a number of Directors in Birmingham, one of which, Mr. Nettlefold, is a Director of Guest Keen & Nettlefolds Ltd. Having regard to the fact that our Bank came from Birmingham, and used to have all its Directors from that City, I do not think it is asking too much to have a second Director. In fact I know that several men in Birmingham who have brought large business to the Bank, have an idea that they might be invited. The advantages of young Keen are that he is the Managing Director of Guest Keen & Nettlefolds which I think is the best industrial concern in the country. He will be a comparatively rich man when his father dies. His age is about 47, and he is an educated man. The gentlemen who were present last week at the Board were strongly of an opinion that the appointment should be made.

Arthur Keen also served as the chairman of Muntz's Metal Co., which made alloy tubes, bolts, nuts and casings nearby in Smethwick. He also accepted the chairmanship of the New Cransley Iron & Steel Co. (a business that he later sought to acquire, p. 190) and held directorships in the steelmakers Bolckow, Vaughan & Co., and the Loddington Ironstone Co.

In the tradition of the eighteenth-century entrepreneur, Keen brought his sons into the business; the eldest, Arthur Thomas Keen (1861–1918), had been called to the Bar, practising for a short time before entering the London Works of the PNB, and ultimately succeeded his father as chairman of GKN (p. 390). In 1881 another son, Francis Watkins Keen (1863/4–1933), was articled to the company as a mechanical engineer and draughtsman.[138] His appointment as

52 Arthur Keen (1835–1915) in 1909 by Ouless commissioned by the Midland Bank of which he was chairman. (*Midland Bank plc*; photograph: *Courtauld Institute of Art*)

competitors and sought alliances with other successful companies. Keen did not draw back from taking major risks. The PNB with its three nut and bolt works, rolling mills, ironworks at Cwmbran and collieries formed an integrated group. There was, however, a weakness. They had been dangerously slow in perceiving the importance of steel, or at least found themselves so heavily committed to wrought iron technology that it was difficult and costly for them to effect a rapid substitution. It was fortunate for the PNB that the mighty Dowlais Iron Co. had remained a family partnership and its proprietor, Lord Wimborne, wished to sell the business – and this despite the fact that they had recently constructed a modern steelworks at Cardiff, and owned an increasingly profitable group of collieries in South Wales.

References

1. *DBB*, Vol. III, London (1985), Edgar Jones, 'Arthur Keen', pp. 570–574.
2. *The Journal of the Iron and Steel Institute*, Part 1 (1915), Obituary, pp. 454–456; *PIME*, Vol. 88 (1915), Obituary, pp. 433–434.
3. *Harrison, Harrod & Co.'s Directory . . . of Staffordshire* (1861), p. 183; *The Post Office Directory of Birmingham . . . with Staffordshire* (1854), p. 789.
4. *DBB*, p. 570.
5. BRL, *Midland Captains of Industry Newspaper Cuttings* (1907–19), 'Mr. Arthur Keen', 7 March 1907, p. 1.
6. BRL, *Familiar Figures from the Birmingham Evening Despatch* (May 1903 – October 1905), No. 729; *VCHS*, Vol. XVII, Oxford (1976), p. 113; *VCHW*, Vol. VII, Oxford (1964), p. 155.
7. *Directory of Birmingham with . . . Staffordshire* (1894), p. 7.
8. *Kelly's Directory of Staffordshire*, Part I (1880), p. 249.
9. D. Morier Evans, *The History of the Commercial Crisis 1857–1858*, London (1895), p. xciii; *MPICE*, Vol. XXXIX (1874–1875), Memoir of Sir Charles Fox, pp. 264–265.
10. *An Outline History of Guest, Keen & Nettlefolds Ltd.* (c. 1925), p. 17.
11. P.L. Cottrell, *Industrial Finance 1830–1914*, London (1980), pp. 115, 125–126; *DBB*, Vol. 1, London (1984), 'David Chadwick', pp. 625–633.
12. PNB Co. Ltd., Minute Book No. 1, June 1864 – October 1879, Memorandum of Association, p. 33.
13. Ibid., 3 June 1864, it. 6.
14. Ibid., Memorandum of Association, p. 49.
15. *The Accountant*, Vol. XXIX, No. 1467, 17 January 1903, p. 66.
16. Ibid., 12 August 1864, the purchase of Weston & Grice was then rejected because 'the present condition of the money market and the terms asked for the business' were considered impropitious, it. 84.
17. *Who's Who of British Members of Parliament, Vol. II, 1886–1918*, Sussex (1978), Sir J.D. Weston was elected Liberal MP for Bristol in 1884, p. 368.
18. *Outline History*, p. 19.
19. PNB Minute Book No. 2, 21 September 1864, it. 93.
20. Ibid., 16 November 1864, it. 99.

21. Ibid., 9 January 1865, it. 126.
22. PRO, BT 31/958/1311C; Cottrell, *Industrial Finance*, p. 119.
23. Ibid., pp. 120–121.
24. Ibid., 25 January 1865, it. 135.
25. Ibid., 15 February 1865, it. 154.
26. PNB Minute Book No. 3, August 1875 – January 1882, 21 March 1876, it. 2661.
27. PNB Minute Book No. 1, 25 January 1865, it. 147, 151.
28. *The Engineer*, Vol. XX, 15 September 1865, 'Visits to the Provinces, The Works of the Patent Nut & Bolt Co. (Ltd.) near Birmingham', p. 161.
29. Ibid., p. 162.
30. Émile Zola, *L'Assommoir*, Paris (1876), Penguin Edition (1970), p. 170.
31. Ibid., pp. 176–177.
32. Smiles, *Industrial Biography*, 'Henry Maudslay', p. 226.
33. Samuel Griffiths, *Griffiths' Guide to the Iron Trade of Great Britain*, London (1873), p. 82.
34. Ibid.
35. PNB Minute Book No. 1, 13 February 1867, it. 488/2.
36. Ibid.
37. Ibid., 20 February 1868, it. 654.
38. PNB Minute Book No. 2, November 1869 – July 1875, 26 February 1870, it. 1144.
39. Ibid., 25 February 1871, Annual Report.
40. BRL, *Midland Captains of Industry* (1907–09), 7 March 1907, p. 1.
41. Ibid., 26 February 1870, it. 1144.
42. Ibid., 10 November 1869, it. 1067.
43. PNB Minute Book No. 3, August 1875 – January 1882, 19 June 1887, it. 2872.
44. Ibid., 18 May 1880, it. 3406; 20 July 1880, it. 3446.
45. Ibid., 24 January 1882, it. 3657.
46. Ibid., it. 3663.
47. PNB Minute Book No. 5, November 1886 – April 1892, 25 February 1887, it. 4514.
48. *The Engineer*, Vol. XLIII, 20 April 1887, 'Wiks' Patent Lock Nut' made by the PNB Co., p. 276.
49. G. Phillips Bevan (Editor), *British Manufacturing Industries, Guns, Nails, Locks, Wood Screws, Railway Bolts and Spikes*, London (1878), W.C. Aitken, 'Railway Bolts and Spikes', p. 66.
50. *The Engineer*, (1865), p. 161.
51. Ibid.
52. Ibid., p. 162.
53. PNB Minute Book No. 5, 26 April 1887, it. 4559.
54. *The Post Office Directory of Monmouthshire and the Principal Towns in South Wales*, London (1871), p. 25.
55. Ibid.
56. PNB Minute Book No. 1, 6 December 1865, it. 214.
57. Ibid., 12 September 1872, it. 1835.
58. *Kelly's Directory of Monmouthshire and South Wales*, London (1895), p. 45; Ordnance Survey Map (1901) Monmouthshire Sheet, XXIII.15, revised 1899.
59. PNB Minute Book No. 2, 21 September 1867, it. 615.
60. PNB Minute Book, 26 April 1887, it. 4559.
61. Ibid., 22 April 1890, it. 5139.

62. Ibid., 1 March 1894, it. 5822.

63. Ibid., 23 October 1894, it. 5951.

64. Ibid., 29 April 1895, it. 6046.

65. GwRO, D 409.0043, Account Book of Rents and Royalties Payable and Principal Debts of the Cwmbran Works 1873–94, pp. 1, 21, 51.

66. Ordnance Survey Map (1882) Monmouthshire Sheet, XXIII.15; Aubrey Byles, *The History of the Monmouthshire Railway and Canal Company*, Cwmbran (1982), p. 71; see also John McKenna and Frank King, *In those Days*, Cwmbran (1976) – a photographic portrait of the Cwmbran Works and recollections of employees.

67. PNB Minute Book No. 1, 10 October 1872, it. 1864.

68. Ibid., 14 November 1872, it. 1884; 12 December 1872, it. 1910; 16 January 1873, it. 1932; 10 April 1873, it. 2015.

69. S.B. Saul, *The Myth of the Great Depression 1873–1896*, London (1969), pp. 12–13.

70. Ibid., pp. 14–15.

71. PNB Minute Book, 15 January 1878, it. 2982.

72. Ibid., 24 March 1886, it. 4332.

73. Ibid., 28 June 1886, it. 4379.

74. Ibid., 16 August 1887, it. 4629; 17 August 1887, it. 4639.

75. Ibid., 28 July 1888, it. 4826.

76. Ibid., it. 4882.

77. Ibid., 25 May 1893, it. 5648.

78. Ibid., it. 5649.

79. Morris and Williams, *The South Wales Coal Industry*, p. 58.

80. *Royal Commission on Coal*, Vol. II (1871).

81. Morris and Williams, *The South Wales Coal Industry*, p. 59.

82. *Transactions of the South Wales Institute of Engineers*, Vol. II (1861), pp. 125–132.

83. *Royal Commission on Coal*, evidence of Matthew Truran.

84. PNB Minute Book, 15 July 1893, it. 5702.

85. Ibid.

86. Ibid., 23 January 1893, it. 5780.

87. Ibid., 23 January 1895, it. 5990.

88. Ibid.

89. Ibid., 16 August 1894, it. 5931.

90. GwRO, D 409.54, Statements of Coal Worked 1 January to 11 March 1899.

91. PNB Minute Book, 16 April 1878, it. 3042.

92. Ibid., 30 July 1885, it. 4216.

93. Ibid.

94. Ibid.

95. Ibid., 14 July 1886, it. 4392.

96. Ibid.

97. Ibid.

98. Ibid., 8 April 1868, it. 692.

99. Ibid., 30 July 1885, it. 4216.

100. Ibid., 12 June 1867, it. 1548.

101. Ibid., 11 December 1867, it. 631.

102. Ibid., 11 October 1871, it. 1546.

103. Ibid.

104. Ibid., 10 July 1867, it. 557.

105. Ibid.
106. Ibid., 12 July 1865, it. 214.
107. Ibid.
108. Ibid.
109. Ibid., 3 October 1866, it. 443/8.
110. Ibid., 20 May 1884, it. 4027.
111. Ibid., 16 September 1884, it. 4068.
112. Ibid., 29 December 1886, it. 4485.
113. Ibid., 21 November 1890, it. 5242.
114. Ibid., 8 April 1868, it. 692.
115. Ibid.
116. Ibid., 13 May 1868, it. 709.
117. Ibid., 12 October 1870, it. 1311.
118. Ibid., 8 May 1867, it. 532.
119. Ibid., 25 February 1869, 5th Annual Report.
120. Ibid., 16 March 1875, it. 2465.
121. Ibid., it. 2466–67.
122. Ibid., 21 March 1876, it. 2661–63.
123. Ibid., 20 March 1877, it. 2818; 18 March 1879, it. 3181.
124. Ibid., 20 March 1895, it. 6019.
125. Ibid., it. 6021.
126. *DBB*, Vol. III, pp. 570–574.
127. BRL, *Midland Captains of Industry* (1907–09), 7 March 1907, p. 2.
128. PNB Minute Book, 14 August 1890, it. 5210.
129. Ibid.
130. R.P.T. Davenport-Hines, *Dudley Docker, The Life and Times of a Trade Warrior*, Cambridge (1984), pp. 235–236.
131. *Journal of the Iron and Steel Institute*, Part 1 (1915), pp. 454–56.
132. MBA, Midland Bank Board Minutes 1880–1900, 2 April 1880; A.R. Holmes and Edwin Green, *Midland, 150 Years of Banking Business*, London (1986), pp. 67, 91, 94, 102, 115.
133. MBA, Midland Bank Board Minutes 1880–1900, 23 September 1898.
134. *DBB*, Vol. III (1985), Edwin Green, 'Sir Edward Holden', pp. 290–297.
135. BRL, *Midland Captains of Industry* (1907–09), 7 March 1907, p. 2.
136. MBA, Letter, Sir Edward Holden to Arthur Keen, 15 February 1908.
137. MBA, Letter, Sir Edward Holden to J. Howard Gwyther, 17 February 1908.
138. PNB Minute Book, 18 January 1881, it. 3527.
139. Ibid., 16 July 1885, it. 4205.
140. Ibid., 23 January 1895, it. 5983.
141. Ibid., 28 January 1896, it. 6158.
142. Ibid., 20 November 1894, it. 5975.
143. Ibid., 21 May 1878, it. 3052.
144. Ibid., 29 October 1885, it. 4246.
145. Ibid., 29 June 1893, it. 5688.
146. Ibid.
147. Ibid., 22 December 1896, it. 6328.
148. Ibid., 23 February 1897, it. 6362.
149. Ibid.
150. Ibid., 28 June 1897, it. 6439.
151. Ibid., 22 November 1899, it. 6892.
152. Ibid., 25 July 1898, it. 6653.

153. Ibid., 13 February 1899, it. 6756.
154. Ibid.
155. Ibid., 24 October 1899, it. 6879.
156. Ibid., 18 November 1899, it. 6887.
157. Ibid., 19 December 1899, it. 6908.
158. GRO, D/DG, C4 'Bar Iron sent from the Dowlais Iron works', 30 March 1861, 21 June 1862, 25 May 1864.
159. PNB Minute Book, 18 July 1899, it. 6842.
160. Ibid., 23 January 1900, it. 6928.
161. Ibid., it. 6929.
162. Ibid., 27 March 1900, it. 7016.
163. Sir John Ponsonby, *The Ponsonby Family*, London (1929), p. 155; *Who was Who 1916–1928*, Vol. II, London (1967), p. 87.
164. PNB Minute Book, 21 April 1900, it. 7033.

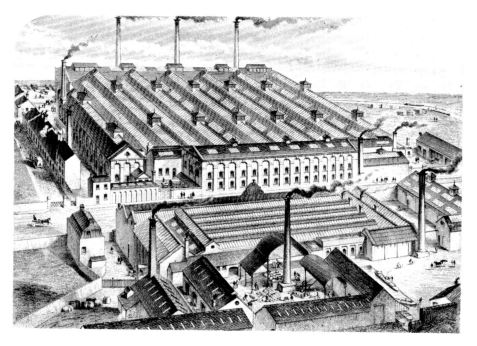

53 A view of Heath Street taken from *Nettlefold Catalogues* of the 1880s, which shows considerable expansion from the works portrayed in 1871 (plate 34). A new two-storey warehouse has been constructed parallel to Heath Street. The Imperial Mills (foreground) have been transferred to the former Patent File Co.'s factory and were served by a short arm from the Birmingham Canal Navigations (right).

7 *Nettlefolds Ltd. and the Screw Industry, 1880–1902*

Nettlefolds had grown at a remarkable pace from the foundation of their mill at Smethwick in 1854. The resignation of Joseph Chamberlain in 1874, and the loss of capital that resulted, did not diminish the firm's dominance of the British woodscrew market. Even the competition provided by the opening of a modern factory nearby, owned by the Birmingham Screw Co. Ltd., had been successfully combated and this rival establishment failed to pose its promised threat. From the formation of Nettlefolds Ltd. in 1880 to their take-over by Guest, Keen & Co. in 1902, the company continued to earn high levels of profit, maintained their position at home, and though they lost ground to German and American competitors overseas and even in imperial territories, remained the world's premier screw maker.

THE FLOTATION OF NETTLEFOLDS LTD.

The passing of the chairmanship to Joseph Henry Nettlefold in 1878 and the desire to take over a number of rival screw-making concerns lay at the root of the flotation. The family partnership had reached its financial limits and if Nettlefolds were to expand further, they needed to draw on the resources of the investing public. The decision to form a limited liability company was taken in the spring of 1880[1] and the prospectus (in some cases an abridged version) was advertised in local and national newspapers and trade publications during April.[2] It is likely that Carter & Carter, the Birmingham firm of chartered accountants, arranged the flotation, since they became the company's auditors once it had come into being. The pattern of investment seems to have been remarkably similar to the Patent Nut & Bolt Co. (p. 168), as the lists of shareholders compiled by the company can be analysed by both occupation and geographical origin. The bulk of the shares were subscribed from the West Midlands (67.01 per cent of preference shares and 78.32 per cent of ordinary shares) including 52.20 per cent and 51.48 per cent respectively from the Smethwick region. The main difference in comparison with the PNB was a lower proportion from the North West (probably because Edwin Chadwick was not involved in this promotion) and a higher one from the South East (19.62 per cent and 12.58 per cent respectively). Curiously, the proportion subscribed by manufacturers was lower (29.23 per cent and 26.06 per cent), because higher percentages had been taken in the case of preference shares by the professions and ordinary shares by merchants. This may have been the result of a broadening in the base of the investing public as shareholding became more widely accepted and involved those groups without a direct connection with industry. The auditors, as was then customary, invested in the new company; Edward Carter purchased twenty two preference and forty seven ordinary shares for £690 and E. Harold Carter nine and twenty respectively for £290.[3]

The extra capital was needed by Nettlefolds in 1880 to enable them to acquire four related businesses. Principal among them was their old adversary, the Birmingham Screw Co. which was valued at £143,000.[4] The other three were: the Manchester Steel Screw Co. Ltd. (£50,000),[5] John Cornforth's wire and nail works in Berkeley Street, Birmingham (£24,000),[6] and Messrs Lloyd & Harrison's screw-making works at Stourport (£21,000).[7] The first (p. 154), which had been set up in direct opposition to Nettlefolds, was to be absorbed within the Heath

54 The former Heath Street entrance; these gates were superseded when Hope Street was acquired. The two-storey warehouse stands in the centre. The overhead telpher was initially installed in 1913 to convey fasteners from the bolt mill to the Heath Street wrapping room. (*European Industrial Services*)

55 J.H. Nettlefold in middle age.

Table 7.1 Regional distribution of Nettlefolds Ltd.'s original shareholding

	Preference Shares %	Ordinary Shares %	PNB %
North	—	—	—
Yorks & Humberside	0.99	1.18	(0.17)
North West	7.38	4.07	(25.46)
East Midlands	0.99	0.31	(4.33)
West Midlands	67.01	78.32	(66.92)
East Anglia	0.60	0.02	—
South East	19.62	12.58	(2.13)
South West	2.98	1.74	—
Wales	0.40	0.37	—
Scotland	—	—	—
Ireland	—	0.16	(0.30)
Foreign	—	1.28	—
Area of Works	52.20	51.48	(65.25)

Figures in brackets are for the Patent Nut & Bolt Co.'s flotation of May 1865.

Source: Nettlefolds Ltd., Directors Minute Book, No. 1, pp. 22–8, and 29–45; and Cottrell, *Industrial Finance*, p. 119.

Table 7.2   Occupational distribution of Nettlefolds Ltd.'s original shareholding

		Preference Shares %	Ordinary Shares %	PNB %
Unoccupied				
Male		24.45	12.17	(24.45)
Female		5.12	1.20	(1.14)
	Sub total	29.57	13.37	(25.59)
Land		—	—	(0.40)
Professions		20.02	5.37	(9.65)
Commerce		—		
Merchants		11.55	37.97	(13.01)
Middlemen & Agents		1.15	6.22	(0.43)
Retailers		2.39	4.76	—
	Sub total	15.09	48.95	(13.44)
Industrial				
Manufacturers		29.23	26.06	(44.43)
Services		1.77	2.54	—
Employees				
Managers		2.92	0.09	(0.21)
Service Workers		1.24	2.70	(0.34)
Industrial Skilled		0.14	—	
Unskilled		—	—	
Unknown		—	—	(5.89)

Figures in brackets are for the Patent Nut & Bolt Co.'s flotation of May 1865.

Source: Nettlefolds Ltd., Directors Minute Book, No. 1, pp. 22–28, and 29–45; Cottrell, *Industrial Finance*, pp. 120–121.

Street complex and was liquidated so that it could become part of Nettlefolds Ltd.[8] In this fashion, the company was able to increase their share of the British market by around twenty per cent and obtained a self-contained, modern extension to their plant. It was, however, situated on the opposite side of the Cape Arm of the canal from the main Nettlefolds' works and, naturally enough, because they had until then been rivals, there was no means of communicating between them; a bridge was erected shortly after the take-over and in May 1913 an overhead telpher was installed initially to convey the output of the bolt mill to the Heath Street wrapping rooms.

As a result of take-over and the purchase of smaller adjacent units for expansion, the Heath Street complex grew steadily throughout the nineteenth and early twentieth centuries. Buildings were extended, re-constructed or added as needs directed.[9] What had started as a

56 The heading
department at St.
George's Works (formerly
the Birmingham Screw Co.
Ltd). These machines
received the wire, cut it to
the required length and
forged a head on one end.
(*European Industrial
Services*)

modern, integrated and compact screw works, became a complex
collection of mills, packaging rooms and warehouses, whose arrangement was dictated by acquisition, market fluctuations and the
availability of land in what was becoming a crowded industrial
suburb.[10] Whilst the success of the company in dominating the British
market obviated the need to transfer to a green-field site (as Lever
Bros. had done at Port Sunlight and Cadbury's at Bournville),
Nettlefolds would have conceivably benefited from being accommodated in a smaller number of large buildings arranged under a single
coherent plan to ensure the rapid and logical flow of manufacturing
processes from reception of raw materials through to despatch of
finished product.

The Manchester Steel Screw Co. Ltd., makers of 'patent steel, brass
and iron woodscrews' at the Bradford Mills, Philip's Park Road,[11]
which appears to have been founded in 1874,[12] had not primarily been
acquired with a view to reducing competition, for the chairman, J.H.
Nettlefold, reported[13]

that for a considerable time he had been of the opinion that steel
was the metal of the future but until he examined the quality of
the wire which the Manchester Steel Screw Co. used he had
never met with any steel sufficiently uniform for screw making.

Now he was convinced it could be made and he desired to be
allowed to alter some puddling furnaces at the Castle Works
[near Wellington, Salop] with steel making furnaces for which
purpose he wished to enter into negotiations with Dr. Siemens.

Ultimately this decision led to the establishment of a steelworks at
Rogerstone near Newport (p. 222), but it revealed that Nettlefolds'
interest in the Manchester company was principally to discover
whether they had made technological progress in the substitution of
steel for bar iron. This appears not to have been the case because the
factory in the Bradford district of Manchester was sold shortly after
the take-over and its stock and machinery shipped to Heath Street
either to be used for iron woodscrews or destroyed.[14]
With the extra capacity provided by the plant of the former
Birmingham Screw Co., Nettlefolds did not need Lloyd & Harrison's
screw works at Stourport and it was soon agreed to remove the
machinery and surrender the premises on the expiry of their lease in
December 1880.[15] There was, nevertheless, a managerial gain as both
Charles Harrison and Sampson Zachary Lloyd were allotted shares to
the value of £10,000 as part compensation for their business,[16] and the
latter, a member of the distinguished family of manufacturers and
bankers,[17] became a leading director of Nettlefolds. As regards John
Cornforth's wire and nail works in Berkeley Street, it was reported in
June 1881 that a fire had damaged amongst other things a box-making
machine and its patterns', but 'as we have other machines doing

similar things at King's Norton' they were not required to replace the loss.[18] The Berkeley Street mills continued in operation until 1907 when they and the Princip Street Wire Works were closed and the work transferred to Coverack Road, Newport (p. 223).

Having inspired the take over of these four related businesses, guided through the flotation of the merged company and seen profits begin to rise (a trial balance for the six months ending 30 September 1880 revealed a net surplus of £27,774,[19] while a profit of £64,204 was recorded for the year ending 31 March 1881),[20] J.H. Nettlefold, in effect chairman since 1878, died on 22 November 1881 at his Highland residence, Allean House, near Pitlochry,[21] where he had travelled to rest, the labour of running the business having contributed to 'the failure of his health'.[22] Aged only fifty-four he succumbed to an apoplectic seizure and Nettlefolds lost one of their ablest leaders. The contribution of J.H. Nettlefold was acknowledged by the other directors, who recorded that it was his 'great business capacity' which had been responsible for the formation and present position of the company'.[23] Educated privately in London at a non-conformist academy, his mathematical abilities, combined with an understanding of engineering principles, enabled him to draw up plans for the extensions to Heath Street, while his administrative skills had been valued during the period of the various mergers.[24] Whilst much of his personality remains a mystery, an obituary suggested that 'both his tastes and his character were too simple to permit ostentation; and he was wholly free from a sense of personal importance which is sometimes associated with the possessor of wealth. One of his characteristics was distinctly marked, his love of works of art'.[25] On his death he gave twenty-five pictures by David Cox, valued at £30,–£40,000 to the Birmingham City Art Gallery, then under construction. The story was told among the older employees that his wife Mary Seaborne (b. 1835) had in fact worked in the warehouse at 16 Broad Street, and that having accepted his proposal of marriage she was sent to France to be educated, returning after three years a cultured and refined lady.[26] She being a Catholic and he a Unitarian, two wedding ceremonies were held; their three children were all daughters, none of their husbands entering the family business. J.H. Nettlefold was succeeded as chairman by his younger brother, Frederick Nettlefold (1835–1913), and his nephew, Edward Nettlefold (1856–1909), was elected to the board to fill the vacancy that had been created.[27]

PROFITS, DISCOUNTS AND CUSTOMERS

After the powerful boom of 1872–73, activity in the British economy slowed as prices fell to a trough in 1896, taking them some ten per cent below the subsidiary peak of 1887; then there followed a relatively modest recovery to 1914.[28] This was accompanied by a declining rate of growth in industrial production. Average annual real growth rates of British industrial production fell from 3.5 (2.4 per head) in the 1850s to 2.1 (0.9 per head) in the 1870s to 1.8 (0.4 per head) in the 1890s to 1.5 (−0.2) in the early 1900s,[29] a pattern which compared unfavourably with Germany and America, where the corresponding figures were considerably higher.[30]

Against this background of relative industrial decline, Nettlefolds,

Table 7.3 Profits earned by Nettlefolds Ltd. 1880–1901

To 31 March	Published[1] (£)	Adjusted (£)	Pre-tax[2] (£)	Adjusted (£)
1881	64204	64853	64204	64853
1882	57240	56673	72759	72039
1883	57634	57063	74824	74083
1884	56925	59921	76330	80347
1885	57260	65068	75579	85885
1886	47534	57270	67867	81767
1887	40415	49895	60471	74656
1888	38418	45736	58744	69933
1889	67830	80750	87362	104002
1890	91739	105447	112235	129005
1891	112130	130383	131064	152400
1892	143096	174507	166203	202687
1893	101569	123865	123210	150256
1894	136830	184905	109976	148616
1895	111555	154938	99597	138329
1896	101871	139549	114966	157488
1897	97876	132265	120655	163047
1898	99111	127065	121173	155350
1899	89619	106689	121158	144236
1900	93133	102344	124164	136444
1901	92265	107285	119694	139179

(Series continued in Table 11.2, p. 371.)

Sources: 1: Nettlefolds Ltd., General Meeting Minute Book, June 1880 – February 1902. 2: BRL 298/14 Nettlefolds Ltd. Annual Accounts General 1880–92; 298/3 Nettlefolds Ltd. Annual Accounts General 1893–1904; 298/15 Annual Accounts General Nettlefolds Dept. 1905–1920. Figures adjusted by the Rousseaux Price Index 1800–1913, average of 1865 and 1885 = 100, Mitchell and Deane, op. cit., pp. 472–3.

the pre-eminent manufacturer of woodscrews in Britain, experienced a rise in their published profits, both in cash and real terms, which increased to a peak around 1892–94 (Table 7.3). Despite the fall from £184,905 in 1894 to £107,285 in 1901, the company's published earnings were well advanced on the £64,853 for 1881. The pre-tax records reveal a similar picture, of rising income up to a peak in 1892, followed by a decline and levelling off. From the higher levels of profits, it confirms that sums were being siphoned off for deposit into a secret reserve. In some years such as 1894 and 1895 when the actual profit was smaller than the published figure, they used the sinking fund to improve their apparent performance. Nevertheless, whether the pre-tax or the published figures are taken, the impression created was that the initiative and drive of the first ten years may not have been maintained during the second decade of Nettlefolds' history and that this was due to increased competition (p. 228) and, it seems likely, to a decline in the performance and determination of the senior management (p. 223), circumstances noted by the acute Arthur Keen who chose the appropriate moment to effect a take-over.

Unfortunately the loss of the company's records has prevented any attempt to correlate profits with production statistics. The only figures which have survived for this period relate to the Bolt Mill and they revealed a rising trend (in grosses): 1905 1,990,000, 1906 2,023,000, 1907 2,502,000, 1908 2,761,000, 1909 2,665,000 and 1910 2,898,000.[31] The general impression survives that output increased throughout the nineteenth century and reached a peak in 1914. The disruption caused by the Great War and the depression which followed resulted in this record not being surpassed until the late 1930s. Table 7.4, therefore, provides an indication of the magnitude of Nettlefolds' business.

A crucial element in the business strategy devised by Nettlefolds &

Table 7.4   Woodscrew sales (per gross) by Nettlefolds 1920–39

	Year	Total	Home	Export
June	1920	18051277	10896505	7154772
March	1923	15681804	9702634	5979170
	1925	17015382	11156434	5858948
	1927	16717879	10904888	5812991
	1929	18245808	12250465	5995343
	1931	14805432	11456846	3348586
	1933	15657490	11569038	4088452
	1935	21197146	14715311	6481835
	1937	25111101	18530184	6580917
	1939	20022586	14700116	5322470

Source: Working papers 'GKN Group Fastener Manufacturers and Traders', November 1975.

Chamberlain, which continued long after the firm had passed into the hands of GKN, was a system of discounts to wholesalers. The list price was not altered from its inception in the early 1850s until 1954. The company did not sell directly to the public but to factors who supplied retailers and the furniture and building trades. Their method of raising or lowering prices was to vary the level of discount offered to these wholesalers according to the state of the market. In the period when the Birmingham Screw Co. was building its works, the discount was reduced to 30–40 per cent (Table 7.5) to build up a financial reserve. When their rival came into operation during the mid 1870s, the discount was raised to 65 per cent and ultimately reached 75 per cent in March 1875.[32] Similarly, when the British Screw Co., a competitor in Leeds, commenced manufacturing in the early 1890s (p. 212), Nettlefolds raised the discount from 57.5 per cent in March 1892 to 72.5 per cent in January 1895, but once they had acquired this company, allowed the rate to fall back to 60 per cent in November 1899. The list price of screws had in fact been set at a high level from the outset, thereby enabling the company to offer such big discounts.

58   A selection of labels printed by Nettlefolds themselves, showing the 'castle' trademark. (*European Industrial Services*)

Table 7.5 Discounts on Nettlefolds' woodscrews sold in Britain 1853–1918

Date			Discount %	Gross Margin Index	Date			Discount %	Gross Margin Index
April	18	1853	50	100	Feb	17	1886	75	0
Nov	17	1853	47½	105	June	23	1888	72½	18
Jan	12	1854	45	109	Oct	9	1888	67½	57
Jan	15	1854	47½	105	March	18	1889	62½	67
Oct	2	1856	52½	95	Nov	11	1889	57½	82
Jan	1	1857	57½	82	April	26	1893	67½	57
Oct	1	1857	60	75	Jan	1	1895	72½	18
April	1	1862	65	47	Oct	19	1898	70	40
Jan	1	1865	70	40	Feb	17	1899	67½	57
Nov	25	1865	60	75	Aug	23	1899	65½	55
Sept	1	1871	50	100	Nov	14	1899	60	75
Jan	22	1872	45	109	Dec	2	1905	70	40
April	9	1872	40	117	March	18	1907	67½	57
June	22	1872	30	128	March	30	1908	72½	18
Jan	18	1873	40	117	Sept	28	1912	70	40
July	1	1874	50	100	Aug	20	1914	67½	57
July	1	1875	60	75	April	14	1915	65	47
April	25	1876	65	47	July	7	1915	60	75
Jan	8	1877	70	40	Dec	11	1915	55	89
Sept	20	1877	72½	18	June	7	1916	50	100
March	21	1879	75	0	Oct	6	1917	45	109
Jan	17	1880	65	47	Feb	9	1918	40	117
March	28	1881	75	0	May	4	1918	35	123
Oct	7	1881	72½	18	Aug	24	1918	30	128
Dec	24	1881	70	40	Nov	9	1918	25	133

Note: These percentages refer in the first instance to wrought iron screws, though steel was substituted during the 1880s.

Source: 'Woodscrew Discounts from 1853' (typescript sheet, May 1954), courtesy of Sela Fasteners Ltd., Leeds.

Given that the list price of woodscrews remained unchanged during the nineteenth and early twentieth centuries, it is possible using the known discounts to calculate a hypothetical profit series. Assuming, for the purpose of argument, that ten gross of screws were listed at 100d., of which 25d. represented manufacturing costs, the effect on profits produced by changes in the discount rate has been computed and expressed as an index. In April 1853, for example, when the discount offered to wholesalers was 50 per cent, the selling price would have been 50d. of which 25d. would have been profit. On the assumption that input and manufacturing costs remained static, the gross margin index (Table 7.5) moves through a considerable range over the period 1853 to 1918 – from 0 to 133 – which suggests that comparatively small changes to the discount rate could have disproportionately significant consequences for the final profit figure. The marketing strategy pursued by the company, therefore, required considerable subtlety in its operation and involved ingenuity in its devising. The hypothetical figures employed in this exercise should not be taken as an accurate measure (the break-even point was probably nearer to a discount of 70 per cent rather than 75 per cent as shown in the Table). If the trends revealed by the gross margin index are related to the actual profits earned by Nettlefolds, a correlation does emerge (Table 7.3). A progressive reduction in the discount rate, for instance, from October 1888 to April 1893 brought higher profits, while an increase in the discount rate from January 1895 until February 1899 corresponded with a fall in the published profit figures. However, the pre-tax results revealed that profits rose from 1895 to 1899, which was most likely the product of expanding output (assuming no great changes in wage and manning levels, the cost of raw materials and the manner in which woodscrews were produced), the difference probably resulting from the siphoning of funds to maintain their secret reserve.

Given that the list price to the consumer remained unchanged from the 1850s until 1954, it is possible to calculate how the price charged to the wholesaler varied over the period to 1918 using three of the most popular sizes of woodscrew: $\frac{1}{2}'' \times 4$ ($8\frac{1}{2}$d. per gross), $\frac{3}{4}'' \times 6$ (1s. per gross) and $1'' \times 8$ (1s. 3d. per gross). In January 1854 with a discount of 45 per cent the factor would have been charged 4.8d., 6.6d. and 8.3d. respectively, a figure which included delivery, while in October 1898 when the discount rose to 70 per cent the price would have fallen to 2.6d., 3.6d. and 4.5d.

Although the original 'A' and 'B' machines constructed to the Sloane patents had been modified to run more efficiently, there was no substantial investment in new technology at Heath Street in the period to 1918. A stocktaking held during 1911 revealed that there were 863 'A' machines arranged in 14 rows with 23 kept as spares. Greater capacity was achieved in the main by increasing the size of the mills and the number of machines employed. In 1911, however, an engineer at the works, P.J. Worsley, designed the 'C11' thread-cutting machine which operated at twice the speed of the existing 'A' and 'B' versions. Despite the fact that it was not a particularly expensive item to build (though a minimum of 60, representing a double row of machines, had to be installed), very few were introduced until the late 1930s. In November 1911, for example, T.Z. Lloyd, the works manager, recorded that 'Mr Nettlefold over the telephone agreed to put in hand 45 more machines to fill up the row. The cost of each machine would be at least £20'. Why so few 'C11s' were installed remains unexplained, though reasonable levels of profit and the success of the company's marketing strategy, may have suggested to the directors that such technical innovation was unnecessary.

The main consumer of woodscrews, whether at home or abroad, was the building trade and, given that Nettlefolds had a virtual monopoly in the UK, its performance was to a large degree instrumental in determining the company's profitability. In the summer of 1897, when presenting the annual report the chairman, J.A. Kenrick, warned the shareholders,[33]

> They had already had two very satisfactory years, and had been able to show very considerable profits, whilst most trades in the neighbourhood had either been languishing or making no profits, so that it appeared hardly likely that they would continue to be as prosperous in the near future. There was another ground for this observation – viz, that when trade was bad builders were busy, and people seemed to think that was the time to invest money in houses, and when houses were being built screws must be used. It appeared to him, therefore, that the building trade would not be so prosperous in the coming year as it had been in the two preceding years.

Until the 1870s the building industry moved in step with the major business cycles of the British economy and, as a result, experienced peaks in the late 1830s, middle 1860s and in 1873–4 when Chamberlain wisely chose to leave the partnership.[34] The third quarter of the

59 An early display case by Nettlefolds for use at a trade exhibition. Contrast this with the more elaborate boards produced in the twentieth century (plate 117).
(*European Industrial Services*)

nineteenth century and the Edwardian period were the times when vast areas of suburban Britain were constructed. Substantial villas, semi-detached residences and streets of terraced houses were erected by the million in the major commercial and industrial cities. However, from 1874 to 1914 much of home investment, and house building in particular, had to take place when foreign investment was low. There was, for example, a small peak around 1889 and a major boom in building centred on 1900, which began in 1895 and continued until 1905. The latter is reflected in the profits earned by Nettlefolds which rose substantially in real terms from £102,344 in 1900 to £272,784 in 1904 but fell back to £207,642 in 1906. The building industry, as Kenrick had recognised, was subject to dramatic fluctuations, which in turn, encouraged Nettlefolds to seek stable markets overseas.

It may have been in an attempt to diversify (to reduce their reliance on the woodscrew) that Nettlefolds manufactured a steam launch in 1888. On show at the Cardiff Exhibition, the engines (manufactured in Smethwick) possessed a number of novelties: 'there are no crossheads or guides, these being replaced by a strong light linkage'.[35] The 25 horse-power engines could be adapted to drive fans, centrifugal pumps or any other machinery which demanded high revolutions. It seems, however, that this excursion into the field of steam-engine design did not prove successful as there are no records of the prototype being put into mass-production.

TRADE WAR: THE BRITISH SCREW CO.

The directors of Nettlefolds must have been considerably concerned to read in a copy of *Chambers's Journal* for 28 December 1889, discovered amongst their files, that,[36]

> The American Screw Company (of Providence, Rhode Island) perfected a machine by which the ordinary screws used by carpenters can be produced with much greater facility than by older methods; and a demonstration of the working of the new machine has recently taken place in London . . . The old-fashioned machine was shown to cut screws at the rate of seven per minute, while the new contrivance showered them forth at the rate of fifty-four in the same time. In the new method the blanks are made by feeding steel wire into a machine which turns them out rapidly, and furnishes them with a head, a slot for the screw-driver, and a point. They are now provided with a screw-thread, not by cutting in a lathe as at present, but by being passed between two fluted rollers. By this new method there is no waste of metal and no weakness caused by cutting, besides which the screws produced by the process possess several structural advantages.

Until the 1880s woodscrews were almost universally manufactured by cutting techniques but then, and the idea seems to have originated in America where it found most favour, engineers began to experiment with thread-rolling methods – using pressure applied through a die to squeeze the thread into the wire. There was much less wasted metal, no need to replace worn cutters at regular intervals and, ultimately, in the mid-twentieth century when the process was perfected, thread-rolling machines were capable of operating at much higher speeds than their screw-cutting predecessors. To borrow an analogy from the textile industry, as mule spinning was to screw cutting, so ring spinning was to thread rolling.

In August 1883 the Harvey Screw Co. of America wrote to Nettlefolds to offer them the British rights to a patent they had taken out on a method of thread rolling woodscrews.[37] J.A. Kenrick, the acting chairman, rejected the invitation, adding that they would only enter this market should a competitor establish himself. Nettlefolds did not entirely dismiss the development and when Charles Steer and Hugh Nettlefold visited Canada and the United States in September–October 1887 they examined a number of thread-rolling machines belonging to the Russell & Erwin Screw Co., New Britain, Connecticut, the American Screw Co. and to Mr. Harvey.[38] In their report they quoted Mr. Edwin G. Angell of the American Screw Co. as saying that 'the rolled screw was very much liked in America, and he was sure of regaining the monopoly of the trade'.[39] Steer and Nettlefold ordered two shares in his company and on their return to Britain started to experiment, building two machines for woodscrews and two for stove bolts.[40] As Mr. T. Ore recalled,[41]

> it was about forty years ago the experiments were started under the direction of Mr. Hugh Nettlefold to roll threads on screw blanks instead of cutting them, with which I had a great deal to do, a great deal of time and money was spent on these experiments, which, however, did not prove a sucess, except for metal threads. This work was particularly interesting to me . . . having to make a journey to Paris with a Smethwick screw cutting machine which had been converted to roll thread work for patent rights.

In November 1889 the chairman of Russell & Erwin wrote to Nettlefolds stating[42]

> that their makers in America had been trying the market with rolled screws but as far as they could learn without much success. They asked our opinion as to the probable chance of substituting in the general market a screw with a rolled thread for one with a cut thread.

The chairman reported that a reply had been sent, informing them that[43]

> we too had been working at rolled screws, not with the view of introducing them, but with the view of protecting ourselves should it prove that there was a demand for them in the future, that we had sent them a sample of a screw which we had made by our machinery exactly similar to the American Screw Co.'s screw. That we did not think that the market would take kindly to a screw and that as far as we could learn the exhibit in Paris had not created much sensation, but that if the American Screw Co. succeeded in creating a demand we could supply it without in any way infringing the American Screw Co.'s patents.

Despite this apparent calmness, Nettlefolds were, in fact, concerned about the possible impact of a rolled-thread woodscrew imported from the United States. They entered into negotiations to purchase the British rights to the patents belonging to the American Screw Co., which were taken out between 1887 and 1892 by Charles D. Rogers (1827–1903), the company's mechanical engineer. Edwin G. Angell,[44] their president, who represented them, suggested that if a trading agreement could not be reached, 'he was ready to establish small works for making screws by the rolling process in England, France and Germany'.[45] After protracted discussions, Nettlefolds offered £50,000 towards the £100,000 being asked for the UK patents,[46] and in June 1891 Angell wrote to them to say that since no agreement could be reached, factories would be constructed in England and Germany.[47] Nettlefolds resolved to resist this competition and 'also to carry the war into the United States market should Mr. Angell be so unwise as to attack us'.[48]

Edwin G. Angell used the threat of the thread-rolled woodscrew to put pressure on Nettlefolds. He hoped to re-negotiate the trade agreement which the two companies had concluded in January 1881 whereby Nettlefolds were to sell no more than 5,000 gross of screws per week to Canada providing that the Canada Screw Co. (based at Hamilton, and the main producer in that country) gave them 'preference for any screw and screw-rods the Canada Screw Factory may wish to purchase'.[49] In addition, neither the Canada Screw Co. nor the American Screw Co. were to sell screws in any of the following countries: Norway, Sweden, Germany, Britain, Holland, Denmark, Belgium and France. Second-quality screws were only to be exported to South America and Mexico. Elsewhere – those European nations upon whom no embargo had been placed, together with Africa, Asia, Australia and New Zealand – the American and Canada Screw Co.'s were to sell at Nettlefolds' prices and conditions.[50] However, by October 1882 the American Screw Co. had become disenchanted with the agreement, particularly with the clause by which they were obliged to give Nettlefolds preference for all screw-rod orders.[51] For their part, Nettlefolds asked that they be permitted to export 7,000 rather than 5,000 gross screws per week. As no new terms seem to have been reached, it appears that the initial cartel of 1881 stood.

It was with a sense of impending battle that the *Practical Engineer* announced that 'an industry of an important character is about to be introduced into Leeds'.[52] This city was selected as being a centre of manufacturing with good communications at some distance from Smethwick, and a site, formerly occupied by the Old Perseverance Ironworks in Kirkstall Road, was acquired. Charles D. Rogers designed the factory, though the plans were revised to conform with local by-laws by Thomas Ambler (1838–1920), the eminent Leeds architect.[53] The works, 344 ft long and 80 ft wide, with a frontage on the Kirkstall Road of 100 ft accommodating the offices, was of two storeys, in contrast to the mills at Heath Street.

The ground floor contained cleaning and heading machines, and the first floor housed those for cutting screws and finishing their

60 The British Screw Co.'s mill under construction at Leeds in 1892.
(*Sela Fasteners*)

heads, together with the packing rooms. A clerestory roof provided clear daylight by which finished screws could be inspected.[54] Its American origin, and the need to erect the factory as quickly as possible, led to a number of architectural novelties. There was a flat gravel roof (provided by a contractor from Providence because this was found to be cheaper, even with the additional transport costs, than employing a local firm), and primitive system of air-conditioning by Sturtevant of Boston, whereby fresh air was drawn through coils and heated, then passed through longitudinal ducts in the walls and then discharged through flues. In warm weather the air was circulated without heating. Electric light, through 50 arc and 500 incandescent lamps, was installed and the provision of flushing lavatories, was also something of a rarity.[55] A siding from the Great Northern Railway's main line at Holbeck Station was laid to the site not simply for the despatch of finished screws but for the construction of the buildings because the materials, machinery and castings were all shipped from America in 204 freight cars. The plant had, in fact, been stripped from the Bay State Mill, Providence, Rhode Island, a factory that had been standing idle for about two years,[56] a situation which resulted not from any lags in technical efficiency, but from surplus capacity in the United States market.

The speed with which the project was undertaken impressed Edward Nettlefold who surreptitiously visited the site in April 1892.[57]

61 The British Screw Co. after it had been acquired by Nettlefolds. The offices fronted Kirkstall Road. Behind, the heading machines and warehouse were on the ground floor and the worming machines on the first floor, lit by a clerestory roof. (*European Industrial Services*)

62 The first-floor of the Leeds factory during the nineteen-twenties. The timber floor and roof ultimately contributed to its destruction by fire in 1948.
(*Sela Fasteners*)

It was estimated that 100–150 workers, chiefly women and girls, would be employed initially, but that expansion would bring these numbers up to 500–600.[58] Output was planned at around 10,000 gross per day and 'every description of metal screw in the market will be turned out, including engineers' screws up to 3 in. in length, rivets, gate and shutter hooks and eyes, pointer hooks and machinery, etc.'.[59]

From 1892, when the works, called the British Screw Co. Ltd., came into operation, until October 1898, when they were finally taken over by Nettlefolds, a fierce price-cutting war was fought. Nettlefolds even went so far as to challenge the Americans' patents (those taken out by Harvey and C.D. Rogers) in the courts, but failed to undermine their validity. In 1898 a newspaper report concluded that,[60]

> Some years of practical test have now confirmed their commercial value, so that at present more than one-half of the screw output of the company consists of screws made by the swaging or forging process [that is thread rolling], whereby a larger product of better quality is produced at a less cost than can be secured by the old cutting process.

Without records detailing the specification of the machines installed at Leeds, it is impossible to confirm this statement. In view of the failure of other manufacturers, both in England and America, to devise adequate thread-rolling techniques until the mid-twentieth century, it appears that this may have been an exaggeration and that Angell simply employed the threat of superior thread-rolling methods as a bargaining lever.

In January 1895, with some patriotic bias, the *American Manufacturer* observed that[61]

> Nettlefolds Ltd, of Birmingham, announced on New Year's day, an increase of 5 per cent in the discount from list prices of iron woodscrews. This is equal to a reduction on the net price of 10 to 15 per cent, and may be regarded as a further attempt . . . to crush the American Screw Company . . . You will remember that some time ago Nettlefolds announced a big reduction as soon as the new Leeds works got into operation, and this is clearly a further attempt to make their trade profitless. Nettlefolds are the last people in the world to reduce prices unless compelled by competition from outside sources.

The effective breaking of their monopoly had compelled Nettlefolds 'to reduce their home prices by 23 per cent, and their export prices 28 per cent. This, however, was not successful in undermining the new competitors, and Messrs. Nettlefolds, Limited, have made a further reduction of 15 per cent on the home trade and 18 per cent on the export trade'.[62] The reductions led the *Leeds Mercury* to speculate that,[63]

> this may give some idea of what their profits must have been until they encountered a healthy opposition, of which the consumer is now reaping the benefit. The British Screw Company . . . with all the reductions, can still manufacture at a fair profit, and so plentiful is work that machinery is still being laid down daily. In fact it is in contemplation to double the size of the works in Kirkstall Road, and if this is done, it will mean employment for near a 1,000 hands.

Despite these brave words, it proved to be a tough battle to disturb the hold Nettlefolds had established over the British market, and in August 1895 Charles L. Rogers, son of C.D. Rogers, visited the Leeds factory to institute economies and improve efficiency still further. Amongst his instructions were:[64]

> All orders for special goods should be avoided as far as practical, they are always attended with a loss of money . . .
> There are too many men employed in out of the way places

without proper oversight . . .

Savings easily made – a reduction in waste to 6% will make a saving of $9,600 per year. 10% increase of product by piece work,

not estimated. Interest on over stock of material, etc. $500 to $8,000. Cut off the losses on special work, this will make a saving of $100 to $1,000.

In an advertisement in *The Ironmonger* addressed to the 'Principal Railway companies', the British Screw Co. set out to challenge Nettlefolds in every department. There they announced their ability to manufacture 'all lengths and diameters of flat, round and raised head iron and brass screws, blued, japanned, electroplated, etc., also Whitworth standard machine screws, flat, round, and raised head iron and brass . . . stone screws, spout bolts, tapped nuts, tyre bolts, rivets, etc.'[65] They had won contracts to supply the Admiralty and India Office. A similar advertisement was authorised for insertion in the *Australian Ironmonger* in August 1896, the Colonies being of particular importance for exports of Nettlefolds' screws.[66]

The sale of the British Screw Co. to Nettlefolds seems not, in fact, to have been determined by the failure of the Leeds factory but by the financial crisis experienced by its parent, the American Screw Co. A special committee appointed to investigate its losses, reported in March 1898 that the deficit of $230,437 for 1897 was primarily caused by a depression in the screw industry, which in turn had forced them to cut prices.[67] The English factory had been unable to meet rising demand and in their current predicament it was considered unwise to invest valuable reserves to expand its output. Two new directors were elected to the board and, as part of their scheme to restore financial stability to the company, it was argued that 'friendly relations' should be re-established with their competitors, enabling them to regulate production and secure fair prices.[68] Clearly this could only be achieved if they sold the British Screw Co. and negotiated trade agreements with Nettlefolds Ltd. Initially, however, the American Screw Co. attempted to interest Arthur Keen in the business. Whilst visiting the United States to research the latest techniques of steelmaking, Keen discussed terms for its acquisition by the Patent Nut & Bolt Co.[69] It was proposed, with the board's approval, that three-fourths of the British Screw Co.'s capital of £100,000 be obtained for $75,000, Arthur Keen was to become its new chairman, and the PNB were to finance any extensions required. Negotiations continued throughout August,[70] but on 6 October, for reasons which were not recorded in the minute books, Keen decided not to effect the purchase but to establish his own screw-making works from scratch.[71] At the time, the PNB had made the question of setting up their own steelworks a priority so that this scheme would have had first call on any funds available for investment, particularly as the Leeds factory required further investment to increase its capacity.

The British Screw Co. was then offered to Nettlefolds who, being anxious to remove their only major competitor in the UK, concluded terms for its acquisition in October 1898.[72] Nettlefolds had recorded a pre-tax profit of £121,173 in June 1898[73] and having created a secret reserve in excess of £50,000 in 1894,[74] paying dividends of 5s. on the 21,000 preference shares of £10 and 10s. on the 42,000 ordinary shares of £10 together with a 10s. bonus on the latter, were in a sufficiently buoyant financial situation to effect the transaction. The sale price is not known, though in 1900 the factory together with stocks was valued at £165,894, which comprised: land £7,573, buildings £21,058, engines and shafting £3,674, boilers £3,173, machinery £76,534, stock of duplicate parts £27,458 and stock of finished goods £26,424.[75] Nettlefolds decided, however, that the Leeds factory should continue to operate under the style, British Screw Co., and its products should continue to be sold under that name, though any thread-rolling machines installed by the Americans were withdrawn from operation while the American screw-cutting machines remained for many years. A *History* of the group, including all its constituent parts, compiled around 1925, deliberately omitted any reference to the Leeds factory.[76] It was said that employees working there never guessed that they were part of the same organisation as Nettlefolds. In this way GKN were able to preserve the illusion of competition long after Nettlefolds had in fact restored their monopoly of the UK woodscrew market.

The sale of the Leeds factory by the American Screw Co. effectively ended all experiment with thread-rolling techniques for woodscrew manufacture in Britain until the mid-twentieth century. The problem lay with the difficulty of designing a die that would provide a gimlet point. There was no difficulty in rolling the thread (machine screws which were blunt-ended were extensively rolled from the 1920s) but engineers were defeated in providing a taper and point without subjecting the screw to an extra operation, despite Angell's confidence in 1887 that this could be achieved.[77] In addition, the consumer objected to having a shank of smaller diameter to the threaded portion, this then being an unavoidable consequence of the manufacturing process unless the thread were carried up to the head.[78] The quality of the thread produced by cutting was superior, being sharper and cleaner to the eye, while rolling techniques demanded a higher quality, and more expensive type of wire. The malleable nature of wire required in thread rolling may well have produced a thread of superior strength to the cut variety, though the head and shank (the most vulnerable parts) would have been stronger in the traditional woodscrew made from a coarser, less refined steel. In the 1880s acid Bessemer steel was selected for woodscrew manufacture because the air blast introduced nitrogen which improved the free-cutting quality of the metal, though the comparatively high levels of phosphorus reduced its malleability and made it unsuitable for thread rolling.

Only when steel was produced by the open hearth method could this problem be overcome. Even the American Screw Co. abandoned experiments with thread-rolled woodscrews and during the inter-war period it and its principal domestic competitor, the Rockford Screw Co. of Illinois, both exclusively employed cutting machines to mass-produce woodscrews.

The published figures produced by the British Screw Co. show that the works declined in profitability once it became a subsidiary. The profits of over £9,000 earned in 1900 and 1901 appear never to have

Table 7.6 Profits earned by the British Screw Co. 1900–28

Year	£	Adjusted £
12 months to 31 March 1901	9941	14619
	9481	12641
15 months to 30 June 1902	15235	21764
12 months to 30 June 1903	8354	12107
1904	8130	11783
1905	5209	7441
1906	5952	8267
1907	300	390
1908	2355	2944
1909	365	500
1910	862	1165
1911	5142	6592
1912	2852	3565
1913	2256	2654
1914	1071	1260
1915	3369	3963
1916	1339	1240
1917	3701	2722
1918	6738	3764
1919	(981)	(511)
1920	(2298)	(1116)
1921	4231	(1686)
1922	(4077)	(2630)
1923	(102)	(78)
1924	1566	1214
1925	492	354
1926	896	659
1927	978	776
1928	(1769)	(1450)

Figures in brackets indicate a loss.

Source: BRL, 298/45 British Screw Co. Annual Accounts 1898–1922; 298/46 Annual Accounts 1923–1928. Figures adjusted by the Sauerbeck-*Statist* index, 1867–77 = 100.

been attained in the subsequent thirty years. GKN were presumably content to keep the factory in operation provided that it returned a small surplus, while concentrating their energies and investment into its much larger parent at Heath Street.

THE CASTLE WORKS, ROGERSTONE

As discussed above, the purchase by Nettlefolds of the Manchester Steel Screw Co. was prompted by a desire to discover more about steel technology, and following this, the board approved an expenditure of £15,000 for a steel-making plant.[79] The project appears to have foundered, for in January 1883 a sum not exceeding £6,000 was authorised for 'the erection of necessary plant for making steel on the Griffiths & Clapps Patent Fixed Steel Converters'.[80] In June 1883, Edward Steer reported that the estimate to put down a steelworks with a capacity of 300 tons per week amounted to £10,000. The board resolved to purchase a smaller installation costing at most £3,000 in order to test the process.[81] Their anxiety and reluctance to commit themselves to steel was understandable. The transition was both extensive and costly. The overwhelming bulk of their products were made from wrought iron rolled into rod and then drawn into wire. That steel possessed superior characteristics was undeniable (it was resistant to wear and had greater tensile strength) and its progressive substitution throughout all branches of engineering suggested that the problem could not be ignored.

In April 1884 Edward Steer announced that the steel plant, erected at the Castle Works, near Wellington, was in operation and that samples of the metal produced had proved to be 'soft and easily worked'.[82] However, to reduce the high running costs, it was necessary to put down another boiler and install a second Bessemer converter.[83] It soon became clear that a steelworks could be operated effectively only if it were located closer to the source of supply of pig iron and constructed on a larger scale.[84] Accordingly, the decision was taken to find a site in South Wales to which the plant at Hadley Castle could be moved.[85] Edward Steer was entrusted with the task of visiting the area[86] and in the meantime the board estimated that it would cost them £42,452 to dismantle the plant and machinery in Shropshire and transfer it to South Wales.[87] By January 1886, draft leases for the Rogerstone and Tydu properties had been prepared, subject to negotiations with the Great Western Railway. In February Benjamin Talbot and his son, Benjamin Talbot Junior, inventor of the continuous method of steelmaking (p. 334), agreed to buy the Castle Ironworks from Nettlefolds for £13,000, which disposed of the need to retain the nearby Ketley collieries, so they resolved to terminate the lease with the Duke of Sutherland.[88] Upon further examination it was discovered, nevertheless, that their lease did not expire until Lady Day 1888 and consequently they decided to continue to operate the mines until then.[89]

Edward Steer moved to Rogerstone (a house being built for him there with a limit of £2,000) to take charge of the construction of the steelworks[90] and the laying down of the rolling mills nearby at Tydu. Just as the Ketley Collieries had supplied Hadley Castle, so they considered buying a small pit to serve the new South Wales works.[91] The acquisition fell through and they subsequently also abandoned the notion of purchasing a larger colliery.[92]

In fact, Nettlefolds never diversified again into coal, this being part of the logic for their merger with Guest, Keen and Co. in 1902. At Rogerstone Nettlefolds erected their acid Bessemer plant and rolling mills, while the hoop mill was set up at Tydu.[93] Pig iron was brought from nearby ironworks on a tender basis.[94] The transfer seems to have been successful: in November 1889 it was agreed to extend the hoop mill at a cost of no more than £5,000,[95] and in 1905 it was decided to transfer the H.P. Wire Nail Works (originally situated at Imperial Mills, Cranford Street) to the Rogerstone site, and they were linked to the main Castle Works by a private railway.[96] Making nails, staples, panel pins, rings and hooks they consumed steel rod which was not of sufficient quality to be drawn for woodscrews.[97] In view of the transport costs, it was rational to site the nailworks beside the steelworks and rolling mills, rather than at Smethwick. With all this activity, the Rogerstone House Property and Investment Co. Ltd. erected a large number of workmen's cottages forming James Street, Charles Street and Edwin Street, together with shops and the Rogerstone Hotel all in close proximity to the works.[98]

After the transfer of the Castle Works from Wellington to Rogerstone, the manufacturing process for steel woodscrews was as follows: pig iron was purchased from various South Wales ironworks; this was converted into steel ingots, rolled into billets and then to wire rod and hoops at Rogerstone; these were then transported by rail to Birmingham, where the rod was drawn into wire either at Imperial Mills, Heath Street, or the two wire works in Berkeley Street and Princip Street. In 1901 the last two were closed and Imperial Mills, Coverack Road, Newport was opened. Situated a few miles from Rogerstone on the River Usk with a wharfage for sea-borne traffic, they also had a direct connection with the GWR, so that wire rod could be sent by freight train direct from Rogerstone to be drawn into wire for screws, nails, bolts, rivets, chains, netting and wheel spokes at Newport before being despatched to Birmingham.[99]

CHANGES IN MANAGEMENT

Frederick Nettlefold (1835–1913), who succeeded J.H. Nettlefold as

63   (left) Charles Steer
(1849–1906), director of
Nettlefolds from 1882, and
of GKN from 1902 to
1906.

64   (right) Edward Steer
(1851–1927), director of
Nettlefolds from 1882, and
of GKN from 1902 to
1927, the last seven years
as chairman.
(*Glamorgan Record Office*)

chairman in 1881, an appointment he held until 1891, was also a
talented leader but he became increasingly involved in the affairs of
Samuel Courtauld & Co. (a connection arising from his marriage to
Mary Warren, a member of the Courtauld family).[100] In 1904 Frederick
Nettlefold was a prime mover in a major re-organisation which
resulted in his appointment as chairman of Courtaulds, a post he
retained until his death in 1913 when his son, F.J. Nettlefold (1867-
1949), succeeded him in that office.[101]

In June 1882 three new directors were appointed at Nettlefolds:
John Arthur Kenrick (1829–1926), whose son John Archibald Kenrick
(1869–1933) subsequently married Grace Nettlefold, a daughter of E.J.
Nettlefold, and the brothers, Charles Steer (1849–1906) and Edward
Steer (1851–1927).[102] The last two were the sons of Charles Steer
(1824–58) who in May 1848 had married Martha Sanderson Nettlefold,
the eldest sister of Edward, John and Frederick Nettlefold.[103] Edward
Steer, who ran operations at Rogerstone, joined the GKN board on its
formation, and later served as its chairman from 1920 to 1927. Charles
Steer Junior, who had joined the Nettlefold board in June 1882, also
became a director of GKN on its formation, retaining the post until his
death.[104]

Kenrick was chairman of Archibald Kenrick & Sons Ltd., the
hollow-ware manufacturers based in West Bromwich, and like the
Nettlefolds was a Unitarian.[105] He, in common with Joseph Chamberlain, had been educated at University College School and owed his

65 (left) Hugh Nettlefold (1858–93), director of Nettlefolds to 1893. (*European Industrial Services*)

66 (right) Godfrey Nettlefold (1874–1918), director of GKN from 1909 until 1918. (*European Industrial Services*)

appointment not simply to this friendship with the Nettlefolds, but to a considerable experience of business. J.A. Kenrick succeeded Frederick Nettlefold as chairman and held the post until the merger with Guest, Keen & Co. in 1902 but in view of his other interests (he was also on the board of Lloyds Bank, the Union Rolling Stock Co. and chairman of William Elliott & Sons Ltd.),[106] he must have assumed something of a non-executive role.

Edward Nettlefold (1856–1909) served as the deputy chairman of Nettlefolds from 1891 until 1902 when he joined the GKN board, holding this directorship until his death. Born in Stoke Newington, he had attended Mr. Case's non-conformist school at Hampstead before taking a B.A. at Cambridge in 1879 shortly after Oxbridge had been opened to dissenters.[107] Joining the family business, Edward Nettlefold was chiefly concerned with the management of the Heath Street mills, while his outside interests included directorships of the LNWR, Lloyds Bank, Birmingham Canal Navigations, and the North British and Mercantile Insurance Co., and membership of the Tariff Commission.[108] He was succeeded on the GKN board in 1909 by Godfrey Nettlefold (1874–1918), who held the directorship until his death.[109] Hugh Nettlefold (1858–93), second son of Edward John Nettlefold, had been in charge of the engineering and machinery departments at Heath Street, and became a director in June 1891,[110] but died shortly afterwards.[111] He had been described as 'a very good engineer, a man of fine appearance, and a perfect gentleman with a charming personality'.[112] Shortly after his appointment as managing director of the Engineering Department of Nettlefolds, he decided to seek election to the Smethwick Local Board, of which Arthur Keen was chairman. Accordingly, Hugh Nettlefold called upon Keen at the London Works to ask his advice on how to win a seat. Keen suggested that he return to the Heath Street Works to secure the support of a member (name unknown) of his own staff who was one of the most popular men in Smethwick and a fine platform speaker. This he duly did and was elected to the board with a sweeping majority.

The other directors during Nettlefolds Ltd.'s twenty years of independent existence were S.Z. Lloyd (1843–1914), who had joined the board after the acquisition of Lloyd & Harrison; Alfred Field (d. 1884), a wholesaler and principal promoter of the Birmingham Screw Co.; Thomas Whitfield Gladstone, who had married Frances Jane Nettlefold in 1881 and died in office in January 1886; Joseph Beattie and G.E. Wilson.

At about the time of the flotation, Reginald Parker (1846–1911) was appointed the chief clerk and in time became the company secretary of Nettlefolds Ltd. He subsequently served as a director of GKN from its formation in 1902 until his retirement in 1906 (p. 366).

67   Reginald Parker (1846–1911), a director of GKN from 1902 to 1906, formerly company secretary and director of Nettlefolds. (*European Industrial Services*)

CONDITIONS OF EMPLOYMENT

While the pieceworker making screws by hand could choose his own hours, the application of steam-powered machinery demanded that employees work according to a regular schedule. Hours in the mills during the period of Nettlefolds' ownership were 7 a.m. to 6 p.m. with thirty minutes for breakfast and an hour for dinner,[113] though under GKN these were revised to 6 a.m. to 5 p.m. with breakfast being taken between 8.30 a.m. and 9 a.m. and dinner from 1 to 2 p.m.[114] In the 1860s, when Nettlefold & Chamberlain were pressing hard to break into the French market, the hours had been from 6 a.m. to 6 p.m. (8 a.m. to 7 p.m. in the warehouse).[115] Office hours were from 9 a.m. to 5 p.m. though staff were expected to remain until the day's tasks were completed. In the warehouse, workers began at 9 a.m. and finished at 6 p.m., except on Saturdays when they departed at 2 p.m. Holidays were limited to two days at Christmas, two-and-a-half days at Easter, one day at Whitsun and a further day for a work's outing (usually a short train journey to Clent, Malvern or Warwick) which included a bonus of two shillings. Wages for men started at eighteen shillings per week and rose by two shillings each year to a maximum of thirty shillings, while females' wages rose from five shillings to ten shillings.

A high proportion of the workforce lived locally in the terraced streets which surrounded the works on three sides, though, unlike some employers in the North of England, they did not build houses themselves. It was not surprising, therefore, that generations of the same families joined Nettlefolds, intensifying the sense of community within the company, nicknamed 'Netts' within the locality. In the St. George's Mill, among the many families who produced employees over the years were the Fords, Bushbys, Smallwoods, Lowes and the Goodwins.[116] In this respect Nettlefolds, long after it had become part of the GKN group, maintained a powerful loyalty among its substantial workforce and was akin to the larger cotton mills of Lancashire which also inspired considerable settlements of brick terraced houses. This close connection between workplace, family and habitation may also have resulted in a certain exclusiveness and resistance to change from outside.

In common with the more paternalistic among Victorian managers, Nettlefolds provided facilities for recreation among their employees. The first sports ground was subsequently the site of St. Cuthbert's Church in Heath Street.[117] In 1894 they acquired a considerable tract of land off Thimble Mill Lane for cricket and football pitches, tennis courts, a bowling green and a fishing pool, which were opened in the spring of 1896 under the supervision of Charles Steer.[118] In addition, in 1895 a recreation ground (comprising a games field, tennis courts and bowling green) had been laid out at King's Norton adjacent to the works. Joseph Chamberlain had built an Institute in Winson Green which served as a schoolroom for the youngest employees and as a

68 The recreation grounds at King's Norton, opened in the spring of 1896. Games of tennis, bowls and cricket are all in evidence, though there appear to be no women present.
(*European Industrial Services*)

meeting place for their elders, though it was also used for political assemblies by its founder.[119]

Whilst there were few industrial disputes at the various fastener mills in Smethwick belonging to GKN, they were not immune from the wave of strikes which spread through the Midlands engineering industry in the spring of 1913. A dispute at the Stour Valley Works resulted in GKN granting an advance of 2s. to the men and offering a minimum wage of 12s. a week for women over twenty-one. Although the works manager reported that many of the employees at Heath Street were 'very restless', the offer of from 6d. to 1s. for women and 2s. for men prevented the outbreak of a strike.[120]

COMPETITION FROM OVERSEAS AND PROTECTIONISM

As early as 1881, J.H. Nettlefold reported 'that he had reason to believe the company's trade was being interfered with by foreign and other competitors' and to combat this the discount on iron wood-screws was increased from 65 per cent to 75 per cent.[121] Their chief rivals were from the United States and Germany. The battle that ensued with the American Screw Co. has already been discussed and their approach to the Germans was conciliatory; the board minutes recall 'that the chairman be empowered to communicate with the German Screw manufacturers offering, if invited, to attend a meeting of the leading makers in order to assist them to form a configuration with the object of raising the price of German screws'. So wary were they of German competition that a plan to purchase Messrs. Lloyd Brothers & Co., screw and rivet makers, was postponed.[122] Soon afterwards they concluded[123]

> it is not desirable at present to take vigorous action to compete with the German makers in Germany, but that it is desirable to meet opposition in their neutral markets and that Mr. E. Nettlefold should go to Copenhagen to ascertain what inroads in that market are being made by the German makers.

His visit revealed that Danish wholesalers would willingly purchase their screws so long as they matched the Germans' lower prices.[124] Concern about the rise of this rival was such that Mr. Sandland, a clerk, was despatched to the chief towns of Norway, Sweden and Russia 'to gain all possible information with regard to German competition in these countries'.[125]

Attempts were made to cut costs at source and this included persistent complaint to the LNWR about freight rates.[126] Screws were charged from two to four times as much as nails according to their value and this, argued Edward Steer, was unfair if Nettlefolds were

69 Labels produced by German screwmakers for use in Britain designed to resemble those of their competitor Nettlefolds. (*European Industrial Services*)

SPECIMENS OF LABELS USED BY GERMAN SCREW MAKERS.

LABEL USED ON I GROSS PACKETS.

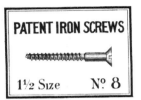

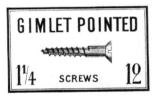

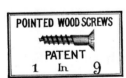

CASING LABEL USED ON PACKETS CONTAINING SIX 1 GROSS PACKETS WRAPPED UP TOGETHER.

prepared to accept the insurance risks.[127] The matter had become important as they[128]

> now suffered severely from foreign competition, the Germans taking a considerable number of export orders, being greatly assisted by the cheapness of their freights to port and it was therefore manifestly the interest of English railways to assist us to keep our trade.

Their anxiety rose when news reached them of German exports reaching the Australian market. To win orders, they were able to take advantage of Australian resentment at greater rates of discount being offered by Nettlefolds for shipments to India.[129] German manufacturers had already obtained a considerable foothold in the Indian market because Nettlefolds had been slow to respond with reductions, so it was decided to act immediately in the case of Australia and increase the discount there from 70 per cent to 75 per cent, which, in turn, 'would render it advisable to take a similar step for South America where the Germans are already well established and South Africa, leaving 70 per cent in force for the UK and Canada'.[130]

A decline in the home trade during 1884 was partly attributed to a general business recession but also resulted from an increasing level of imports from Germany[131] as they were 'continually getting fresh customers in the United Kingdom'. They considered increasing the discount on iron woodscrews from 70 per cent to 75 per cent. The question was deferred, partly because they believed that a new screw made by a 'new patent rolled process' might prove cheaper than German imports, but also because they were close to the break-even point.[132] In February 1886, when a further increase in the discount became unavoidable, a ten per cent reduction in wages had to be imposed on the Heath Street mills. This enabled Nettlefolds to sell best quality screws with a discount of 75 per cent, plain label screws at $77\frac{1}{2}$ per cent and those delivered free to Germany, with their import duty paid, would carry a discount of 68 per cent.[133]

In May 1886, meetings were held with their German opposition in an attempt to establish a cartel.[134] The discussions continued until June 1888 when Edward Steer succeeded in arranging a meeting of French, Belgian and German makers in Brussels, at which an experimental International Union had been set up for a year. The parties agreed to sell at the English price ($72\frac{1}{2}$ per cent discount), and a system of fines was arranged for those who transgressed this limit.[135]

The International Woodscrew Union remained a body of major importance for the regulation of the industry and Nettlefolds, as the largest single manufacturer, played a leading part in its organisation, Godfrey Nettlefold being elected president in 1911. Meetings were arranged on average twice a year in the period to 1914, often being held at the Grand Hotel in Brussels. In essence members agreed not to

Manchester Guardian, Leeds Mercury, Scotsman, Glasgow Herald, Ironmonger, and *Hardware,* pp. 4–5.

3. Ibid., 30 April 1880, p. 12.
4. Ibid., 30 April 1880, p. 12; *Nettlefolds Limited, Prospectus* (1880), p. 2; *Nettlefolds Limited, Memorandum and Articles of Association,* p. 27.
5. Ibid., 30 April 1880, p. 14.
6. Ibid., p. 15.
7. Ibid., p. 9; *Lloyd & Harrison, Stourport, Sample Card, Patent Pointed Wood Screws.*
8. Ibid., p. 13.
9. Plan, Guest Keen & Nettlefolds, St George's Works, Heath Street Works and Imperial Mills, 5 January, 1922.
10. Ordnance Survey, Sheet XIII 3.25, 10.5 feet to One Mile (1888).
11. *Slater's Directory of Manchester* (1879), p. 254.
12. *Slater's Directory of Manchester* (1874), first mention of the company, p. 149.
13. Nettlefolds Ltd., Minute Book, 4 January 1881, p. 84.
14. Ibid., 7 June 1881, p. 100.
15. Ibid.
16. Ibid., 30 April 1880, p. 9.
17. Humphrey Lloyd, *The Quaker Lloyds in the Industrial Revolution,* London (1975), pp. 255–60.
18. Nettlefolds Ltd., Minute Book, 7 June 1881, pp. 99–100.
19. Ibid., 7 December 1880, p. 80.
20. Ibid., 7 June 1881, p. 107.
21. *PIME,* Vol. 33 (1882), Obituary, pp. 9–10; *DBB,* Vol. 4, London (1985), J.H. Nettlefold, pp. 428–31.
22. BRL, Obituary Notices Birmingham & District 1864–1904, collected by E.H. Osborne, *Birmingham Post,* 24 November 1881, p. 19.
23. Nettlefolds Ltd., Minute Book, 6 December 1881, p. 121.
24. *PIME* op. cit., p. 10.
25. BRL, Obituary Notices, *Post,* p. 192.
26. Mr Hughes, 'Recollections', p. 2.
27. Nettlefolds Ltd., Minute Book, 21 December 1881, p. 127.
28. Saul, *Great Depression,* p. 13.
29. Ibid., p. 37.
30. Ibid., p. 39.
31. Works Manager's Common Place Book 1910–1917, 22 November 1910, item 302.
32. 'Woodscrew Discounts from 1853' (typescript, May 1954).
33. Sela Fasteners, press cuttings 'Public Company Meetings'.
34. R. Church (Editor), *The Dynamics of Victorian Business,* London (1980), E.W. Cooney, 'The Building Industry', p. 147; E.W. Cooney, *EcHR,* Vol. XIII (1960–61), 'Long Waves in Building in the British Economy in the Nineteenth Century', pp. 262–70.
35. *The Engineer,* Vol. LXVI, 26 October 1888, p. 349.
36. *Chambers's Journal of Popular Literature, Science, and Art,* Vol. VI, No. 313, 28 December 1889, p. 829.
37. Nettlefolds Ltd., Minute Book, 22 August 1883, p. 245.
38. *Abstract of Reports of the Visit of Messrs. C. Steer and H. Nettlefold to Canada and the United States* (1887), pp. 5–7.
39. Ibid., p. 6.

40. Mr. Thomas, Burns, 'Recollections', p. 5.
41. Mr. T. Ore, 'Recollections', p. 1.
42. Ibid., 5 November 1889, p. 159.
43. Ibid.
44. Ibid., 6 January 1891, p. 217.
45. Ibid.
46. Ibid., 16 April 1891, p. 232.
47. Ibid., 22 June 1891, p. 244.
48. Ibid.
49. Ibid., 2 November 1880, p. 76; 4 January 1881, p. 83.
50. Ibid., p. 76.
51. Ibid., 3 October 1882, p. 183.
52. *Practical Engineer*, 'A New Industry for Leeds', 10 July 1891.
53. Edgar Jones, *Industrial Architecture in Britain 1750–1939*, London (1985), p. 164.
54. *Practical Engineer*, 'New Industry', 10 July 1891.
55. *The News*, Providence, 12 August 1892, Willard I. Lancing, 'An American Innovation'; *The Illustrated Carpenter and Builder*, 21 October 1892, pp. 293–4.
56. George Barton, 'A Bit of Yorkshire Visited' (typescript history of the British Screw Co.), p. 3.
57. Nettlefolds Ltd., Directors Minute Book, 13 April 1892, p. 202.
58. *Illustrated Carpenter*, p. 293.
59. Ibid., p. 294.
60. *Evening Telegram*, Providence, 10 March 1898, 'American Screw Co. not Mismanaged'.
61. *American Manufacturer*, 18 January 1895, 'Our English Letter'.
62. *Industries and Iron*, London, 25 January 1895.
63. *Leeds Mercury*, 19 January 1895, 'The Screw Trade in Leeds'.
64. Sela Fasteners, Typescript dated 21 August 1895, pp. 1–7.
65. *The Ironmonger*, 30 March 1895, p. 61.
66. Sela Fasteners, Advertisement with handwritten note.
67. *Evening Telegram*, Providence, 10 March 1898, 'American Screw Co. not Mismanaged'.
68. Sela Fasteners, Newspaper cutting 'American Screw Stockholders Received Committee's Report', March 1848.
69. PNB & Co., Minute Book No. 7, November 1897 – July 1900, 25 July 1898, it. 6653.
70. Ibid., 9 August 1898, it. 6661; 30 August 1898, it. 6670.
71. Ibid., 6 October 1899, it. 6683.
72. Details of the negotiations are unknown as Nettlefolds Ltd. Minute Books have been lost for the period 1894–1902.
73. *Birmingham Daily Post*, 23 June 1898.
74. Nettlefolds Ltd., Directors Minute Book, op. cit., 1 August 1893, p. 375; Nettlefolds Ltd., General Meeting Minute Book 1880–1902, 25 September 1894, p. 50.
75. BRL, 298/45 British Screw Co. Annual Accounts 1898–1922, March 1900.
76. *Guest, Keen & Nettlefolds Ltd., An Outline History of this Group of Companies* (c. 1925), lists of subsidiaries and factories, pp. 8–14.
77. *Abstract of Reports of the Visit of Messrs. C. Steer and H. Nettlefold to Canada and the United States* (1887), p. 6.
78. Dickinson *TNS* (1941–42), p. 87.

79. Nettlefolds Ltd., Minute Book, 1 March 1881, p. 88.
80. Ibid., 2 January 1883, p. 198.
81. Ibid., 5 June 1883, p. 221.
82. Ibid., 1 April 1884, p. 290.
83. Ibid., 27 May 1884, p. 295.
84. Ibid., 7 April 1885, p. 343.
85. Ibid., 5 May 1885, p. 346.
86. Ibid., 2 June 1885, p. 352.
87. Ibid., 5 August 1885, pp. 359–60.
88. Ibid., 2 February 1886, pp. 378–9.
89. Nettlefolds Ltd., Minute Book No. 2, 1886–1894, 5 April 1887, p. 25.
90. Ibid., 1 June 1886, p. 398.
91. Ibid., 6 November 1888, p. 109.
92. Ibid., 4 December 1888, p. 109.
93. Ibid., 1 October 1887, p. 154.
94. Ibid., 4 November 1890, p. 209.
95. Ibid., 5 November 1889, p. 160.
96. *An Outline History*, p. 37.
97. *Price List of Wire Nails, Staples, Panel Pins manufactured by Castle Works, Rogerstone* (1907).
98. *Johns's Directory of Newport* (1890), p. 284.
99. *Outline History*, p. 37.
100. D.C. Coleman, *Courtaulds, an Economic and Social History*, Vol. I, Oxford (1969), pp. 178–9.
101. Ibid., Vol. II, Oxford (1969), pp. 123, 208; Crofton, *The Nettlefolds*, pp. 49–50.
102. Crofton, *The Nettlefolds*, p. 30.
103. Elsa Steer, *Threads from the Family Tapestry* (1957), p. 5.
104. *Guest, Keen & Nettlefolds Ltd., Second Report and Balance Sheet*, 30 June 1902.
105. R.A. Church, *Kenricks in Hardware, A Family Business: 1791–1966*, Newton Abbot (1969), pp. 78, 80, 81.
106. Church, *Kenricks*, p. 80.
107. *The Engineer*, Vol. CVII, 16 April 1909, Obituary, p. 394.
108. R.S. Sayers, *Lloyds Bank in the History of English Banking*, Oxford (1957), p. 350.
109. *GKN, Ninth Report and Balance Sheet*, June 1909; Crofton, op. cit., p. 35.
110. Nettlefolds Ltd., Minute Book No. 2, 9 June 1891, p. 389.
111. Ibid., 2 January 1894, p. 393; he died on 23 December 1893.
112. Typescript 're Mr. Hugh Nettlefold "Managing Director" ' (n.d.); J.B. Trotman, 'Recollections', pp. 1–2.
113. John Dinnis, 'Recollections of the Screw Department' (typescript), p. 3.
114. *Guest Keen & Nettlefolds Ltd. Rules*, No. 1 (c. 1913).
115. Mary A. Burns, 'Recollections', p. 1.
116. 'St. George's Mill' (typescript).
117. Mr. John Rose, 'Recollections'.
118. *An Outline History*, pp. 29, 64–65; *VCHS*, Vol. XVII, p. 135.
119. H. Rosa Lusty, 'Recollections', p. 2; *VCHS*, Vol. XVII, p. 140.
120. Works Manager's Common Place Book 1911–17, May 1913, item 936.
121. Nettlefolds Ltd., Minute Book, 23 March 1881, p. 91.
122. Ibid., 4 April 1882, p. 145.
123. Ibid., 7 March 1882, p. 141.

124. Ibid., 2 May 1882, pp. 153–4.
125. Ibid., 3 October 1882, p. 184.
126. Ibid., 4 December 1883, p. 269; 4 March 1884, p. 286.
127. Ibid., p. 286.
128. Ibid.
129. Ibid., 7 October 1884, p. 317.
130. Ibid.
131. Ibid., 4 November 1884, p. 321.
132. Ibid., 1 September 1885, p. 363.
133. Ibid., 2 February 1886, pp. 379–80.
134. Ibid., 1 June 1886, p. 397.
135. Ibid., 22 June 1888, p. 89.
136. Minutes of International Woodscrew Union (1908–1926), No. 123, 26 September 1910.
137. Ibid., No. 132, 21 April 1911.
138. Ibid., No. 85, 7 December 1908.

Part III

Steel and Coal in Wales, 1850–1914

8   Transition at Dowlais, The 1850s and 1860s

By March 1848, when after the death of Lord Bute it became clear that his Trustees would renew the lease, the ironworks at Dowlais had been allowed to fall into a state of considerable disrepair. Little had been spent on maintenance and renewals in the immediate past and, in view of Lord Bute's implacability and consistent refusal to reach an agreement, there had been virtually no substantial investment in new plant and technology over the recent five years. The plight of the Dowlais Iron Co. was compounded by the debilitating effect of Sir John Guest's illness. Just when he was needed to invigorate his managers with fresh enthusiasm and set about re-building the ironworks and modernising the mines, Guest suffered from growing ill health. He was forced to spend increasing periods in the unpolluted air at Canford where he could rest without being overly troubled by the pressing problems of his family business. Who, then, would occupy Dowlais House, take responsibility for negotiating the renewal of the lease and make the decisions needed to rejuvenate the ailing iron and coal company?

RENEWAL, NEW MANAGEMENT AND RECONSTRUCTION

Initially Sir John Guest himself undertook the task of reconstructing the Dowlais Ironworks; in March 1849 Lady Charlotte recorded that No. 14 blast furnace was again in operation and that a total of 17 were in blast, whilst No. 9 was being rebuilt.[1] But despite jubilation over the prospect of the renewal of the lease and the gradual recovery of the works, all was by no means well. 'I do more than ever feel', wrote Lady Charlotte in December 1848, 'the want of some assistance for poor Merthyr who really has more work upon him now than it is possible for him to accomplish without any great exertion and he is often fatigued and worn beyond his strength, but it will be very difficult to find anyone capable of helping him'.[2] He did, however, make less complicated the question of who was to succeed him, and

70 A part view of the furnaces at Dowlais (*c.* 1865–70), the furnaces in operation standing in front of their predecessors are (left to right) No. 13, No. 12 and No. 14. The building under construction is No. 2–3 blowing engine house, next to it, in derelict condition, is No. 4, while the right, still in operation is No. 5; above the line of the furnaces, No. 6 blowing engine house stands. The single storey building in the foreground is the smith's shop. (*Glamorgan Record Office*)

in doing so fulfilled a life-long ambition, by acquiring the outstanding seven-sixteenths shares in the company. Five of them were held by Wyndham William Lewis (d. 1855) who had inherited the shares from the Revd. William Price Lewis (d. 1848) and those Sir John purchased in August 1850 for £200,000.[3] This did not entirely sever the connection which had existed from Thomas Lewis, founder of the Dowlais Iron Co., as G.T. Clark, a trustee appointed under Sir John's will, had married Anne Price Lewis, a sister of Wyndham William Lewis (p. 45).

The other two-sixteenths belonged to his nephew, Edward John Hutchins (1809–76), whose father had married Sarah, a sister of Sir John Guest. In April 1850 Hutchins had become the Liberal M.P. for Lymington, a seat from which he retired in 1857.[4] Sir John considered him unsuited for the responsibilities of senior management and determined to keep him from Dowlais. Hutchins, nevertheless, wished to take command of the ironworks and discussed the possibility with Lady Charlotte.[5]

> We went fully into the questions of the Dowlais management . . . and I gave him my views (as unauthorised) of what Merthyr might probably agree to, viz: that each should take his own department. Merthyr, the London House with the general supervision of all the branches, Edward the manufacture, residing nine months in the year at Dowlais, on a fixed salary.

71 In the centre is the Goat Mill (*c.* 1864), when completed in 1859 the largest and most powerful rolling mill in the world. The roll house stands on the left with a number of rolls standing around it. In the foreground (right) stands Little Mill. The chimney, dated 1840, has louvres fitted at the top to regulate the draught. The shorter chimneys with dampers are probably for re-heat furnaces. (*Glamorgan Record Office*)

72 Middle Forge (built in 1847) photographed in 1870. The shorter chimneys here are for the various puddling furnaces. The two-storey building in the centre of the picture is the Caersalem Chapel, East Street. (*Glamorgan Record Office*)

> Then I told him that we should pay occasional visits to the Works
> . . . and being the senior partner, and by far the largest
> proprietor, Merthyr should be at liberty to go and reside at
> Dowlais if ever he wished it for two or three months.

Hutchins agreed to these proposals though made an allusion to a
desire to run the London House whenever her husband was out of
town.[6] The arrangement, it appears, was not acceptable to Sir John,
who feared the consequences, should his nephew ever gain command
at Dowlais. Accordingly, in July 1851 he purchased the two-sixteenths
share belonging to Hutchins for £58,000 – part of which was used to
settle Hutchins' overdraft of £8,000 and the £20,000 which he owed
to Mr. Lewis.[7] Hutchins subsequently became a director of the
Rhymney Iron Co. and when he resigned in 1875 had served as its
chairman for over twenty years.[8] For his part, Sir John Guest had
secured absolute control of the Dowlais Iron Co. but had little more
than a year to live.

In the meantime, the work of rebuilding the ironworks continued
unabated. In November 1850 Lady Charlotte estimated that it would
cost at least £100,000 to bring the company into 'tolerable order'.[9]
However, the absence of Sir John at Canford placed many executive
decisions, together with the daily management, in the hands of Lady
Charlotte, while his death in November 1852 made this *ad hoc*
arrangement formal. From that date until the spring of 1855 she lived
at Dowlais House and was in command. It was an arduous period,
characterised by the entry in her journal of 10–11 December 1852:
'work, work . . . Nothing but the hard work, and the feeling that I am
endeavouring in all things to carry out my darling's wishes.'[10]

Among the improvements that Lady Charlotte supervised was the
installation in 1851 of an enormous blowing engine.[11] At the time it
was said to have been the largest of its class in Britain or abroad.
Originally it supplied blast to eight furnaces, but by 1857, with the
assistance of three much smaller engines, it served twelve furnaces,
whose average weekly make of forge pig iron was estimated at 2,000
tons. With the exception of the cylinders which were purchased from
the Perran Foundry, Truro, the engine and its boilers were made at
Dowlais and assembled to the design of Samuel Truran, the
company's engineer.

In addition, the company's brick-making facilities were improved by
re-siting them as near to the Upper Branch Incline as possible. There
four kilns with a capacity of 18,000 bricks and stoves capable of holding
12,000 bricks were constructed, and thereby raised the works' weekly
output to 72,000.[12] Unlike Cyfarthfa and Penydarren, which manufactured house bricks for sale to local builders, the Dowlais Co., because
of its size and the scale of its own consumption, restricted itself to
refractories. In November 1854 the company calculated that they had
spent £125,727 on new work since 31 May 1848;[13] the largest items of

expenditure included mine openings and roadways (£47,833), the Dowlais Railway (£33,309), repairs to and the rebuilding of blast furnaces (£7,245), the Upper Branch Incline (£6,798), the Ivor New Mill (£8,369), and the new brick yards (£3,814).

Despite the hiccup produced by uncertainty over the renewal of the lease, the Dowlais Iron Company remained the leading ironworks in Merthyr. With the improvements initiated by Sir John and carried through by Lady Charlotte, its capacity, as Truran confirmed, was almost equal to that of its Merthyr rivals combined (Table 8.1).

Table 8.1 Output at Merthyr's ironworks in 1855

Ironworks	Number of blast furnaces	Weekly make per furnace (tons)	Total Annual make (tons)
Dowlais	14	116	84448
Ifor	4	116	24128
Cyfarthfa	7	100	36400
Ynysfach	4	100	20800
Penydarren	7	100	36400
Plymouth	5	100	26000

Source: William Truran, *Iron Manufactures*, p. 172.

EXPANSION AT THE PITS

The principal difficulty facing Lady Charlotte was not at the ironworks, but concerned the supply of raw materials. In November 1852 she lamented that,[14]

> Our works seems falling behind hand – and I am most anxious to try and press matters so as to keep up to our full make – I fear however we shall barely be able to raise coal enough to do much good. Last week our quantity of coal was very inadequate – only about 7,300 tons – It should have been 9,100 – [John] Evans and I are scheming (as they call it here) to bring our make up to 1,500 tons of finished iron per week – But I almost fear that we shall not succeed.

The problem had been apparent for some years and in 1857 Sir John Guest had asked Mr. Thomas E. Wales, their mining engineer, to compile a report on the state of the collieries at Dowlais.[15] He calculated that coal was costing them upwards of 4s. 6d. per ton, which was excessive for the district, and that this high price was attributable to the following causes: first, the expense of repairing a large number of workings, many of which were situated in tiers making intercommunication difficult and inefficient, and secondly the long distances that horses were required to haul loads of coal, particularly where seams were on different levels.[16] In an attempt to increase production without incurring the enormous cost of sinking new pits he suggested that shifts be staggered:[17]

> instead of all the men going to work at six o'clock in the morning, I would recommend that half of them go at say 2 o'clock in the morning . . . my object . . . is to get double the number of men applied to the same area of extent of workings and consequently get double the quantity of work or coal [during each day]; this would in great measure reduce the working of so many seams at the same time.

Wales also advocated the replacement of all the iron trams by lighter wooden wagons as horses would then be capable of hauling an additional 20–30 per cent.[18]

In view of the continuing problems, Wales was asked in January 1852 to produce a second report on the basis that the collieries' daily output be raised to 1,500 tons[19] as the works were then consuming 1,400 tons of large and 100 tons of small coal each day.[20] Whilst such demand could be readily accommodated with their existing pits and levels, he calculated that the subsequent exhaustion of the Bargoed Big Coal Pit and the Brewhouse Big Coal Pit would reduce the total by 240 tons per day.[21] The only means of making up this deficiency, he argued, was to sink new pits.[22] By December 1852 the situation had deteriorated and they were averaging 31,200 tons per month, or 7,800 tons per week.[23] Wales promised to increase the output to over 36,000 tons (or 9,100 tons a week) by February–March 1853, but even then Lady Charlotte calculated that they would be short by 2,200 tons a week, or at very best 1,000 tons. The only solution was to purchase supplies from other mines in South Wales, notably from Aberdare.[24]

As a longer-term solution, John Evans proposed in March 1853 that two collieries be opened, which he calculated would cost £35,725.[25] The first, which was to be sunk into the Big Coal level at a depth of 280 yards, had an expected capacity of 1,420,000 tons, which over a period of $15\frac{3}{4}$ years would produce a yield of 300 tons per day. The second pit, 275 yards deep into the Upper Four Feet coal, had an estimated life of six and a quarter years, with an output of 572,500 tons at 300 tons per day.[26]

Before proceeding with this capital-intensive project, Lady Charlotte Guest decided to call in an expert mining engineer to advise them on exactly where these two pits should be sited and the methods by which they should be worked.[27] Nicholas Wood, FRS (1795–1865) of Newcastle, 'who is considered the highest authority' was commissioned to survey and report on the Dowlais coal deposits.[28] First he calculated that the existing reserves (3,491,240 tons), being worked at the current rate of 1,500 tons a day, or 469,000 tons a year, would only last for a further 7½ years (Table 8.2).[29] Given that those reserves of coal suitable for the furnaces amounted to 1,352,920 tons and those for the forges 1,425,720 and that the former consumed 5,000 tons of coal a week and the latter only 4,000 tons, it became clear that the shortfall was particularly acute in the case of the furnaces, so that the 712,600 tons in the Rhas Las bed, suitable for either department, would have to be employed to make up the deficiency.[30]

Table 8.2   Quantity of coal to be worked at Dowlais in each bed by existing levels and pits

Locations	Total reserves (tons)	Consumed by
Upper Four Feet Coal	912480 ⎱	Blast Furnaces
Big Coal	440440 ⎰	
Rhas Las Coal	712600	either furnace or forge
Little Vein Coal	723158 ⎫	
Lower Four Feet Coal	646222 ⎬	forges
Various beds	56340 ⎭	
	———	
TOTAL:	3491240	

Source: 'Coal Reports', Nicholas Wood, p. 53.

Moreover, the problem was compounded by the actual methods of extraction. Although it might appear that the total reserves would last for an average of seven and a half years, in practice this was not the case. The Rhas Las, Lower Four Feet, Buxton's and Cwmbargoed Pits (which together provided 900 of the 1,500 tons consumed daily) could be expected to last a further eleven years, while the other levels and pits, producing 600 tons per day had not much more than a year's coal in them. The question of shortages was therefore both pressing and serious.

The required output and specific demands of forge and furnace could be met, Wood demonstrated, by sinking two new pits into the Big Coal Level, each to have a capacity, without being pushed, of 400 tons per day.[31] In addition, the Cwmbargoed Pit (constructed in 1839 and opened in 1842) could be improved to provide 500 tons per day. These three mines would supply the basic needs of the ironworks (1,300 tons) while the remaining 200 tons would come from the Rhas

Table 8.3   Nicholas Wood's strategy for coal at Dowlais

	Total reserves	Daily output first 12 years (tons)	Subsequent output (tons)	Duration (years)
Lower Four Feet, No. 3 and Buxton's Pits	1206560	300	—	12
Rhas Las Pit	2615200	200	—	42
Cwmbargoed Pit	7321586	400	500	50
No. 1 New Pit No. 2 New Pit	13766810	600	800	55

Source: 'Coal Reports', Nicholas Wood, p. 64.

Las (1850), Lower Four Feet (1850), No. 3, and Buxton's Pits (1820) (Table 8.3).[32]

Further, these greater outputs could, suggested Wood, be combined with savings in the cost of extracting the minerals. 'I am well aware', he confessed,[33]

> of the difficulty of introducing any novel system of working to colliers generally, and . . . still more of the Welch colliers – who are probably more retentive of old habits and prejudices than most other colliers – and therefore I do not think it is advisable that any violent or extensive change should be made nor does it appear almost necessary.

The current problems stemmed in large measure from the pillar and stall method of mining the coal. Headings were driven from newly opened levels at distances of about 100 yards and stalls dug on each side for a distance of 50 yards, the roof in each case being supported by pillars of coal which were then lost to the colliery owner. The weight on the pillars caused the side walls to disintegrate making those headings used as roadways expensive to maintain.[34] Further, the coal worked in close proximity to the pillars was also subject to pressure and produced a 'great quantity of "sluck" or small coal unfitted for the furnaces'.[35]

To avoid these drawbacks, Wood suggested that they increase the dimensions of the pillars in those places where they supported roadways to prevent crushing, and, more important, that a diluted system of longwall working be introduced.[36] He felt that it would be too radical a change to adopt the method in its entire vigour and concluded that 'there are modifications of the system which are extensively practised in the North of England, by which such coal as that of Dowlais would I think be quite as cheaply and with as great a degree of perfection worked as the Long Wall method.'[37] Alas, the details of this technique were not included in his report. In May 1853, Martin, Wales and Matthew Truran had, in fact, visited the North of England to study the latest methods and returned in the belief that a modification of longwall working would prevent them from continuing to waste about one-third of the coal deposits in pillars.[38]

In addition, costs could be reduced, and greater outputs achieved, Wood argued, by improving the means of conveying coals from the face to the ironworks. 'With the exception of the engine on the Slope Level', he observed,

> lifting to the surface is done entirely by horses and manual labour. The cost is consequently very great, the daily average duty or performance of a horse is about 6 tons per day or 1s. per ton – The daily cost for 1,500 tons would be £75 per day, or nearly £20,000 per annum.[39]

Much of the expense resulted from the lengthy and circuitous nature of the levels, the pit openings generally being on the edge of the coalfield so that the roadways often had to be laid across its entire breadth.[40] To facilitate the transport of materials in these circumstances, Wood advocated the employment of steam-driven machinery in place of horses.

Obstacles hindering the introduction of new methods to Dowlais' pits included: the crooked and tortuous lines of the different levels, the poor condition of the roads and rails, and the type of wagons used.[41] Initially, therefore, Wood proposed that machinery be installed in the Brewhouse Level communicating with Buxton's Pit and Blind Engine Pit. At that time 420 tons of coals were conveyed daily along the level requiring thirty eight horses at an annual cost of £3,500; a figure, he estimated, which could be reduced to £500.[42] Further, in the Engine Plane Drift, Wood calculated:[43]

> about 300 tons of coals, mine and rubbish is daily brought out, at a cost of about 4½d. per ton or £5 12s. 0d. per day or £1,680 per year. The cost of this, if done by machinery, should not exceed £380 per annum by which a saving might be made of £1,300 per annum. So that if machinery was employed in these two Levels a saving might certainly be made of something like £4,000 per annum.

However, should steam power be employed, the old system of wagons with loose wheels running on tram rails needed to be replaced by round-top rails of malleable iron and trucks with wheels attached to axles to ensure the trains would not be de-railed. The cost of this improvement was estimated at £2,593 for the Brewhouse Level,[44] a sum, he calculated that would soon be recouped not only by the lower level of operating expenses, but also by reduced maintenace costs as the old cast iron rails and primitive wagons were prone to breakage and very likely had a shorter working life.[45]

Furthermore the transport network for the collieries, Wood argued, could be made far more efficient if machinery were also applied to drawing wagons from the Brewhouse Level to the forges and hauling the empty wagons back again, thereby entirely eliminating the need for horses in this section of the works.[46] This innovation would cost a further £3,304 and the expenditure of a further £800 would permit all the iron transported from the blast furnaces to the forges and all the ashes carried from the forges to be conveyed by engine power, saving the employment of nine horses. To implement the entire scheme, Wood recommended that a single engine be erected at the end of the Brewhouse Level, near Buxton's Pit, and that a double engine, or two singles, be installed at the mouth of the Level near the blast furnaces.[47]

Finally, additional savings could be obtained by using a greater proportion of small coal, and this, in turn, would prolong the life of the pits.[48] Out of the 1,580 tons of large coal raised each day, between 350 and 400 tons of small coals were then left underground, since only 100 tons could be consumed by the steam engines and other uses. Wood suggested that, if mixed with other coals, it would be suitable for coking and could then be fed into the blast furnaces. The deposits of small coals deliberately left in the mines would not be subject to an extraction charge (as that was already borne by the large coal) and could be conveyed to the furnaces for under 1s. per ton. As small coals were exempt from the royalty agreement, they could be converted to coke and delivered to the furnace for a total cost of 2s. 10d. per ton, which compared favourably with the figure of 5s., being the cost of mining and delivering large coals to the ironworks.[49] Wood calculated that 2s. per ton would be saved on all coals to be coked if the small coals were employed for this purpose. The total sum accumulated in this fashion would have been considerable given that 200–300 tons of coal were converted into coke daily.[50] Lady Charlotte assented to this scheme and Wood agreed to send a foreman from Newcastle to erect and manage the special coke ovens (barrel-shaped rather than domed) needed for small coals.[51]

In consultation with John Evans, Lady Charlotte Guest decided, with the exception of sinking the two new pits, to accept Wood's proposals. They agreed to install engines to draw the wagons in the Rhas Las, Lower Four Feet, Bargoed Big Coal, and Bargoed Upper Four Feet Pits.[52] In total the winding engines were expected to cost £1,000 which was infinitely cheaper than opening two fresh collieries. 'Mr. Wood on consideration agrees to this being the most economical and advantageous mode of our working the coal', wrote Lady Charlotte in May 1853, 'especially as we have but little time for sinking new pits and could scarcely keep up our supplies until they were ready'.[53] As regards changing the means of working the coal, Lady Charlotte held lengthy discussions with Wood on the longwall method. By this technique, she was convinced that they would be able[54]

> to bring out the whole of our coal – instead of as at present leaving a great deal in the ground – sometimes we lose to the extent of two-thirds. In the Lower 4ft we do not attempt to get the lowest seam, which is always sacrificed but in talking it out with Mr. Wood, Evans thinks he sees his way to saving the whole of this vein (as of all our others) in future. We are to try this method first in the working of the Drift Incline to the Dip of the Rhas Las, which is all prepared for proceeding with.

Whilst most of the improvements advocated by Wood were implemented, the sinking of the two new pits, the most capital-intensive of his reforms, was delayed until 1857 when William Menelaus, the works manager, had delivered his report on the entire operation of the ironworks and its ancillary activities (p. 251). Sited at Fochriw, No. 1 Pit, 443 yards in depth, was opened in June 1863, and No. 2 (433 yards) in September 1866, the cost of sinking and machinery being £83,000.[55] They were the first of the modern collieries at Dowlais and over the following decades proved to be sound investments.

Much of the organisational groundwork for these improvements had been cleared in 1846 by Sir John Guest when he abolished the sub-contract system of mining coal. Henceforth, employees were paid directly by the Dowlais Iron Co. At the time of change, no fewer than forty contractors had agreements with the company. Not all were discontinued, but the sub-contracting was limited to the smaller levels and patches. A hierarchy of agents, managers and overmen in the direct employ of the company was introduced, and thereby facilitated tighter supervision.[56] The introduction of salaried management corresponded with the sinking of deeper, capital-intensive pits which required more precise running.

In expanding their output, the Dowlais Iron Co. were considerably assisted in 1859 by the offer of the Penydarren Ironworks, together with its two coal and single iron ore fields,[57] which had fallen behind in the technical race and was no match for its larger rivals, Dowlais and Cyfartha. William Forman (d. 1829), formerly an ordnance agent at the Tower of London, had charge of the works from 1813, executive authority then passing to William Thompson (d. 1854), a Lord Mayor of London, and then to Messrs Fothergill and Hankey who decided to sell the business. Although the package included an estimated reserve

73 The Penydarren
Ironworks in a ruined
state *c.* 1870.
(*Cyfarthfa Castle Museum*)

of 1,500,000 tons of furnace coal and iron ore which could be extracted
more cheaply than their own, Lady Charlotte thought the asking price
of £50,000 excessive, though finally agreed to pay £59,875, the
purchase being completed in June. However, the acquisition of this
extra capacity (135,700 tons of coal and 6,900 tons of ore were raised in
the first year)[58] prompted a fundamental change in the attitude of the
Dowlais Iron Co. towards it mineral reserves. Until then, as William
Jenkins recorded in November 1861,[59]

> previous to June 1859 our sales of coal were confined to the trade
> of the neighbourhood of Dowlais and Merthyr . . . soon after the
> purchase of Penydarren, we commenced selling coal on a large
> scale. After June 1859 we made several large contracts for coal
> sent to Cardiff, Swansea, Liverpool, London, Hereford,
> Shrewsbury &c.

To increase coal sales further, in May 1861 their Cardiff agency was
expanded to deal with minerals as well as iron. In June 1861 Mr. D.
James was appointed as the company's agent in Swansea, and in
August of that year Mr. M.A. Johns was engaged to represent the
company in Liverpool. The London office had also been instructed to
win orders for coal and had succeeded in selling to St. Petersburg and
other Continental nations.

   In addition, William Menelaus had written to Clark on the same
subject a few weeks before to recommend that the Dowlais Iron Co.

enter wholeheartedly the 'sale coal trade'.[60] He confirmed that deposits of sufficient quality and quantity existed to accommodate the ironworks and yet leave a substantial surplus to be disposed of in the market place. For Martin had estimated that the reserves would provide 3,000 tons of coal a day for sixty years, though in practice Menelaus felt it safer to assume that 2,500 tons would be raised every day. Menelaus calculated that the works would continue to turn out 2,000 tons of finished iron per week, and since the yield was constantly improving, he predicted that the company would soon be able to produce a ton of finished iron with four tons of large coal, should 'a sufficient supply of small coal . . . be obtained to take the place of large under the new system of mixing with bituminous coal and applying fan blast'.[61] Such levels of consumption would require 8,000 tons of large coal a week leaving, with a weekly output of at least 15,000 tons, upwards of 1,000 tons a day for sale.

'If we can compete in price', Menelaus concluded, 'there is no doubt that we shall have a certain demand for our coal'. He argued that the ironmaster who owned collieries could always work coal more cheaply than the coal owner who possessed no ironworks, as the former could give his men more regular employment. Another justification for entering the sale trade concerned the balance of power within the company:[62]

> when an ironworks only raises sufficient coal for daily use in iron making the men [in the pits] have always the power to inflict grievous loss upon the master by simply idling, keeping the furnaces and forges short of coal . . . Dowlais has on several occasions suffered severely from the conduct of the colliers in this way. If, however, the works raises a considerable quantity of coal beyond its requirements for iron making the power of the men to inflict loss is lessened.

If diversification into the sale coal trade could be considered as an insurance policy against potential labour difficulties, it was also seen as a counterbalance to periodic depressions in the iron market. The 1860s and late 1870s were, in general, difficult years for ironmasters and no small number sank pits to provide an extra source of income during times of falling demand.[63]

REJUVENATING THE IRONWORKS

Although Sir John and, subsequently, Lady Charlotte had spent over £100,000 in re-establishing the works after 1848, a detailed survey of plant undertaken in June 1856 revealed that much remained to be done. The 'Dowlais Works Report' was compiled by William Menelaus in November 1857 and concluded,[64] within the last four years, at nearly every works in Wales, the makes and yields of furnaces have been improved and rapid strides were making in the way of producing cheaper pig iron. Dowlais is standing still instead of taking the lead as from her site and position she ought; she was quietly falling into the rear. To remedy this state of things a great effort is necessary and also a considerable outlay of capital.

In the summer of 1856 there were seventeen furnaces in blast, making on average 107 tons of pig iron per week, a quantity that had not been improved upon for several years.[65] For the year ended June 1856, 53 cwts of coal (or 57 cwts including fuel for the blast engines) were needed to produce a ton of iron, which was consistently higher than at many well-managed furnaces in this district. Further the quality of iron produced was 'very irregular and often inferior'. 'It was obvious', wrote a senior manager, possibly Menelaus,[66]

> that the works could only be restored to a fair condition by a very large expenditure. The means for meeting that expenditure were not present – the large sums retired from the concern by Sir John Guest before his death had left very little capital, in reality, insufficient to carry on an establishment of such magnitude. On the other hand it was equally obvious that, when prices fell to anything like their natural level the duration of Dowlais [its continued existence] must be measured by months and finally there were grounds for belief that by expenditure in the restoration of the works, development of the coal resources and by general reforms in the management, the works might be placed in a condition to compete with any of their neighbours in the manufacture of iron.

The first problem to which they had to address themselves, if they wished to increase both output and efficiency, was the irregular supply of raw materials. Large contracts for red ore (p. 257) were made, most of them in Westmorland, to compensate for dwindling local supplies. Arrangements for transporting the ore from Cardiff to Dowlais were greatly improved by the purchase of sixty new wagons, while thirty of a cheaper construction were acquired to handle the cinder and other traffic within the works, thereby allowing all the Cardiff wagons to be employed continuously on ore trains. A consequence of these reforms was that the furnaces were regularly supplied and that a stockpile of 10,000 tons was accumulated on the furnace tops.[67]

As the pits then in operation were still considered unable to cope with any increase in output, a contract was concluded with Thomas Joseph of Aberdare to supply the company with 200 tons of coking coal per day for five years, such a quantity being able to 'make up for

74 The other half of Middle Forge in 1870. The works office is directly behind the forge and the bay window lit the manager's office and was, therefore, where William Menelaus would have had his desk. In the skyline, St. John's Church is visible on the left, while the Dowlais stables stand to the right and behind them the Ifor Works.
(*Glamorgan Record Office*)

75 To the right is No. 6 Puddling Forge showing the puddling furnaces (built in 1847) and to the left a light merchant bar mill. In the foreground steam-powered cropping shears are being used to trim lengths of bar iron which will then be arranged in piles for consolidation and shaping in one of the larger rolling mills. Mounds of pig iron are at the base of the photograph. To the right behind the forge are first Dowlais House and then the Guest Memorial Hall.
(*Glamorgan Record Office*)

any deficiency that may arise in our own supply until the new pits are fairly at work'.[68]

Several of the blast furnaces having fallen into a poor state needed to be repaired – Numbers 4, 6, 7, 10 and 18, while No. 17 was entirely rebuilt. To improve their efficiency further, three new boilers were added to the blast engines – two at No. 7 Ifor, and one at No. 6 Old Works.[69] As a result of these improvements the weekly make of iron rose to 160 tons, while the consumption of coal required to make a ton of pig iron fell to 41 cwts (or 44 cwts including the blast engines). Menelaus did not regard these achievements as final and reported in 1857 that the average make for the week ending 14 November was 176 tons per furnace in the Old Works and 172 tons at the Ifor Works.[70] He thought that a figure of 200 tons per week represented a reasonable target. In all, the improvements, when compared with figures for 1855–56, showed an increase of 48 per cent in output with a fuel saving of almost 22 per cent. The reduction in costs, (with coal at seven shillings per ton) amounted to 4s. 6d. per ton of pigs or 6s. 6d. per ton of finished wrought iron. Given that their weekly make of pig iron was 2,400 tons, Menelaus calculated that the annual saving on their fuel bills could reach £28,000 a year.[71]

Further reductions in costs, amounting to 1s. 4d. per ton, were secured by modifying the recipe for making iron – principally an increase in the percentage of red ore from Westmorland and a decrease in the three local ores (Table 8.4). With an annual make of 2,400 tons this represented an economy of £7,801 a year, while also improving the yield and quality of pig iron. To facilitate the supply of the other ingredients (limestone and coke), three additional lime kilns had been constructed which ensured regularity at a 'materially reduced cost'. In addition, 116 coking ovens were constructed,[72]

Table 8.4   Composition of ore at Dowlais and its cost

| | Cost per ton | 52 weeks ending | | | | | |
| | | 6 May 1856 | | | 16 September 1857 | | |
		£	s	d	£	s	d
Welsh mine	14/5d	1	2	$6\frac{2}{10}$	0	18	$4\frac{9}{10}$
Thomas's mine	13/6d		1	$6\frac{3}{10}$			$7\frac{1}{10}$
Black Band	14/–		2	$3\frac{7}{10}$		1	$10\frac{4}{10}$
Red ore	24/–		11	$2\frac{3}{10}$		15	4
Forge Cinders	11/6d		5	$5\frac{3}{10}$		5	$6\frac{2}{10}$
Finery	11/6d			$11\frac{1}{10}$			$11\frac{2}{10}$
		2	3	$11\frac{8}{10}$	2	2	$7\frac{8}{10}$

Source: GRO, D/DG 'Report on the Dowlais Works' by William Menelaus, p. 5.

which, though involving a considerable expenditure, would enable the company to increase their coke stocks by an estimated 20,000 tons.[73] This insurance against dramatic swings in demand was considered prudent because coke, unlike coal, was not subject to violent fluctuations in value.

Moreover, there existed a serious discrepancy between the Dowlais Iron Co.'s ability to make pig iron and their capacity to convert it into bar iron. Their puddling furnaces and mills had a weekly capacity of just 1,200 tons which fell far short of the output from the improved blast furnaces able to make almost 3,000 tons of iron. That such a mismatch arose was understandable enough. Puddling was both a skilful and arduous occupation, while rolling-mill plant was parti-cularly costly. Nonetheless, Menelaus calculated that the company's profitability depended upon raising the output of the puddling furnaces and rolling mills for they earned disproportionately large surpluses; the 'value-added' at the capital-intensive blast furnace was little in comparison with the refining and finishing processes. Menelaus calculated that they needed to increase their capacity to 2,000 tons of finished iron per week in order to consume the surplus of pig iron.[74] Whilst it proved possible to raise the efficiency and flexibility of rolling mills, the puddling furnace proved largely resistant to technical change and increases in output could only be achieved by duplication. Accordingly, he advocated that No. 6 mill be converted into a forge and that more puddling furnaces be installed in the Middle Forge and an additional forge be constructed in the Ifor Works. These alterations would raise the number of puddling furnaces to 149½ and thereby increase the capacity of the works by about 800 tons to 2,000 tons per week.

This, in turn, required that they improve rolling facilities and Menelaus recommended that a new mill sufficiently powerful to roll 1–1,500 tons of iron a week be erected in the Old Works.[75] He demonstrated considerable foresight in estimating the working requirements of this mill. 'In the production of wrought iron' observed Menelaus,[76]

> the means of producing large sizes and great lengths has not kept pace with the requirements of engineers. It may be fairly anticipated that when machinery of sufficient power has been erected a demand for large sizes will follow which will command a high price from the difficulty of obtaining iron of this description. With this in view the New Mill is designed of thrice the power of any mill in the kingdom.

Called the Goat Mill (probably because many of the men who worked there belonged to the Dowlais Company of the Glamorgan Engineers whose coat buttons showed the head of a goat in relief),[77] it was a vast undertaking which took two years to construct, being completed in 1859. Although the overall conception originated with Menelaus, the practicalities were entrusted to Samuel Truran.[78] The motive force was provided by two high-pressure engines with cylinders 45 ins in diameter and fed by six Cornish boilers. The engine beam was carried entirely by cast iron framing, as was the huge driving wheel, the first time that the material had been employed in this fashion.[79] This enormous machine, double the power of any existing engine in Britain, drove three mills, one capable of turning out 1,000 tons of rails per week, another with a capacity of 700 tons, and a third, a bar or roughing-down mill capable of making 200 tons.[80] One of the principal mills was fitted with finishing rolls one above each other, rotating in opposite directions so that the red-hot iron could pass through the bottom rolls in one direction and then be lifted to the upper set to be passed back. As bar iron could only be shaped while red hot, any delay necessitated re-heating and additional costs. The larger the section (and the tendency was for heavier and longer rails) the more urgent was the need to process the bar iron as quickly as possible.[81] The introduction of a two-directional mill reduced the number of men required to manipulate the bar iron as it was converted into rails. Menelaus correctly anticipated that the mill would be able to roll rails 70ft in length, and to fashion such sections before they cooled it was necessary to run the bars through at high speed which, in turn, required engines of considerable power.[82]

The total cost of the Goat Mill and its engines was not recorded; it would have been substantial, possibly as much as £50,000. Whatever the figure, it proved to be a sound, possibly vital, investment; the ability to earn profits at Dowlais in the second half of the nineteenth century rested firmly on their capacity to make rails more cheaply than their competitors without impairing the quality. The Goat Mill was the means by which rails of heavier weight and greater length could be mass produced. 'Unless a rolling mill turns out a regular and uniform quantity of finished iron', Menelaus asserted in 1861,[83] 'there is an end to all economy . . . It is because rails are required in large quantities of the same section, that they can be produced at the lower price for which they are sold'. In addition, enormous power was needed to roll girders and deck beams of great lengths, which placed the Dowlais Iron Co. in an almost unassailable position to tender for such work. They had, for example, rolled the deck beams (49 to 50 feet in length) ordered by the government for floating batteries just before the end of the Crimean War.[84] By foreseeing these developments and having the courage to install expensive equipment, Menelaus played a master card. Although situated at the end of a stream of productive processes, the Goat Mill was a crucial piece of machinery. Without it, the company's ability to earn profits would have been handicapped and the labour and skill which went into the manufacture of wrought iron would have been largely wasted.

By November 1857, when Menelaus compiled his report, the various improvements initiated over the previous year had cost £23,643.[85] 'The whole of this sum', he recorded, 'has been charged upon the cost of production; this divided over 89,148 tons, the quantity made since June 1856, amounts to 5s. $3\frac{6}{100}$d. per ton.[86] This did not include the figure of £31,557 (incurred in the construction of coke ovens and the forge at the Ifor Works, together with a small sum for new mine openings) which was to be charged against running costs in 1857–58. The enormous expense involved in opening new pits and laying down the Goat Mill was to be spread over the next ten years.[87] However, even these figures understated the scale of the investment required to bring the Dowlais Iron Co. back into a competitive state. Writing ten days after Menelaus had completed his report, Lady Charlotte complained in her Journal,[88]

> I do not like the state of our finances at all, although *au fond*, we are sound. Still I grieve to find nearly £100,000 has been lost or sunk in new works since I gave up the management [April 1855]; and besides the immediate pressure for ready money there seems no hope of any profit being made for a long time to come.

The figure of £100,000 was composed of the £23,643 already charged, the £31,557 to be incurred, leaving about £45,000 for the Goat Mill and new pits, although it is conceivable that a number of improvements were introduced during 1855–56 which Menelaus failed to mention in his report.

NEW SOURCES OF IRON ORE

The decision taken in 1856 to increase the proportion of red ore from Westmorland considerably eased the pressure on dwindling local supplies (p. 80). Although it cost considerably more than the local black band (24s. as against 14s. per ton, a difference which, in part, resulted from the higher transport cost), the higher yields of iron which this rich ore produced served as compensation. The problem at Dowlais was not simply that nearby deposits were running thin but, as the miners were paid by the quantity of mineral extracted, there was a flow of labour from the ore mines to the coal pits:[89]

> the men have comparatively low wages – by becoming colliers they can easily earn more money, this keeps up a continual drain of men from the mine works to the collieries, which will end in raising permanently the cost of the mine. To meet this scarcity we are using as little mine as possible . . . by substituting red ore for Welsh mine, the cost has been reduced 1s. 4d. per ton of pigs, while at the same time we have not lowered the quantity.

The report commissioned in 1853 from Nicholas Wood on the state of the Dowlais' collieries also included reference to the 'iron-stone workings' and concluded that improvements, principally the application of machinery to the conveyance of minerals, were equally necessary.[90]

The Dowlais Iron Co. had actually begun to purchase ore from Lancashire and Cumberland in the late 1820s and 1830s,[91] though the trade did not assume substantial proportions until the 1840s when the construction of the Furness Railway's lines to the haematite fields of the region had a dramatic impact upon its output.[92] In July 1842, for example, Henry William Schneider wrote to Thomas Evans to say that 5,000 tons of ore had been shipped on board a merchant vessel at Ulverston for delivery to Cardiff, leaving 1,400 tons of the present contract to be despatched.[93] The price, nine shillings per ton, Schneider observed, was extremely low, offered 'for the sake of keeping up the valuable connection we have formed with your house, and to obviate the necessity of reducing our hands'.[94] Schneider was a businessman of standing in the Furness region, his firm owning three pits in 1849 with an output of 25,000 tons per annum.[95] The completion of the local railway network in the mid-1840s resulted in Whitehaven and Barrow becoming the principal ports for the shipment of iron ore to South Wales. Considerable quantities were involved as the following contract between the Dowlais Iron Co. and Messrs. Tulk and Ley revealed:[96]

> We agree to supply you with 20,000 tons of good merchantable iron ore, delivered free on board at Whitehaven at 10/– per ton . . . The amount in store not to exceed 1,000 tons at a time, and we agree to make no further contracts for ore after this date excepting to the Haematite Iron Company or to a Company in our own neighbourhood, until the above is delivered or otherwise terminated . . . Payments per bill of 3 months from date of delivery or $2\frac{1}{2}$ per cent by seven days Bills.

Other suppliers working from Barrow and Whitehaven during the 1850s included, Harrison Anishe & Co., George Ashburner & Co., Town & Rawlinson, and the Cleator Iron Ore Co.[97]

Another mine partnership which consistently supplied the Dowlais Ironworks was the Hodbarrow Co. formed in 1855.[98] The ore was transported to South Wales either by rail to Whitehaven and then by ship or more directly by sea from Borwick Rails, its principal customer being those ironworks which lay in an arc on the edge of the South Wales coalfield between Merthyr and Blaenavon.

The decision to purchase an increasing quantity of ore from Cumberland and Lancashire, in an era before steam-powered freighters, on occasion presented Dowlais with problems of supply, and required them to maintain substantial reserves. This they usually did, but in December 1852, as Lady Charlotte recorded in her Works Journal, the margin of safety was small:[99] 'We have about 4,000 tons [of iron ore] in stock – and though our requirements, 1,500 to 1,800 tons per week, will soon run that down, we think it best to take the chance of the changes of weather, [and of] other vessels on their way coming in'. To compensate for over-reliance on a few areas of supply, the Dowlais Iron Co. took a lease on coal and ore mines in the Forest of Dean. They were not, however, of substantial size and could never compare with local deposits or purchases from the North-West. In February 1853 a further interruption to sea traffic gave Lady Charlotte cause for concern that their stocks had fallen below 40,000 tons (a reserve figure which they sought to maintain) for this also put them[100] 'too much in the power of the miners – besides the even greater disadvantage of our having them use it too green – under these circumstances it seemed necessary to make every effort to get down Red Ore from the North'. These problems continued until 1873 when, in the face of dwindling reserves in the Westmorland and Furness region, the Dowlais Iron Co. in conjunction with the Consett Iron Co. and Krupp formed the Orconera Iron Ore Co. to obtain huge quantitites of haematite from Spain (p. 310).[101]

THE RETIREMENT OF LADY CHARLOTTE AND THE APPOINTMENT OF THE TRUSTEES

During January 1854 Lady Charlotte Guest became troubled over the future of the works. Its very size brought onerous managerial responsibilities. John Evans, with whom she shared much of the burden, had fallen into ill health and the strain of executive office was beginning to show in both of them. No obvious successor existed, as Lady Charlotte's sons were still quite young and none had been allowed to learn the business. Moreover, new competition loomed: 'other districts, with apparently better resources, are opening up', she observed,[102]

> and unless we keep quite ahead as to improvements and the most advantageous and enlightened system of working we shall be quite unable to keep any position at all – much less than we now occupy at the head of the trade – and this will involve continuous labour and immense skill and energy.

Accordingly, and somewhat surprisingly given the heartache and effort that had gone into renewing the lease, she decided to sell the Dowlais Iron Co. Her solicitor, Mr. Bircham, agreed that this was the sensible course and suggested that the works should be valued and an inventory prepared.[103] When the scale of the transaction became apparent, the possibility of an outright purchase receded, making a

76 Dowlais House (c. 1870) was built in 1817–18 for Josiah Guest who had married Maria Rankin in 1817. It was considerably smaller and less grand than Cyfarthfa Castle occupied by the Crawshays. It was occupied by Lady Charlotte Guest and then G.T. Clark, but became offices when he retired in 1892. Without regard for its historical importance, the building was demolished in 1973. (*Glamorgan Record Office*)

leasing arrangement with a fixed annual rental more likely to prove an attractive proposition.[104] Nevertheless, her advisers doubted whether many would be able to contemplate such a deal given 'the immense magnitude of the concern'.[105] Having striven to retain the ironworks in the face of Lord Bute's intransigence, it seemed that Lady Charlotte would subsequently be thwarted in her intention to dispose of her dearest possession. In February 1854 the works were valued at £400,000, exclusive of stocks of iron or raw materials.[106] George Kitson, the Dowlais agent, whose advice Lady Charlotte sought, wrote to say that the depressed state of the money market made it unlikely that a scheme for selling the works would succeed,[107] and at a meeting on 15 March in Lady Charlotte's house in No. 7 Suffolk Street, London, it was concluded that the most feasible plan was to let the works at a yearly rental.[108] But, then, as it had done over the lease, fate intervened. On 29 March Britain found herself locked into conflict with Russia over the Crimea.[109] A further meeting was held in Lady Charlotte's London house at which Nicholas Wood, Bircham, Evans, Kitson and Locke announced that they had 'made no progress in finding a tenant for the works and now only had to report their conviction that the present state of the money market and following the declaration of war it was hopeless to attempt to carry out any scheme'.[110] Consequently, Lady Charlotte 'determined to suspend and discard from my mind' any proposal to dispose of the Dowlais Ironworks.[111]

Shortly afterwards she appears to have conceived of the idea to involve the two trustees (appointed by her late husband's will) more in the daily running of the works. G.T. Clark (1809–98) had already moved into Dowlais House to keep a watchful eye on daily events, so

77 G.T. Clark (1809–98) in the uniform of a Lt. Colonel of the Dowlais Rifle Corps, a volunteer unit. (*Merthyr Central Library*)

78 H.A. Bruce, Lord Aberdare (1815–95), appointed trustee of the Dowlais Iron Co. Originally a barrister, he subsequently entered politics and became Home Secretary. (*Glamorgan Record Office*)

Lady Charlotte invited H.A. Bruce, who was later to succeed Edward Divett as the other trustee, to take a 'general directional supervision and in fact share the London management with Kitson'.[112] Two days later Bruce agreed to the arrangement and on 20 May 1854 Lady Charlotte's spirits brightened further:[113]

> [James] Walkinshaw [their accountant] is here about the closing of the books which show a profit this year of some £43,000, which considering all the improvements made and the outlay thereon, speaks pretty well for my management. But for the strike [in 1853 p. 276] it would have been much more, but I must not boast. Indeed I feel very unequal now to doing anything, and long to resign the reins of government.

By June the strain was beginning to tell: 'how do I manage', she asked, 'to keep *au courant* of all that is doing at the works, and all on Ivor's landed property?'[114] Although she was spending increasing lengths of time away from Dowlais, either at Canford or in London, she still kept close contact with the ironworks and scrutinised any important contracts and approved major items of expenditure.[115]

The retirement of Lady Charlotte Guest from the management of the Dowlais Iron Co. was gradual, though the period of gentle withdrawal seems finally to have been concluded by her marriage on 10 April 1855 to Charles Schreiber (1826–84).[116] The son of Lt. Colonel James Schreiber of Melton, Suffolk, and a former Fellow of Trinity College, Cambridge, he had been engaged in December 1852 at a salary of £400 a year to teach Sir John's eldest son, Ivor, who not liking Harrow required further tuition before going himself to Cambridge. Lady Charlotte's first impressions of the man that she was later to marry were revealing: he 'has taken high honours and seems altogether to be a very desirable person for the office – I like what I see of him very much'.[117] Henceforth, she divided the greater part of her time between the estate at Canford and developing an absorbing interest in collecting English china, and later fans and fan leaves.[118] Sir Ivor Guest, who based himself at Canford and at 22 Arlington Place in London, became a Member of Parliament first for his father's party, the Liberals, but switched to the Conservatives. He sat for Poole (1874) and Bristol (1878 and 1880), before his ennoblement to the Lords. Under the influence of his formidable wife, Lady Cornelia, elder sister of Lord Randolph Churchill, he re-joined the Liberals in 1903 in reaction to the fiscal policies advocated by Joseph Chamberlain.[119]

John Evans, who had been the works manager during Lady Charlotte's period of control, felt that she had married too hastily after the death of her first husband, whom he had known since childhood. Accordingly, Evans resigned from the company and retired to Sir John's former house at Sully. His departure and the retirement of Lady Charlotte compelled the trustees and senior managers to take greater responsibility. First among them was George Thomas Clark, who proved to be one of the outstanding leaders at Dowlais. On the surface, he appeared to have little to recommend him. Son of George Clark (1777–1848), chaplain at the Royal Military Hospital, Chelsea, he was educated at Charterhouse and soon abandoned a medical career in favour of civil engineering.[120] During the construction of the Great Western Railway, Clark worked under Brunel and in the mid-1840s spent several years in India as a consultant engineer where he reported on sewage systems for Bombay and advocated the building of the first railway there. Although offered the post of chief engineer to the Great Indian Peninsular Railway, he decided to return to England in 1848 to take up an appointment with the Board of Health, first as a superintending inspector and subsequently as one of three Commissioners. His selection as a trustee of the Dowlais Iron Co. owed much to his close friendship with Sir John Guest rather than any expertise or experience, for he had no knowledge of iron-making, the extractive industries or business. He may well have been introduced to the Guests by his wife, Ann Price Lewis, who was the niece of Wyndham Lewis, MP, a partner in the Dowlais Co.[121] Sir John had

Table 8.7 Output and yields of finished iron at Dowlais 1853–57

	53 weeks ending June 1853	53 weeks ending June 1856	55 weeks ending September 1857
Output (Tons)			
Puddled bars	77870	76254	111392
Rails made	42767	46267	66190
Total make of finished iron	61212	59883	89148
Average per week	1155	1130	1371
*Yields** (Tons)			
Roughed iron	7.0	8.2	7.0
Puddled bars	25.2	25.1	25.1
Pigs on finished iron	30.1	30.0	29.2
Coal in mills	18.3	18.3	15.1

Notes:
*Yields indicated the tonnage of coal required to produce one ton of the given product.

Source: GRO D/DG, Section C, Box 4, No. 3, Comparative Statement of Yields of Iron and Coal at Dowlais Iron Works 1853–57.

and it may be gratifying to some who have begun almost to believe in the alarming reports of foreign competition to learn that we saw 10-inch rolled girders passing through this mill for delivery *in Holland*, and we may add that the price of the girders was but £9 per ton, free on board at Cardiff. The girder mill is called a diagonal mill.

However, the trade proved unremunerative and Dowlais abandoned the girder trade during the 1870s.[140] This was not on account of technical backwardness, but because British architects proved reluctant to substitute wrought iron girders for timber or cast iron.[141] 'They had orders of 10 tons or 12 tons at a time', recalled Menelaus, 'some wagon-builders had ordered as much as 50 tons; but the trade would not answer'.[142] Less conservative Continental designers generated a healthy market there which was captured by the Belgians, who, with lower transport costs to customers, successfully undercut Dowlais,[143] and the diagonal rolling mill was converted to other uses.

MECHANICAL PUDDLING AND BESSEMER STEEL

Whilst blast furnaces became bigger and more economical and rolling mills had both reduced their unit costs and were able to handle ever larger sections, there had been virtually no advance in the crucial intermediate process, the conversion of pig iron into puddled bars. 'Puddling' observed Menelaus in his presidential address to the South Wales Institute of Engineers in October 1857,[144]

> has remained . . . since its invention, almost without improvement . . . Science and practice have alike failed . . . Here is a process which absolutely costs nearly one half of the value of the material operated upon, to change very slightly its chemical condition, a large proportion of the cost being for manual labour of the most severe kind, of which the supply barely keeps pace with the demand. When iron makers went mad with excitement about the Bessemer invention, it was only an indication of how strongly they felt the necessity for improvement.

The failure to obtain any further gains in productivity from the puddling method was compounded at Dowlais by three related problems: the need to expand output, the necessity of increasing the size of the bloom produced in order to make longer and heavier rails, and a shortage of suitable labour. The capacity of the puddling furnaces had to be multiplied to keep pace with the company's ironmaking and rolling plant. The simple, and only, solution was duplication. Menelaus increased the number of puddling furnaces steadily during the early 1850s,[145] so that by 1865 there were a total of 146 at Dowlais.[146] Because of the skilled and arduous nature of the job, puddlers were among the highest paid workers in the ironworks, earning on average twenty eight shillings per week; piece rates enabled some to earn even more.[147] They remained in a comparatively strong position to negotiate rates in the prevailing employment market: 'one thing is certain' wrote Lady Charlotte in March 1853, 'viz that labour is becoming daily scarcer, owing to the emigration to Australia and consequently dearer'.[148]

Menelaus was particularly troubled by the shortage of young men coming forward to be trained as puddlers. 'A lad of ordinary strength', he wrote in 1866,[149]

> may begin puddling at 15 to 16; it requires five years practice at least to learn puddling, so that at 21 he is fit to take a furnace as a first hand puddler . . . Owing partly to the system of school education pursued in the South Wales works, few or no lads take to puddling; the educated boys aspire to something better, and in consequence very few boys are now in training for puddlers, this of itself is a matter so serious, that unless some scheme is devised for puddling by mechanical means, it is not easy to see how the present make of wrought iron in England can be maintained.

As a result, herculean efforts were made to improve the puddling process. In March 1853 Lady Charlotte recorded that they proposed to mix '$\frac{3}{4}$% of metal to the charge in the puddling [process] by way of getting out an increasing quantity of puddled bars in preference to going to the enormous expense that a new forge would entail'.[150] In the early 1860s it was discovered that small coals could be employed on the puddling process if added to cheap bituminous coal and subjected to a fan blast. Experiments, Menelaus calculated, showed that costs were significantly reduced: 20 cwts of small coal at 2s. 6d. per ton would 'do as much work as 15 cwts of large at 5s.'.[151]

Although these modifications achieved considerable savings, they did little to increase output, the answer to which Menelaus rightly believed lay with mechanisation. 'If we consider', he argued in 1857,[152]

> what has been done in other branches of manufacture, the great ingenuity that has been displayed in designing machinery for our factories, surely the same amount of skill and invention brought to bear upon our mines and manufactures must produce an amount of labour-saving machinery that will more than compensate for the rapidly increasing values of labour – reduce the amount of drudgery and hard work, and keep the price of iron within reasonable limits.

Some advances had already been achieved in this respect. In December 1853, following in the footsteps of a Mr. Beasley of Staffordshire, Menelaus designed a mechanical squeezer which consolidated wrought iron bars by steam-powered cylindrical rolls thereby eliminating almost all the physical labour normally involved.[153]

The earliest attempt to mechanise the puddling furnace had been undertaken at Dowlais where, to a design by Tooth, an iron drum lined with firebricks was constructed. The whole rotated while the pig iron inside was subjected to an oxidizing blast of hot air.[154] Menelaus unsuccessfully attempted to improve the machine by making the drum elliptical to break open the balls of iron which tended to form inside the Tooth furnace and then erode the lining. 'The chief difficulty', he observed 'in puddling in revolving vessels is to get a lining which will withstand the chemical action of the melted metal and cinder and the mechanical [erosive] action of the iron'.[155]

In May 1868 Samuel Danks (d. 1913) of the Cincinnati Railway Ironworks experimented with a small rotary furnace which was successfully scaled up and exhibited at the Great Industrial Exposition at Cincinnati in 1870 where it won a gold medal.[156] Danks furnaces were subsequently installed at the Indianapolis Rolling Mill Co.'s works and at the Albany Rolling Mill Co. After the news had been digested by the Puddling Committee of the Iron and Steel Institute, it was Menelaus himself who suggested that a commission be set up and its members travel to America to study the process at first hand. Three delegates – J. Snelus, chief chemist at Dowlais, J. Lester of Wolverhampton, and John Alcock Jones of Middlesbrough – were selected and sailed for Baltimore, taking with them samples of pig iron from various parts of Britain to be tested at Cincinnati. In December 1870 they telegraphed the Iron and Steel Institute to say that the Danks furnace was a complete success and that preparations should go ahead for the erection of several 10 cwt converters. The Danks furnace, having a fixed firebox, a rotating hearth and a flue which was fitted in such a way as it could be swung clear of the hearth for loading pig iron and extracting the bloom, stood in the technical tradition started by Tooth and developed by Menelaus.[157] By the end of 1872 there were 72 Danks furnaces being built in Britain, the first having been constructed at the Tees Side Ironworks, Middlesbrough, of Messrs. Hopkins, Gilkes & Co.[158]

In 1874, as president of the Iron and Steel Institute, Menelaus concluded that rotary puddling was close to being perfected.[159] 'Mechanical puddling, in the hands of so many distinguished men who are now at work upon it', he suggested,[160]

> will soon be brought into successful operation; and, further, I opine that it has been clearly demonstrated that the revolving puddling machine, of whatever type, if properly fettled and managed, produces far better results than hand puddling.

The system devised by Samuel Danks then represented the best so far and a prototype was erected at Dowlais. However, it was in the mid-1870s, when mechanical puddling appeared to be about to establish itself, that the volume of steel produced by the Bessemer method accelerated and overtook puddled iron. Henceforth, finance and inventive energies were channelled into making steel rather than wrought iron. J.S. Jeans wrote in 1882 that,[161]

> it will probably not be denied that the skill, experience and inventiveness of practical men have seldom been so barren of useful results . . . The ordinary puddling process has outlived all attempts to improve it out of existence. The puddling furnace of a generation ago is in all its essential features the puddling furnace of today.

Although the production of Bessemer steel did not begin in any quantity at Dowlais until 1865 and first surpassed that of wrought iron in 1878,[162] experiment had begun at Dowlais as early as 1856. *The Times* for 14 August 1856 carried a report of Henry Bessemer's paper, three days after it had been delivered.[163] Lady Charlotte saw the report while in Winchester and readily appreciated that if the technique proved to be a practical proposition, then it would quickly supersede puddling.[164] On reading this, Menelaus, accompanied by Edward Riley, the chemist at Dowlais, hurried to London for discussions with Bessemer. As a result, on 27 August 1856, they secured the first licence to use the Bessemer patent,[165] others subsequently being granted to the Butterley Iron Co., John Brown of Sheffield and Dixon of Govan.[166] For this permission the Dowlais Iron Co. paid £10,000 and were permitted to produce 20,000 tons per annum for the next ten years, any additional quantity being subject to royalty payments of one farthing per ton providing the total output remained below 70,000 tons.[167]

On their return Menelaus and Riley immediately set about building a converter according to the Bessemer specifications. However, their experiments in steel making did not justify the original excitement or expectations. In essence, the patent required that a blast of hot air be passed through a brick-lined furnace filled with molten iron from the refinery. A violent chemical reaction, producing intense heat, occurred, by which the pig iron was purified into steel. Although Bessemer had established the principle on which steel could be made, it remained far from being a practical proposition, let alone a commercial success. When the first steel rail was rolled at Dowlais in 1858 (from an ingot supplied by Henry Bessemer's St. Pancras Works), it broke while still hot, to the undisguised rejoicing of the assembled puddlers.[168] Experiment continued, but as the science of metallurgy had scarcely progressed very far, no solutions were forthcoming.

Repeated failure to rid the brittleness from steel in the late 1850s was due to the chemical composition of the pig iron fed into the early converters. The 'acid' process required ores with very low phosphorus and sulphur contents, that is below 0.06 per cent.[169] The ingots produced at Dowlais in this experimental period vastly exceeded these percentages as Riley's analysis showed: sulphur 0.068 per cent and phosphorus 0.753 per cent. The resultant metal was liable to crack and could not be rolled. Similarly, if too great a quantity of silicon were present then yields were low.

It took almost ten years to isolate the problem, and the appropriate ore to be used in the blast furnace having been identified, in July 1865 the steel forge at Dowlais began operations.[170] The bars it produced were then rolled into rails for tests by the London & North Western Railway, though it was confidently predicted that they would soon replace their wrought iron counterparts. 'If this proves to be the case', observed *The Wigan Examiner*, 'of which there is hardly any doubt, the demand will be so huge that there is every possibility that steel forges will be added to the principal ironworks of South Wales'.[171] Caution remained the railway companies' watchword. Although John Ramsbottom and F.W. Webb of the LNWR at Crewe began laying small numbers of steel rails in the 1860s, they also manufactured and laid over 18 miles of compound or laminated rails in which a steel-bearing surface was welded to a wrought iron web and foot, thereby combining the hard-wearing properties of steel with the ductile qualities of iron.[172]

When Kohn visited Dowlais in 1869 they had installed six 5-ton converters, making it one of the principal Bessemer plants in Britain.[173] In 1866 the company produced 2,257 tons of steel, of which 762 tons was rolled into rails,[174] but by 1870 these figures had risen to 21,179 and 16,967 tons respectively (Table 8.8). Henceforth, the days of the wrought iron rail were numbered.

Table 8.8 The output of wrought iron and steel at Dowlais 1857–80 (tons)

Year	Puddled Bars	Rolled Iron	Bessemer Steel	Siemens Steel	Rolled Steel
1857	93913	75208			
1858	98719	75996			
1859	110626	83825			
1860	114283	88682			
1861	122857	96983			
1862	112570	83984			
1863	107566	89425			
1864	114959	94857			
1865	117199	99224			
1866	122545	99508	2257		762
1867	119872	94387	6206		5176
1868	138628	89471	9162		7634
1869	117993	84660	9737		8124
1870	124364	118390	21179		16967
1871	115477	100827	25958	581	22305
1872	121165	94432	37516	3034	31321
1873	81264	63842	28246	5032	30688
1874	94586	77864	40197	10579	38421
1875	66548	54264	27853	8944	31810
1876	72032	43867	35453	14175	38860
1877	64040	48738	54660	17938	63257
1878	49049	35014	70403	19040	76360
1879	41497	29521	87014	17787	90652
1880	34530	53609	83460	18621	88776

Source: Owen, *History of the Dowlais Iron Works*, Appendix 'G', p. 143.

Speaking in 1868 at the Institution of Civil Engineers in London, Menelaus argued forcefully that,[175] 'even the best wrought-iron ever made was far inferior to Bessemer metal, at least for rails. In adopting steel for Bessemer rails there was one great security; bad steel, in the sense of impure steel, could not be made into rails'. Initially steel rails were more expensive to produce than their wrought iron counterparts. At one works in June 1869 the former cost £70 per ton and the

Table 8.9 The Dowlais workforce, by age, May 1866

Place of work	Under 10 M*	F+	10–13 M	F	14–18 M	F	Over 18 M	F	Total
Forges & Mills:									
Old Works	7	—	44	5	160	55	1091	67	1429
Ifor Works			48	20	98	21	573	15	775
Furnaces			13	16	32	59	559	123	802
Steel Works			3	—	2	—	39	—	44
Fitting, Pattern & Smiths Shops, Foundry, Carpenters & Boilermakers			5	1	78	1	310	2	397
Engineers:									
Forge & Blast			8	—	16	—	130	1	155
Locomotive					3	—	18	—	21
Pits					12	—	126	—	138
Collieries			237	15	358	34	1342	37	2023
Mine Works, Limestone Quarries			95	—	122	41	1248	200	1709
Masons, Roadmen & Navvies			19	—	2	—	288	1	310
Church building			2	—	5	—	24	—	31
Farms							19	13	32
Stables			2	—			82	—	84
Railway Station					—	—	3	1	4
Warehouse					1	—	3	—	4
Traffic					3	—	48	1	52
Weighters, Croppers					11	—	32	5	48
Offices, Library, Post			—	7		22	9	17	55
Cardiff Yard					6	—	58	—	64
Edge Hill Mines			28	—	58	—	195	1	282
London & Liverpool Houses							23	—	23
Totals	9	—	505	64	968	233	6237	484	8500

(*Male +Female)
Source: GRO, D/DG, Section C, Box 5, 'Report on the Employment of Women and Children in the Ironworks of South Wales' by William Menelaus, 16 May 1866.

the expedient of raising by subscription a fund, out of which they offered the colliers a small gratuity per head to be paid on due condition that they resumed their work [before 12 September].

Over the next few days the striking miners returned to the pits. By 4

September, 215 were at work,[205] and three days later the total had risen to 597. *The Times* for 12 September announced that the dispute had ended, the colliers having accepted the *status quo*, and agreed to the existing increase of thirty per cent granted since the autumn of 1852.[206]

The strike had been lost. From the outset Lady Charlotte had demonstrated a determination lacking in her neighbours. 'I am not afraid of the men', she wrote on 11 July 1853; 'I will be their master'.[207] Had the ironmasters shown a similar resilience at Cyfarthfa, Penydarren and Plymouth, the colliers in the district would not have been encouraged to seek ever greater increases. Firmness from the management at the outset, it may be concluded, may have prevented expectations outstripping what could practically be offered. For the men undoubtedly deserved an advance to compensate for rising food prices, and if a fair increment had been decided amongst the four ironworks and adhered to, the acute hardship suffered by the Dowlais colliers and their families would have been avoided. Weak management at the lesser three was the principal cause of the strike which brought Dowlais Iron Co. to the brink of ruin.

What, then, was the nature of employment at Dowlais? In May 1866 Menelaus conducted a detailed survey of the company's labour force and presented the results in a report which he claimed 'may be taken as a fair sample of the South Wales Ironworks generally'.[208] There were at that time 7,719 males (1,482 under eighteen) and 781 females (297 under eighteen) working at Dowlais (Table 8.8).[209] Although his findings appear shocking by twentieth-century standards, they represented an improvement on the conditions prevailing during the late eighteenth and early nineteenth centuries and at some of the less well-managed ironworks of the 1860s:[210]

> practically no children are employed under 10 years of age. There are no girls under 10 and the few boys, nine in all, are the sons of very poor parents to whom their earnings are of importance. The labour at which these children are employed is healthy; they either work in the open air or under large and airy sheds, and the employment is by no means hard; as they are for the most part taken on as a help to their parents, and very little work is expected of them. Of [the] children between the ages of 10 and 13 years, there are employed 505 boys and 64 girls. Most of the boys work in the collieries and mine works.

He concluded that a great improvement had taken place in conditions of employment over the last twenty years.[211] Females were generally being replaced by men or machinery and because wages were slowly rising it was no longer necessary to send children to work at such young ages. Women were increasingly able to devote their time to bringing up their offspring rather than supplementing their husband's income at the ironworks.[212]

The reluctance of young men to train as puddlers (p. 270), the withdrawal of women and children from the works and the emigration of colliers to Australia, had combined to produce shortages of labour in the South Wales ironworks, which in turn raised its cost. In France and Belgium, where they still had ample numbers of labourers, it was proving possible to manufacture rails more cheaply and even sell into the British market.[213]

SUMMARY

The twenty years from 1850 saw the transformation of the Dowlais Iron Co.: from a predicament in which its very existence was in real doubt, the company advanced to a position where it led the world in rail technology and earned consistently high and rising profits. Matters could scarcely have been worse in 1850–52. The ironworks had been run down and needed modernising; the collieries produced insufficient coal to supply the furnaces and steam engines; the death of Sir John Guest in 1852 created a hiatus at the highest level of management. The company was operating at a loss and much of its reserve capital had been withdrawn to purchase Canford Manor at Wimborne. When the colliers went on strike during the summer of 1853, Lady Charlotte Guest must have doubted the wisdom of trying to continue to run the ironworks. Had the miners not capitulated, it seemed inevitable that all production would have come to a halt and the Dowlais Iron Co. forced to close. The return to work enabled a programme of innovation and expansion to continue.

During the interregnum between Sir John Guest and the rule of professional managers under the executive control of G.T. Clark, Lady Charlotte was responsible for authorising a policy of reforms. Although not entirely convinced of its efficacy and disturbed by the capital expenditure that it entailed, she backed the judgement of her senior engineer, William Menelaus, and consulted outsiders, such as Nicholas Wood, where expertise was lacking within the company. The reconstruction of the ironworks also provided an excellent opportunity to introduce the latest plant and working practices. New methods of extracting coal were introduced to the pits and a degree of mechanisation was applied to the conveyance of minerals from the face to the furnace. Bigger and larger blast furnaces were constructed and the number of puddling furnaces increased, though the disproportionate advance occurred in rolling technology with the completion of the massive Goat Mill in 1859 which allowed the Dowlais Iron Co. to mass-produce rails of great length and virtually any required section. Revitalised in this fashion, the company was able to raise output and earn consistently high profits throughout the 1860s.

The brake on greater productivity could be completely released only if a means of improving or circumventing the puddling process could be discovered. The publication and acquisition of the Bessemer patent in 1856 seemed to provide the answer, but the steel ingots produced by the first converters were brittle and unsuitable for rolling into rails. Menelaus, and other engineers experimenting in the iron industry, persisted with the idea of devising a mechanical puddling furnace and, ironically, appear to have been on the point of perfecting a rotary converter at about the time that metallurgists solved the problem of making good quality steel. Perceiving its advantages over wrought iron, new investment was funnelled into steel technology and henceforth the number of puddling furnaces fell steadily.

New management operating new methods was not, however, sufficient to ensure the continued profitability of the Dowlais Iron Co. Just as in the late eighteenth century, congestion on the roads to Cardiff had forced the ironmasters to construct the Glamorganshire Canal, so in the mid-nineteenth century, crowding on the Taff Vale Railway compelled the company to seek an alternative route. Their Colly Line, a private railway designed to serve their modern pits, was sold to the Great Western Railway on condition that it was extended down the Bargoed Taff valley to join the existing network near Llancaiach. In this way, the Dowlais Iron Co. secured a second route to the port of Cardiff and the railway network to England. In 1870 they were poised to enter a strikingly successful period in their history, one that would compare favourably with the growth of the 1830s and early 1840s.

References

1. Lady Charlotte Guest, 'Journal', Vol. VIII, March 1848 – February 1851, 17 March 1849, p. 286.
2. ıbid., 24 December 1848, p. 212.
3. Ibid., 20 November 1850, p. 760; GRO, D/DG Miscellaneous, Box 1, Dowlais Works Accounts 1831–48, 31 May 1848, p. 77; Owen, *Dowlais Iron Works*, p. 44.
4. Guest, 'Journal', 22 April 1850, p. 577; Bessborough, *Lady Charlotte Guest*, p. 241; M. Stenton (Editor), *Who's Who of British M.P.s, Vol. I, 1832–1885*, Hassocks (1976), p. 206.
5. Ibid.
6. Ibid., p. 578.
7. Ibid., Vol. IX, February 1851 – September 1853, 5 July 1851, pp. 89–90.
8. E.E. Edwards, *Echoes of Rhymney*, Risca (1974), p. 27.
9. Guest, 'Journal', Vol. VIII, 20 November 1850, p. 760.
10. Ibid., 10–11 December 1852, pp. 517–518.
11. *PIME*, Vol. 8 (1857), William Menelaus, 'Description of the Large Blowing Engine and New Rolling Mill at Dowlais Iron Works', p. 112.
12. Guest 'Journal', Vol. IX, 14 July 1853, p. 731.
13. GRO D/DG, Box 8, Miscellaneous, 'Summary of Expenditure on New Works Since 31 May 1848 to 11 November 1854'.

14. Guest 'Journal', Vol. IX, 8 November 1852, pp. 464–65.
15. 'Coal Reports, C.E.G., 1851–53' (Manuscript volume in the possession of the Dowager Viscountess Wimborne), 30 April 1851, p. 1.
16. Ibid., p. 8.
17. Ibid., p. 10.
18. Ibid., p. 13.
19. Ibid., p. 17.
20. Ibid., Mr. Evans' Report, 9 January 1852, p. 43.
21. Ibid., p. 25.
22. Ibid., p. 26.
23. GRO, Microfilm Reel No. 129, Lady Charlotte Guest's Works Journal 1852–55, 8 December 1852, p. 3.
24. Ibid., 28 December 1852, p. 11.
25. Ibid., Mr Evans' Report on Proposed New Coal Pits, March, 1853, pp. 39–40.
26. Ibid., pp. 37–38.
27. GRO, Microfilm Reel No. 129, Lady Charlotte Guest's Works Journal, 1852–55, 16 March 1853, p. 27.
28. Ibid., p. 16.
29. 'Coal Reports', Mr Nicholas Wood's Report, 22 April 1853, p. 52.
30. Ibid., p. 54.
31. Ibid., p. 63.
32. Ibid., p. 64.
33. Ibid., p. 69.
34. Ibid., p. 70.
35. Ibid., p. 71.
36. Ibid., p. 72.
37. Ibid.
38. GRO, Works Journal, 6 May 1853, p. 51.
39. Ibid., p. 74.
40. Ibid.
41. Ibid., p. 76.
42. Ibid., p. 78.
43. Ibid.
44. Ibid., p. 80.
45. Ibid., p. 81.
46. Ibid.,
47. Ibid., p. 82.
48. Ibid., p. 86; see also GRO, D/DG, 'Works Journal', 18 April 1853, p. 44.
49. Ibid., p. 86.
50. Ibid., p. 87.
51. GRO, Works Journal, 16 March 1853, p. 27.
52. GRO, Works Journal, 28 May 1853, p. 62.
53. Ibid., p. 63.
54. Ibid., 1 June 1853, pp. 64–65.
55. Owen, *Dowlais Iron Works*, p. 136.
56. R. Walters, *The Economic and Business History of the South Wales Steam Coal Industry*, New York (1977), pp. 158, 162; Church, *Coal Industry*, p. 418.
57. Guest 'Journal', Vol. XI, January 1856 – January 1863, 3 February 1859, pp. 217–18; The Earl of Bessborough, *Lady Charlotte Schreiber, Extracts from her Journal 1853–1891* London (1952), p. 98.

58. Owen, *Dowlais Iron Works*, pp. 60–61.
59. GRO, D/DG, Section D, Collieries, Letter from William Jenkins to G.T. Clark, 15 November 1861.
60. GRO, D/DG, Section D, Letter to G.T. Clark from W. Menelaus, 7 November 1861.
61. Ibid.
62. Ibid.
63. Church, *Coal Industry*, p. 405.
64. GRO, D/DG, Box 6, Section C, Miscellaneous, 'Report on the Dowlais Works' 14 November 1857, from William Menelaus.
65. Ibid., p. 1.
66. GRO, D/DG, Section E, Box 2, Letter to G.T. Clark from H.A. Bruce, 26 July 1860.
67. GRO, D/DG, 'Report', p. 2.
68. Ibid.
69. Ibid., pp. 2–3.
70. Ibid., p. 4.
71. Ibid.
72. Ibid., p. 6.
73. Ibid., p. 7.
74. Ibid.
75. Ibid., p. 8.
76. Ibid., p. 9.
77. Owen, op. cit., p. 58.
78. Ferdinand Kohn, *Iron and Steel Manufacture*, London (1869), p. 87.
79. *JISI*, Vol. I (1869), W. Menelaus, 'On Improved Machinery for Rolling Rails', p. 187.
80. *PIME*, Vol. 8 (1857), Menelaus, 'On Improved Machinery', p. 114.
81. Ibid., p. 115; Owen, *Dowlais Iron Works*, p. 58.
82. Ibid., p. 117.
83. *TSWIE*, Vol. II (1861), W. Menelaus, 'On Rolling Heavy Iron', pp. 77–78.
84. Ibid., p. 79.
85. GRO, D/DG, Report, p. 16.
86. Ibid.
87. Ibid., p. 17.
88. Guest 'Journal', Vol. XI, 24 November 1857, p. 14; Bessborough, *Lady Charlotte Schreiber*, p. 14.
89. GRO, D/DG, 'Report November 1857', W. Menelaus, p. 18.
90. 'Coal Reports', Nicholas Wood's Report, p. 88.
91. Elsas, *Iron in the Making*, William Chessell to James Wise, 1827 (I), f. 104, p. 90; William Chessell to Richard Wood, 1833 (I), f. 189, p. 93.
92. J.D. Marshall, *Furness and the Industrial Revolution*, pp. 187, 194, 197.
93. GRO, D/DG, Letter Book 1842 (2), 14 July 1842, f. 389; Elsas, op. cit., pp. 95–96.
94. Ibid., p. 96.
95. Marshall, *Furness*, pp. 194, 202.
96. GRO, D/DG, Letter Book 1846 (I), 22 January 1846, f. 572; Elsas, op. cit., p. 98.
97. GRO, D/DG, Section C, Notebook, 'List of Contracts at Dowlais House', 1852–54.
98. GRO, D/DG, Miscellaneous, Assay Book 1865–69, 6 December 1866,

Hodbarrow Ore, p. 68; A. Harris, *Cumberland Iron, The Story of the Hodbarrow Mine 1855–1968*, Truro (1970), pp. 27–31, 49.

99. GRO, D/DG 'Works Journal', 27 December 1852, p. 9.
100. Ibid., 19 February 1853, p. 20.
101. Owen, op. cit., p. 77.
102. GRO, D/DG, Works Journal, 18 January 1854, p. 203.
103. Ibid., 20 January 1854, p. 204.
104. Ibid., 1 February 1854, p. 208.
105. Ibid., 3 February 1854, p. 209.
106. Ibid., 9 February 1854, p. 211.
107. Ibid., 12 February 1854, p. 212.
108. Ibid., 15 March 1854, p. 220.
109. Ibid., 29 March 1854, p. 230; Bessborough, *Lady Charlotte Schreiber*, p. 33.
110. Ibid., 4 April 1854, p. 232.
111. Ibid.
112. Guest 'Journal', Vol. X, September 1853 – June 1855, 6 May 1854, p. 258; Bessborough, *Lady Charlotte Schreiber*, p. 34.
113. Ibid., 20 May 1854, p. 264; Ibid., p. 35.
114. Ibid., 6 June 1854, p. 37.
115. Guest, 'Journal', Vol. X, latter part of 1854 and 5 December 1854; Ibid., p. 44.
116. Guest, 'Journal', 10 April 1855; Bessborough, *Lady Charlotte Schreiber*, p. 45.
117. Ibid., 20 December 1852, p. 525.
118. Montague Guest, *Lady Charlotte Schreiber's Journals*, 2 vols., London (1911), *passim*.
119. David Watkin (et al.), *A House in Town, 22 Arlington Street, Its Owners and Builders*, London (1984), pp. 139–40.
120. Wilkins, *Iron, Steel, Tinplate*, p. 302; *DBB*, Vol. 1, London (1984), L.J. Williams, 'G.T. Clark', pp. 686–89.
121. Roger L. Brown, 'The Lewis' of Greenmeadow' (typescript history 1984), p. 4.
122. Stenton, *Who's Who of MPs*, Vol. I, p. 111.
123. *PIME*, Vol. 34 (1883), Memoir, W. Menelaus, p. 20; *JISI*, Vol. 1882 Part II, Obituary, p. 633.
124. Guest 'Journal', Vol. VIII, 20 November, 1850, p. 759; Bessborough, *Lady Charlotte Guest*, p. 251.
125. Ibid., p. 760; Ibid., p. 251.
126. Guest 'Journal', Vol. IX, 30 January 1851, p. 271; Bessborough, *Lady Charlotte Guest*, p. 288.
127. Bessborough, *Lady Charlotte Guest*, pp. 297–98.
128. GRO, D/DG, Works Journal, 16 March 1853, p. 25.
129. Ibid., 10 February 1854, p. 211.
130. Ibid., 29 March 1854, p. 230.
131. GRO, D/DG, Section E, Box 2, Letter to G.T. Clark and H.A. Bruce, presumably from W. Menelaus, 26 July 1860.
132. Ibid.
133. Ibid.
134. Ibid.
135. Guest 'Journal', Vol. XI, 24 November 1857, p. 14; Bessborough, *Lady Charlotte Schreiber*, p. 73.
136. GRO, D/DG, Section E, Letter to G.T. Clark, op. cit., July 1860.

137. GRO, D/DG, Section C, Box 4, Report, W. Jenkins Dowlais Office, to W. Menelaus, 14 November 1857.
138. GRO, D/DG, Section C, Box 4, William Jenkins to W. Menelaus, 'Comparative Account of Makes and Coal Yields at Dowlais 1856–1857', 6 November 1857.
139. Ferdinand Kohn, *Iron and Steel Manufacture*, London (1869), p. 90.
140. *PIME*, Vol. 31 (1880), W. Menelaus, p. 322.
141. Jones, *Industrial Architecture*, pp. 162–63, 173–75.
142. *PIME*, Vol. 31 (1880), p. 323.
143. Ibid., Edward Williams, p. 321.
144. *TSWIE*, Vol. 1857–1859, President's Address, p. 6.
145. GRO, D/DG, Works Journal, 16 March 1853, p. 26.
146. *Webster & Co's Postal and Commercial Directory of the City of Bristol and County of Glamorgan* (1865), p. 494.
147. *Good Words*, 1 January 1869, 'The Merthyr Iron Worker', p. 42.
148. GRO, D/DG, Works Journal, 14 March 1853, pp. 24–25.
149. GRO, D/DG, Section C, Box 5, 'Report on the Employment of Women and Children', by W. Menelaus, 16 May 1866.
150. Guest, 'Journal', Vol. IX, 9 March 1853, p. 364.
151. GRO, D/DG, Letter to G.T. Clark from W. Menelaus, 7 November 1861.
152. *TSWIE*, Vol. (1857–59), p. 3.
153. GRO, D/DG, Works Journal, 16 June 1853, p. 76; 10 December 1853, p. 188.
154. *Cleveland Iron and Steel*, J.K. Harrison, 'The Production of Malleable Iron in North East England and the Rise and Collapse of the Puddling Process in the Cleveland District', pp. 142–43.
155. Ibid., p. 155.
156. Ibid., p. 145.
157. Ibid., pp. 145–47.
158. Carr and Taplin, *British Steel Industry*, pp. 56–57.
159. *JISI*, Vol. 1875, Presidential Address, pp. 17–18.
160. Ibid., pp. 23–24.
161. *JISI*, Vol. 1882, Part 1, p. 144.
162. Owen, *Dowlais Iron Works*, Appendix G, p. 143.
163. Carr and Taplin, *British Steel Industry*, p. 20; Derry and Williams, *A Short History of Technology*, p. 482.
164. Guest, 'Journal', Vol. XI, 15 August 1856, p. 140.
165. Owen, *Dowlais Iron Works*, p. 52.
166. J.S. Jeans, *Steel: Its History, Manufacture, Properties, and Uses*, London (1880), p. 62.
167. GRO, D/DG, Section C, Box 2, Draft Agreement with respect to Patent Rights for the Manufacture of Iron, 1857, pp. 5–6; Letter Books 1857 (I), 19 January 1857, f. 48; Elsas, *Iron in the Making*, p. 195.
168. Owen, *Dowlais Iron Works*, p. 53.
169. Ibid.
170. *The Wigan Examiner*, Vol. XII, No. 605, 7 July 1865, p. 6.
171. Ibid.
172. David Brooke, *Journal of Transport History*, Vol. VIII (1986), 'The Advent of the Steel Rail 1857–1914', p. 21.
173. Kohn, *Iron and Steel Manufacture*, p. 88.
174. Owen, *Dowlais Iron Works*, p. 143.
175. *MPICE*, Vol. XXVII (1867–1968), Christer Peter Sanberg, 'The Manufacture

98   The interior of
Carmen VII station on the
aerial ropeway.
(*British Steel Corporation,
Northern Region Records
Centre*)

99   Luchana shipping
staithes, No. 3 station in
1925. Steamers would
depart from here to the
Roath Dock at Cardiff for
unloading.
(*British Steel Corporation,
Northern Region Records
Centre*)

limestone to complete the smelting process and produced a larger volume of slag.[78] In his presidential address to the Institution of Mechanical Engineers, E.P. Martin observed that because between $3\frac{1}{2}$ and 5 tons of iron ore were required to make a single ton of pig iron, it was imperative to obtain regular supplies of quality ores at low prices. He calculated that in 1905, 110 million tons of ore had been exported from the Bilbao district over the previous twenty-seven years.[79]

The very success of the Dowlais Iron Co. in securing these deposits of Spanish haematite may well, if Sir David Dale is to be believed, have contributed to the company's mixed profit record in steelmaking, for it discouraged them from adopting basic methods until after Dowlais-Cardiff was rebuilt in a large scale in 1934–36. Had they switched from acid to basic linings in their open hearth furnaces they would then have been able to purchase ore from fields within Britain. Whether the cost of shipping ore from Spain by sea was any more expensive than by freight train from the Midlands or Lincolnshire is doubtful. Had there been a marked difference, the Dowlais Iron Co. would doubtless have reorganised their ore gathering organisation. What was probably of far greater importance was the sustained inventive attention which others focussed on the basic method. Since both American and German steelworks were predominantly organised around the basic system and were responsible for generating a host of innovations, it is likely that British concerns which remained wedded to acid technology fell progressively behind in the race for efficiency.

THE DOWLAIS COLLIERIES

If steelmaking at Dowlais was not the profitable activity that it should have been, then there can be no doubting that the company's coal mines were an increasingly important element in the success of the business. Table 9.2 showed that the contribution made by coal sales rose in both absolute and percentage terms between 1870 and 1894. Clark and Menelaus had taken the decision in the early 1860s (p. 250) to expand their mining operations, not simply to provide plentiful supplies of coal for coking and their many steam engines, but to sell to domestic consumers. The revenue gained from this activity could then be employed to modernise Dowlais and provide the enormous capital investment required to construct the Dowlais-Cardiff steelworks.

To expand output still further, in 1874 work began on the sinking of the Bedlinog Colliery. No. 1 Pit (582 yards deep) was opened in June 1881, and No. 2 Pit (580 yards) followed in June 1883, the total cost of their construction, including machinery, being £131,000.[80] Unfortunately, and probably because of the destruction of records at the time of nationalisation, it has proved impossible to assemble a complete picture of productivity at all of the Dowlais Collieries. The statistics which survive (Tables 9.3 and 10.2) reveal a steady rise in

Table 9.3 Output of Dowlais collieries 1893–96 (large coal tons)

	1893	1894	1895	1896
Fochriw Colliery	285640	313974	314614	306573
South Tunnel	108374	124594	137354	139758
Long Work	77045	80533	76374	78495
Bedlinog No. 1	95587	122133	132366	115601
Bedlinog No. 2	128962	149970	157131	174984
Nantwen*	—	177606	179169	165087
Black Vein Drift	14089	16799	16273	22932
Abercynon	—	—	—	4610
Total	709697	985609	1013281	1008040

Notes:
*Including small coals.

Source: GRO, D/DG, Section D, Annual Reports (1894–96), compiled by Henry William Martin.

100 Bedlinog Colliery in 1895. Note the timber pit props piled in the foreground. (*John A. Owen*)

output, though labour productivity (Table 10.4), did not follow in a steady upward trend.

Having made the decision to build an integrated steelworks in Cardiff, it became clear that the Dowlais Iron Co. needed to sink another pit to supply it with coking coal;[81] the cost was estimated at around £270,000.[82] Moving south down the Taff Valley to Abercynon, the company started work on a new colliery in 1890.[83] The two shafts finally reached the 'nine feet coal' in 1896 – some 740 yards beneath the surface, then the deepest in Wales.[84] In comparison with the drift workings of earlier periods, the decision to open a modern mine containing substantial reserves involved a considerable capital outlay and a lengthy period of gestation before any returns could be expected. In 1897, seven years after the scheme had been inaugurated, output had attained 650 tons per day, though it was anticipated that it could reach 2,000 tons when the pits were fully developed.[85]

The financial success of the Dowlais Collieries owed much to the Martin family. George Martin (d. 1887) son of Edward, who had been the principal mining agent for the Duke of Beaufort's Welsh estates, joined the Dowlais Co. in the days when coal working was a subsidiary activity.[86] He was responsible for opening up many of the existing levels and pits, while his last major undertaking was the sinking of the Fochriw Colliery in the late 1850s. His two sons both entered the company, E.P. Martin as successor to Menelaus and Henry William, his younger brother, as manager of the collieries. The latter served in a junior capacity in the mines before working under Sir George Elliot in County Durham. Having gained both knowledge

101 Abercynon Colliery in 1898. Opened in 1894, pits were eventually sunk to a depth of 740 yards, which then represented the deepest in Wales. The Glamorganshire Canal is in the foreground, while the Taff Vale Railway is just beyond the colliery out of sight.
(*John A. Owen*)

and experience, in 1873 H.W. Martin was commissioned by the Japanese government to open various collieries there. He remained abroad for seven years returning to Wales to manage a portion of the Powell Duffryn Co., but in 1884 resigned to take up the post of chief colliery manager at Dowlais,[87] and as such was responsible, together with John Vaughan, a mechanical engineer, for sinking the Abercynon Colliery.[88]

E.P. Martin, addressing the South Wales Institute of Engineers in 1888, noted that the volume of coal passing through the port of Cardiff had increased by five times from 1857, rising from $2\frac{3}{4}$ million tons to $13\frac{3}{4}$ million in 1887.[89] Amongst the innovations applied to the coal industry, he mentioned the installation of electric lighting, shot firing, the use of compressed air and water to damp down dust. Timber pit props were being replaced by rolled steel beams of 'H' section (which provided a further outlet for the rolling mills at Dowlais-Cardiff). Improvements had been made in washing, crushing and preparing small coals for sale. 'The question of delivering our coal abroad in the best possible condition', Martin concluded, 'is now of even greater importance than it was formerly as a new rival has sprung up in mineral oil'.[90] The output of the South Wales coalfield more than tripled over the last thirty years of the nineteenth century, rising from 13,590,000 tons in 1870 to 39,320,000 tons in 1900.[91] By being fully involved in this movement, the Dowlais Iron Co. was able to take advantage of one of the industry's most profitable phases.

There was one major dispute during this period which brought production at the Dowlais Collieries to a halt for almost four months. A depression in 1875, following five extremely profitable years (Table 9.2), prompted the company to cut wage rates which, in turn, caused the miners to strike. G.T. Clark bemoaned the attitudes of his workforce:[92]

> Of late years the great mass of men employed in the ironworks and collieries have been content to do as little work as possible and . . . often done in a slovenly manner. All this, if curable at all, can only be cured by years of financial distress, and by such personal privation, out of which and out of which alone, a more healthy state of things can be expected to rise.

As chairman of the Board of Guardians, he instituted a policy of denying out-relief (payments to those living in their homes rather than in an institution) to strikers, though not to those who had widowed or elderly parents who needed their support, on the grounds that the thrifty could manage without parish assistance. After three months Clark remarked: 'they have ample wages . . . they are pretty well-to-do and can hold out, I dare say for three months . Those locked out were offered relief on condition they took a labour test, but even this was withdrawn in the third month, a tactic to force the miners back to work at one of the re-opened Dowlais collieries. In the fourth month, when the strike collapsed, not one able-bodied collier or underground haulier was receiving relief in any form.[93]

CHANGES IN MANAGEMENT

On 30 March 1882 Dowlais lost the first of its great engineers. William Menelaus had been in poor health for several years and died while on holiday at Tenby aged 64.[94] He left £250,000, but had no children to succeed him for, although he had married Miss Rhys of Tegabor Faur in 1852,[95] she died only nine weeks after their wedding, having succumbed to a fever.[96] Subsequently, Menelaus adopted his two nephews, the eldest Charles Darling (1849–1936), later Lord Langham, becoming MP for Deptford and a judge. Although he spent much of his life in various ironworks engaged on practical engineering questions, Menelaus was no philistine. He built up a considerable collection of pictures which were given to Cardiff Town Council and now form part of the National Gallery of Wales.[97]

The many achievements of Menelaus received official recognition. He had been among the first to apply Bessemer's technique of making steel, previously having striven to devise a successful method of mechanising the puddling process, while advances in rolling mill practice had been pioneered under his supervision. He was one of the principal founders of the South Wales Institute of Engineers and served as its first president in 1857–8, and subsequently in 1864–5.[98] Menelaus was also a leading figure in the setting up of the Iron and Steel Institute in 1868, and in the following year, when the body was formally constituted, he was elected a vice president. Then in 1875 Menelaus became the Institute's fourth president in succession to the Duke of Devonshire, Sir Henry Bessemer and [Sir] Isaac Lowthian Bell respectively. For his contributions to the iron and steel industry, he was awarded the coveted Bessemer Gold Medal in May 1881.[99] Menelaus was also a member of the Institution of Civil Engineers[100] and the Institution of Mechanical Engineers, being voted on to the council of the latter in 1868 and as a vice president in 1870. Although elected to serve as the president for 1881, Menelaus declined the post because of ailing health.[101] His obituary in the *Journal of the Iron and Steel Institute* summarised his professional achievement:[102]

> it is perhaps no exaggeration to say that there was no more indefatigable worker in the manufacture of iron and steel, no one who had more thoroughly mastered it in the best practical way, and few if any who enjoyed at Dowlais and elsewhere a stronger and better reputation.

Any executive hiatus created by the death of Menelaus was avoided

102 E.P. Martin (1844–1910), who succeeded Menelaus in 1882 as the general manager at Dowlais. (*Institution of Mechanical Engineers*)

by G.T. Clark's continued presence as the resident chief executive and by the return of E.P. Martin early in 1882. Destined to become a leading figure in the steel industry, Edward Pritchard Martin (1844–1910) had been born at Dowlais and was educated there and in Paris; at the age of sixteen he was apprenticed to Menelaus, served as Edward Williams' assistant in the London office and then returned to Dowlais to take up the appointment of deputy general manager.[103] To further his career and gain wider experience, E.P. Martin left Dowlais in 1870 to become manager of the Cwmavon Works, but four years later secured the post of general manager at the Blaenavon Iron Works for which he designed a large Bessemer steel plant. Whilst there he befriended Sidney Gilchrist Thomas and his cousin Percy Carlisle Gilchrist, allowing them facilities to experiment on the dephosphorisation of steel, and also interested Menelaus in the endeavour sufficiently that he, too, provided assistance. Convinced of the soundness of this research, Martin, together with E. Windsor Richards, did much to bring the process into commercial operation, and for this contribution they were both awarded the Bessemer Gold Medal in 1884. In this way, 'basic' technology was born and subsequently diffused throughout Britain. In 1881, with Menelaus' health failing, Martin returned to Dowlais and when the former died in the following year, it was clear that he would be offered the general managership. Under his auspices, the Dowlais-Cardiff scheme was inaugurated and carried through, while a programme of modernisation and re-building was initiated at Dowlais to improve its efficiency and to introduce steel technology in all its ramifications.

In the way that Coalbrookdale had served as an informal seminary for the diffusion and development of iron technology during the early eighteenth century, so Dowlais became one of the industry's leading training centres in the Victorian period. Some of the finest engineers and metallurgists either gained their initial knowledge there or journeyed to the town to acquire practical experience. In this fashion, the company assumed a significance beyond its mere commercial standing. Among those who were trained by William Menelaus were Edward Williams, later of Bolckow, Vaughan & Co., William Jenkins of Consett, D. Evans of Barrow, William Davis of Cyfarthfa,[104] and Samuel Truran.

Edward Williams (1826–86), for example, was born at Merthyr Tydfil and was educated at his father's school there before entering the Dowlais Iron Co. in 1842. By the time he left in 1865 to take the post of general manager at Bolckow, Vaughan & Co. in Middlesbrough, he was deputy to Menelaus.[105] Williams had alerted Menelaus to the report in *The Times* outlining the Bessemer patent, and was subsequently responsible for the complete rebuilding of the Middlesbrough plant and in 1884 designed and superintended the erection of a steelworks for Messrs. Crawshay Brothers at Cyfarthfa. He too was awarded a Bessemer Gold Medal. E. Windsor Richards (1831–1921), subsequently to become a director of GKN and one of the outstanding engineers in the steel industry, had been born in Dowlais.[106] Although never employed by the Dowlais Iron Co. (his first job was with the Rhymney Iron Co.), he became a friend of Menelaus and E.P. Martin and succeeded Edward Williams as general manager of Bolckow, Vaughan. Through bodies such as the Iron and Steel Institute and the South Wales Institute of Engineers, based in Cardiff, engineers and metallurgists could meet to discuss ideas, present papers and assess the competence and abilities of their friends and rivals. By such professional and informal links, ideas were disseminated, managers recruited and problems solved. It is possible, in this fashion, that loyalty to a particular works or company became less important than pursuing one's individual career and making a contribution to the universal sum of knowledge.

Enoch James (1846/7–1908), who in 1890 was appointed manager of the Dowlais-Cardiff works had, for example, previously worked for the Rhymney, Ebbw Vale, Solway Haematite and Blaenavon Iron Works. He was a member of the Institute of Mechanical Engineers, the South Wales Institute of Engineers and a Fellow of the Imperial

Institute.[107] In the eighteenth and early nineteenth century, after the disappearance of the itinerant ironmasters, it was less likely that a man should be employed by so many companies. The gradual application of professional standards and scientific attitudes to managers in the steel industry encouraged an exchange of technical information and prompted notions of a career traced through various works and departments to acquire experience and promotion.

In 1892 G.T. Clark, who had been the effective executive head of the Dowlais Iron Co. from 1854 and possibly before, decided to retire from active management. The gap created by his withdrawal was only partially filled by Lord Wimborne taking a greater interest in policy and the town itself. Although he succeeded in improving social conditions there to a marked degree, it may be argued that his intervention as a man of no business experience and certainly no technical knowledge of the iron, steel and coal industries, played a crucial part in the sale of the partnership to Arthur Keen's Patent Nut & Bolt Co.

DISSOLUTION OF THE PARTNERSHIP AND TAKE OVER

It is difficult to piece together the events leading up to the conversion of the Dowlais Iron Co. into a private limited liability company, this being a prelude to its take over by Arthur Keen. Those who had exhibited the greatest commitment to the firm died, placing Lord Wimborne in a position of almost unchallenged authority. Lady Charlotte Schreiber, who conceivably would have been implacably opposed to the sale of the family business, died on 15 January 1895 at Canford.[108] In retirement at his home in Talygarn, G.T. Clark, who had recently opposed a flotation, died on 2 February 1898.[109] Among the senior executives, this left only E.P. Martin, whose views on the sale and merger are not recorded.

In January 1898 *The Western Daily Mercury* carried a story headed 'Report of Impending Sale Confirmed'.[110] It continued:

> The company is a private one, and therefore no balance sheets are published, but a general impression has prevailed that, since the new works were laid down at Cardiff and improved plant introduced at Cardiff, the proprietors were able to compete with any other iron and steel firm in the UK or America, and turn over a handsome profit. If such be the case, why, it is asked, is Lord Wimborne anxious to dispose of the property? There are many reasons which could be advanced for such a step, but, probably, the most potent will be found in the fact that the responsibility is becoming too great for one man.

It appears from correspondence concerning the disposal of the

103 Ivor Bertie Guest, Lord Wimborne (1835–1914), who sold the Dowlais Iron Co. to form Guest, Keen & Co. (*Cyfarthfa Castle Museum*)

Dowlais Iron Co. that the threat of American competition was a factor in Lord Wimborne's thinking. A letter to E.P. Martin in April 1899 mentioned that[111]

> the Standard Oil Company of America (i.e. Mr. Rockefeller) have at length come to a working agreement with Mr. Carnegie and they are contemplating an onslaught on the English steel market this autumn. I know for a fact a similar scheme is in hand in respect of the coal trade for the largest London firm of coal merchants have been asked to act for the Pennsylvanian Anthracite Coal Trust.
>
> It is obvious that American competition by reducing prices would affect most seriously the prospects of English steel companies and it therefore seems to me that advantage should be taken of the present exceptionally favourable time and if Dowlais is to be bought out as a company, no time should be lost.

Preliminary negotiations with Arthur Keen were already underway. In September 1899, the Dowlais Iron, Steel & Coal Co. Ltd. was formed with a registered capital of £1,100,000 to take over Lord Wimborne's industrial properties.[112] Under his chairmanship, five other directors were appointed: Lord de Ramsey, Edward Ponsonby, Viscount Duncannon (later to become 8th Earl of Bessborough), the Hon. Ivor Churchill Guest (subsequently Viscount Wimborne), E.P. Martin and Frederick Gordon. Viscount Duncannon (1857–1920), who had made a name for himself in the City and held a number of industrial directorships including the chairmanship of the London, Brighton and South Coast Railway,[113] was elected vice-chairman.[114] He had apparently been responsible for persuading Lord Wimborne to sell the firm though the discussion which took place between them remains a secret.

The formation of a private limited liability company allowed Lord Wimborne the opportunity to clarify the firm's affairs and to divorce his personal holdings from those of the business. For example, all the depositors' holdings in the Dowlais Savings Bank, a sum amounting to £13,000, were paid up.[115] As a partnership, there had been no legal requirement for the Dowlais Iron Co. to appoint a firm of accountants to perform an annual audit, but on becoming a limited liability company, the law and convention dictated a change. The eminent City practice, Turquand, Youngs & Co. were elected and subject to 'Mr. Young's views as to depreciation' calculated that the profit for the half year ending 30 September 1899 was £132,500.[116] In the summer months of the following year, discussion came to an end and a new public limited liability company, called Guest, Keen & Co., was formed to take over the interests of the former Dowlais Iron Co. and the Patent Nut & Bolt Co.[117] Although Lord Wimborne, Viscount Duncannon and E.P. Martin all joined the Guest, Keen & Co. board, no longer was this a family business and no longer was it run by those whose interests were exclusively attached to South Wales and to coal, iron and steel. In 1902, when Nettlefolds joined Guest, Keen & Co., Lord Wimborne retired from the board and the former Dowlais membership was confined to Lord Duncannon, E.P. Martin and Frederick Gordon.[118]

SUMMARY

The hard-won acquisition and progressive application of steel technology by competitors were crucial in trimming the mighty empire of the Dowlais Iron Co. So different were the requirements of a modern steelworks that it was a herculean task to try to convert an historic ironworks, whose situation was determined by the demands of water power and the provision of local ores and coal, into an integrated steel plant whose raw materials were imported from Spain and many of whose finished products were sold abroad by sea. The answer, as G.T. Clark and E.P. Martin understood, was to build a steelworks from scratch on Cardiff's coastal flats in an area of moorland beside the docks. The one criticism that may be raised of their scheme was that it was not sufficiently ambitious. The Dowlais-Cardiff works never succeeded in dominating its parent in Merthyr until the 1930 slump ended steelmaking at the latter. In fact the Dowlais-Cardiff steelworks, as it was originally conceived, had a comparatively short life, for in 1934–36 it was completely rebuilt at a cost of £3 million and converted to 'basic' technology.[119]

There were two factors inhibiting vital innovation and change. First, Lord Wimborne was loath to do anything that would bring even temporary complaint to the people of Dowlais. It is easy to sympathise with his viewpoint. Within living memory the population had lived in appalling housing conditions, suffered from fevers and cholera, experienced harsh working conditions and periods of financial stringency. To have compelled so many families to move to Cardiff would have seemed scant reward for their services. But delay, as the inter-war period was to demonstrate, only compounded these problems, and much of the hardship endured in the 1930s, when unemployment rose to 64 per cent of the insurable population (12,460 of £19,570) in Dowlais, might have been avoided.

The second factor was of a contractual technical nature. Having committed themselves to 'acid' steelmaking for both their Bessemer converters and open hearth furnaces at Dowlais and in Cardiff, and then engaged in a major enterprise to import phosphorus-free ore from Spain, it would have taken a considerable effort and an imagination of breadth and foresight to have switched to basic methods. In a sense, the Dowlais Iron Co. was penalised by being among the very first in the acid technology race. Later entrants could change with less difficulty; many were not so fully committed, while newcomers could simply adopt basic methods from the outset.

It is interesting to contemplate what might have happened had Lady Charlotte Schreiber or G.T. Clark lived longer, or had Lord Wimborne remained steadfast in his resolve to run the family business. The firm could have used its rising revenues from coal to fund further expansion at Cardiff or to have opened an integrated steelworks elsewhere in Britain, whilst running down operations at Dowlais. In the event, Lord Wimborne, apparently taking the advice of Viscount Duncannon, sold the entire enterprise to Arthur Keen. Henceforth, both the steelworks at Dowlais and Cardiff, together with their various mineral holdings, became part of a major and diversified manufacturing company beholden to shareholders and subject to a broader and sometimes conflicting range of interests. The effect of the new arrangements on the company's behaviour and performance form the subject of the next chapter.

References

1. *JISI*, Part I (1897), p. 230; Owen, *Dowlais Iron Works*, p. 87; D. Morgan Rees, *Historic Industrial Scenes, Wales*, Ashborne (n.d.), plate 38.
2. Ibid., p. 143; Robert Forester Mushet, *The Bessemer-Mushet-Process, of Manufacture of Cheap Steel*, Cheltenham (1883), p. 8.
3. Owen, *Dowlais Iron Works*, p. 76.
4. Ibid., p. 75.
5. Ibid., pp. 76, 143.
6. *JISI* (1897), 'Notes on Works Visited', p. 230.
7. Owen, *Dowlais Iron Works*, p. 80.
8. Ibid., p. 81.
9. Ibid., p. 82.
10. *JISI*, Part (18), p. 226.
11. Ibid., *PIME*, Vol. 68 (1905), E.P. Martin, 'President's Addresses', p. 357.
12. Ibid., p. 357.
13. Owen, *Dowlais Iron Works*, p. 83.
14. Sir Lowthian Bell, *The Iron Trade of the United Kingdom*, London (1886), p. 20.
15. Gourvish, *Railways and the British Economy*, p. 25.
16. R.J. Irving, *The North East Railway Company 1870–1914*, Leicester (1976), pp. 132–34.
17. David Brooke, *Journal of Transport History*, Vol. VII (1986), 'The Advent of the Steel Rail 1857–1914', pp. 22–24.
18. Morgan, *Civil Engineering: Railways*, p. 136.
19. Vamplew, 'Railways and the Iron Industry', p. 39.
20. *Herapath's Railway Journal*, 18 March 1871.
21. I.L. Bell, *Memorandum as to the Wear of Rails*, N.E.R. (1895), p. 29.
22. Brooke, 'The Advent of the Steel Rail', p. 23.
23. Ibid., p. 27; 1900 (Edition), p. 76; see also H.J. Skelton, *Economics of Iron and Steel*, London (1892), p. 241.
24. Owen, *Dowlais Iron Works*, p. 80.
25. Ibid., p. 143.
26. Carr and Taplin, *British Steel Industry*, p. 101.
27. G.R. Walshaw and L.H.J. Behrendt, *The History of Appleby-Frodingham*, Bradford (1950), pp. 63–68.
28. *TSWIE*, Vol. XIII (1882–83), p. 10.
29. *TSWIE*, Vol. XVI (1888–89), Inaugural Address, p. 6.
30. Jeans, *Steel*, p. 35.
31. Owen, *Dowlais Iron Works*, p. 83.
32. *Guest Keen Baldwins Iron & Steel Co. Ltd.*, London (1937), p. 26.
33. Owen, *Dowlais Iron Works*, p. 84; *GKN Dowlais-Cardiff Works, Visit of H.R.H. The Prince of Wales, 22 February 1918*, p. 1.
34. *PIME*, Vol. 71 (1906), p. 599.
35. *JISI*, Part I (1892), p. 399; *The Engineer*, Vol. LXXII, 13 November 1891, pp. 396, 404.
36. Ibid., pp. 400–410.
37. *JISI*, Part I (1892), p. 399.
38. *PIME*, Vol. 71 (1906), p. 600.
39. *Visit of Prince of Wales* (1918), p. 3.
40. *JISI*, Part II (1892), p. 233.

41. *PIME*, Vol. 71 (1906), p. 599.
42. Wilkins, *Iron, Steel, Tinplate*, p. 300.
43. *TSWIE*, Vol. XVII (1888–90), p. 8.
44. Davies, *Economic History of South Wales*, p. 65.
45. *Guide to Cardiff and District, The Institute of Journalists*, Cardiff (1892), p. 60.
46. Wilkins, *Iron, Steel, Tinplate*, p. 299.
47. GKN Minute Book, Vol. 2 (1905–16), 5 October 1905, it. 1189.
48. J. Stephen Jeans, *The Iron Trade of Great Britain*, London (1906), p. viii.
49. Ibid., p. ix.
50. Saul, *The Great Depression*, p. 15.
51. GRO, D/DG, Section E, Box 2, Statement of Profits 1864–1894.
52. *Leaves from the Consett Iron Company Letter Books 1887 to 1893*, Consett (1962), W. Jenkins to W.H. Hedley, 18 August 1892, p. 227.
53. Jeans, *Iron Trade*, p. x.
54. *TSWIE*, Vol. XVI (1888–90); E.P. Martin, p. 7.
55. *Leaves from the Consett Iron Company Letter Books 1887 to 1893*, Consett (1962), W. Jenkins to G.T. Suches, 15 January 1887, p. 7.
56. Jeans, *Iron Trade*, p. xiv.
57. Quoted from Saul, *The Great Depression*, p. 39.
58. Carr and Taplin, *British Steel Industry*, p. 209.
59. *Metallurgical Review*, Vol. I, December 1877, pp. 332–33; quoted from Alfred D. Chandler, *The Visible Hand*, Harvard (1977), p. 260.
60. Jeans, *Iron Trade*, pp. 100–101.
61. Saul, *The Great Depression*, p. 40.
62. Edwards and Baber, p. 149.
63. Jeans, *Iron Trade*, pp. 100–102.
64. *JISI*, Part 1, (1895), p. 44; Carr and Taplin, *British Steel Industry*, p. 177.
65. Ibid., p. 52; Ibid., p. 178.
66. 'Eleventh Special Report of the Commissioners of Labour', *Regulation and Restriction of Output*, Washington (1904), p. 752; quoted by Saul, op. cit., p. 48.
67. Saul, *The Great Depression*, p. 48.
68. S.R. Lysaght, *My Tower in Desmond*, London (1925), p. 110.
69. Charlotte Erickson, *British Industrialists, Steel and Hosiery 1850–1950*, Cambridge (1959), p. 18.
70. P.L. Payne, *British Entrepreneurship in the Nineteenth Century*, London (1974), p. 27.
71. GRO, D/DG Section C, Box 3, *The Orconera Iron Ore Co. Ltd., Incorporated 17 July 1873, Memorandum of Association*.
72. Owen, *Dowlais Iron Works*, p. 78.
73. Skelton, p. 34.
74. W.H. Greenwood, *Steel and Iron*, London (1887), p. 35.
75. Bell, *Iron Trade*, p. 11.
76. Jeans, *Iron Trade*, p. 12.
77. *JISI*, Part I (1881), Thomas Joseph, 'The South Wales Claybed Ironstone or "Mine" ', p. 218.
78. *JISI*, Part II, (1881), p. 580.
79. *PIME*, Vol. 68 (1905), p. 347.
80. Owen, *Dowlais Iron Works*, p. 78.
81. *PIME*, Vol. 68 (1905), E.P. Martin, p. 346.
82. Owen, *Dowlais Iron Works*, p. 85.

83. Ibid.
84. *JISI*, Part II (1897), p. 234.
85. Ibid.
86. Wilkins, *South Wales Coal*, pp. 240–41.
87. Ibid., p. 242.
88. Wilkins, *South Wales Coal*, p. 301.
89. *TSWIE*, Vol. XVI (1888–90), p. 4.
90. Ibid., p. 5.
91. Evan J. Jones, *Some Contributions to the Economic History of Wales*, London (1928), p. 70.
92. Smith, 'Social Control and Industrial Relations', p. 175; Church, *British Coal Industry*, p. 298.
93. Ibid., p. 176.
94. Wilkins, *Iron, Steel, Tinplate*, p. 245; obituaries of William Menelaus were included in *Nature*, Vol. XXV, p. 337; *The Times*, 31 March 1882, p. 106; *Engineering*, Vol. XXXIII, pp. 347, 398; *Iron*, Vol. XIX, p. 250; *Athaeneum* (1882), p. 409; *JISI*, Part I (1881), p. 6; *TSWIE*, Vol. XIII (1882–83), p. 2.
95. NLW, W.W. Price Card Index, W. Menelaus.
96. Guest, 'Journal', 4 November 1852, pp. 462–63.
97. *Western Mail*, 7 April 1882.
98. *TSWIE*, Vol. VII (1872), p. x.
99. *JISI*, Part II (1882), pp. 634–65.
100. *MPICE*, Vol. XXVII (1867–68), p. 353.
101. *PIME*, Vol. 8 (1857), p. 55; Vol. 19 (1868), p. 19; Vol. 21 (1870), p. 18; Vol. 34 (1883), p. 22.
102. *JISI*, Part II (1882), p. 635.
103. *JISI*, Part II (1910), Obituary, pp. 368–69; *The Engineer*, Vol. CX, 30 September 1910, Obituary, p. 363; *PIME*, Vol. 79 (1910), Memoir, pp. 1707–08.
104. Wilkins, *South Wales Coal*, p. 241.
105. *JISI*, Part I (1886), Obituary pp. 213–14; *PIME*, Vol. 37 (1886), Memoir pp. 264–65.
106. *DBB*, Vol. 4, London (1985), p. 897.
107. *Contemporary Portraits and Biographies, Men and Women of South Wales and Monmouthshire*, Cardiff (1896), p. xxiii; *JISI*, Part III (1908), pp. 467–8.
108. Bessborough, *Lady Charlotte Schreiber*, p. 206.
109. Wilkins, *Iron, Steel*, p. 302; *JISI*, Part I (1898), Obituary, pp. 313–14; *The Engineer*, Vol. LXXXV, 4 February 1898, Obituary, p. 116.
110. The *Western Daily Mercury*, 8 January 1898.
111. GRO, D/DG, Section E, Box 8, Correspondence concerning sale of the Dowlais Iron Co., to E.P. Martin from Arthur Radford, 21 April 1899.
112. Owen, *Dowlais Iron Works*, p. 89.
113. Sir John Ponsonby, *The Ponsonby Family*, London (1929), p. 155.
114. Dowlais Iron Steel & Coal Co. Ltd., Minute Book (1899–1974), first meeting, 20 October 1899.
115. Owen, *Dowlais Iron Works*, p. 90.
116. Dowlais Iron Steel & Coal Co. Ltd., Minute Book, 24 November 1899.
117. Henry W. Macrosty, *The Trust Movement in British Industry*, London (1907), p. 37.
118. *GKN, Second Report and Balance Sheet*, 30 June 1902.
119. *Guest Keen Baldwins Iron & Steel Co. Ltd.*, London (1937), pp. 55–63.

10 South Wales: More Steel and Coal, 1900–14

Having merged with the Patent Nut & Bolt Co., the managers of the collieries and manufacturing plant of the former Dowlais Iron Co. discovered that they were no longer autonomous leaders. Not only were there other interests to consider, but, despite their size and historical importance, they found themselves being junior partners in the union. They were faced with the prospect that their policies might conflict with those decided upon by other members of the Guest, Keen group. Would the personalities that the amalgamation had brought together be prepared to co-operate with one another? Whilst at first sight the activities of the Dowlais Iron Co. complemented those of the PNB and provided for a chain of vertical integration, on closer inspection it was apparent that the links fitted together far less closely than might be supposed. There were considerable difficulties following the merger, as formerly unconnected units had to sever established business relationships and attempt to form trading and supply relationships with those consumers within the group of whom they had little knowledge and, on occasion, because of personality clashes and the strength of former company loyalties, scant liking.

MODERNISATION AT DOWLAIS; EXPANSION AT DOWLAIS-CARDIFF

Although a modern steelworks had, in effect, been laid down in the middle of the old ironworks, the onward march of technology had overtaken the established ironmaking and rolling activities at Dowlais. If the works were to compete, and keep pace with its younger offshoot in Cardiff, wholesale rebuilding was required. The directors of GKN were concerned that costs were rising: in August 1902 Dowlais had produced 8,250 tons of rails at 93s. 3d. per ton and in August 1903 made 7,158 tons at 99s. 4d. per ton.[1] They concluded that a rising percentage of waste products was responsible for the adverse trends. Whilst a powerful case could be argued for closing Dowlais

104 Building 'A' blast
furnace and the blowing
engine house in June
1906. Dowlais House is to
the right.
(*Glamorgan Record Office*)

and shifting production to the Cardiff site, the magnitude of such a
transfer and the disruption and hardship that it would have caused to
the residents of Merthyr discouraged the implementation of such a
policy. With this in mind, a major investment programme was
authorised at Dowlais in 1904 for the erection of two blast furnaces of
the most modern American design. They were the first in Britain to be
fully mechanically charged and featured the 'Pohlig' system which
had originally been developed in Germany, but perfected at the
Mayhill Steelworks in Ohio.[2] Construction commenced in July 1905[3]
and was supervised by a consultant, David E. Roberts, a Dowlais
trained engineer based in Cardiff.[4] The furnaces, called 'A' and 'B'
were 80ft in height and 20ft in diameter at the boshes. The bunkers
situated to their rear for the storage of coke, ore and limestone, had a
capacity of 371,000 cubic feet. In addition, nine Cowper hot blast
stoves, a new blowing house accommodating three engines, and pig
beds served with two cranes and an electrical pig breaker were
constructed. 'A' furnace came into operation on 12 November 1909
and was so successful that it served as a model for similar schemes
elsewhere in Britain.[5]

The other area of concern at Dowlais was its rolling operations.

Figure 12 The Dowlais Ironworks in 1900

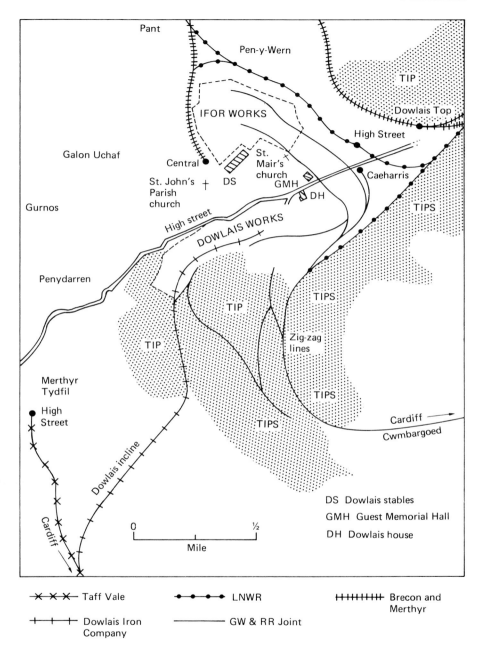

E. Windsor Richards, who had been appointed to the board of GKN, stated in January 1902 that 'for some time past he had been seriously considering the heavy losses which the mills had been and were making'.[6] He recommended that

105   'A' blast furnace at Dowlais under construction in March 1908.
(*John A. Owen*)

several rolling mills which were situated in various parts of the Dowlais Works should be stopped, broken up and converted into money . . . and that in their place, one good rolling mill, capable of turning out 150,000 rails per annum should be employed.

Mr Richards also explained that when the whole of the furnaces at Dowlais were in blast they could produce enough pig iron to keep the [projected] rolling mill going at the rate fixed upon, viz 150,000 tons per annum, and supply a small quantity of pig iron which would be required for the Siemens-Martin furnaces to enable the crop ends and other scrap to be used up on that department and converted into special billets.

Following this report it was decided to install a new rail mill with a weekly capacity of 5,000 tons and worked by fewer men than had been necessary under the old system, whereby 600 tons of iron rails were produced a week.[7] Constructed in 1905, it required three engines, one each for the cogging, roughing and finishing processes. The task of transferring the hot metal from the cogging to the roughing rolls and then on to the finishing rolls was performed, in each case, mechanically by nine rollers on either side of the rolls, assisted by an Evans & Lewis manipulator, the whole needing just the attention of two boys. As a result of this extra rolling capacity, the Bill Mill engine was scrapped in 1906 after seventy-six years continuous service.

Having introduced measures to improve their iron-making and

106 'A' blast furnace completed. It was mechanically charged by the 'Pohlig' system and had Cowper hot blast stoves with hexagon regenerator linings. The sand pig beds are in the foreground.
(*British Steel Corporation*)

107 The blast furnace site at Dowlais *c.* 1927; (left to right) 'A', 'B' and No. 11 blast furnaces. In the foreground are the pig beds with an electrical pig breaker and two ten-ton overhead cranes to transport the iron into wagons.
(*Glamorgan Record Office*)

rolling methods, the managers of GKN also considered ways of raising productivity in their steelworks. The tilting furnace, an innovation which promised much (George Snelus in the *Journal of the Iron and Steel Institute* for 1900 described it as the greatest advance in the manufacture of steel for some years),[8] but whose impact has yet to be quantified by historians, was devised by Benjamin Talbot (1864–1947). Born in Shropshire and apprenticed at Ebbw Vale, Talbot emigrated to America in 1890 and nine years later as superintendent of the Pencoyd Steel Works, Pennsylvania, introduced the continuous method of steelmaking to which he gave his name.[9] In 1901, returning to England and becoming managing director of the Cargo Fleet Iron Co., Middlesbrough, Talbot continued to promote his new process. In essence, it involved adding pig iron to much greater quantities of molten mild steel. An equivalent amount of steel would be tapped by tilting the furnace initiating a continuous manufacturing process, while slag too could be removed by a similar operation. The conversion of the metal was swift, and it allowed a lower grade of pig iron to be refined than in a fixed furnace and much more economically as very large, deep-bathed furnaces of 250 to 300 tons capacity were employed.[10]

There were no tilting furnaces in Britain before 1900, but Talbot's return from America stimulated interest and in January 1902 the first continuous tilting furnace was introduced at Frodingham by Maximilian Mannaberg. Guest, Keen & Co. had made enquiries as early as November 1900 when E.P. Martin explained that[11]

108   The interior of the new blowing engine house at Dowlais in 1912; it contained three vertical compound condensing engines.
(*British Steel Corporation*)

negotiations had been in progress with Mr. Harbow of Englefield Green, Surrey, the agent in this country for Mr. Talbot, with a view to obtaining a license on preferential terms to work this process and that to build the necessary furnace to make a trial would involve an expenditure of about £10,000.

Whilst in America, Arthur Keen and E. Windsor Richards visited Pencoyd and secured an agreement from Talbot that a licence be granted to the company with a maximum royalty of 6d. per ton.[12] This was formally ratified in August 1901.[13] Construction proceeded at Cardiff and in June 1904 William Evans reported that 'everything was ready for the furnace to be put to work'.[14] By January 1905, when 10,949 tons, 15 cwts of steel had been manufactured by the process, £273 14s. 10d. was owed in royalty payments to the Talbot Continuous

109 An aerial view of Dowlais-Cardiff steelworks in May 1920. The blast furnaces are to the left and the melting shop containing the open hearth furnaces are in the centre of the photograph. (*Aerofilms*)

110 The laboratory at Brymbo *c.* 1920. The photograph suggests that the science of metallurgy had still not developed far.

Steel Process Ltd.[15] Unlike those tilting furnaces installed at Frodingham and at Cargo Fleet which operated using basic ores, as advocated by Talbot in his pioneering experiments, GKN introduced haematite pig iron to their furnace, thereby retaining an unswerving adherence to acid technology. Whether, indeed, the Talbot process actually exercised a 'great effect for the future of British basic steelmaking' as Carr and Taplin have suggested,[16] is unclear. Reference to the Dowlais-Cardiff example does not answer the question. The overwhelming bulk of its steel was produced by acid open hearth furnaces and only under the rebuilding scheme of 1934–36 were three 230-ton tilting furnaces and two 90-ton fixed furnaces installed, though a further 250-ton tilting furnace was added shortly afterwards.[17] It seems, moreover, that the switch to basic technology, rather than the introduction of a continuous facility, was the crucial innovation.

In 1899 E.P. Martin drew up a report on coke ovens and coal washing machines at Dowlais-Cardiff, in which he recommended the adoption of a system devised by the Belgian, Evence Coppée.[18] The ninety ovens and washing machines, argued Martin, should be erected at Cardiff because[19]

   1. The foundations for the ovens at Dowlais would be on ground that had been mined; and the washing machines would be

Table 10.1 Numbers employed at the Dowlais-Cardiff steelworks, East Moors in 1902

Department	Men Over 18 Yrs.	Men Under 18 Yrs.	Women
Blast Furnace	216	32	—
Siemens open hearth furnaces	209	4	—
Rolling Mills	317	34	3
Docks	13	—	—
Total	800	70	3

Source: GRO, D/DG, Letters Dowlais-Cardiff Works 1902, Letter from E.H. James, 9 May 1902.

erected on land having only a short lease to run – at Cardiff the lease would be about 90 years.

2. Since a certain quantity of coal for the ovens would have to be purchased, Cardiff offered a better market for such purchases.

3. The by-products would be more easily disposed of as Cardiff was a port.

Without separate profit figures it is difficult to assess the overall commercial success of the steelworks at Dowlais and East Moors, Cardiff. The reported GKN figures provide little an indication of how the Guest portion of the business fared, for they also comprise the nut, bolt and woodscrew elements, together with the Rogerstone steelworks (formerly Nettlefolds) and Cwmbran ironworks (formerly Patent Nut & Bolt Co.). All that can be said is that there were no dramatic fluctuations in profits between 1902 and 1914 (Table 11.2) the highest profit being £471,511 in 1907 and the lowest £348,093 in 1910. In real terms the plateau-effect is modified by a slight decline in reported profits falling from a peak of £809,000 in 1907 to £641,000 in 1914.[20]

Dowlais-Cardiff steelworks appears to have benefited from a policy of re-armament and in particular the expansion of the Royal Navy. In 1912 A.K. Reese, the general manager, wrote to Arthur Keen to impress on him the importance of Dowlais being able to supplement their own production of coke:[21]

in view of the heavy demand for plates and the tonnage we have on our books for delivery we consider it of great importance to keep our plate mill running as full as possible, but it will be impossible to do this unless we are able to keep our No. 2 furnace in blast to supply our Talbot furnace with molten metal.

Should we be compelled to bank No. 2 furnace it would be necessary to stop the Talbot furnaces only, which would reduce our output from 2,000/2,100 tons per week to 1,500/1,600 tons per week, which, besides increasing our costs owing to the lower tonnage, would prevent our meeting our obligations . . . to our customers, which is of considerable importance owing to the large number of specifications which we have in hand.

Among those to whom Dowlais-Cardiff sold were Vickers, Sons & Maxim Ltd.,[22] Cammell Laird & Co.[23] and the Admiralty,[24] while Harland & Wolff were described as being 'such good customers of ours'.[25]

RECONCILING MANAGERIAL DIFFERENCES

The mergers which brought together the Guest, Keen and the Nettlefold interests were for the most part prompted by a desire to secure a measure of vertical integration (in its simplest form this theoretical chain ran as follows: coal and iron ore converted into pig iron and steel and then rolled into billets by the Guest element; the billets then rolled into rod by the Nettlefold element for conversion into woodscrews by them, or their manufacture as nuts and bolts by the Keen element). Nevertheless, there were in practice considerable difficulties in reconciling the differences between the three principal constituents, and many years were to elapse before this system was actually implemented. The advantages accruing from amalgamations have been widely publicised (not least by the dominant partner in question) but also by business historians and the management schools, and it seems that due weight has often not been given to the drawbacks, bitterness and rivalries that they often generated.

A crucial part of the great scheme devised by Arthur Keen was that the Dowlais-Cardiff steelworks should provide the fastener factories in the group with their basic material, pig iron – and, in time, steel rod, though this stage was not achieved until the mid-1930s with the progressive transfer of the Castle Works from Rogerstone to the Cardiff site. Yet neither Dowlais, which specialised in the manufacture of rails, nor Dowlais-Cardiff, which had been designed to roll plate, had any recent experience in making products for the fastener trade. Nettlefolds continually complained that the pig iron despatched from East Moors to their Bessemer steelworks at Rogerstone[26] was unsuitable, since it contained levels of phosphorus and manganese higher than were desirable in machining woodscrews.[27] In July 1906 Edward Steer, then general manager of the Castle Works, wrote to Arthur T. Keen, then joint managing director of GKN, to complain that[28] in order to procure satisfactory material for the screw works, we ought to have pigs running from .03 to .04 phosphorus, with an average say .035 low in sulphur, and 2% to $2\frac{1}{4}$% silicon. We have gradually lowered our standard and practically confined our purchases to Dowlais iron until we eventually agreed to take as 'best' iron .05 phosphorus, and for second grade .06 phosphorus.

On the same day he also wrote to the general manager at Dowlais to inform him that[29]

we are not receiving any iron fit for screw rods from Dowlais or Cyfarthfa [which GKN had taken over in 1902]. Our stock of best iron from other districts is practically worked off as we have had to draw upon it unduly on account of the inferior quality of iron we have lately received from you. Unless we receive good deliveries – at least 800 tons – next week, of your better quality . . . we shall not be able to keep our Birmingham screw works going, and the result to the firm will be disastrous.

Although a certain amount of friction seems to have arisen over the matter, the managers at Dowlais and Cardiff were not so ill-disposed towards their new Midlands owners that they were deliberately ignoring their requests, rather their system of supply and manufacture had never been geared towards making the types of iron required by the fastener trade. In order to reduce the percentage of phosphorus and manganese in the pig iron, it was necessary[30]

to use more expensive ore mixtures and select our coke using only low-phosphorus coke on one furnace and this of course would mean we would have to use all the high-phosphorus coke on the other furnace, which would cause the iron from that furnace to be too high in phosphorus for our use and sales.

As a result of pressure from Nettlefolds, they were forced to purchase high quality ores from the Hodbarrow mine in Westmorland[31] which undermined the logic of having concluded contracts with the Orconera Co. for bulk supplies of cheap ironstone.

Considerable disruption to the manufacturing schedules at Dowlais-Cardiff resulted from the requirement to produce iron for Nettlefolds.[32]

in reference to our discontinuance of sending hot metal [from the blast furnace] to Siemens [open hearth furnace] since October. Our object in stopping this practice was to aid us in filling the requirements of Nettlefolds, which, at about that time, was . . . 2,000 tons per week, and as we were afraid we would have some difficulty in supplying them we did not like to send 3–4,000 tons of iron suitable for them to the Siemens furnace.

Thus, the character of the additional demand presented by Nettlefolds was not in the short-term conducive to greater economies of scale at Dowlais-Cardiff. These difficulties endured throughout the Edwardian period and were probably not resolved until the mid-1930s.

Problems had also been created by those who now supplied Dowlais-Cardiff with its basic materials. The Cyfarthfa steelworks (p. 352), owned and operated by GKN between 1902 and 1910, together with Dowlais provided the company's works at Cardiff with supplementary deliveries of coke. This too caused difficulties. Because the managers at Cardiff lacked direct control over the type of coal being coked by the steelmakers in Merthyr, they often received deliveries of coke containing levels of phosphorus and sulphur such that they would render the pig iron produced unsuitable for use by Nettlefolds. Furthermore, the construction of extra furnaces at Cardiff, which depended upon Cyfarthfa and Dowlais for part of their coke supply often led to shortages. A letter, typed with a red ribbon to indicate the urgency, which was sent to Dowlais by A.K. Reese in October 1908, read:[33]

> Coke situation still very serious. While we had a good lot on Saturday evening, and in consequence started up No. 3 furnace yesterday morning, very little came in this morning and the situation does not look at all promising for keeping both furnaces going. It is of course very bad for the furnace to be started up and stopped again at such frequent intervals.

It appears that the closure of Cyfarthfa in 1910 forced Dowlais-Cardiff to seek coke supplies from the Cwmbran ironworks, formerly belonging to the Patent Nut & Bolt Co. Again, there were problems over quality and regularity of deliveries. 'We have your letter of 14 inst', wrote A.K. Reese on 17 June 1912,[34]

> advising that after July 1st Cwmbran Works will be blowing their furnace in, and will not be able to send us more than 2/3,000 tons per week. This . . . will bring our receipts of coke, exclusive of German coke, considerably below our consumption though it is possible that Great Western and Llanbradach [collieries] may by that time have increased their shipments sufficiently to make up the difference.

In August 1914 the complaints made by the managers of Dowlais-Cardiff of Cwmbran focussed on a rise in the phosphorus levels due to a change in the quality of the coal, thereby making the coke unsuitable for iron destined for Nettlefolds. 'This alteration', observed Reese,[35]

> in Cwmbran coke reduces us to Lewis Merthyr [colliery] as the

only low phosphorus coke received, Great Western being the next . . . This is particularly important at the present time owing to the desirability of using a proportion of the washed Orconera and Obregon ores which are both high in phosphorus, on both of our furnaces owing to the restricted receipts of the rough ores.

Moreover, the Dowlais-Cardiff steelworks was reliant upon quarries in the Merthyr district for its supplies of limestone and these, by the late nineteenth century, appear to have been subject to fluctuations in quality and quantity. In December 1907 Reese reported to Dowlais 'our stone stock is dangerously low owing to the irregular supplies we have been receiving from Dowlais and Craigeau'.[36] Such difficulties were not overcome quickly for a year later Thomas R. Martin wrote to confirm that[37]

> with the small shipments we have been receiving from Craigeau lately, this quantity will be entirely inadequate for our requirements this week. Our limestone stock is completely out and we shall require from 1,900 to 2,000 tons of stone to see us over.

He concluded by asking Dowlais for 12,000–14,000 tons of limestone otherwise the rate at which the blast furnaces were worked would have to be slowed down. Later in 1908, Reese was forced to complain that large lumps of limestone were still being found in shipments from Dowlais, though there had been improvements in the quality of those sent from Cyfarthfa.[38]

FURTHER EXPANSION OF COAL

When Arthur Keen's acquisitive eyes fell upon the Dowlais Iron Co., he was not simply looking for a steelworks to complete the manufacturing chain, but he was also interested in the firm's extensive and profitable holding in coal mines which added to the attractions of a take-over. At a board meeting in March 1901, shortly after the merger, Keen[39]

> referred to the importance of the company's mining properties, and recommended that the monthly report made by Henry W. Martin to Mr. E.P. Martin should be laid before the board for their consideration and that typed copies of the reports should be sent to the directors as early as possible each month.

Soon afterwards, in October 1902, a 'Colliery Committee' was set up to look in more detail at the coal mining activities of the group.[40] To assess whether any improvements could be introduced or whether rationalisation might be required, in November 1901 Keen appointed

Mr. T. Forster Brown whom he had known for thirty years, as 'consulting mining engineer for the whole of the company's collieries'.[41] Formerly a Durham mining engineer who had become a partner in a firm which specialised in deep mining, especially in South Wales, Forster Brown was given the brief to[42] 'give his opinion and advice with regard to the manner in which the different collieries should be worked, and the expenditure to be incurred, so as to ensure the best possible results'. Keen clearly believed that the new company had a valuable commodity in coal and was determined, through investment and attention to management, to secure the maximum commercial advantage from their many holdings.

In the decade before the Great War, there was little mechanisation of coal cutting. The longwall system, or at least variants on the theme, was widely employed in GKN's mines and extraction was by sheer hard labour in confined spaces using picks and shovels. Coal-cutting machines were not in general introduced in South Wales until the inter-war period and then in an unsystematic fashion. Such machinery as had been introduced underground was for ventilation and to convey coal from the face to the shaft, though it had not proved possible to calculate the respective percentages of coal moved by steam power, and by human or animal muscle. In 1901, when the Dowlais and Abercynon Collieries already employed 500–600 horses, it was concluded that the current number was insufficient and more pit ponies should be purchased.[43] In October 1902, Henry W. Martin was instructed to discover the reason why eleven to twelve per cent of the coal extracted at the Dowlais Collieries was consumed by internal operations such as winding engines, compared with five to six per cent at the Abercynon pit.[44] The latter was more modern than the others and so could be expected to be more efficient, but not to such a large extent.

The nature of the geology of South Wales made mining an unpredictable activity. H. Stuart Martin (possibly no relation of H.W. Martin, and who resigned in 1908 to work in South Africa) reported in December 1904 that the fall in the percentage of 'large coal' being extracted was partially[45] 'due to our having lost a large number of faces throughout the Dowlais and Abercynon Collieries, faces having been cut out by faulty ground and other faces having been worked up to the boundary'. When a seam suddenly narrowed, making coal cutting an arduous task and reducing the quantity that could be mined, the labour productivity of the pit would of necessity fall, and decisions had to be made as to the advisability of searching for a new face and the capital investment that its establishment would involve.

Another problem, in a period before the universal introduction of steel pit props and arches, was the provision of pit wood. As H.S. Martin explained to his managers in 1906[46]

we consider that about 4,000 tons stock is a fair quantity [for the

Dowlais Collieries] and we always try to avoid exceeding this figure, as when the pit wood is allowed to remain on the ground for a very long time it depreciates very much in value and gets too rotten to be used underground. When the stocks are very heavy . . . the older timber cannot be used first as it is often at the bottom of the stocks. At Abercynon, we have about 2,300 tons in stock, which will last us about six weeks.

Attempts were made to raise the efficiency of coal extraction though to little effect. In February 1909 a coal-cutting machine was purchased from Messrs. Mavor & Coulson and set to work in Fochriw No. 1 Pit,[47] and shortly afterwards, Howell R. Jones wrote to them to say that the medium-size coal-cutting machine on order was now required for the Long Work Pit, Cwmbargoed.[48] Unfortunately there is no record of their cost or output and what percentage was extracted by manual labour and what by machinery. The faulted nature of seams throughout the South Wales coalfield discouraged the introduction of new technology. 'It would be quite rash and quite wrong to suppose', argued the Chief Inspector of Collieries in 1919,[49]

that mechanical coal-cutters can be employed broadcast in all coalfields. They are quite impossible of application in a great number of Welsh coalmines . . . because the coal will not stand to be cut. No sooner does the machine proceed to work on the face than the coal falls upon it.

The nature of the coal itself and the existence of geological faults or slips eased the difficulty and labour of extracting the coal by human effort.[50] In view of the particular circumstances in Wales, one inspector would not 'anticipate a great increase in the employment of machinery in coal cutting for some time to come, as most of the steam coal seams now being worked are thick, and as the "slips" or lines of cleavage occur with such great regularity there is not much [sic] labour required in working the coal'.[51] Nevertheless, the introduction of the Eight Hours Act in 1910 (p. 347) had sufficient an impact on output to encourage companies to purchase machines in an attempt to offset the effect of the shorter working day.[52]

An overwhelming proportion of coal was still mined by pure physical labour, using the simplest tools and methods. In the Victorian and Edwardian periods employment in a coal mine was for most part extremely exhausting toil combined with a serious element of danger and high risk of ill-health; in spite of these conditions, it was not well rewarded although during the Great War was considered an honourable alternative to fighting in the trenches.

Mechanical aids were more readily applied to the sorting and cleaning processes situated above ground. In his report presented to the Guest, Keen board in December 1901, H.W. Martin demonstrated that[53]

> except at No. 1 Pit Fochriw, where the company has two side tipplers and two cleaning bands, the company had no special plant for cleaning coal at any of the Dowlais Collieries, and stated that to prepare coal for sale (especially from the lowest and inferior seams), cleaning machinery of some description was necessary.

Because it was more modern, Abercynon Colliery appears to have been mechanised above ground from the outset, though the system had its defects. In March 1904 Fifoot, Ching & Co., coal merchants, complained that they had found large pieces of slag and stone in deliveries of coal from the pit. H.W. Martin wrote to explain how the mechanised screens should have prevented such oversights and privately admitted that the occurrence of many faults in the coal seams was the primary cause.[54] The cost of installing modern processing plant seems to have been regarded as prohibitive during this period. Mr. Bruce Jones, manager at Abercynon, received an unenthusiastic response to his proposal in February 1909:[55] 'I fear that your idea of putting down a washery and aerial railway to deal with the shale, and the necessary plant to partially clean the coal, will be considered too large an outlay by the firm'.

Whilst the colliery side of GKN continued to earn substantial profits by simply expanding output, and labour remained plentiful and not expensive, there was no great incentive to install cost-cutting machinery. Further, the work of sorting and preparing the coal for sale was commonly performed by boys too young to work below ground or older men whose health was no longer sufficiently robust to perform the arduous tasks of mining. To have mechanised these jobs on the surface would have taken away their livelihoods and, in view of the low wages paid, would have resulted in only minimal savings to the company. It might, too, have been unpopular amongst families who relied on the additional earnings of children or elderly relations.

Records of output for the many collieries owned by GKN are patchy and unsystematic. In 1886 it was calculated that the Dowlais Iron Co. raised 1,025,236 tons of coal, which made them one of the largest coal owners in South Wales, only the Powell Duffryn Coal Co. with an output of 1,072,012 tons exceeding their capacity.[56] A fair measure of total output (that is large and small coals) was provided by the annual summaries published by the Monmouthshire & South Wales Coal Owners' Association (Table 10.2). The figures refer to the tonnage for which the individual companies were assured, that is the amount on which the Association would pay compensation should the company suffer from a strike. From 1889 onwards, the total was based on the output during the last full year; the assured tonnage for March 1902–3, for instance, would represent the actual output in 1901. Totals were rounded up to the next 5,000 or 10,000 tons. Nevertheless, the series provides evidence of increased output at many of the pits owned by the Dowlais Iron Co. and subsequently GKN from 1887 to 1914. This picture was corroborated by evidence from the company's own letter books which recorded gross output in relation to the consumption of pitwood (Table 10.3).

Table 10.2   Output (tons) at selected Dowlais collieries (large and small coal) 1887–1914

Year	Nantwen	Bedlinog		Cwmbargoed	Fochriw		Abercynon
1887	180000	117000		69000	253000		
1888	180000	127000		69000	253000		
1889	161100	157523		76716	335988		
1890	155779	207991		79515	328080		
1891	139984	218258		84023	331146		
1892	155554	269986		98706	369965		
1893	184862	329435		112092	412195		
1894	180521	354667		102542	412733		
1895	170000	375000		160000	400000		50000
1896	168030	370000		102569	415347		160000
1897	144450	354733		77354	415000e		380000e
1898*							
1899	157961	378051		70612	385237		349936
1900	140000	190000	120000	71000	190000	200000	420000
1901	140000	190000	120000	50000	160000	200000	420000
1902	120000	200000	110000	50000	160000	200000	440000
1903	125000	240000	155000	50000	135000	220000	470000
1904	130000	230000	160000	50000	135000	230000	540000
1905	140000	230000	170000	45000	135000	230000	600000
1906	155000	232000	175000	40000	100000	220000	610000
1907	155000	245000	185000	30000	100000	220000	610000
1908	155000	250000	190000	30000	100000	200000	620000
1909	150000	260000	180000	50000	100000	200000	600000
1910	150177	282651	192475	63918	99856	197608	563420
1911	150000	260000	160000	65000	125000	225000	580000
1912	150000	250000	160000	60000	135000	225000	620000
1913	160000	180000	160000	55000	150000	240000	650000
1914	170000	160000	140000	60000	140000	220000	625000
		(No. 1)	(No. 2)		(No. 1)	(No. 2)	

Notes:

e indicates given as an estimated figure in original.

* The assured figures for year to March 1900, which would have been based on output for 1898, were in fact identical to those for 1987 since this was the best estimate of each colliery's capacity given the strike of 1898.

Source: Monmouthshire and South Wales Coal Owners' Association records, Annual Summaries, 1888–1915, National Library of Wales, Aberystwyth.

Table 10.3   Output at Dowlais and Cyfarthfa collieries 1905–12

| Year | Dowlais | | Cyfarthfa | |
	Gross output (tons)	Tons of coal raised per ton of pitwood used	Gross output (tons)	Tons of coal raised per ton of pitwood used
1905	979083	33.7	17765	95
1906	978678	32.1	18455	215
1907	934998	30.4	18593	224
1908	965618	30.9	19547	264
1909	995872	28.8	23006	307
1910	999185	28.9	25967	356
1911	1020426	30.3	25043	334
1912	—	—	22129	312

Source: GRO, D/DG, Letters Dowlais Collieries, Mr. Howell R. Jones and Mr. Tudor Davies, 1912–15, Statements from H.R. Jones, 8 May 1912.

Table 10.4   Labour productivity at selected South Wales colliery companies (annual output per man, tons) 1902–13

Year	Crawshay Bros (Cyfarthfa)	GKN	PNB (Cwmbran)	Powell Duffryn
1902	252	252	288	322
1903	249	261	—	299
1904	250	260	257	299
1905	246	261	249	282
1906	233	259	218	292
1907	207	248	200	303
1908	189	225	206	304
1909	181	207	201	301
1910	—	206	170	279
1911	—	202	160	283
1912	—	207	162	288
1913	—	214	175	299

Source: Rhodri Walters, *The Economic History Review*, Vol. XXVIII (1975), 'Labour Productivity in the South Wales Steam-Coal Industry, 1870–1914', p. 301.

Figures recently compiled to assess the labour productivity of South Wales mining companies reveal a downward trend from 1902 to a low in 1911 with a slight recovery in 1913.[57] The colliery companies belonging to GKN were no exception (Table 10.4). Within this period the highest output per man (above and below ground combined) was achieved in 1905 (261 tons) and the lowest in 1911 (202 tons). A major

Table 10.5   Coal output at Dowlais and Abercynon, 1909–11

	Year	Large coal	Small coal	No. of men	Tons per day	Tons per day per man
Dowlais	1909	751544	242569	4812	3465	14.4
Collieries	1911	746391	271740	5547	3428	12.35
Abercynon	1909	432731	406143	2470	2088	16.9
Colliery	1911	164565	171842	2667	1953	14.64

Source: GRO, D/DG, Letters Dowlais Collieries 1909–11, Howell R. Jones to William Evans, 25 July 1911.

reason for the fall in the productivity of individual miners was the legislation designed to shorten the working day. The introduction of the Eight Hours Act in 1910 prompted the company to calculate its effect upon output and productivity (Table 10.5). In 1909, 751,544 tons of large coal and 242,569 tons of small coals were mined from the Dowlais Collieries by 4,812 men working 287 days. This represented an average output per man per day of 14.4 tons.[58] At Abercynon Colliery, 432,731 tons of large coal and 164,565 tons of small coals were extracted by 2,470 men working 286 days, which produced an output per man per day of 16.9 tons. After the introduction of the eight-hour day the figures fell to 12.35 tons at Dowlais and 14.64 tons at Abercynon per man per day. Nevertheless, the Eight Hours Act cannot be relied upon to provide the entire explanation for declining productivity as a trend of falling output was already well established before the legislation came into force.

Some evidence suggests that the proportion of underground workers not engaged in cutting coal rose and that the productivity of the hewers themselves stagnated or fell slightly. It was tough physical labour and there was a limit to the amount that individual miners could cut, given unchanging tools and techniques. The chief reasons given by contemporaries for a decline in effort by underground workers were rising wage rates and the system of piecework. These were directly tied to selling price of large coal at Cardiff, so that a gradual increase in the price of coal brought higher wages to those hewing coal at the face. The arduous and unpleasant nature of the job discouraged miners from maintaining output when wage rates rose. One mining engineer told the Sankey Commission that 'their tendency for years has been to reduce their rate of exertion, and, personally I do not think they will exert it. Increased wages has always had this effect as regards exertion and has always increased voluntary absenteeism'. This response was established in the 1870s; 'it is not' said H.W. Martin 'that the men want to get very large wages. I do not believe that they do; but they want short hours, and a higher price for their piecework'.[59] Since the collier was paid by the ton of coal hewn, he could always increase his output in times of low prices and maintain his wages by less effort in times of higher prices. The exceptionally high productivity achieved in 1899, for example, was to compensate for the loss of time during a five-month strike which had ended in September 1898.[60]

High voluntary absenteeism was also a feature of South Wales coalmining and this too was affected by fluctuations in piecework rates. In the 1840s many of the Dowlais colliers took four days every month, others one week in four, a pattern which had not changed by the 1870s.[61] Being paid at lengthy intervals, miners were likely to absent themselves for several days after they had received their wages.

The increasing age of the collieries owned by GKN also served to reduce productivity. Each year the face retreated from the shaft, making the problem of transporting coal to the pit head that more difficult. Most of the pits within the Dowlais Collieries had been sunk in the 1870s and 1880s, and only Abercynon, which came into production in 1896, was really modern. As has been seen, there was little attempt to mechanise production (either within GKN or throughout the whole South Wales coalfield) to counteract the effects of stagnation in the hewers' output. This did not necessarily reflect an inherent conservatism or refusal to consider innovation, as many of the new coal-cutting machines were not easily able to cope with the faulted nature of Welsh seams, a characteristic which made them particularly suited to traditional hewing methods. In a region in which labour was plentiful, no great pressure fell upon management to mechanise coal-cutting. Indeed, for such machinery to produce significant economies, it was also necessary to introduce conveyor belts to speed the flow of coal from the face to the shaft. The cost of installing such a range of mechanical equipment discouraged colliery owners from any action; not an unreasonable decision as they were able to respond to rising demand and continue to increase their profits by employing larger numbers, albeit with a falling level of productivity. The inherent problems of the South Wales coalfield were not, in fact, to reveal themselves until the market began to contract in the inter-war period.

A growing proportion of the coal mined in South Wales by GKN was sold to domestic consumers. Among their principal customers were the major railway companies (such as the London & South Western, London Brighton & South Coast and Great Western) whose locomotives were specifically designed to burn coal from the region,[62] while the Admiralty purchased considerable quantities of steam coal from Abercynon.[63] However, the destruction of historical records has prevented the production of statistics detailing that coal sold to outsiders and that consumed internally.

Records of employment have, however, survived with greater

Table 10.6   Dowlais Collieries – employment figures, 1888–1914

Year	Nantwen b	Nantwen a	Bedlinog No. 1 b	Bedlinog No. 1 a	Bedlinog No. 2 b	Bedlinog No. 2 a	Cwmbargoed b	Cwmbargoed a	Fochriw No. 1 b	Fochriw No. 1 a	Fochriw No. 2 b	Fochriw No. 2 a
1888	331*		519				272		1199			
1891	322		840				332		1200			
1894	298	27	1183		159		329	40	637	94	606	94
1895	295	26	1244		189		323	46	624	96	602	99
1896	290	27	1226		176		277	50	667	99	656	99
1897	263	28	1223		178		217	50	665	114	648	117
1898	297	28	524	87	794	105	224	50	606	122	625	116
1899	269	41	494	79	614	95	213	48	596	121	598	116
1900	254	40	596	100	476	96	228	43	500	118	661	122
1901	242	30	636	97	427	96	244	45	531	124	695	124
1902	237	49	842	109	372	81	252	45	551	131	738	128
1903	242	46	886	85	463	74	227	44	492	109	843	127
1904	249	48	888	114	583	78	203	44	533	111	881	129
1905	320	47	907	118	587	79	193	44	462	97	889	127
1906	316	49	950	129	620	90	169	49	427	97	819	141
1907	313	46	1019	136	624	99	155	49	424	87	847	150
1908	303	60	1210	136	795	103	130	42	455	92	885	165
1909	319	59	1331	152	951	120	208	40	497	85	984	154
1910	326	54+	2283		302		257	41**	541	83	1013	158
1911	330	53+	2209		276		301	43**	579	86	1096	162
1912	323	54+	2128		288		232	46	586	128	1057	197
1913	358	54+	1962		252		239	45	1666		313	
1914	347	54+	1804		254		279	45	1738		280	

Notes:
+ Includes Danyderi   ** Includes Penydarren   * Includes Colliery Levels

b – below ground   a – above ground

Source: Dr. Trevor Boyns, from the Annual *List of Mines*, 1888–1914.

frequency. The employment figures (Table 10.6) relating to four of the pits in the Dowlais group reveal that greater output was achieved in the main by increasing the number of men beneath ground. In the absence of the introduction of machinery and set against a background of legislation designed to shorten the working day, this was the only way that output could have been raised.

In 1902 when GKN was created, and before the Cyfarthfa collieries were acquired, 4,528 men were employed underground in the various collieries formerly belonging to the Dowlais Iron Co. with a further 669 on the surface (Table 10.6). A breakdown of those at Abercynon

Table 10.7 Average number of persons employed at the Dowlais Collieries in 1902

Colliery	Underground	Surface	Total
Bedlinog No. 1 Pit	643	100	743
Bedlinog No. 2 Pit	450	42	492
Fochriw No. 1 Pit	552	67	619
Fochriw No. 2 Pit	719	77	796
South Tunnel Pit	450	60	510
Longwork Pit	245	45	290
Black Vein Drift	35	4	39
Water Levels	32	4	36
Nantwen Pit	248	30	278
Abercynon Colliery	1154	240	1394
Total	4528	669	5197

Source: GRO, D/DG, Dowlais Collieries 1902–03, Letter from H.W. Martin to GK Dowlais, 28 July 1902.

Table 10.8 Number of persons working at the Dowlais-Cardiff Colliery, Abercynon, 1902

	Men	Boys	Girls	Total
Colliery managers, under-managers, overmen, firemen, surveyors	20	—	—	20
Cutting coal	385	30	—	415
Day wagemen: underground	634	11	—	645
Day wagemen: surface	87	10	—	97
Underground mechanical department	53	2	—	55
Surface mechanical department	101	8	1	110
Timekeepers, weighers, croppers and colliery office department	14	2	—	16
Masons department	7	—	—	7
Quarry department	9	1	—	10
	1310	64	1	1375

Source: GRO, D/DG, Letters Dowlais-Cardiff Works 1902, Statement, 26 April 1902.

revealed the overwhelming majority were engaged either on cutting coal or transporting it to the shaft – 1,019 or 74.1 per cent of the total[64] (Table 10.7).

Sixty-four boys were employed at Abercynon in 1902, of whom at least forty-three were underground. In 1906 H.W. Martin reported that, according to the shift, they worked either 'ten hours per day for four full days and seven hours per day for the two customary short [sic] days equal to fifty-four hours per week' or 'ten hours per day for five days equal to fifty hours per week', though a few totalled 57 hours.[65]

There is some evidence that men and unions resisted change, fearing that their wages would suffer should new work practices be introduced. The abiding impression of the South Wales coal industry in the late nineteenth century is one of impasse, with men and masters locked into mutually defeating attitudes. Although in his novel *Germinal* Zola was referring to the French coal industry during the 1880s, his observations also apply to the Welsh experience. Speaking of a coal strike much in the character of that which had afflicted Dowlais in 1853, the fictional Monsieur Hennebeau, manager of the mine, though not touched by hardship himself, described the stalemate which had arisen in these terms,[66]

> When I think that in our pits these chaps could make as much as six francs a day, double what they earn nowadays! And they lived well, too, and developed a taste for luxuries. Now of course they think it hard to go back to their former frugality . . . We [the Company] are very hard hit as well . . . Since the factories have been closing down one by one we have been having the devil of a job to rid them of our stocks, and in view of the decreasing demand we are obliged to lower our prices. That's what the workers simply refuse to understand.

Such statistics as have survived indicated that the total number of workers rose over the period. In 1910 Howell R. Jones reported that there were 7,250 employed at the Dowlais and Abercynon Collieries (comprising 162 firemen and overmen, 3,215 at the face, and a further 3,873 underground), together with a further 2,905 at the Cyfarthfa Collieries (51, 1,763 and 1,091 respectively).[67] This total represented a considerable increase on the figure of 5,197 for 1902 which included 669 surface workers.

Whilst British iron and steelworks could be considered as having lost the lead in the race for technical excellence, by the last two decades of the nineteenth century, to their American and German competitors, this was not then true of her coal mines. In 1880 output per man was not approached by any Continental nation. The gap in productivity was then twenty per cent which the Germans did not succeed in closing to achieve parity until 1914, and even then UK output per miner remained at thirty per cent above that of France and Austria and sixty per cent above Belgium and Russia.[68]

THE ACQUISITION OF CYFARTHFA

What had once been the mightiest ironworks in South Wales, if not in Britain and possibly the world, experienced an inauspicious end. Having failed to adopt steel technology when first it was publicised, Cyfarthfa slipped far behind Dowlais in terms of output and profitability. By 1880 it had become clear that unless a steelworks was added within the complex of blast furnaces, forges and rolling mills, the firm's future was bleak. To raise the necessary funds, the Crawshays promoted a local Act of Parliament, which was enacted in 1882,[69] and, under the superintendence of Edward Williams of Middlesbrough and formerly of Dowlais, four Bessemer converters were installed at a cost of £150,000.[70] Such was the strain imposed on the business by the rebuilding programme and the heightened competition from abroad that financial ruin was warded off only by flotation, and in 1890 they sought incorporation as a limited liability company called Crawshay Bros. (Cyfarthfa) Ltd.[71] They were to begin with a nominal capital of £600,000 divided into 60,000 shares of £10 each. Without the advantages which accrued to the most modern, large-scale steelworks situated beside a port or an ore field, Cyfarthfa had no greater prospect of survival than Dowlais. Arthur Keen, perceiving their predicament, opened negotiations with the Crawshays

111 'Evening view of Cyfarthfa Works from Cefn Bridge' by T. Prytherch in 1896, a few years before the steelworks was purchased by GKN. (*Cyfarthfa Castle Museum*)

not long after he had formed Guest, Keen & Co.[72] It would appear that his interest lay primarily in acquiring their collieries, but he was also aware of the value of reducing excess capacity and may have been planning to recruit William Evans, the general manager at Cyfarthfa who subsequently took control at Dowlais (p. 354). In a board minute, however, Keen detailed his reasons:[73]

> A. The company would be entitled to a larger proportion of the Pool of the Rail Association namely 10% of 115%.
>
> B. The company would be able to obtain its supplies of coke much cheaper, Messrs. Crawshay Bros. being practically the only competitor in the purchase of small coal in South Wales for coking purposes.
>
> C. The difficulty of dealing with the workpeople at Dowlais would be less, as at present the employees at the works and collieries of one company obtain employment at the works of the other company when disputes arise or when they consider it advisable to make a change.

On this basis they decided to press the negotiations and in March 1902 it was recorded that the purchase had been completed for an unspecified sum.[74]

Once Cyfarthfa had become part of GKN, as the smallest and least efficient of the three integrated steelworks in the group, it was the most vulnerable, should there be shortages in raw materials or a fall in demand. In August 1903, for example, when orders declined, William Evans advised the board that No. 3 furnace at Cyfarthfa should be blown out 'as this would relieve to some extent the pressure which was being experienced in getting adequate supplies of coke owing to a strike at North's Navigation Collieries and Powell Duffryn pits'.[75] Although £3,000 had been spent on improvements at Cyfarthfa since the acquisition, the works recorded a loss of £3,105 for the 13 months to 28 March 1903.[76] In November A.T. Keen explained that it[77]

> only had one order on its books for rails and fishplates (approximately 5,000 tons) delivery of which extended over the year 1904 and that as respects tin bars, on the manufacture of which the works were now relying, the Germans and Americans were importing into this country at prices about 80/– to 81/6d. per ton c.i.f. Newport, which figures were [several] shillings per ton below the Cyfarthfa cost.

William Evans had been asked to calculate the cost of closing the works and to compare this figure with the loss which would accrue if the mill were to continue operating at prices equivalent to those charged by American and German exporters. As there appeared to be little difference in the two sums, it was resolved to continue operating

Cyfarthfa 'for a time' as a producer of tin bars.[78] In the event, matters did not improve and the works was closed by GKN in 1910, though its collieries continued to flourish, and the 'Castle' rolling mill (named after the nearby Cyfarthfa Castle) and blast furnace were re-opened to help supply the immense demands created by the Great War.

CHANGES IN MANAGEMENT

In November 1901, E.P. Martin, a leading figure at Dowlais at the time of the merger, resigned as deputy chairman and managing director of Guest, Keen & Co.[79] Nevertheless, he agreed to remain on the board and continued to act in that capacity until his death at the age of sixty-seven, at Harrogate on 25 September 1910.[80] Devoting less time to GKN, in his later years he had served as president of the Institution of Mechanical Engineers (1906–07), and had also been elected president of the Iron and Steel Institute (1897–98). He was a director of the Orconera Iron Co., the Rhymney Railway Co. and of the South Wales Electrical Power Distribution Co., and, in 1903, was appointed High Sheriff of Monmouthshire.[81] Martin had served as president of the South Wales Institute of Engineers and of the Monmouth and South Wales Colliery Owners' Association and had chaired the South Wales Iron and Steel Workers' Sliding Scale Board.[82] His gradual withdrawal from the business, and subsequent death, represented the loss of one of the ablest managers in the history of the company. E.P. Martin was the only great Dowlais man to occupy a senior position in GKN.

Almost as soon as the acquisition of Crawshay Bros. was agreed, William Evans (1843–1915) was appointed general manager of both Dowlais and Cyfarthfa.[83] He had received his earliest training at Dowlais where, at the age of twenty-eight, he had become a blast furnace manager. He moved to a similar post at the Rhymney Co. in Cardiff and was, for a short period, works manager at the Erimus Works, Stockton-on-Tees but returned to South Wales to take up the general managership of the Cyfarthfa Iron & Steel Works. Evans continued to be the chief executive at Dowlais until his sudden death at Merthyr on 12 February 1915 at the age of seventy-two when he was succeeded by Howell R. Jones (p. 392).[84]

To what extent the fortunes of the former Dowlais Iron Co. were affected by becoming a subsidiary of GKN, remains matter for conjecture. With the death of E.P. Martin in 1910, representation of Dowlais on the main board ended. In 1900 when Guest, Keen & Co. was formed, Martin had been their sole spokesman, the other directors being Viscount Duncannon, Frederick Gordon, E. Windsor Richards (a close friend of Arthur Keen), J. Weston Stevens, A.T. Keen and F.W. Keen.[85] The chairmanship of the Dowlais Iron, Steel & Coal Co. Ltd. (which continued in existence to deal with detailed questions concerning the Dowlais Works) also fell to Arthur Keen and the membership of its board corresponded with that of its parent company.[86] Keen dominated GKN until his death in 1915 (p. 367) and, because he consistently failed to bring forward men of ability, it seems likely that the strategic development of the group's holdings in steel and coal could have been hampered, for he had no deep theoretical knowledge of steel or coal matters and relied on E. Windsor Richards, an eminent consultant, to advise him on policy. The situation appears to have been exacerbated by the failure of Dowlais to produce a new generation of innovative managers in the mould of Menelaus and E.P. Martin.

SUMMARY

All was not entirely well in South Wales on the outbreak of the Great War. Whilst significant and substantial steps had been taken to ensure the survival of the steel industry by building a modern works on the coast, the maintenance of considerable manufacturing capacity at other sites in the valleys was to result in both financial loss to individual companies and considerable suffering to the local population during the inter-war period. For GKN, these dangers were to a large extent obscured by the buoyancy of the group's extensive holdings in coal. Their mines produced ever greater quantities of coal, for which there seemed ever expanding domestic and export markets, but the substitution of oil in the 1920s and 1930s, combined with a world-wide depression, would show that unlimited faith could not be placed in this aspect of GKN's operations.

From the 1880s, the feature for greatest concern was the persistence of import penetration by Germany and America and though that initiated by the former was temporarily halted by the Great War, this remained an enduring characteristic of the British economy, and especially its staple industries. Although the UK's comparative performance could not inspire overwhelming confidence, the continued growth of GNP in absolute terms, albeit at a slower rate than its main competitors, prevented the problem from assuming the dimensions of a major crisis. As the various Royal Commissions on Trade and Industry illustrated many politicians and public figures were aware of these worrying developments but they proved powerless to reverse these trends.

At the company level, industrialists could not fail to see that their traditional export markets were no longer safe while manufactured goods continued to flood into Britain. Nevertheless the self-esteem that they had justly won in the earlier part of the century, combined with a pervasive conservatism, discouraged many businessmen from attempting to correct fundamental flaws in their methods of training, introducing new technology, managing the workforce, and marketing and selling products. The deep and prolonged slump that was to come in the inter-war years exposed any cases of complacency and revealed further weaknesses in many sectors of the British economy.

References

1. Guest Keen & Nettlefolds Directors' Minute Book, Vol. I 1900–05, 8 October 1903, it. 754.
2. Owen, *Dowlais Iron Works*, p. 92.
3. GKN Minute Book, Vol. I, 6 July 1905, it. 1128.
4. Owen, *Dowlais Iron Works*, p. 92.
5. Ibid., p. 95.
6. GKN Minute Book, Vol. I, 28 January 1902, it. 399.
7. Owen, *Dowlais Iron Works*, p. 93.
8. *JISI*, Part 1 (1900), B. Talbot, 'The Open Hearth Continuous Steel Process', pp. 33–61.
9. Carr and Taplin, *British Steel Industry*, p. 216.
10. Ibid.
11. GKN Minute Book, Vol. I, 1 November 1900, it. 41.
12. Ibid., 25 June 1901, it. 225.
13. Ibid., 29 August 1901, it. 255.
14. Ibid., 2 June 1904, it. 899.
15. Ibid., 5 January 1905, it. 1032.
16. Carr and Taplin, *British Steel Industry*, p. 215.
17. *Guest Keen Baldwins*, p. 60; *East Moors Album, Portrait of a Steelworks 1888–1978*, Cardiff (1978).
18. Dowlais Iron Steel & Coal Co. Ltd., Minute Book, 28 October 1899.
19. Ibid., 23 July 1900.
20. *GKN Annual Reports 1902–1914.*
21. GRO, D/DG, Letters Cardiff Works 1911–1915.
22. GRO, D/DG, Letters Dowlais-Cardiff Works 1908–10, Letter from A.K. Reese, 29 October 1909.
23. Letter to A.K. Reese, 23 March 1911.
24. GRO, D/DG, Letters Cardiff Works 1911–15, op. cit., 4 February 1911.
25. GRO, D/DG, Letters 1908–10, Letter from E.H. James, 9 December 1910.
26. GKN Minute Book Vol. I, 2 July 1903, it. 716.
27. GRO, D/DG, Letters Dowlais-Cardiff Works 1902–03, Letter from E.H. James, 30 April 1903; D/DG, Letters Cardiff Works 1911–15, Letter from A.K. Reese, 5 December 1912.
28. GRO, D/DG, Supplementary Letters, London Works – Crawshay Brothers, 1902–13, Edward Steer to A.T. Keen, 20 July 1906.
29. Ibid., E. Steer to Dowlais Iron Co., 20 July 1906.
30. GRO, D/DG, Letters Dowlais-Cardiff Works 1902–03, 30 April 1903.
31. Ibid., Letter from E.H. James, 21 May 1902.
32. Ibid., Letter from A.K. Reese to William Evans, general manager at Dowlais, 8 December 1902.
33. GRO, D/DG, Letters Dowlais-Cardiff Works 1908–10, 12 October 1908.
34. GRO, D/DG, Letters Cardiff Works 1911–1915, A.K. Reese to Cwmbran, 17 June 1912.
35. GRO, D/DG, Letters Cardiff Works 1911–15, Letter from A.K. Reese, 19 August 1914.

36. GRO, D/DG, Supplementary Letters 1902–13, op. cit., A.K. Reese to GKN Dowlais, 31 December 1907.
37. GRO, D/DG, Letters Dowlais-Cardiff Works 1908–10, Thomas R. Martin to GKN Dowlais, 7 January 1908.
38. Ibid., A.K. Reese to GKN Dowlais, 31 October 1908.
39. GKN Minute Book, Vol. I, 26 March 1901, it. 154.
40. GKN Minute Book, Vol. I, 2 October 1902, other committees established at the same time were 'Works', 'General Purposes', 'Finance' and 'Nettlefolds', it. 540–544.
41. Ibid., 26 November 1901, it. 357.
42. Ibid.
43. Ibid., 17 December 1901, it. 370.
44. Ibid., 2 October 1902, it. 536.
45. GRO, D/DG, Letters Dowlais Collieries 1904–07, from H.S. Martin, 10 December 1904.
46. Ibid., Letter from H.S. Martin, 9 October 1906.
47. GRO, D/DG, Letters Dowlais Collieries, Mr. Howell R. Jones 1909–11, 15 February 1909.
48. Ibid., 20 February 1909.
49. PP 1919, XL, 603 (Sankey Commission, evidence of Sir R.A.S. Redmayne).
50. Rhodri Walters, *EcHR*, Vol. XXVIII (1975), 'Labour Productivity in the South Wales Steam-Coal Industry 1870–1914', p. 297.
51. PP 1907, XIII, 535.
52. Walters, 'Labour Productivity', p. 297.
53. GKN Minute Book, Vol. I, 17 December 1901, it. 366.
54. GRO, D/DG, Letters Dowlais Colieries 1904–07, from H.W. Martin to GKN Dowlais, 8 March 1904.
55. GRO, D/DG, Letters Dowlais-Cardiff Colliery, Abercynon 1909–1915, Letter to Bruce Jones from GKN Dowlais, 12 February 1909.
56. Wilkins, *South Wales Coal*, pp. 323–24.
57. Rhodri Walters, *EcHR*, Vol. XXVIII (1975), 'Labour Productivity in the South Wales Steam Coal Industry 1870–1914', p. 301.
58. GRO, D/DG, Letters Dowlais Colieries 1909–11, Statements from H.R. Jones to William Evans, 25 July 1911.
59. PP Select Committee 1873, X 52.
60. Walters, 'Labour Productivity', p. 289.
61. Ibid., p. 293; P.P. 1847 XVI, 418; 1873 X 52.
62. GRO, D/DG, Letters Dowlais Collieries 1904, 1907, From Bruce Jones to H.W. Martin, 3 March 1904; GKN Minute Book Vol. I, 26 March 1901, it. 150.
63. GRO, D/DG, Letters Dowlais Collieries, Mr. Howell R. Jones 1909–11, 15 February 1909.
64. GRO, D/DG, Letters Dowlais Cardiff Works 1902, Statement on 26 April 1902.
65. GRO, D/DG, Letters Dowlais Collieries 1904–07, Letter from H.W. Martin to GKN Dowlais, 31 December 1906.
66. Émile Zola, *Germinal*, Paris (1885), Harmondsworth (1954), p. 203.
67. GRO, D/DG, Letters Dowlais Collieries, Mr. Howell R. Jones 1909–11, Letter to GKN Dowlais, 9 September 1910.
68. Saul, *Great Depression*, pp. 44–45.
69. *Cyfarthfa Works Act* (1882).
70. *JISI*, part II (1897), 'The Cyfarthfa Iron and Steel Works', pp. 237–39.

71. Addis, *Crawshay Dynasty*, pp. 148–49.
72. GKN Minute Book, Vol. I, 29 August 1901, it. 258.
73. Ibid., 5 November 1901, it. 319.
74. Ibid., 6 March 1902, it. 428.
75. Ibid., 6 August 1903, it. 724.
76. Ibid., 8 October 1903, it. 762.
77. Ibid., 5 November 1903, it. 771.
78. Ibid.
79. Ibid., 26 November 1907, it. 359.
80. *PIME*, Vol. 79 (1910), Memoir E.P. Martin, pp. 1706–08; *The Engineer*, Vol. CX (1910), obituary, p. 363.
81. *PIME*, p. 1707.
82. *JISI*, Part II (1910), obituary, p. 369.
83. GKN Minute Book, Vol. I, 3 February 1902, it. 408.
84. *JISI*, Part I (1915), Obituary, p. 454.
85. GKN Minute Book, Vol. I, 20 August 1900, it. 1.
86. Dowlais Iron Steel & Coal Co. Ltd., Minute Book, 1900–15, *passim*.

However, nothing further appears in the company minute books about the project. Whether it foundered because the parties could not agree over a particular point, or because of insufficient commitment, is not known. The failure of this scheme did not extinguish Arthur Keen's appetite for take-over, as he swiftly switched his attention to a company much closer to home.

Whilst the merger between the Guests and the Keens had been carried through with amity and goodwill, this could not have been said of the events of 1902. For a long time, Keen had cast envious eyes on the Heath Street mills of his neighbours, Nettlefolds Ltd. They had consistently rebuffed his suggestions of a union. At a special meeting of Guest, Keen & Co., held in January 1902, he outlined the circumstances which led to the merger:[16]

> In September last I made up my mind to make a final effort to amalgamate the interests of Guest, Keen & Co. Ltd. and Nettlefolds Ltd. on fair and equitable grounds, and if this could not be done, to abandon it for all time, and decided to seek an interview with Mr. Edward Nettlefold for this purpose . . . I explained . . . the principal advantages that would accrue to Nettlefolds Ltd., which were, that it would make them in a business sense (like ourselves) practically self contained, which at the present they were not, as they had to commence with the manufacture of their products from all bought raw materials whereas we should enable them to commence at the base, which referred to our iron ore, coal, limestone and all other materials necessary for the manufacture of pig iron.

Compelling as the logic of this argument might appear, its implementation caused considerable practical difficulties (p. 365), and it was not to have been the reason for Nettlefolds' compliance, for legend has it that Keen purchased several modern machines for making woodscrews from America and had them ostentatiously conveyed into his London Works and then secretly removed to be brought back repeatedly to create the impression that he was about to manufacture woodscrews on a large scale. The threat of further competition, at a time when Nettlefolds' profits had established a pattern of slow decline (doubtless from the remorseless pressure applied by German manufacturers in world markets, p. 228), was sufficient to propel a weakened management towards the negotiating table.

The capital of Nettlefolds Ltd. was valued at £630,000, though they also possessed an internal reserve fund of £300,000, 'which does not appear in the accounts'.[17] Under the terms of the take over, Edward Nettlefold, Charles Steer, Edward Steer and Reginald Parker, who had been the company secretary, all became directors of the merged organisation,[18] which was entitled Guest, Keen & Nettlefolds. Arthur Keen explained the union in the following way:[19]

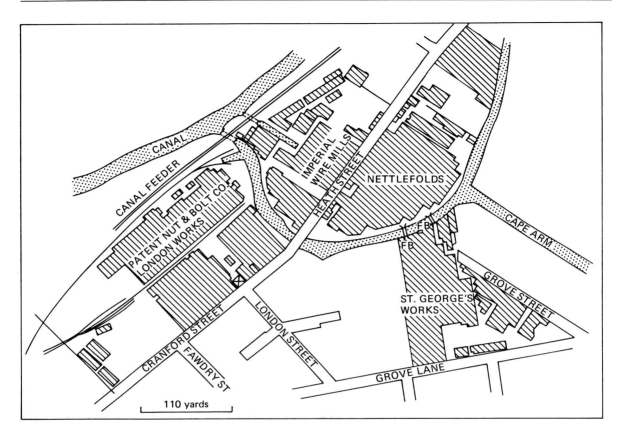

Figure 13 Smethwick in 1902

Messrs. Nettlefolds were not only screwmakers but manufacturers of goods so similar to their own in many cases that the line of demarcation between the two was so obscure that it could hardly be explained. In addition, to that they were steelmakers on no small scale, and, in many instances, produced the same classes of steel which Guest, Keen & Co. manufactured, and had been regularly selling in competition to each other.

The accuracy of this statement was open to considerable doubt. First, the degree of product duplication was very limited; Guest, Keen & Co. manufactured very few woodscrews at Cwmbran, while the range of nuts and bolts made by Nettlefolds was narrow; the type of pig iron and steel made at Dowlais and Dowlais-Cardiff was, as events showed, unsuitable for woodscrews and must therefore have been of a very different nature to that manufactured by Nettlefolds at Rogerstone. The merger was actually and privately justified on grounds of diversification into related products, for it broadened and consolidated the group's fastener holdings in Smethwick.

In the successful conclusion of the mergers between the Dowlais Iron Co. and the PNB, and more particularly between Guest, Keen & Co., and Nettlefolds, the role of the Birmingham chartered accountants, Carter & Co., was of subtle and seemingly crucial importance. The firm, established in 1827, were elected as the first auditors of the PNB on its flotation in 1864 when Edward Carter, a founder council member of the Institute of Chartered Accountants in England and Wales,[20] was appointed by Arthur Keen.[21] By coincidence, Carter & Co. also became the auditors of Nettlefolds on their incorporation in 1880,[22] doubtless because the practice had attracted a considerable clientele amongst Midlands manufacturers, which included Rubery Owen and Averys. Carter & Co. would have been responsible for settling the financial details of the first merger with Turquand, Youngs & Co., the eminent City firm who served as auditors to the Dowlais Iron, Steel & Coal Co.[23] Significantly, Edward Carter took the opportunity provided by the take-over to resign as a director of the PNB and thereby removed any conflict of interest which might have occurred following the appointment of his firm as the auditors of Guest, Keen & Co.[24] Discussions on a possible amalgamation between Guest, Keen & Co. and Nettlefolds took place in Eric Carter's dining room in order to be on neutral ground and to preserve secrecy; he may well also have served as an arbitrator or as a referee between the two parties. It was natural that Carter & Co. should be elected as auditors of the new combine and the appointment remained in their name until 1960 when the firm became part of Cooper Brothers, who in 1973 changed their style to Coopers & Lybrand.

ORGANISATION AND MANAGEMENT

Although the events of 1902 resulted in a change of title and an amalgamation of the two main boards of directors, it was not initially a deep-seated union. Partly because of the manner in which Keen had forced Nettlefolds' hand, a residue of ill-feeling prevented complete co-operation between all members of senior management.

The task of co-ordinating the activities of GKN, albeit in a decentralized fashion, was not helped by the existence of the London offices established by the various parent companies. The PNB had premises at 66 Cannon Street, Nettlefolds at 2 Fen Court, Fenchurch Street, and the Dowlais Iron Co. at 13 King's Arms Yard, and from 1914 at King William House, 2A Eastcheap.[25] These continued to function, serving the interests of their former businesses until 1920, when the last was closed, and in 1924 they all moved to 66 Cannon Street.[26] Nevertheless, the importance of these divisions should not be overstated, as the group as a whole was managed from Smethwick and individual companies allowed to continue functioning almost as autonomous units.

In order to attempt to co-ordinate activities and break down established loyalties, Arthur Keen created a series of specialist committees in October 1902 for the purpose of presenting reports to each meeting of the main board. These comprised the Colliery, Works, General Purpose, Nettlefolds and Finance Committees;[27] Keen was to be an *ex officio* member of them all. They formed an intermediate layer of management, above individual subsidiary companies, but below the main board. However, membership of these committees was limited to directors and it was a way, in effect, of giving them specific responsibilities without tying them exclusively to one or two subsidiaries. In 1905, for instance, the Colliery Committee was composed of A.T. Keen, F.W. Keen, E.P. Martin, Edward Nettlefold, E. Windsor Richards, J. Weston Stevens and Edward Steer; the Nettlefolds Committee comprised A.T. Keen, F.W. Keen, Edward Nettlefold, Reginald Parker, J. Weston Stevens, Charles Steer and Edward Steer.[28] In this fashion, former PNB and Nettlefolds executives were involved in the affairs of Dowlais, whilst the Heath Street mills of Nettlefolds included among their board members several ex-PNB directors. The Finance Committee included directors from all three constituents of GKN.[29] Significantly, Viscount Duncannon, a man of little practical business experience, was appointed to only one of these bodies, the General Purposes Committee.[30] The creation of this secondary level of management clearly played a major part in welding together the various components in the GKN group, though it was probably not until the 1920s that a satisfactory level of harmony was achieved. It also served a more obvious purpose: following the two mergers, the company had attained such a size and embraced such a range of activities that it would have been virtually impossible for a single board of directors to exercise proper executive control without some division of responsibilities. Decisions requiring a detailed knowledge of individual factories or plant were, in effect, taken by the specialist committees and ratified by the main board. Matters were discussed by the latter only if high levels of expenditure were to be incurred, or if agreement could not be reached at the lower level. The full board could take an overview of the group's operation, having only to resort to detailed debate on questions of finance, trading results, acquisitions, capital expenditure and senior appointments; the remainder of its time was in fact occupied with comparatively tangential matters, such as charitable donations, inquiries from institutions and public bodies and minor legal questions.

A further attempt to lighten the administrative burden which fell to Arthur Keen was made in 1901, when three managing directors were appointed, E.P. Martin, A.T. Keen and F.W. Keen. 'The chairman explained', on 1 October,[31]

that as the company's business now necessitated his frequent

vast manufacturing group, he must also accept some criticism for causing the power vacuum from which the Berry brothers were able to benefit when they obtained control of GKN during the nineteen-twenties.

PROFITS AND PERFORMANCE

As in the case of British industry as a whole, the Edwardian era did not witness an outstanding performance by GKN. Using the published annual accounts, the profits of the group experienced a gentle decline, between 1902 and 1914, a trend that was slightly accentuated in real terms (Table 11.1). Profits of £447,000 in 1902 were only surpassed once during this period (£453,000 in 1913). This represented £798,000 in real terms, a figure which, with the exception of the recovery in 1907 (£809,000), was not to be bettered until 1925, when a published surplus of £841,000 was earned by GKN. Whilst it has rightly been concluded that the laxity of company legislation during this period permitted businesses considerable leeway in the presentation of figures for scrutiny, it would seem that the trend

Table 11.1 GKN's profits and equity interests 1902–19 (£000s)

Year	Profits	Adjusted*	Equity Interest	Adjusted*
1902	447	798	3305	5723
1903	410	727	3363	5963
1904	404	711	3514	6187
1905	408	723	3669	6505
1906	427	757	3843	6814
1907	471	809	4061	6977
1908	455	763	4215	7073
1909	372	624	4286	7191
1910	348	580	4333	7222
1911	383	628	4416	7251
1912	396	628	4511	7149
1913	453	718	4664	7391
1914	402	641	4765	7600
1915	384	491	4852	6205
1916	424	459	4972	5381
1917	433	388	5100	4570
1918	447	348	5242	4083
1919	417	307	6255	4599

*Figures adjusted by Bank of England's Index of Consumer Prices 1930 = 100.

Source: *GKN Annual Reports and Balance Sheets, 1902–20.*

114 The coal arch: constructed of substantial blocks of coal it remained as the entrance to Dowlais House until demolition in 1956–57.
(*John A. Owen*)

revealed by this series was accurate, even if the record of individual years may be open to doubt.

Confirmation of this view is provided by the profit figures produced for Nettlefolds (Table 11.2). These reveal that in 1902 Nettlefolds would have been contributing about twenty five per cent of the group's profits, even allowing for the fact that the published figure of £447,000 would have probably understated the group's true surplus. The importance of the screw-making company rose, for in 1912 it was contributing around fifty per cent of the total group profit. The fact that the Nettlefolds' figure for 1918 was £537,210 and yet GKN's profits as a whole were recorded as being £447,000, is explained by the workings of Excess Profits Duty (p. 387). The reported profits for 1916–19 were not an accurate measure of GKN's earnings, distorted by the effect of wartime demand and inflation.

Given that there were economies of scale to have been gained from the merger of the three companies, and that the whole union was justified at the time on grounds of compatibility and a greater degree of vertical integration, together with the removal of wasteful competition and overlapping, why, then, did the group fail to improve on the results recorded in 1902, when by all the arguments advanced at the time, it should have lead to considerable growth and greater profitability? First, it took time to eliminate areas of

Table 11.2 Nettlefolds' profits 1902–19

Year	Gross £	Adjusted £	GKN published (after tax) £
1902	176724*	256122*	447204
1903	186411	270160	410181
1904	190949	272784	404023
1905	164664	228700	407557
1906	159884	207642	427156
1907	184993	231241	470511
1908	201644	276225	454716
1909	195438	264105	371724
1910	213325	273493	348093
1911	207750	259688	383009
1912	214484	252334	395586
1913	173425	204029	453093
1914	198317	233314	401722
1915	189621	175575	384400
1916	302416	222365	424480
1917	478206	267156	433453
1918	537210	279797	446645
1919	397923	193166	417140

*15 months

Source: BRL, 298/2 Nettlefolds Ltd. Annual Accounts General 1893–1904; 298/15 GKN, Nettlefolds Dept. Annual Accounts General 1905–20. Figures adjusted by the Rousseaux price index, average of 1865–1885 = 100.

115 No. 41, 'Sandyford' built at Dowlais in 1908. 'Sandyford' was the name of Arthur Keen's house in Birmingham. The various locomotives turned out from the Ifor Works were used to transport raw materials and finished products around the extensive sites leased by the company.
(*British Steel Corporation*)

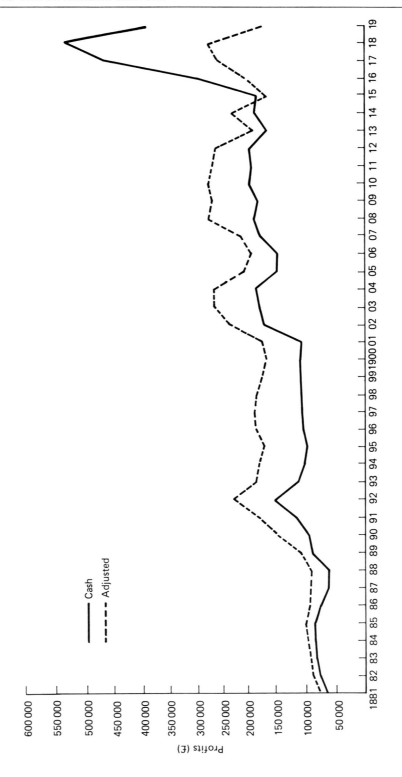

[Figures adjusted by the Sauerbeck-*Statist* index, 1867–1877 = 100.]

Figure 14 Profits earned by Nettlefolds 1881–1919

duplication. Each constituent of the company continued to maintain an office in London until the 1920s and there appears to have been widespread resistance among the various subsidiaries to sacrifice autonomy in favour of the group as a whole. The expected economies of scale, therefore, did not materialise as soon as expected. Secondly, the extent to which various operations could be fitted together in a neat manufacturing chain was exaggerated (p. 363). The complexity and specialist requirements of certain processes prevented works from being able, at the touch of a switch, to divert output to new customers within GKN. Again it was a lengthy and difficult process to rationalise production throughout the many subsidiaries.

But possibly just as important as any of these internal factors in levelling out the company's profits was the continuing impact of competition from overseas. The German and American economies continued to grow at a much faster rate than the British, surpassing it in absolute terms. In spite of established imperial loyalties, UK exporters found it increasingly difficult to sell in world markets. The Tariff Commission reporting on screws, bolts and nuts, quoted one English bolt maker as saying,[38]

> our manufacturers are gradually being pushed out through low prices of German, French and American goods. We find German, Belgian and American competition in Australia, Egypt, India and South Africa. In Australia and New Zealand American goods are

116   The general office staff in 1912 photographed outside Dowlais House. (*John A. Owen*)

117 An elaborate display of Nettlefolds woodscrews, nuts, bolts, cotters, nails and hooks prepared for a trade exhibition.

imported to suit the American imported vehicles. In South Africa, French, German and American goods compete with ours at low prices.

Worse still, German manufacturers, as the 1909 *Tariff Commission* concluded, were able to undercut British producers supplying the domestic market:

118 A delivery van (No. 1) used by Nettlefolds in Birmingham, possibly pre-1914.

nails and screws can now be obtained from Germany at about 25% less than the average British price. This refers more particularly to brass screw nails and iron wire nails and is caused by a determined effort on the part of German manufacturers to obtain a sure footing in our market.

In areas such as fasteners and steel where it seems that surplus capacity had arisen, the British were in a weak position. By industrialising late and with larger individual plants, the Germans and Americans could undercut their competitors. As a result, British manufacturers adopted a defensive strategy and called for a policy of Imperial protection. The cause was taken up publicly by Joseph Chamberlain, who in 1895 began to press for a *zollverein* or a system of free trade within the Empire. This was opposed by the self-governing dominions, who already protected their infant industries and refused to expose them to the overwhelming might of British competition. Chamberlain then turned to a form of Imperial preference, by which trade within the Empire would be encouraged by the imposition of taxes upon goods supplied by foreign manufacturers. The Tariff Reform League was formed in 1903 to advocate the policy and was financed by businessmen suffering from the impact of American and German exports.[40] Arthur Keen, for example, was a member of the Tariff Commission and, although unable to attend its London meetings, he submitted evidence in 1914 and was a firm supporter of Chamberlain's policy.[41]

In face of rising competition and surplus capacity, British manufacturers formed cartels with their Continental rivals in an attempt to control the market. As has been seen, Nettlefolds were leading members of the European Woodscrew Union (p. 230),[42] and GKN Dowlais entered into a similar arrangement with German and Belgian rollers of rails.[43] Declining orders at Dowlais had forced them to reduce the make of iron and enforced intermittent operation of the rolling mills which increased costs considerably. In his presidential address to the Iron and Steel Institute (1895) David Dale observed that Britain's output of steel rails had peaked in 1882 when 1,235,000 tons had been manufactured, a figure which had fallen dramatically to 579,000 tons in 1893. This was, in part, the result of a declining world market but it also reflected the success of their American and German rivals who in 1893 turned out 1,040,000 and 483,000 tons of steel rail respectively.[44] To reduce the degree of uncertainty, a Rail Makers Association was formally established in October 1904.[45] Representatives from Britain, Germany, Belgium and France agreed on quotas and set up a system of fines for those who transgressed these limits. The fact that two of its major products, rails and woodscrews, were subject to restrictive trade agreements may explain why GKN did not experience growth in the first twenty years of its existence. With capacity being generated by the leading industrial nations faster than it could be absorbed by world demand, individual manufacturers could increase output only if they cut prices and reduced the level of surplus. Coal seems to have been the sole area of GKN's activities which expanded and earned consistently high profits, these being used to subsidise its less successful operations at Dowlais and build a new integrated steelworks at East Moors, Cardiff.

SUMMARY

Despite the continuing threat imposed by aggressive American and German manufacturers, the situation in which GKN found itself on the outbreak of war in August 1914 was nevertheless strong. As one of Britain's few industrial giants, GKN controlled vital imports of iron ore, possessed extensive and highly profitable coal mines, owned three steelworks, one of which could compete with any rival in Britain, and enjoyed an unassailable monopoly of the UK woodscrew market, while being one of the nation's leading manufacturers of nuts and bolts. It was diversified and had established a considerable measure of vertical integration. A healthy financial situation ensured its protection against take-over and provided the option of further acquisition or expenditure on capital-intensive projects. Unfortunately, the age of many of its directors and the failing health of its autocratic chairman were to precipitate the company into a leadership crisis during 1915. A determined resolve to innovate and compete aggressively was dissipated with the death of Arthur Keen. But for the moment, as conflict swept across Continental Europe, the country was drawn into a crisis of far more horrific and devastating consequences. How GKN fared during the Great War is the subject of the next chapter.

References

1. P.L. Payne, *Economic History Review*, Vol. XX (1967), 'The Emergence of the Large-Scale Company in Great Britain 1870–1914', p. 519.
2. Ibid., p. 539.
3. Leslie Hannah, *The Rise of the Corporate Economy*, 2nd Edition, London (1983), pp. 186–88.
4. Ibid., Table A.5, pp. 189–90.
5. Henry W. Macrosty, *The Trust Movement in British Industry, A Study of British Organisation*, London (1907), p. 38.
6. GKN Minute Book Vol. I, August 1900 – August 1905, 1 November 1900, it. 60–61.
7. *The Financial News*, 14 June 1900, 'The Great Iron Combination'.
8. GKN Minute Book, Vol. I, 28 September 1900, it. 21; 1 November 1900, it. 26; 26 March 1901, it. 158; 21 May 1901, it. 182.
9. Ibid., 29 July 1901, it. 242. Lord Wimborne's property was to be transferred to Guest, Keen & Co. after the meeting of 7 August 1901, it. 247.
10. *The Financial News*, 14 June 1900, 'The Great Iron Combination'.
11. Ibid., 26 March 1901, it. 155.
12. Ibid., 25 June 1901, it. 210.
13. Ibid., 25 June 1901, it. 244.
14. Ibid.
15. Ibid., 29 August 1901, it. 257.
16. Ibid., 20 January 1902, it. 391.
17. Ibid.
18. Ibid., it. 393.
19. Macrosty, *The Trust Movement*, pp. 39–40.
20. *Institute of Chartered Accountants in England and Wales, List of Members*, London (1881), p. 102; *The Accountant*, Vol. XXIX, No. 1467, 17 January 1903, p. 66.
21. *C & L Journal*, No. 31, June 1979, p. 26.
22. *Nettlefolds Ltd., Prospectus* (1880), p. 1.
23. Edgar Jones, *Accountancy and the British Economy 1840–1980, The Evolution of Ernst & Whinney*, London (1981), pp. 33–35.
24. GKN Minute Book, Vol. I, 2 August 1900, it. 15.
25. *The Post Office London Directory, Commercial for 1902*, p. 1198.
26. *The Post Office London Directory, Commercial for 1924*, p. 1659.
27. GKN Minute Book, Vol. I, 2 October 1902, it. 540–544.
28. GKN Minute Book, Vol. 2, October 1905 – February 1916, 5 October 1905, it. 1168, 1170.
29. Ibid., it. 1169.
30. Ibid., it. 1171.

31. GKN Minute Book, Vol. I, 1 October 1901, it. 286.
32. Ibid., 17 December 1901, it. 359.
33. GKN Minute Book, Vol. I, 27 November 1900, it. 55; Vol. II (1905–16), 9 March 1906, it. 1254.
34. MBA, Edward Holden's Diary 1905–07, 27 June 1907, p. 67.
35. GKN Minute Book, Vol. II, 4 July 1912, it. 2236.
36. Ibid., 4 March 1915, it. 2508.
37. Various newspaper cuttings 4–5 July 1918, Obituaries of A.T. Keen. He had, according to one report, 'been greatly over worked on account of the war, and on May 13 [1918] entered Grandbourne Nursing Home. He was then suffering from nervous breakdown and depression'. A temporary attack of insanity was given as the explanation for his suicide.
38. BLPES, TC7 19/1 Tariff Commission Collection (B) 24, p. 29.
39. BLPES, TC1 4/1 *Report from the Tariff Commission, Vol. 4, The Engineering Industries*, London (1909), paragraph 756.
40. *Government and Opposition*, Vol. 16, No. 4 (1981), Nicholas A.H. Stacey, 'Entrepreneurship in Politics', p. 503.
41. BLPES, Ref. TC6 1/19 Tariff Commission Collection, Correspondence from Arthur Keen, 23 December 1903–04, 4 November 1914.
42. GKN Minute Book, Vol. II, 2 November 1905, it. 1185.
43. GKN Minute Book, Vol. I, 7 July 1904, it. 917.
44. *JISI*, Part 1 (1895), pp. 39–40.
45. Ibid., 4 November 1904, it. 988.

12   *GKN and the Great War 1914–18*

Whilst trade rivalry itself neither triggered the Great War in August 1914, nor can it be seen as the principal cause of the conflict, the economic battle which had been fought over the previous thirty years created an atmosphere of mutual hostility and distrust, so making resort to war more likely. Many Germans argued that their undermining of Britain's industrial hold over the European nations from the mid-1870s and eventual supremacy (ousting British exporters from first place in Austro-Hungary, Russia, Sweden, Denmark and Rumania) left her no alternative but to shatter their new-found manufacturing and commercial might in a Continental war.[1] After 1895, the dominance of trade achieved by Germany was undeniable in chemicals, dyestuffs, optics, plastics and artificial fibres and this was also true of engineering by 1914; in textiles and coal mining, the UK offered a comparable performance, while a supremacy in quantity, if not always quality, was retained only in shipbuilding, Britain constructing 61 per cent of the world's tonnage in 1910–14. Having overtaken Britain in the production of steel in 1893, Germany was making double her output in 1914, and in a war which was to be determined not just by manpower, but the ability to manufacture munitions, this lead proved to be of vital consequence. Such growth, often at the expense of British exports, had encouraged a leader in *The Times* for 1895 to argue that[2]

> Germany is by far the most dangerous of our industrial competitors at the present moment all the world over, and one cannot but regret that the influence of German competition upon British industry has not yet received the full amount of official attention which [it] . . . deserves.

'BUSINESS AS USUAL'

Hostilities were greeted with a sense of release and even excitement, as men flocked to recruitment offices to serve king and country;[3]

popular, political and military circles felt that the fighting would be mobile and decisive, settling matters at an early stage – possibly before Christmas. The state munition factories were, therefore, thought adequate for the provision of the required quantities of shells, explosives and weaponry; it was expected that private armaments manufacturers would meet the extra demand for artillery.[4] It, therefore, seemed unnecessary to make any elaborate plans to regulate the civilian population. Indeed, such a course, the government believed, would be positively harmful, instilling panic and stifling the natural forces of enterprise. Hence, they deliberately fostered the policy 'business as usual' (a phrase that first appeared in the *Daily Chronicle* on 11 August 1914, appearing in Harrods' shop window two days later).[5] Although public control had been established over the railways, shipping and other vital areas of the economy under the wide-ranging Defence of the Realm Act ('DORA') of 8 August 1914, state intervention was limited to placing extra orders for arms and munitions with engineering companies currently short of work, for, as in 1939, war broke out at a time when Britain was entering the downward phase of the trade cycle after a period of prosperity.[6] Until the movement of large bodies of troops and skirmishing solidified into a continual battle of attrition conducted over long lines of trenches, it seemed that these *ad hoc* arrangements could adequately meet the needs of the military planners. Armstrong Whitworth, Vickers Engineering and Cammell Laird & Co., for example, had for some time been contracted to supply an expanding Royal Navy and were able to respond well to the initial pick up in orders. Yet once they were flooded with an additional demand for field artillery and high explosive shells desperately needed by the Army, they found that their resources, maintained during peacetime with a margin should any conflict break out, were inadequate.[7] When the trench system had stabilised from the Alps to the English Channel, and the movement of the first few months of combat had drawn sluggishly to a halt, it became painfully clear that the unforeseen strategy of this war required industrial planning on a scale never before contemplated.

During the opening phases of the Great War, when almost everyone thought that a victory was close at hand, GKN were scarcely touched by the hostilities. The only inquiry affecting their manufacturing operations concerned Cwmbran.[8] Recognising that the demand for high explosives would rise, the government wrote in February 1915 to ask whether the company would install a plant to enable them to make benzol from the by-products of their coke ovens. They offered to pay for the plant, the cost of manufacturing benzol and a guaranteed profit from five per cent to fifteen per cent on working expenses. After discussions, the GKN directors replied that they would prefer to incur the initial installation cost, estimated at £15,000, and then enter into fixed contract to supply benzol at a given price for an agreed timescale. They subsequently suggested that the War Office should undertake to purchase the plant's entire output at the current market price for a period of four years after its completion.[9] Mr. J.B. Deakin, manager of the Cwmbran coke ovens, who had enlisted in the Birmingham Second City Battalion, was to be released from military duties to take charge of the new works. Thus, GKN, in common with other manufacturers, resisted state intervention (even though it would involve them in substantial capital investment) preferring to supply legitimate war needs by traditional peacetime arrangements. However, the intrusive demands of modern warfare soon proved to be so pressing that the government had to act decisively and, when the occasion warranted, ignore the wishes of the private sector.

GKN AND THE MINISTRY OF MUNITIONS

The foundation of the Ministry of Munitions in May 1915 marked the practical end to the policy of 'business as usual' and its active intervention in the economy represented a novel element in the behaviour of government during wartime.[10] Lloyd George, who was largely responsible for its creation, realised that the repeated and heavy barrages used to prepare the way for frontal infantry assaults could only be supplied by co-ordinated volume production: the quantities fired in prolonged artillery engagements were so grossly underestimated that in 1914 Britain's total munitions output was insufficient to sustain even a single major offensive. The real crisis in manufacturing output centred on the shortage of shells. Hence, the Ministry of Munitions set about mobilising the country's industry. It assumed responsibility for the purchase, supply and distribution of raw materials needed by factories engaged on war work and diverted others to manufacture ammunition, weapons, vehicles, equipment and uniforms; it reorganised the labour force and productive processes to maximise output and at the same time, through the employment of an army of accountants, installed checks to see that costs were kept within reasonable levels after the price rises caused by shortages in the first year of fighting.

The impact of the formation of the Ministry of Munitions on GKN's many works was initially slight, and confined, apparently, to the establishment of an administrative framework. In June 1915 the main board recorded that[11]

> The Earl of Plymouth, at the request of Lord Kitchener, had undertaken the work of organising the South Wales and Monmouthshire area in connection with . . . increasing the production of munitions of war. A public meeting had accordingly been held in the Town Hall, Cardiff, on Thursday 17 May,

which had been attended by Mr. Edward Steer, also by Mr. A.K. Reese of the Cardiff Works, when as a preliminary step a committee of twenty to twenty-five representatives of the district . . . had been appointed, who would . . . appoint a management committee to have control of the direction and management of the work . . . Mr. A.T. Keen explained the action to be taken by the Munitions Committee recently formed in Birmingham, of which he had been appointed a member, also what was being done at the company's Heath Street Works as regards the manufacture of fuses.

The crucial change came in November 1915 when those GKN factories and steelworks engaged upon government work became Controlled Establishments, which in practice affected all their subsidiaries except a number of colliery companies.[12] A misunderstanding arose over Crawshay Bros. (Cyfarthfa) Ltd. It had been included among the Controlled Establishments so that a letter had to be sent to the Ministry of Munitions to explain that 'the works had not been running for a number of years, the business being that of colliery proprietors, supplying Admiralty coal';[13] the company was subsequently removed from the list.[14]

In total, twenty-four works were included under the regulations of the Munitions of War Act in November 1915:[15]

London Works, near Birmingham,
Stour Valley Works, West Bromwich,
Birmingham Bolt & Nut Works, Smethwick,
E. Lewis & Co. Ltd., Albert Square Works, Tipton,
Cwm-Bran Works, near Newport,
Cwm-Bran Colliery, near Newport,
Viaduct Colliery, Pontnewydd,
Henliss Firebrick & Retort Works, near Newport,
Upper Cwm-Bran Brick Works, near Newport,
Newport Wharf, Newport,
Dowlais Works, Dowlais,
Dowlais and Dowlais-Cardiff Collieries,
Dowlais-Cardiff Works, East Moors, Cardiff,
Dowlais Wharf, Roath Dock, Cardiff,
Broad Street, Birmingham,
Heath Street, Birmingham,
St George's Works, Grove Lane, Smethwick,
Stirchley Street, Birmingham,
Imperial Mills, Cranford Street, Smethwick,
Imperial Mills (Wire Department), Cranford Street, Smethwick,
Castle Steel Works, Rogerstone, near Newport,
Imperial Mills, Coverack Road, Newport,
British Screw Works, Leeds.

Companies with government contracts were controlled to maximise output, eliminate wasteful duplication, and to try to ensure that excessive profits were not earned in the face of desperate need and grave shortages (p. 387).

The prime material of war was steel. Besides having only half the capacity of German production in 1914, British steelworks were particularly deficient in the manufacture of high-grade alloy steels. Until the outbreak of war, they had been largely imported from Germany.[16] British steelmakers, recorded the *History of the Ministry of Munitions*, were 'behind other countries in research, plant and method',[17] and concluded that it was only the ability to import American steel and shells that saved the Allies in the first two years of the war.

The Ministry of Munitions set about boosting output and encouraging the production of special grades of steel. Although works such as Dowlais were suffering from a 'great shortage of orders . . . for rails, fishplates, tin bars' during 1915, it was not a simple matter of diverting its furnaces and mills to the materials of war.[18] The particular type of pig iron, and hence steel, that they produced was unsuitable for rolling as shells. In July 1915 they had executed a trial order for 20 tons of '$3\frac{1}{2}$ inch round steel for shrapnel shells' but from the unenthusiastic nature of the Ministry's reply it seems that the metal was not suitable.[19]

During November 1915 W.R. Lysaght (1853–1945), whose official position was Spelter Adviser to the Ministry of Munitions, was instructed to estimate the supply and demand figures for steel in the coming year. After allowing for possible imports, he calculated that some 9,360,000 tons could be manufactured, but that civil and military orders would total 12,051,000 tons leaving a deficit of over 2,500,000 tons.[20] Hence, the Ministry of Munitions urged steelmakers to increase production and effect extensions to their plant. The departure of so many volunteers for the armed forces, caused a shortage of labour to construct the new works; more problematical still was the fact that pig iron output and blast furnace capacity lagged behind the potential for making steel. To try to overcome these shortages, the flow of pig iron was diverted from other uses and focussed on the steelworks, while new blast furnaces were erected. The latter, however, took much longer to complete than open hearth furnaces, and had in many cases been started later than most of the extensions to the steelworks and on financial terms less favourable to the producers. It was only in the latter stages of the war that the imbalance in the production of pig iron began to be corrected.

Another result of the munitions famine was a continuous revision in the official War Office and Admiralty specifications for shell steel. In January 1915 the permitted percentage of phosphorus was raised from .04 per cent to .05 per cent and by October 1915 the Army Council agreed that .06 per cent was acceptable. In April 1916 it gave way further to .07 per cent for some sizes of shells and finally in February 1917, after many tests, .08 per cent was permitted for high explosive shells on land service.[21] Initially shell steel had to be made by the acid open hearth process, though the Ordnance Committee did consent to trials with steel made by basic open hearth, basic Bessemer and acid Bessemer during 1916, the result of these wider definitions and experiments being to bring increasing numbers of steelworks within the orbit of government contracts and raising the nation's productive capacity.

While the Dowlais-Cardiff Works continued to make plate urgently needed in ships, it also made shell and special steels, output being boosted in 1917 by the installation of two extra 60-ton open hearth furnaces.[22] However, the Ministry of Munitions was concerned to reduce both its, and the company's, reliance on imports of ores from Spain. The supply to Cardiff was continually being interrupted as merchant vessels were torpedoed[23] and the cost of transport rose. In January 1916 stocks of ore at Dowlais-Cardiff fell to such a point that supplies intended for Dowlais were temporarily diverted to their East Moors steelworks.[24] The only answer was to install basic open hearth furnaces so that the works could accept supplies of indigenous ores. The Ministry of Munitions proposed this step in November 1916[25] (which also had the advantage of easing the demand for pig iron). The existing acid open hearth furnaces at East Moors could only be charged with pig iron, whereas a basic furnace was commonly worked with at least fifty per cent scrap. In addition, GKN were asked to consider the possibility of laying down a basic open hearth plant at Dowlais. A joint report, compiled by Howell R. Jones, A.K. Reese, John Williams and J. Faenor Jones, calculated the cost of installing basic technology at Dowlais.[26] They recommended that two 200-ton Talbot furnaces (capable of producing 2,600 tons of steel per week), three 60-ton fixed furnaces, with one as a spare (1,400 tons per week) and, if the Bessemer plant were to be removed, a further three 60-ton fixed furnaces (2,100 tons per week) be built, together they would provide the works with a total capacity of 6,100 tons of basic steel ingots a week. The total expenditure, £547,798, was reached by the following calculation: clearing ground and excavation (£25,000), two 500-ton gas-fired mixers (£80,000), two 200-ton Talbot furnaces (£150,000), six 60-ton basic-lined fixed furnaces (£242,988), together with ten per cent for contingencies. In addition, to roll the ingots, it would be necessary to lay down a new merchant mill in place of the existing Big Mill, another capital-intensive scheme. Speed of construction depended upon 'the supply of labour and delivery of material and machinery' but was estimated at twelve months. After discussions, the board agreed in principle to the adoption of the scheme. Whether the Ministry of Munitions considered that the price was too high or that such an ambitious plan would take too long to complete was not recorded. Suffice it to say that none of this work was actually undertaken at Dowlais.

Nevertheless, considerable steps were taken to raise output at other GKN works, notably that at Cyfarthfa. In November 1915, Messrs. Richard Thomas & Co. asked to purchase the cogging and finishing mill that was standing idle there.[27] Anxious to stimulate production, the Ministry of Munitions raised no objections to the transfer, though GKN suggested that it be loaned at rental of £100 per week for the period of the war.[28] At this point, the arrangement seems to have collapsed and in March 1916 the notion of re-starting the Castle rolling mill at Cyfarthfa to roll ingots for shell steel was discussed by the board.[29] The total cost, to be paid by the Ministry of Munitions, was estimated at £29,572, together with £4,000 for two new heating furnaces, and 'it was understood that the company would be indemnified both against any loss and on working, and that at the end of the war the company would have the option of taking over the plant at a valuation'.[30] On 19 February 1916, the Castle Mill at Cyfarthfa began again to roll billets, the ingots being supplied by the Ministry of Munitions from various works.[31]

The next request from the Ministry concerned the two blast furnaces at Cyfarthfa, and it was suggested that they be blown in to make basic pig iron with Northamptonshire ironstone.[32] GKN were reluctant to undertake this step and argued that 'the production of a low silicon basic pig iron was considered practically impossible', given the very high silica content of this class of ore. This may have been an excuse, for the Ministry pointed out that the Ebbw Vale Co. had been successfully making pig iron from this material. In July 1917, a further request was received from the Ministry of Munitions explaining that[33]

> the position with regard to the requirements of basic pig iron for steel production had become a very serious one owing to the falling off of foreign ore imports [for acid steel] and the great reduction in the stock of pig iron, and pressing for one at least of the Cyfarthfa furnaces to be blown in.

The difficulty arose because of the shortage of trained workers. Howell R. Jones and A.K. Reese reported that seven or eight men could be spared from Dowlais or Cardiff, though a considerable number would still have to be recruited from other sources.[34] However, the Ministry had its way and on 28 October 1917 No. 3 furnace at Cyfarthfa resumed operations.[35] For the same reasons, on 6 December 1917 a scheme was approved to bring the third blast furnace at Dowlais-Cardiff back into blast for the production of basic pig iron,[36] and an expenditure of £7,619 was authorised in February 1918.[37]

The desire to raise output was in evidence at other GKN sites. In October 1915 management at the Imperial Mills, Coverack Road, Newport, which drew wire from rods supplied by the Castle Works at Rogerstone, received a government inquiry for considerable quantities of wire needed in the manufacture of weapons and munitions.[38] Since the mills were working at full capacity to cope with increased orders of screws and nails, the only solution was to purchase extra machinery. Such a scheme also required extensions be undertaken at Rogerstone to raise the weekly output of wire rods by 500 tons. The cost was estimated at £30,000, though GKN asked the authorities whether the sum could be charged against revenue so that it would pre-empt any calculation of liability for Excess Profits Duty (p. 387).[39] In fact, the Ministry of Munitions agreed that the company should reclaim 75 per cent of expenditure out of excess profits and conditionally allowed a further 7s. 6d. per ton on all rods over and above the quantity agreed at the standard output.[40]

In view of the urgency, the government had to offer financial concessions to companies as an encouragement to take courses of action which they might otherwise have rejected. In October 1915, for example, GKN agreed that the land adjoining Imperial Mills, Coverack Road, could be used by the government to erect a shell factory, provided that the building suit their future needs 'and at a cost not exceeding twenty thousand pounds'. They indicated their willingness to purchase the works on the resumption of peace, provided proper allowance was made for depreciation and the inflation generated by war-time shortages.[41]

At Smethwick in July 1915 part of the bar shop was diverted to the manufacture of fuses and aircraft work, the new equipment costing £5,670,[42] while extensions were authorised in August 'having regard to the present orders for government work and the future prospects of running the shop on ordinary work'.[43] Such expansion and the general increase in demand for woodscrews created by the war encouraged GKN to consider the purchase of a 1,000 kwt Belliss-Siemens turbo generator to be installed in a new reinforced concrete power house.[44] The cost was not settled[45] and the scheme was not finally authorised until October 1917, when the figure was fixed at £21,900.[46]

The imposition of greater levels of government control and the provision of incentives revealed itself throughout British manufacturing. Joseph Sankey & Sons, makers of all types of pressed metal goods, who were taken over by GKN in 1920, were approached by the War Office with a request to produce helmets of steel capable of stopping a revolver bullet at close range. A number of Sheffield companies claimed that material of this strength was too hard to press and for the moment the Army had to take helmets of a second-best, mild steel. George Sankey (1865–1934), acting chairman, with his eldest son at the front and a nephew, Sidney Sankey, having been killed in action',[47] refused to accept defeat and after many failures developed a method of pressing hard steel. The Albert Street works of Joseph Sankey, a Controlled Establishment from 1 November 1915,[48] finally supplied 5½ million manganese steel helmets to the troops, nearly the Army's entire requirement.[49] The helmet saved many lives and its value was widely acknowledged, not least by Robert Graves in *Goodbye to All That*.[50] The company's Hadley Castle Works, near Wellington, manufactured field kitchens, mine hemispheres, wagons, paravanes and smoke-making apparatus. Towards the end of the war an aluminium bomb case, six feet long and two feet in diameter, was built there in great secrecy, though before it could be dropped on Berlin the peace was signed.[51]

COST ACCOUNTING AND EXCESS PROFITS DUTY

Because the government was spending huge sums of the public's money on factory extensions and munitions contracts, it attempted to devise methods to prevent overcharging, without impeding the rapid production of war material in the quantities demanded. The effect of shortages and the urgency with which orders had to be executed created ample opportunity for profiteering. A manufacturer whose components were desperately needed at the front or in other factories could exaggerate the costs of production or the difficulties entailed in the process of manufacture to force up the price. In an attempt to prevent such fraud, the Ministry of Munitions sought to impose standing charges and margins, for which each stage of manufacture had to be costed and a reasonable level of profit computed. This work was undertaken by an army of accountants recruited from private practice and much was learned about cost accounting as a result. Businesses, too, benefited from a systematic attempt to measure the financial performance of their productive processes and many cost accountants recruited during the war remained in industry once the peace had been signed.

When a works became a Controlled Establishment, the government sought to establish a standard profit level. This was based on an average calculated from the period 1913–14; any profit earned in excess of this amount was subject to taxation at the rate of 80 per cent.[52] The negotiation of an agreed profit benchmark brought much additional work for company auditors, and Carter & Co. were continually involved with the GKN accounts throughout the Great War.

In May 1916, Carter & Co. raised the important issue of the valuation of stocks. In order to raise the level of profits in the pre-war period and therefore reduce the final bill for Excess Profits Duty, Mr. Eric Carter, the partner responsible for the GKN audit, suggested that the stocks at Dowlais in 1913–14 had been seriously undervalued. He argued that the extra income tax that this revision would entail would be far less than the savings which would follow from a higher profit 'standard' by which GKN would be judged over the period of Control.[53] The matter involved considerable negotiation with the authorities, and though discussions were still proceeding in December 1916, a letter from the auditors advised that[54] 'as important questions such as stock valuation and depreciation were involved, and precedents were being established . . . no action should be taken with a view to hurrying on a decision'. In June 1917, the auditors reported further meetings between themselves as the company's representatives and the Ministry of Munitions, when questions such as depreciation, subsidiary companies and stocks were debated. The board suggested that stocks should be valued following the practice of previous years, while the Ministry argued that the figures should be inflated to reflect current market prices, which, in turn, would raise the company's profits and liability for Excess Profits Duty. To strengthen their hand in such a crucial dispute, GKN decided to consult [Sir] Albert Wyon (1869–1937), senior partner of Price, Waterhouse & Co., the City accountants, for an expert opinion.[55] On 13 June 1917, Eric Carter and Mr. Birley of Carter & Co., together with A.T. Keen and Edward Steer, travelled to London to meet Wyon, who subsequently journeyed to Birmingham to make a more detailed investigation.[56] They consulted Wyon because he had served as a member of the board of referees appointed by the Treasury under the Finance Act of 1915 and possessed an intimate knowledge of the provisions for Excess Profits Duty. As a result of these deliberations, the auditors prepared the accounts valuing stocks as in previous years with no allowance for inflation. Shortly afterwards the Ministry of Munitions agreed to the following compromise:[57]

> With regard to stocks . . . the company should continue to take those on the same basis as previously, leaving the question to be re-opened on either side at the end of the period of control, and as respects depreciation, the authorities were willing to allow an annual charge of £90,000. The questions of special wear and tear and extra depreciation owing to the higher cost of replacements had also been discussed and the authorities had offered for the year ending 30th June 1916 to allow a further sum of £30,000 in respect of these items.

The certainty that they would be liable to an undecided sum in Excess Profits Duty, together with the flood of substantial government contracts commanding rates beyond those of peacetime, provided both the means and the incentive for companies to amass considerable financial reserves and in this GKN was no exception. These were not disclosed in the published accounts and in the 1920s, when the sums actually demanded by the revenue proved smaller than expected, most companies continued to maintain secret reserves from funds accrued during the war years.

Too much reliance should not therefore be placed on precise accuracy of the profit figures published by GKN during the Great

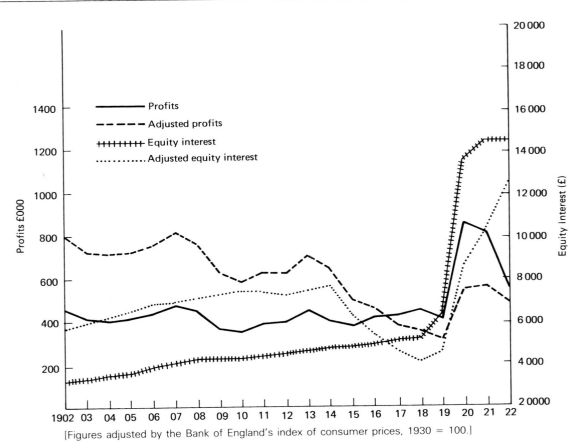

[Figures adjusted by the Bank of England's index of consumer prices, 1930 = 100.]

Figure 15 GKN's profits and equity interest 1902–22

War. As has been discovered, there were strong pressures acting on the group to understate its profits during these years and to overstate the surplus in the period 1913–14. Table 11.1 (p. 369) reveals that the published profit figures for 1914–18 were all lower than 1913, a fall all the more marked when expressed in real terms. Whilst they doubtless reflect a degree of manipulation, the extent of the decline seems to have been so marked as to suggest that the Great War did not benefit GKN financially. Despite accusations in the popular press and a number of political and other groups that industrialists were getting fat at the expense of the taxpayer, there is no evidence that GKN prospered as a result of the war, despite the profiteering that occurred elsewhere. It is not difficult to see why this should have been so. The disruption caused to the company's export markets and customers at home, the loss of skilled labour to the forces, the requirement to expand production in areas inappropriate to the needs of a peacetime economy, the extra wages occasioned by inflation, the need to pay dependants of employees disabled or killed in the conflict, and the request to push machinery to the limit to raise output at whatever cost all conspired to undermine sound business principles.

Table 12.1   GKN profit and loss account 1918

Income and expenditure	2 months ending 31 August £	3 months ending 30 September £	4 months ending 31 October £
Dowlais, Dowlais-Cardiff and Collieries	(113644)	(120685)	(10204)
London, Stour Valley and Cwmbran Works	12481	17269	32246
Nettlefolds	44165	60789	148726
Investments and Bank Interest	22890	34285	45680
Sub-total:	(34108)	(8342)	216448
Less: Income Tax and Head Office Expenses	27000	40500	54000
Total:	(61108)	(48842)	162448

Figures in brackets indicate a loss.

Source: GKN Minute Book, Vol. III, 30 October 1918, it. 3163; 7 November 1918, it. 3184; 5 December 1918, it. 3208.

Credence is lent to this conclusion by a series of calculations made by GKN for 1918 (Table 12.1), which revealed that the Dowlais, Dowlais-Cardiff steelworks and their associated collieries were operating at a serious loss throughout 1918. The group was kept afloat in the main by Nettlefolds, which continued to earn substantial profits, and by the company's investments and interest from bank deposits. For the three months ending 30 September 1918, the manufacturing side of GKN made a loss of £42,627; income from investments reduced this to £8,342 but their liability for tax and other expenses increased the deficit to £48,842.[58] By successfully reducing the loss suffered by the former Dowlais Iron Co. to £10,204 for the four months ending 31 October 1918, they calculated that the company could expect to earn an overall profit of £162,448.

MANAGEMENT DURING THE WAR

The major change was the death on 8 February 1915, of Arthur Keen who was succeeded by his eldest son Arthur T. Keen.[59] There appears to have been no contest for the chairmanship, as his son had long been the heir apparent and no rival of wide business experience sat in the boardroom. Lord Wimborne had in any case died on 22 February

119 Edward Ponsonby, the eighth Earl of Bessborough (1851–1920), chairman of GKN from 1918 to 1920.

1914, after a long illness. In April 1917 Godfrey Nettlefold, who had become a joint managing director when Arthur T. Keen assumed the chairman's post, asked to resign on the advice of his doctor, Sir J. Mackenzie,[60] but remained a board member until his sudden death on 30 March 1918.[61] Sir Joseph Weston-Stevens also resigned as a director in 1916–17. As a result, the number of main board directors had fallen to five: the Earl of Bessborough, F.W. Keen, Edward Steer, E. Windsor Richards and Sir John Field Beale (1874–1935). The latter had been appointed to the board in 1918; he was the senior London partner in the firm of solicitors, Beale & Co. whose Birmingham office under C.G. Beale had advised the Patent Nut & Bolt Co. Their Westminster office was managed by James Beale, his brother and father of Sir John. C.G. Beale had married Alice Kenrick, sister of Florence, Joseph Chamberlain's second wife, while James Beale married a member of the Field family which had owned the Birmingham Screw Co. Sir John Field Beale, appointed to replace Godfrey Nettlefold who had died in office, was filling a Nettlefold vacancy and was probably put forward by Edward Steer.

The death of Arthur T. Keen in July 1918 resulted in the Earl of Bessborough taking the post of chairman.[62] Shortly afterwards, on 22 August 1918, J.H. Jolly (1887–1972) attended his first board meeting as company secretary in succession to H. Probyn who had originally worked for the Patent Nut & Bolt Co. Probyn became a director in July

1918, a post he retained until 1921, while Lt. Colonel The Hon. C.H.C. Guest (1874–1957), MP, was appointed to the board in 1919. Jolly, who was subsequently to serve as chairman from 1947 to 1953, was a chartered accountant.[63] Working in Cardiff for W.B. Peat & Co., he had been instructed to prepare a report on the Blaenavon Co., a steelworks with colliery interests, and having suggested certain managerial changes, asked Peats whether he could leave to carry them into effect. Whilst working there, he encountered Edward Steer, who lived nearby in Monmouthshire, and he suggested that Jolly might consider joining GKN, as their current secretary, Probyn, suffered from poor health.

When Lord Bessborough became chairman, an 'Executive Committee' was formed alongside those responsible for Nettlefolds, the Collieries, Works and Finance. Unlike the other committees which were exclusively composed of board members (the only exception being Probyn who initially sat on the Finance Committee as company secretary), a number of senior managers attended. Howell R. Jones (Dowlais), T.Z. Lloyd (1872–1939) (Smethwick), A.K. Reese (Cardiff), W.H. Whitehouse (Cwmbran) and John Williams (Rogerstone) were all members of the Executive Committee.[64] It was probably formed to discuss the detailed implementation of policy decided upon by the main board, and the involvement of the works managers was to provide Lord Bessborough with a better understanding of what was involved. The only other directors with any industrial experience were F.W. Keen, E. Windsor Richards and Edward Steer.

The death of William Evans in 1915 resulted in Howell R. Jones (1860–1941) being appointed as general manager of the Dowlais steelworks and collieries. Born at Dowlais, he attended Taunton School, becoming a pupil in the company's collieries and obtained his manager's certificate in 1883. After serving as manager of the Penydarren Pits, in 1894 he became assistant to H.W. Martin, colliery agent, and seven years later when Crawshay Bros. Ltd. were acquired, became agent of the Cyfarthfa collieries. On the retirement of Martin in 1909, he served as agent to both groups of collieries, a position he held until 1915. Thus, his experience and training was essentially in coal. It is significant that by 1915 the balance of power had switched away from steel in favour of coal; in the nineteenth century no colliery engineer would have been placed in overall charge of Dowlais. Although Jones was not of the calibre of those eminent men who had preceded him, he had obtained his position by loyal hard work and had as his newspaper obituary stated: 'devoted himself entirely to his work and took little part in public affairs, but all charitable movements found him a generous supporter'.[65]

T.Z. Lloyd, the son of S.Z. Lloyd, had been educated at Clifton College and as a mechanical engineer at King's College, London, but did not complete his studies there, entering Heath Street in about 1892. Serving in a variety of departments, he became assistant to

Charles Steer, whom he succeeded as general manager when the latter died unexpectedly in 1906. Although Lloyd ran Heath Street, then the most profitable enterprise within GKN, he was not appointed to the main board until 1930, a delay which may be explained by his comparative youth on becoming general manager and the requirement to invest £5,000 in the company, a stipulation in the articles of association.

The war years had not seen a strengthening of GKN's management team. Most of the elderly men who had died or retired had not been replaced by younger executives of drive and expertise. The death of so many talented officers and NCOs in the trenches of Europe must have further damaged the company's prospects of improving the calibre of its management, whether at board or factory level.

Having acknowledged that there was little change in the strategy pursued by GKN, one event, had it come to fruition, would have produced dramatic consequences. During 1914 Dudley Docker (1862–1944) had attempted to persuade Arthur Keen that an amalgamation with his Metropolitan Railway Carriage, Wagon & Finance Co. (also formed by merger in 1902),[66] the only other Midlands combine that compared in size with GKN, would be an attractive initiative. However, Keen's death and the onset of war scuppered Docker's plans: the former's son and successor, Arthur T. Keen, proved to 'so nervous, [and] so full of settling his father's affairs and taking over the business' that, Docker's solicitor concluded, 'it would be premature to push him'.[67] Had such a union been effected, the resultant group would have ranked as Britain's largest engineering company and it was likely that the forceful Docker would have been chosen to lead it. In this event, the merger between GKN and John Lysaght in 1920 would probably have never taken place because the Berry brothers, who organised the amalgamation, benefited from a power vacuum that had developed in GKN's higher echelons. As a mammoth Midlands-based engineering group with steelworks at Cardiff and Dowlais, rather than steelmakers with engineering interests, it is interesting to speculate how this united body might have fared.

LABOUR PROBLEMS

Just as there were few in 1914 who foresaw that the Great War would be protracted, so, too, many failed to appreciate its inherent industrial character. The Secretary of State for War, Lord Kitchener, was almost alone in the Cabinet when he argued that the conflict would be long-drawn-out and wide-ranging.[68] He urged companies making vital supplies for the Armed Forces to discourage their employees from joining up. For example, in September 1914 Kitchener wrote to Kirkstall Forge, manufacturers of axles, that[69]

I wish to impress upon those employed by your establishment the importance of the government work upon which they are engaged. I fully appreciate the efforts which the employees are making and the quality of work turned out. I trust that everything will be done to assist the military authorities by pushing out orders as rapidly as possible. I should like all engaged by your establishment to know that it is fully recognised that they, in carrying out the great work of supplying munitions of war, are doing their duty for their king and country equally with those who have joined the army for active service in the field.

Yet the call to arms was so compelling that many workers ignored Kitchener's pleas and reported to enlistment centres. Hence, when Lloyd George became Minister of Munitions in June 1915, skilled workers (and later labourers as well because of their experience and physical strength)[70] engaged on government contracts were issued with a brass badge, depicting the shield of the Royal Army Ordnance Corps and the words 'On War Service', and a card to certify this fact.[71] Even so, between July and December 1915 over 7,000 men from the steel industry alone volunteered for the forces, though this represented a considerable reduction 'on previous figures'.[72]

Large numbers of employees from GKN enlisted in the early years of the Great War. By 5 November 1914, 2,926[73] men had volunteered; by 1 July 1915, the total had risen to 4,818.[74] When conscription had to be introduced in 1916, a system of 'certified occupations' was devised. Skilled mechanics, operators of lathes or supervisors in steelworks and factories could be more effectively employed in running munitions works than making up the numbers in the trenches, and a scheme of deployment was needed to ensure that they remained at home in industry.

The same was true of the coal mines. Large numbers of colliers employed in GKN's many pits volunteered for military service in 1914–15 and this rapidly had a significant impact on output. Managers were soon compelled to refuse to let men leave. Tudor Davies wrote to the head office at Dowlais about three potential volunteers in December 1915: 'we cannot afford to do without the services of these men as we are very short handed'.[75] In 1916 efforts were made to encourage soldiers to return to the pits. Davies wrote a number of letters to the authorities to secure the services of former colliers, who had been in particular demand at the front as tunnellers, to lay mines under enemy trenches:[76]

It is stated that Blunt is certified for home service only and is desirous of returning to his former occupation: he was engaged as a collier at Bedlinog before his enlistment and we are prepared to offer him similar work should he be discharged. With regard

63. *DBB*, Vol. III, London (1985), Edgar Jones 'J.H. Jolly', pp. 523–6; Interview J. Cockroft with J.H. Jolly, 25 July 1972.
64. Ibid., 3 October 1918, it. 3156, it. 3161.
65. GKN Scrapbook, Obituaries, February 1941, pp. 100–01.
66. R.P.T. Davenport-Hines, *Dudley Docker*, Cambridge (1985), pp. 46–70.
67. SRO, ASM 193/165/1/544 Steel-Maitland Papers, Memorandum of conversation with R.A. Pinsent, 25 April 1915.
68. *History of the First World War*, Vol. 4, No. 53 (1970), Sir Philip Magnus, 'The Death of Kitchener', p. 1463.
69. Rodney Butler, *The History of Kirkstall Forge*, York (1954), p. 208.
70. Carr and Taplin, *British Steel Industry*, p. 313.
71. Butler, *Kirkstall Forge*, opposite p. 208.
72. Carr and Taplin, *British Steel Industry*, p. 313.
73. GKN Minute Book, Vol. II, 5 November 1914, it. 2482.
74. Ibid., 1 July 1915, it. 2575.
75. GRO, D/DG, Letters Dowlais Collieries 1912–15, Tudor Davies to GKN (D), 16 December 1915.
76. GRO, D/DG, Letters Dowlais Collieries 1916–18, Tudor Davies to GKN (D), 14 July 1916.
77. Ibid., Tudor Davies to GKN (D), 21 August 1916.
78. Arthur Marwick, *Women at War 1914–1918*, London (1972), p. 12; Milward, 'The Allies', p. 672.
79. Butler, *Kirkstall Forge*, pp. 209–10.
80. Ibid., p. 210.
81. Owen, *Dowlais Iron Works*, p. 100.
82. Marwick, *Women at War*, p. 162.
83. Ibid.
84. GKN Minute Book, Vol. II, 27 August 1914, it. 2466.
85. Ibid.
86. Ibid., 6 May 1915, it. 2552.
87. Ibid., 7 October 1915, it. 2611.
88. Ibid., 4 November 1915, it. 2623.
89. Ibid., 2 December 1916, it. 2649.
90. GKN Minute Book, Vol. III, 4 May 1916, it. 2704.
91. Ibid., 9 August 1917, it. 2926.
92. Ibid., 30 October 1917, it. 3169.
93. GKN Minute Book, Vol. II, 1 April 1915, it. 2535.
94. Ibid., 6 May 1915, it. 2551.
95. John Keegan, *The Face of Battle*, Harmondsworth (1976), pp. 217–19.
96. *Unveiling and Dedication of a War Memorial, Guest, Keen & Nettlefolds at Smethwick Recreation Grounds*, 26 June 1924, p. 7.
97. 'Sankey Story', p. 28.
98. GKN Minute Book, Vol. III, 6 June 1918, it. 3093.
99. Ibid., 6 December 1917, it. 2999.

13 *Conclusions*

In November 1918, when peace returned to Europe, GKN, though essentially healthy, had developed a number of minor complaints which could, if unattended, threaten its vital constitution. Whilst the group comprised a unified and coherent collection of manufacturing subsidiaries, embracing the various processes between coal mining, steel making and the production of fasteners, some of its plant was outdated and had only been kept alive by war-inflated demand. It would soon be difficult to earn a respectable profit at Cyfarthfa, Dowlais and Cwmbran, and before long the first two would close. The collieries belonging to the company, once a source of great wealth, were to experience declining fortunes. To balance the picture, the screw and bolt works in Smethwick were very successful. The steelworks at East Moors, though modern, had been designed to roll plate and would soon find that the market for its products had shrunk considerably. Possibly most serious for the well-being of GKN were the gaps that retirement and death had opened in the highest levels of management. The great entrepreneurs and engineers of the late nineteenth century had departed and the reconstituted board of 1918 lacked broad industrial experience and technical expertise.

Yet to summarise events at this point is, in effect, to present the reader with a false ending. There was a great deal more to come. Volume Two of this history will take the story of GKN through the inter-war years, across the Second World War and on to the post-1945 economy. Nevertheless, it would be foolish not to attempt to draw conclusions from the first hundred and fifty years of GKN's existence, as many questions have been raised by the group's longevity and diverse activities.

'Now, what I want is Facts. Teach these boys and girls nothing but Facts. Facts alone are wanted in life', urged Mr. Thomas Gradgrind, formerly of the wholesale hardware trade in the mythical Coketown of Charles Dickens' novel *Hard Times* (1854).[1] Facts remain at the very heart of this study of GKN, for one of its aims is to provide a narrative of the journey that the group and its main constituent parts have taken from the foundation of the Dowlais Iron Co. in 1759. However, the criticism implicit in Dickens' portrayal of Gradgrind, a man for whom facts were deemed sufficient in themselves, has implications for the writing of company histories. Interpretation and imagination were an anathema to this cynosure of Victorian humbug and he dismissed them as mere 'fancy'. Yet a study of business which fails to attempt to explain success and failure, the motives for action, the context in which decisions were taken and to delineate the various forces acting upon companies at specific times, is a work of scant value. Whilst history may not in fact repeat itself, there are always parallels to be drawn with the present, and the very act of considering a contrast is at least to add a further dimension of understanding to current problems. The company history will not enable businessmen to solve their difficulties, but it will provide them with a reference point (ideally showing them how and why they have arrived at their present position) and should present the options which had been applied to past problems, albeit in the context of different historical circumstances.

Whilst not intending to suggest recipes for business success, it appears from the example of GKN, a large-scale company, that profitability for the manufacturer lay in consistently associating oneself with the truly dynamic areas of the economy. The rapid growth of Dowlais Iron Co. in the 1790s, for example, owed itself principally to the installation of puddling furnaces and rolling mills, which enabled them to enter the highly profitable market for bar iron. Demand for products fashioned from bar iron expanded swiftly and offered ample opportunities for commercial exploitation. Because much of the tedious experimental work in devising an efficient manufacturing process had been undertaken by the Crawshays at Cyfarthfa, who had incurred the research and development costs, having already adopted the inferior 'potting and stamping' method, the Guests with an element of luck were able to innovate at the optimum time. Had they lingered any longer the moment would have passed, as their rival ironworks in Merthyr closed ranks around the market. Timing, therefore, was as crucial as knowing which technology to purchase, particularly as plant in this industry was comparatively expensive.

Similarly, the decision by John Sutton Nettlefold to purchase the very latest machinery for mass-producing the gimlet-pointed wood-screw from Thomas Sloane of New York was of equal importance. Nettlefold & Chamberlain were not responsible for devising the technical breakthrough, but they can claim credit for its commercial exploitation. Had they delayed in building a modern mill at Heath Street to house the new machines, then the initiative would undoubtedly have been taken by a rival, and the cost advantages generated by mass production would have made it impossibly difficult to establish themselves, as the Birmingham Screw Co. found in the

of the economy and the influences of society. Successful companies are fully integrated within their industry and community. Only then can they acquire or sell new technology, attract the most talented students and managers and raise capital for expansion. Businesses exhibiting a laager mentality, which stand apart, considering themselves too powerful to be affected by their rivals or economic trends, court disaster and have often died. The fall of the Cyfarthfa ironworks in the late nineteenth century may be ascribed to such causes. By failing to recruit leaders of ability, the firm had slipped down the rankings of South Wales works, and foolishly refused to enter the market for steel until the costs had risen to such a level that they were precipitated into financial crisis which not even public flotation could solve. They were taken over by GKN who soon discovered that the steelworks was unprofitable and closed it to reduce capacity. Cyfarthfa had once been among the leading ironworks in Britain, but by not keeping pace with its competitors, technological innovation and changing patterns of demand, it lapsed into inevitable decline.

Implicit throughout this study has been an assessment of the value, whether high or low, that society placed on its entrepreneurs and success in business. During the Industrial Revolution, the ironmaster was often an outsider, commonly Non-conformist in religion, working at the forefront of technology at sites remote from established centres of population; he was a pioneer. Drawn from the artisan or yeoman class and without formal education, his ambition was to earn a good living and establish his own business. He was not particularly interested in what society thought of his achievements and sought neither title nor preferment to match his wealth; the trappings of land and architecture that accompanied such formal approval held no attraction. His children, however, were not always immune to these considerations. By virtue of his grandfather's and father's efforts, Josiah John Guest inherited a firm worth a fortune and though he remained committed to its management, spending the greater part of his life at Dowlais House situated in the heart of the ironworks, he married Lady Charlotte Bertie, the daughter of the Earl of Lindsey, and agreed to contest the parliamentary seat of Glamorgan, on condition that he be awarded a baronetcy. Although he lost the election, the honour was duly conferred, though Lady Charlotte, sensitive to these matters, felt that a peerage at least was deserved. The reluctance to reward industrialists with honours also applied later in the century to Arthur Keen. The *Birmingham Gazette & Express* for 1907 speculated that,[3] 'though wonder has often been expressed that he has never been raised to the dignity of a knighthood or baronetcy, it is extremely doubtful whether he would accept any such honour. It cannot be claimed that he is an ambitious man in that direction'.

The many children of Sir John Guest were educated not at Dowlais and Bridgnorth Grammar School as he had been, but privately. The eldest boy, Ivor Bertie Guest, who became Lord Wimborne in 1880, attended Harrow School and Trinity College, Cambridge. Whilst Lady Charlotte wished him to train as a manager at Dowlais, his entry was blocked by G.T. Clark and he took up residence at Canford, taking charge of the estate. Marrying Lady Cornelia Churchill in 1868, he sold the business in 1900, fourteen years before his death. His son, Ivor Churchill Guest (1873–1939), created Viscount Wimborne in 1918, having been a Liberal MP for both Plymouth and Cardiff, served as Lord Lieutenant of Ireland between 1915 and 1918, but never took any part in the affairs of GKN.

The children of entrepreneurs, whether able or otherwise, were often more interested in attending the ancient universities (which with the exception of scholarship places were not yet meritocratic institutions) or entering the professions than acquiring vocational skills and qualifications. Although many members of the Nettlefold family entered the business, a large number were attracted to the armed forces. Edward Nettlefold, educated at Caius College, Cambridge, became Nettlefolds' deputy chairman and subsequently served on the GKN board. His eldest son, Edward John Nettlefold, of Eton and Trinity College, Cambridge, was commissioned into the 5th Dragoon Guards, and his younger brother, Joseph Henry Nettlefold, who also went to Eton, entered Sandhurst and became a regular officer. The sons of Frederick Nettlefold, one-time chairman of Nettlefolds, were: Frederick John (1867–1949), educated at Eastbourne College, and Corpus Christi College, Oxford, chairman of Courtaulds Ltd.; Archibald (1870–1944), a farmer in Yorkshire and owner of the Comedy Theatre in London.[4]

The evidence of GKN suggests, therefore, that the children of successful businessmen appeared to be increasingly reluctant to enter industry, once the family had amassed sufficient income to fund a career elsewhere. And that in itself may have been no bad thing. It is unlikely, for example, that Lord Wimborne, had he been allowed to take charge at Dowlais, would have run the firm as profitably as did G.T. Clark and his team of professional managers. Talented fathers by no means always produce talented sons, or even sons who would wish to join the family business. Of greater significance for British manufacturing was the establishment of the notion that employment in industry carried a lower cachet than the professions, a commission in the Army or Royal Navy, or a position in a financial institution in the City of London. Accordingly, young men, whose parents had no direct connection with manufacturing and who sought a rewarding career, were seldom likely to consider employment in an ironworks or textile mill. Possibly they were further discouraged by the obvious signs of dynastic succession. In a professional firm, where entry and promotion were to a significant extent determined by examination results and practical competence, the outsider might feel that he had a reasonable chance of promotion, while in a business owned by a family, where relatives were traditionally preferred for posts of responsibility, the recruit would judge his opportunities for advancement more limited.

Nations which industrialised later, such as America, Germany and Japan, do not appear to have adopted such attitudes. For them, there was nothing ignoble or inferior about being associated with 'trade'. Given that Britain recognised its manufacturing might and seemed in the mid-Victorian period to be proud of it (the 1851 Great Exhibition was, in part, designed to reveal this superiority over other countries), adopting the slogan 'the workshop of the world', it is difficult to explain why this damaging snobbery developed.

Victorian society, and in particular its business community, may be judged to have failed in not establishing management as a professional occupation. It remained a 'practical' job where knowledge was acquired by watching and doing; there was little theoretical understanding of business principles, no examination, written or otherwise, of competence and expertise and no institute in which problems could be debated and research discussed and publicised. Even in science-based industries, such as chemicals, where academic research had a direct and obvious role, businessmen were slow to adopt its ideas and techniques. The British steel industry, too, lagged behind the Americans and Germans in this respect. The failure to appreciate the value of rigorous scientific training is revealed in the opinions expressed by John Wigham Richardson (1837–1908), the Newcastle shipbuilder, who argued that[5] 'technical education can surely only mean the teaching of an art . . . I can conceive of no better school than the workshop. You have there the experience and skill of the best artisans . . . you are in the very atmosphere of your craft . . . you are learning by doing'. As British industry fell behind its major competitors and found itself being squeezed out of world markets, profit levels fell and the rewards also declined. By the end of the nineteenth century, there were also strong financial reasons why young men selecting a career would choose the professions in favour of industry.

The attitudes which prompted the ambitious and able to prefer the professions also had a deleterious effect on those who remained in manufacturing. Because society so little valued the industrialist as an industrialist, he was forced to adopt a different persona to win esteem, commonly seeking recognition as a squire or gentleman.[6] Relatives who inherited managerial positions often spent considerable sums building country homes and gaining acceptance with the country circuit. The construction of Cyfarthfa Castle in 1825 by William Crawshay II at a cost of £30,000, much to the disapproval of his father, was an early example of this desire for social elevation.

In the late eighteenth and first three-quarters of the nineteenth centuries, the withdrawal into the rural pursuits of the gentry by the wealthy sons of entrepreneurs may, in fact, have had a beneficial effect, for it cleared the upper ranks of industry for a succession of talented and ambitious, but lower-born, managers. Men such as John and Thomas Evans, William Menelaus and E.P. Martin were able to take their chance because Sir John Guest did not insist on his sons entering the family business. The system appears to have worked well until the 1880s, when the combination of 'gentleman amateur' and 'practical man' came into competition with professionally-qualified managers from Germany and America.

Complementing the 'practical man' on the shop floor, senior executives and proprietors now felt most at ease with the image of the 'educated amateur'. Their background was increasingly that of the public school (only six per cent of pupils at Marlborough entered industry in 1846, but twenty-three per cent in 1906; six per cent from Merchant Taylors in 1851 but forty-two per cent in 1891, and nine per cent from Clifton in 1867, but twenty-five per cent in 1907)[7] and if fortunate, Oxbridge as well. The ancient universities were not then distinguished for their teaching and research, but for most, existed as a form of finishing school where undergraduates learned how to be a certain kind of person. Jude Fawley, the gifted, but low-born, scholar of Hardy's novel, was advised to abandon his academic ambitions:[8] 'It is an ignorant place . . . You are one of the very men Christminster [Oxford] was intended for when the colleges were founded; a man with a passion for learning, but no money, or opportunities, or friends. But you were elbowed off the pavement by the millionaire's sons'. Indeed, most of those who had attended Oxbridge and then entered the steel industry read arts, not science.[9] Such men had a distrust of any theoretically grounded knowledge and strengthened the resistance to science-based innovation. 'Economics, management techniques, industrial psychology', observed Coleman, 'all were frequently looked upon with grave suspicion, for they represented attempts to professionalise an activity long carried on jointly by "practical men" and gentlemanly amateurs.'[10]

In the opening decade of the twentieth century, GKN, in tune with most manufacturing companies in Britain, reached a plateau in terms of profitability and seemed unable to grow any larger. This was undoubtedly due to the pressure of foreign competition, and, in part, the inability of British manufacturers to fight back must have been an implicit criticism the calibre of management. The competence exhibited by entrepreneurs in the early and mid-nineteenth century had been diluted by the rise of the professions and proliferation of commercial and financial institutions syphoning off so many talented leaders. Whilst GKN, like other major companies, did recruit and retain able managers, it appears that their numbers were reduced. The impact of the rise of new professions and the expansion of the established ones would have been greatest on middle management. The restricted number of places on the board or at the head of factories or works could still be filled by leaders of ability, but the ranks of middle management would have suffered. The performance of the British economy as a whole and the profit record of individual companies supported this judgement.

But, whatever generalisations can be made about the comparatively poor calibre of British management at the turn of the nineteenth century, there remain a number of outstanding figures in the story of GKN. Sir John and Lady Charlotte Guest, in their different ways, were characters of eminence in Victorian Britain. Contemporary accounts of Sir John's personality are few; even Lady Charlotte's journals do not afford a full view of him. She described visitors and colleagues but in view of their close relationship did not seek to portray her husband directly. Nevertheless, he appears not to have been boastful or to have sought publicity overtly. Although a Member of Parliament and married to an aristocrat, he had no enduring interest in high society or following a political career. His home was Dowlais and it was to protect the interests of his ironworks and the people of the town that Josiah John Guest became Merthyr Tydfil's representative. The well-being of his firm was his driving ambition. He was born at Dowlais and, though forced by a debilitating illness to rest at Canford, Sir John Guest travelled back to the town when he felt death close at hand, so that he might die and be buried there.

Lady Charlotte Guest possessed high intelligence and, if not classically beautiful, had an attractive face of perception and interest. Possibly because she had been disillusioned at too young an age by the death of her elderly father and by a mother who appears not to have offered her sufficient affection, when twelve, Lady Charlotte turned to study and literature for consolation. She determined to be a scholar and master many of the pursuits commonly thought exclusively male. Perhaps she was attracted to a life at Dowlais among the blast furnaces and rolling mills because it was so very different from her unhappy childhood as an aristocrat in rural England. Lady Charlotte could scarcely have chosen a more alien environment, but entered fully into its culture – even to the extent of learning Welsh so that she could converse with the workers and inhabitants of Merthyr. It was only in her early forties that she seems to have come to terms with her upbringing and background. Then Lady Charlotte married Charles Schreiber MP, a former fellow of Trinity College, Cambridge, and son of a cavalry officer, moved to Canford and pursued a life-style which contemporaries would have regarded as fitting her station and wealth. Schreiber was fourteen years younger than she, so that their marriage would have been regarded as just as unconventional as that to Josiah Guest who was twenty-seven years her senior.

Although outwardly a different type of person from Sir John or Lady Charlotte Guest, Arthur Keen, like them, had experienced a tough childhood. Keen was in essence a determined, hard-working Midlands businessman who obtained wealth and power by sheer single-minded dedication to his task. With little formal education, no professional qualification nor a substantial inheritance, his marriage and a chance acquaintanceship with Francis Watkins produced the opportunity he required to enter manufacturing on his own account. Rapid growth, combined with a series of skilfully managed take-overs and amalgamations, brought Keen to the point where he could consider the acquisition of the Dowlais Iron Co. Had his subsequent scheme to merge Guest, Keen & Co. with the United States Steel Corporation come to fruition, then events would have followed a discernably different path. The collapse of this proposal prompted him to turn his attention to Nettlefolds, whom Keen pressurised into a take-over in 1902.

Unlike the eminent engineers who repeatedly achieved gains in technical efficiency at Dowlais, Arthur Keen's role was that of strategist, fixer and motivator. He appears to have been a leader whom men feared rather than revered. 'No one', observed the *Birmingham Evening Despatch*, 'will ever carry off his hat by mistake for he takes a seven and three-quarters – Gladstone's size'.[11] In contrast to Sir John and Lady Charlotte, he was probably something of a loner, without true friends. It was widely believed, for example, that he was an orphan, several obituaries referring to this supposed fact. Whether this rumour gained credence from his behaviour, or because he encouraged its circulation, is not known, though its widespread acceptance suggests that Keen was a remote figure. He appears to have been wary of professional advisers and distrusted managers of ability and ambition, believing perhaps that they would wrest power from his hands in a moment of weakness. This largely explains why Keen failed to appoint a deputy who possessed the qualities to succeed him and could not, though he had reached his late seventies, bring himself to retire from the business.

Joseph Chamberlain possessed sufficient talent and determination to have become an outstanding industrialist. He had the ability to plan ahead and yet retained a capacity to solve detailed problems. It was only his over-riding desire to become a politician of national consequence which prevented this from happening. After his withdrawal from the partnership in 1874, the dynamism exhibited by the firm was largely generated by J.H. Nettlefold who was responsible for floating the business as a limited liability company. His premature death in 1881 robbed Nettlefolds of one of their most gifted executives.

The Dowlais Iron Co. produced two distinguished engineers and one outstanding manager: William Menelaus, E.P. Martin and G.T. Clark respectively. Menelaus occupied such a position of pre-eminence in the iron industry that he was awarded the Bessemer Gold Medal in 1881 and as his obituary in the *Proceedings of the Institution of Mechanical Engineers* concluded:[12]

> Mr. Menelaus' professional history during the past thirty years may be said to be the history of Dowlais. How the works grew

Helve   The helve used for 'shingling' was a hammer lifted up and then allowed to drop down by the operation of a cam.

Hot blast   Invented by J.B. Neilson, this was a technique of heating the blast of air (by passing it through chequer bricks) before it was injected into the blast furnace. The heated result of this innovation was to raise the efficiency of the blast furnace.

Ingot   Molten steel cast into a mould of square or rectangular shape and allowed to solidify before re-heating in a 'soaking pit' before rolling.

Longwall method   This method of mining coal enabled the mineral to be removed in a single continuous operation. The space from which it was taken, known as the 'gob' was then packed with rock and debris to support the roof. No coal was lost in pillars and more men could be employed along a given length of face to produce a greater proportion of large coal.

Mine   A name for iron ore.

Open hearth furnace   A means of making steel devised by C.W. Siemens. Unlike the Bessemer converter, the open hearth furnace had a lengthy operating cycle which was capable of greater control. The furnace resembled a large puddling furnace, the heat being applied by burning coal gas at either end of the furnace alternately about every twenty to thirty minutes. An important innovation was the application of the regenerative principle by which waste heat was recovered and used. By having two sets of firebricks (or regenerator chambers), each with one chamber for air and one for coal gas, it was possible to employ the hot gasses evolved from the decarburising processes to reheat one set while the other was heating the molten metal. By reversing the operations, the air could be heated to very high temperatures and effect savings of 70–80 per cent in fuel.

Pass   A pair of grooves or other shapes cut into the rolls in a rolling mill, or the term applied to the movement of a piece of iron or steel through them. If the metal is shaped during the pass it is called a 'live' pass, otherwise it is a 'dead' pass.

Pig bed   A flat area of sand in front of a blast furnace in which channels were made to allow the molten iron to flow and then solidify in conveniently sized shapes.

Pig iron   Cast iron run from the blast furnace and allowed to solidify in a pig bed.

Pillar and stall   The means of excavating coal which preceded the 'longwall' method. A heading was driven into solid coal and at right angles opened into a stall, or wide working space from which the bulk of the mineral was removed. Pillars of coal, usually rectangular in shape, were left between the stalls to support the roof. The distance between each heading could be as much as one hundred yards.

Pot sleepers   Circular cast iron discs attached to each chair in place of the traditional timber sleeper.

Potting and stamping The ¨rocess of making bar iron which was superseded by Cort's puddling and rolling patents. By this method, pig iron was taken from the refinery and broken into small pieces. These were placed in clay crucibles or pots with a flux (to absorb the sulphur) and heated in a coal-fired reverberatory furnace. The high temperature oxidised the carbon and broke the pots, the metal being removed from the furnace to be re-heated in a coal-fired 'chafery' and consolidated by hammering. The process was introduced at Cyfarthfa in 1766 by Charles Wood.

Puddling A technique invented by Henry Cort, by which a brick-lined bath of pig iron is heated, refined and stirred until a molten ball of wrought iron is prepared. A lengthy and skilled process it proved itself largely immune to technical innovation and was eventually rendered obsolete by steel-making. The 'gentleman puddler' was an aristocrat among workers in the iron industry.

Refinery A type of furnace in which pig iron was heated and refined before being puddled. The pig iron was partly decarburised and desiliconised before being converted into wrought iron.

Regenerator A method of recovering waste heat, see 'open hearth furnace'.

Reverberatory Furnace A furnace (unlike the blast furnace) in which the metal to be heated or melted is separated from the fuel. The flames are directed to beat down on the metal or 'reverberate' from the sloping roof. A puddling furnace is an example of the application of this technique.

Reversing Mill A mill which can be run in either direction, thereby removing the need for 'dead' passes.

Roughing An early stage in rolling.

Rounds Iron or steel bars, round in section, slightly above 1in in diameter.

Shingle, shingler To hammer a ball of puddled iron to expel any slag that remains and to consolidate it into a bloom for rolling.

Slab The stage in rolling a piece of iron or steel between an ingot and plate or sheet.

Slag The waste material formed either during the smelting of iron in the blast furnace or the making of wrought iron or steel.

Smelting To fuse or melt ore in order to extract the metal.

Spiegeleisen An alloy of iron, manganese and carbon, used to improve the quality of steel.

Tap To tap a furnace is to let the molten metal or slag run out of it.

Teem To pour molten steel from a ladle into an ingot mould.

Thread rolling A method of producing a thread on a woodscrew or bolt by squeezing the wire within a die, rather than by removing metal with a cutter.

Throat The opening at the top of a blast furnace through which the charge is placed.

Tilt hammer A hammer driven up and allowed to fall down by a cam usually powered by a water wheel.

Tuyère The nozzle, set within the blast furnace, which directs the blast into the area of combustion. They were cooled by a continuous flow of water.

Universal mill A rolling mill capable of rolling all sides of a piece of steel.

Wrought iron Iron produced by puddling. Unlike cast iron it is capable of being rolled and shaped.

McKenna, John, and Frank King, *In Those Days*, Cwmbran (1976).

Merthyr Teachers' Association, *The Story of Merthyr Tydfil*, Cardiff (1932).

Merthyr Teachers' Centre Group, *Merthyr Tydfil, A Valley Community*, Merthyr (1981).

Minchinton, W.E. (Editor), *Industrial South Wales 1750–1914, Essays in Welsh Economic History*, London (1969).

Mitchell, B.R. and P. Deane, *Abstract of British Historical Statistics*, Cambridge (1962).

——, *Economic Development of the British Coal Industry 1800–1914*, Cambridge (1984).

Morgan, Bryan, *Civil Engineering: Railways*, London (1977).

Morgan, Kenneth O., *Keir Hardy, radical and socialist*, London (1975).

Morris, J.H. and L.J. Williams, *The South Wales Coal Industry 1841–1875*, Cardiff (1958).

Nef, J.U., *The Rise of the British Coal Industry*, 2 Vols., London (1932).

Newport Encyclopaedia, Coronation Year and Royal Visit Souvenir, Bristol (1937).

North, F.J., *Coal and the Coalfields in Wales*, Cardiff (1931).

Owen, John A., *The History of the Dowlais Iron Works, 1759–1970*, Newport (1977).

Owen-Jones, Stuart, *The Penydarren Locomotive*, Cardiff (1981).

Payne, P.L., *British Entrepreneurship in the Nineteenth Century*, London (1974).

——, *Colvilles and the Scottish Steel Industry*, Oxford (1979).

Ponsonby, Sir John, *The Ponsonby Family*, London (1929).

Pressnell, L.S. (Editor), *Studies in the Industrial Revolution Presented to T.S. Ashton*, London (1960), W.H. Chaloner, 'Isaac Wilkinson, Potfounder'.

Raistrick, Arthur, *Quakers in Science and Industry*, Newton Abbot (1968).

Rattenbury, Gordon, *Tramroads of the Brecknock and Abergavenny Canal*, Oakham (1980).

Reed, M.C. (Editor), *Railways and the Victorian Economy*, Newton Abbot (1969).

Rees, D. Morgan, *Mines, Mills and Furnaces, An Introduction to Industrial Archaeology in Wales*, London HMSO (1969).

——, *The Industrial Archaeology of Wales*, Newton Abbot (1975).

——, *Historic Industrial Scenes, Wales*, Ashborne (n.d.).

Roberts, C.W., *A Legacy from Victorian Enterprise, The Briton Ferry Ironworks and the daughter companies*, Gloucester (1983).

Rowe, Malcolm, *East Moors Album, Portrait of a Steelworks 1888–1978*, Cardiff (1978).

Saul, S.B., *The Myth of the Great Depression 1873–1869*, London (1969).

Snell, J.B., *Mechanical Engineering: Railways*, London (1971).

Steer, Elsa, *Threads from the Family Tapestry*, (1957).

Thomas W. Gerwyn, *Welsh Coal Mines*, Cardiff (1979).

Walshaw, G.R. and C.A.J. Behrendt, *The History of Appleby-Fordingham*, Bradford (1950).

Walters, R., *The Economic Business History of the South Wales Steam Coal Industry*, New York (1977).

Watkin, David and Anthony Ratcliff (et al.), *A House in Town, 22 Arlington Street, Its Owners and Builders*, London (1984).

Wiener, Martin J., *English Culture and the Decline of the Industrial Spirit 1850–1980*, Cambridge (1981), Harmondsworth (1985).

Williams, Glanmor (Editor), *Merthyr Politics: The making of a Working-Class Tradition*, Cardiff (1966).

Williams, Gwyn A., *The Merthyr Rising*, London (1978).

Wrenn, Dorothy P.H., *Welsh History Makers*, London (1976).

Index